FIELDING
TRAVEL GUIDES

FIELDING'S
VIETNAM

Fielding Titles

Fielding's Amazon
Fielding's Australia
Fielding's Bahamas
Fielding's Belgium
Fielding's Bermuda
Fielding's Borneo
Fielding's Brazil
Fielding's Britain
Fielding's Budget Europe
Fielding's Caribbean
Fielding's Europe
Fielding's Far East
Fielding's France
Fielding's Guide to the World's Most Dangerous Places
Fielding's Guide to the World's Great Voyages
Fielding's Guide to Kenya's Best Hotels, Lodges & Homestays
Fielding's Guide to the World's Most Romantic Places
Fielding's Hawaii
Fielding's Holland
Fielding's Italy
Fielding's London Agenda
Fielding's Los Angeles Agenda
Fielding's Malaysia and Singapore
Fielding's Mexico
Fielding's New York Agenda
Fielding's New Zealand
Fielding's Paris Agenda
Fielding's Portugal
Fielding's Scandinavia
Fielding's Seychelles
Fielding's Southeast Asia
Fielding's Spain
Fielding's Vacation Places Rated
Fielding's Vietnam
Fielding's Worldwide Cruises

FIELDING'S
VIETNAM

The Adventurous Up-to-the-Minute Guide to the World's Newest Tourist Destination

by
Wink Dulles

Fielding Worldwide, Inc.

308 South Catalina Avenue

Redondo Beach, California 90277 U.S.A.

Fielding's Vietnam

Published by Fielding Worldwide, Inc.

Text Copyright ©1994 Fielding Worldwide Inc.

Icons & Illustrations Copyright ©1994 FWI

Photo Copyrights ©1994 to Individual Photographers

FIELDING WORLDWIDE INC.

PUBLISHER AND CEO	Robert Young Pelton
PUBLISHING DIRECTOR	Paul T. Snapp
PUBLISHING DIRECTOR	Larry E. Hart
PROJECT DIRECTOR	Tony E. Hulette
ACCOUNT EXECUTIVE	Beverly Riess
ACCOUNT SERVICES MANAGER	Christy Harp

EDITORS

Linda Charlton   Kathy Knoles

PRODUCTION

Tina Gentile   Chris Snyder

Craig South

COVER DESIGNED BY	Digital Artists
COVER PHOTOGRAPHERS — Front Cover	Mike Yamashita
Background Photo, Front Cover	Mike Yamashita
Back Cover	Mike Yamashita
INSIDE PHOTOS	Wink Dulles, Mike Yamashita

Inquiries should be addressed to: Fielding Worldwide, Inc., 308 South Catalina Ave., Redondo Beach, California 90277 U.S.A., ☎ *(310) 372-4474*, Facsimile *(310) 376-8064*, 8:30 a.m.–5:30 p.m. Pacific Standard Time.

ISBN 1-56952-055-0

Library of Congress Catalog Card Number

94-068338

Printed in the United States of America

ABOUT THE AUTHOR

Wink Dulles

Wink Dulles, 36, is the Southeast Asia correspondent for Fielding Worldwide. His articles have appeared in numerous national publications and his travel writings on Southeast Asia have been published in newspapers across the U.S. including *New York Newsday*, the *Salt Lake Tribune* and the *Santa Barbara News-Press*. Additionally, Dulles is a contributing editor for *AAA World* magazine, *Escape* magazine, and was Asia editor for *UFM* magazine. His travels through Cambodia, Thailand and Vietnam will continue to provide Fielding with an invaluable prospective on this burgeoning region of the world.

Ironically, Dulles, now a welcome part-time inhabitant of Vietnam, is the cousin of the late CIA Director Allen Dulles and former Secretary of State John Foster Dulles, who sent the first American military advisors into Vietnam in the 1950s after the French defeat in the First Indochina War. John Foster Dulles was considered "an enemy of the state," by Hanoi during his eight-year tenure as Secretary of State under President Dwight D. Eisenhower.

Dulles likes to think he lives in Bangkok, Thailand but he's usually somewhere in Southeast Asia faced with the grueling job of keeping Fielding's *Far East*, *Southeast Asia* and *Vietnam* the most up-to-date guides on the market.

Letter from the Publisher

In 1946, Temple Fielding began the first of what would be a remarkable new series of well-written, highly personalized guide books for independent travelers. Temple's opinionated, witty, and oft-imitated books have now guided travelers ever since we guided travelers through post-war Europe. More important to some was Fielding's humorous and direct method of steering travelers away from the dull and the insipid. Today, Fielding Travel Guides are still written by experienced travelers for experienced travelers. Our authors carry on Fielding's reputation for creating travel experiences that deliver insight with a sense of discovery and style.

Wink Dulles personifies the Fielding attitude: seasoned, bright, obsessed with detail, and born to seek out new experiences for travelers. Wink Dulles has created the most enlightening travel guide available on post-embargo Vietnam. Wink bought a beat up 500cc motorcycle and drove down muddy roads and cow paths looking for the real Vietnam.

We are working with the Vietnamese government and local tour operators to build tourism from the ground up. Working closely with the only Vietnamese company based in the U.S. we have set up a selection of tours all custom-designed for the adventurous traveler. We have gained permission for access to old battlefields and set up military tours for Vietnam Vets, diving tours from Vietnamese junks that will impress even the most jaded and more. Just look in the back of the book for the selection of tours and give us a call.

Fielding Nam Hai is the name of our Vietnamese office based in Ho Chi Minh City. From here, we cover the Far East to keep our books up to date and relevant. When you are in Vietnam don't be shy about looking Wink up and telling him about your experiences. Write us and tell us what you think should be in subsequent updates.

Welcome to the new Fielding.

RYP

Robert Young Pelton
Publisher and C.E.O.
Fielding Worldwide, Inc.

ACKNOWLEDGEMENTS

The number of people I wish to thank for the preparation of Fielding's *Vietnam* in the countries of Vietnam, the U.S. and Thailand is vast, but they all deserve to be included in these pages. First and foremost I wish to thank Do Trong Tu, now the tourism and marketing specialist at Ho Chi Minh City's Dai Nam Construction, Trade & Tourism Co. Ltd., and formerly with Saigon Railway Tourist Company. Known by his American-given name "Johnny" during the Vietnam War, Tu provided an invaluable amount of time and expertise in the preparation of this publication. He is a guide of unequaled abilities in this large nation of more than 70 million people. His knowledge of all areas of Vietnam is unsurpassed by Vietneamese guides in my opinion. By motorcycle, we explored the deepest regions of the Mekong Delta and traversed the coastal route National Highway 1 from Saigon to Hue. It seemed that every kilometer he wanted to stop and explain the cultural customs, topography and history of the area. We crossed rivers on tiny, dilapidated ferries unknown to tourists during monsoons. I dumped my Honda motorcycle on several occasions in the muddy delta without complaint from him. He was able to secure Vietnamese prices at hotels and restaurants each place we stopped for food or rest (as a foreigner I would be required to pay at least twice the amount that Tu was able to negotiate). This is a man who knows personally two of every three persons living south of Saigon. The other one third are members of his extended family. Money was never an issue. He was simply in Nirvana to travel with me. Traveling without such a man in Vietnam is like crawling through the old Viet Cong Tunnels without light. He was able to renew visas at a fraction of the cost of conventional travel agents. His life is travel in his beloved homeland, and the number of years he spent in the States during the 1960s gave him such an acute ability of the English language that the vast majority of Vietnamese he runs into believe he is "Viet Khieu," an Overseas Vietnamese from the United States. Tu was my guide and is now my trusted friend. Trust is the first thing that needs to be established in working with the Vietnamese people. With Tu, the trust came quickly, and our friendship negated any suspicions of selfishness I might have encountered with men of lesser human qualities. This is a man who is a true Vietnamese. Vietnam is not a war, but a country of friendly inhabitants who wish namely for the best fortune to be bestowed on their friends. Tu's human and professional qualities and qualifications transcend even the typically hospitable intentions and sentiments the Vietnamese have for visiting Americans. The war is over, long over, and Tu is perhaps the man in Vietnam who truly knows this. Thank you (*com on*) Johnny, Mr. Tu. Tu can be reached at Dai Nam Construction, Trade & Tourism Co. Ltd., located at *422 Hai ba Trung Street, 1st District, Ho Chi Minh City, Vietnam.* ☎ *84.8.442937; FAX: 84.8.230132.* Or write him at his home: *322 Pham Van Hai Street, Ward 3, Tan Binh District, Ho Chi Minh City, Vietnam.* He'd love to hear from you if you're planning a visit to Vietnam, and will enable you to get the most out of your visit.

I'd also like to thank Mr. Yellow River of the Hai Van Hotel in Saigon. His gracious hospitality and help in allowing me to communicate with the U.S. were essential to the success of this project. Also greatly helpful here were Miss Mai and Mr. Kong. If you come to Saigon, spend at least one night at the Hai Van Hotel (see WHERE TO STAY IN HO CHI MINH CITY). You'll be blown away by the friendliness of the staff. Also thanks to Khan, who introduced me to the sights of Ho Chi Minh City. Especially, I'd like also to thank Mr. Tran Phan Ngoc Hue and his lovely wife Hue, whose help in allowing me to utilize his computer equipment at both his shop and home in Saigon while my own was being repaired in Bangkok saved weeks of time in preparing this manuscript. Also thanks to Nguyen My Chau and Mamason Miss Long of Saigon. There are countless others in Vietnam I'd like to mention, but the list would constitute a book in itself. In Thailand, I'd like to thank Mr. Pham Manh Hai, press attache at the Vietnamese embassy in Bangkok, as well as the staff at the 27 Hotel, a brothel on Sukhumvit Soi 22, that permitted me to keep mega-kilograms of luggage at the hotel for nearly 6 months at no cost.

In the U.S., I'd particularly like to thank Robert Young Pelton, an adventurer and the publisher of the Fielding guidebooks, who gave me the lifetime opportunity of preparing Fielding's *Vietnam*. Although his deadlines rival that of a major newspaper's city desk editor, he is a man of the world, who fully realizes the future connections that all nations of the globe will eventually share. Also at Fielding (in Redondo Beach, California), I received major support from Paul Snapp, director of publishing, as well as from editor Kathy Knoles, who handles my American affairs (like sending me nasty faxes about credit card bills I haven't paid) while I'm away from the country. I'd also like to especially thank Beverly Riess. If it wasn't for her, I'd still be driving a beer truck around Santa Barbara County. Also at Fielding, thanks to Larry Hart and Tony Hulette, the computer wizards (i.e., propeller heads) who, working 18-hour days, have made Fielding's *Vietnam* the first and the best guidebook to Vietnam since the lifting of the U.S. trade embargo against Vietnam. To the countless others that have helped prepare this book, I say *Yo!*

And special thanks to my parents, Win and Patsy—who were there without being there.

AUTHOR'S PREFACE

The day U.S. President Bill Clinton lifted the nation's debilitating trade embargo against Vietnam, I was scouring Ho Chi Minh City's dark alleys and market stalls in search of an elusive pair of earplugs in an effort to mute the din of progress, celebration and hope that was emitting from this bustling city of more than 5 million people. The cacophony of building construction swirling in the same audio cocktail with the ceaseless blasts of millions of deafening firecrackers marking the Tet New Year had become too much. Sleep had become merely brief, unrewarding windows of semiconsciousness; the Vietnamese were winning this Tet offensive.

Occasionally, I'd feel a tug on my sleeve. *"Hoa Ky?"* the passersby would inquire, usually adorned in a Chicago Bulls ball cap or an American flag covered T-shirt.

"Toi la nguoi Hoa Ky," I'd respond. "Yes, I'm an American."

"Did you hear? America, Vietnam friends. President Clinton dropped the embargo I heard. Is this true?" Boom! Another fusillade of fireworks.

"I'm not sure," I'd say. "I've heard it, too."

The news stayed only a rumor, and derivatives of, for almost a full day. A cyclo driver approached me, said the embargo had been dropped, but that Clinton had only moments before rescinded the order after it was learned some tattered American POWs were still being held captive in caves in northwestern Vietnam. Then a motorcade whooshed down Central Saigon's Le Loi Blvd., past the Rex Hotel, accompanied by a dozen policemen on siren-spewing motorcycles. "See, they're still negotiating," another man said. "The man in the limousine, that was Premier Vo Van Kiet."

There's no shortage of subjects for photo buffs throughout Vietnam.

It hadn't been Vo, but rather the mayor of Saigon, more than likely on his way to dinner. But the Vietnamese on the street were caught up in the moment. This was historic, and suddenly the bursting of the firecrackers in the street took on a different context, and more than a few Saigonese were aware of it.

It was the next day at a computer store when I received confirmed information about the dropping of the embargo. It wasn't from the television. Nor the newspaper. Rather it was in the form of a huge sign that had been posted above the store, which hadn't been there the day before, and it was no less conclusive of the embargo's lifting than the opening of a U.S. embassy in Hanoi. The three letters beamed in a deep, freshly-painted lake blue, and they read "IBM."

The beggars still held their bowls in front of me, and the pickpockets continued to clamor for a better angle at my watch. Babies glazed with the milky, sickening white of advanced cataracts still groveled naked in the slick brown sludge on the sidewalk.

Yet, somehow, things were different. Not with the instantaneousness of a bomb, but rather with the expectancy of comfort that ensues after taking a time release medication. In Vietnam, that incubancy has persevered and festered through 15 years of war and another 20 of economic and social isolation and depravity.

GUERILLAS IN THE MIDST

Any world leader who chooses to self exile himself in New Jersey, as did Vietnam's Ngo Dinh Diem during the First Indochina War between 1945 and 1954, has left a place that's got a problem.

Conscripted Americans and soldiers of other aligned nationalities such as Australia, South Korea and Thailand—as well as the Viet Cong and the untold millions of civilians—had in these paradisiacal surroundings probably the most gut-wrenching experiences ever confronted by those mentally and physically displaced by war. Armed men in this culturally and topographically idyllic Southeast Asian nation were ordered to burn, napalm, bulldoze and otherwise raze an area three times the size of Montana, hectares responsible for more then 60 percent of the Eastern Hemisphere's chlorophyll production.

Yet there is not a lot of evidence left of the war in Vietnam. There are the craters left by B-52s near Cu Chi. Scrap metal shops line portions of National Highway 1 in the south near the shells of former U.S. military installations—still offering for sale rusted drivetrains and wheels scavenged from discarded American trucks and personnel carriers.Occasionally, one can spot bunkers in the sand dunes and gun turrets on the beach. There are Viet Cong tunnels in the south and near Quang Tri in central Vietnam.

But surprisingly, there is little testament left to the carnage, both on the ground and in the hearts of the Vietnamese people. What had been defoliated 30 years ago is now lush and verdant. North of Phan Thiet, the visitor notices a drastic change in the countryside—which turns from electric green to sunbaked brown—and often asks if the area had been defoliated. No, it hadn't been. It's simply an arid part of the country. The evidence of Agent Orange (nearly two tons were used during the war), if there is indeed any, is contained in the people rather than in the topography—children born in the south tend to be smaller than those in the north.The horrors of this pesticide seem to have seeped as deep into the soil as has Vietnamese animosity toward Americans.

Do we owe the Vietnamese a debt? It's a question most Americans to this day struggle with. But suffice it to say that each year dozens of Vietnamese are killed in search of mortar shells and dud grenades and other petty war materiel to sell to American tourists for the equivilant of a stick of gum. I don't see a lot of sodbusters from Lawrence, Kansas crawling around on their hands and knees in corn fields looking for Chinese or Russian shell casings to hawk at their produce stands to tour bus loads of ethnic Cambodians, Laotions and Vietnamese donning Minoltas and camcorders.

Though I've spent the first few pages of this book outlining a war that has polarized even to this day a populace to such a degree it makes Rush Limbaugh and Howard Stern seem like a couple of color commentators on Monday Night Football, Vietnam should be perceived as a country, not a war. There is no war in Vietnam, save that which is happening behind Windsor knots and Waterman pens. The new aggressor in Vietnam is the fusillade of foreign investment poised to the transform the nation as no B-52s could hope to do. It is an inner war between an antiquated and isolated ideology and the magnetlike pull of a free market destiny, a balancing act between socialism and capitalism.

Most of Vietnam's population of around 70 million is under 30. An Irish woman in Saigon remarked that she was amazed at the age disparity of the Vietnamese people. People seemed very young or very old, she said. And she was mostly correct in that observation. While much the same scenario can be seen in neighboring Cambodia's Phnom Penh, it is for two very different reasons. Whereas Cambodia's missing generation ended up in shallow, pungent graves outside Phnom Penh after being bludgeoned by the axes of Pol Pot's heinous henchmen, Vietnam's missing generation ended up in Southern California, Minnesota, Virginia and Australia after the capitulation of Saigon to NVA troops in 1975.

They left in droves, some 280,000 alone in 1979. Many died at sea under abhorrent conditions, including cannibalism and subsistence on human waste. Pirates combed the seas for the refugees' dilapidated vessels, raping the women and murdering entire boatloads of Vietnamese. Many of the fleeing Vietnamese vessels were ordered back out to sea by the nations they were adrift to. Malaysia turned 40,000 refugees back to sea in one six-month period alone in the late 70s. By the end of that decade, there were nearly 350,000 Vietnamese in detainment camps in East Asia. Even today, under the United Nations' Orderly Departure Program, an estimated 100,000 Vietnamese leave their homeland each year.

And the collapse of the former Soviet Union and the tumbling of Eastern blocs like a Thai garment factory didn't help matters. Vietnamese exports went to hell and a handbasket. Although real growth continued to inch upward at a six-percent clip by 1989, inflation soared to a staggering 75 percent. The former USSR was the recipient of nearly 60 percent of Vietnamese trade. Conversely Vietnam received nearly 75 percent of its imports from the former Soviet Union.

Vietnam today remains one of the most deeply impoverished nations in the world. Its per capita income still fails to exceed US$200 per year. Policemen, the watchdogs of the communist streets, rarely make in excess of $100 per month; they can be seen on the outskirts of every population center stopping bus drivers for kickbacks. In 1991, child malnutrition stood at 60 percent. The monthly rice ration was a mere 13 kgs.

Gratefully, this is all beginning to change. Countries such as Singapore, Hong Kong, Taiwan and Japan have pumped more than US$5 billion into the economy since 1989, a figure that is bound to soar with the lifting of the U.S. embargo.

The demise of the Cold War and the breakup of the former USSR has had a tremendous impact in the thawing of Washington-Hanoi relations. Hanoi began a limited move to a free trade system in 1966 and, by 1989, she opened her doors to relatively unrestricted tourism in the hope of luring desperately needed hard currency. Additionally, the 1991 Paris Peace accords and the subsequent May 1993 free elections in Cambodia have played major roles in reducing tension in the Indochina region.

These events, as well as Hanoi's largely detailed accounting for missing American servicemen (no previous American foe in war has been as thorough), have helped American businesses succeed in pushing the Clinton administration to establish ties with Hanoi, as American companies will no doubt realize enormous profits in helping Vietnam to establish a viable communictions, transportation and public utilities infrastructure once they transcend the growing pains of the red tape so endemic in communist administrations.

The negative effects of the impending overcommercialization of Vietnam will be profound—the annihilation of offshore reefs, the inevitable extinction of perhaps hundreds of species of both land and sea creatures. There will be the enormous cranes atop the skeletons of skycrapers bearing the massive blocks of foreign investment and turning them into hotel rooms and conference centers.

But the curtain is lifting, and the carpet bombing by American planes of this beautiful country will again resume—as will the textiles, consumer goods and the fast food that will drop from the sky along with the rugs.

But neither the Vietnamese nor others should fool themselves into thinking that normalized relations between Washington and Hanoi will be the savior of Vietnam. There are many who have beaten the Americans to Hanoi and Saigon. Although the Vietnamese welcome the return of Americans, their welfare is no longer as dependent on that return as many have traditionally and still currently believe.

Japanese motorbikes and consumer goods, everything from televisions to toothpaste, are making the Vietnamese quite satiated. "American dollars don't necessarily need to come from America," as one Thai writer noted. Many believe the embargo, in its latter stages, was no longer significantly impacting the Vietnamese. Land prices, which as recently as 1993 were skyrocketing in anticipation of the lifting of the embargo, have largely stabilized—and even dropped to some extent. Japanese products face no real threat with the introduction of American consumer goods into Vietnam, save for perhaps the legitimate entry of Coca-Cola. Recent surveys indicate that most Vietnamese believe the Japanese make the best household products in the world. The Americans will have to work hard to create a campaign to change that impression.

It would be tempting to call it Hearts and Minds, wouldn't it?

Wink Dulles
Ho Chi Minh City

AUTHOR'S NOTE: FLASH!!!

In a dramatic and somewhat confusing shift in Vietnam's tourist and business travel economy, as of October 1, 1994, hotels in Vietnam have been required by law to accept only Vietnamese dong in payment for rooms. Whereas the American dollar had previously not only been the preferred currency for hoteliers, many establishments across the country—especially the finer ones—required payment in U.S. currency. How this will affect tourism is not known at press time, but what is known at any time is that the highest Vietnamese monetary note is the 50,000 dong bill, which is about as readily available as a personal meeting with the Pope. Sounds like a lot, but it's worth about five U.S. bucks. That's it, folks. Five dollars. Lines at hotel cashiers' counters are bound to rival the queues at Ticketmaster for Madonna tickets as clerks will be forced to count barrel-loads of dong notes, especially at the higher-ticket hotels.

The move is part of the Vietnamese government's effort to replace the U.S. dollar with the dong for most currency transactions. It's scaring some foreign businesses and may send some shivers up the spines of tourists planning to visit Vietnam, as the dollar has remained stable with the dong since the government began opening up the economy in the late 1980s. Foreigners generally have paid for higher-priced goods and services with the dollar during the past seven years. Many experts believe that as much as US$2 billion is floating around the country in U.S. dollar notes. Authorized businesses that have previously accepted or required U.S. dollars in payment are now required to reapply for their licenses. Banks and hotels will be required to set up more currency exchange booths. Airlines are continuing to accept U.S. dollars. Credit cards are still accepted at the time of this writing, but may become more difficult to use. The question is how vigorously the law will be enforced.

Consider this: US$150 in "large" 5000 Vietnamese dong notes is about as thick as this book. That's just for one night in an upscale hotel. Well-heeled tourists planning on visiting Vietnam better pay a visit to a camping shop and get some advice from the grisly-faced, earring-donning youths pricing backpacks.

Fielding Rating Icons

The Fielding Rating Icons are highly personal and awarded to help the besieged traveler choose from among the dizzying array of activities, attractions, hotels, restaurants and sights. The awarding of an icon denotes unusual or exceptional qualities in the relevant category.

RATINGS: Fielding Award, Author Selection, Money Saver, Expensive, Quality, Warning, Danger, Inexpensive, Mild Disapproval, Spacious, Cramped

CULTURAL: Museum/Art, Interesting Architecture, History, Book Reference, Artistically Important, Musically Interesting, Cultural Archeology, Crafts, Theatre

SIGHTS: Picturesque, Great Scenery, Market, Beaches/Resorts, Cultural, Fortress, Castles, Church

WHERE TO STAY: Simple, Luxurious, Cottage, Bed & Breakfast, Scenic, Business, Honeymoon, Chateau

TRAVEL TIPS: Arrival/Departure, By Air, By Water, By Train, By Car, Bus/Local Transit, Barge, River Boat, Calendar, Itinerary, Compass, Kids

ACTIVITIES: Downhill Skiing, X–country Skiing, General Sports, Water Sports, Sailing, Scuba Diving, Snorkeling/Diving, Deep-sea Fishing, Freshwater Fishing, Swimming, Hiking, Walking, Relaxing, Golf, Tennis, Horseback Riding, Cycling, Workout

SPECIAL INTEREST: Mystery, Singles, Romantic, Nude Beaches, Lecture, Spectacular Cuisine, Wine Tasting, Shopping, Nightlife, Cafe Stops, Gardening, Pro Sports

TABLE OF CONTENTS

LIST OF MAPS

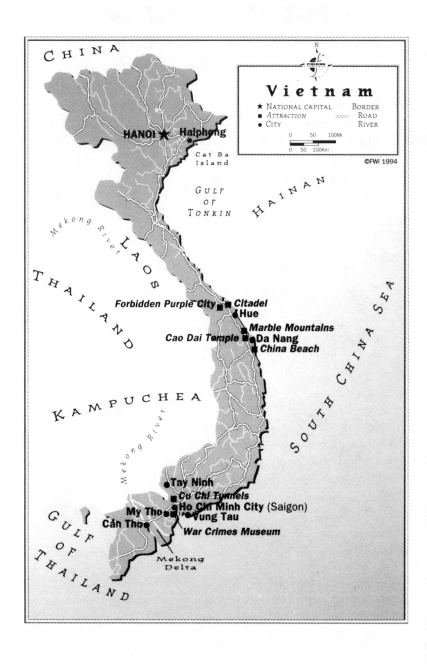

INTRODUCTION

Traditional Vietnamese dance and theatre depicts Vietnam's history.

If any books in the Fielding series of world travel guides require constant updating they are the ones that are written about Southeast Asia.

The Far East, particularly Southeast Asia, is the world's fastest changing region. From Myanmar to Mindanao, from Telukbetung to Na Trang, Southeast Asia is exploding. Economic prosperity is rapidly transforming the face of countries such as Vietnam, as it makes the transition from an agrarian-based, Soviet-aided litany of economic failure to a manufacturing and export giant.

So it is with some trepidation that we prepare this intro to Fielding's *Vietnam*, because as these words are committed to paper, they become out of date. Asia has a maddeningly invigorating habit of doing exactly what you expect the least. Gentle people stage bloody uprisings. Nations hurl themselves from capitalism to religious fanaticism overnight—and vice versa. If one thing is the same in Asia it is change.

For 49 years, Fielding has been renowned for our expertise of the globe's less strife-torn regions—such as Europe, Hawaii and the Caribbean. But now our pioneering books also explore the remote cultures of Borneo, Kenya, Mexico and Brazil. And, of course, the Far East.

WHO IS THIS GUIDE FOR?

Fielding's *Vietnam* is designed to be more fun than the penurious tones and dull squeaking of the backpacking guides, with less air-conditioned sterility of the business guides. It's more exciting than the white bread guides, and more opinionated than all of them combined. Fielding's *Vietnam* is for the person with a lust for the foreign but with a healthy fear of the unknown. You're college educated, have traveled before and really want to get into Vietnam. Not just surf. This is the guide to lean on when you get confused, tired or hurried—and the one to ignore when you're on a roll.

A WORD ABOUT GUIDEBOOKS

Guidebooks, even this one, aren't the end-all for managing your Vietnam adventure. Southeast Asia is a highly dynamic and constantly changing environment. Although Fielding's *Vietnam* listings are up-to-date right up to press time, businesses, eateries, hotels and tour companies both in and pertaining to the Far East are in a constant state of flux. Phone numbers change. Faxes are installed. Businesses boom and bust. Tour companies come and go on the scene as fast as lip-synching pop stars. In fact two calls to Asian tour companies based in the U.S. that are listed in one 1993 guide to Vietnam were greeted with disconnection announcements. A third was answered by a bubbly but bemused receptionist at a carpet store in Fountain Valley, California.

WHERE THE HECK IS VIETNAM?

For most Westerners it's on the other side of the world. Twenty-four hours aboard a plane or two or three and you're there. Sure it's a haul. But while Aunt Tess and Uncle Bill are getting toured to death on a bus in Belgium, you're checking out shrines built before there *was* a Europe—cultures and monuments so old they predate written history.

WHAT'S IT LIKE?

Vietnam offers some of the world's most mysterious and exotic attractions. It possesses a beautiful topography—ranging from rainforests not unlike those found in the deepest jungles of Central America and vast deltas to boulder strewn mesas of the variety found in Mexico's Baja peninsula. And if the country has had its fill of Western colonialism and domination, it is still very much the virgin for economic exploitation. (But to its credit, Vietnam plans to plant 120,000 hectares of new forest and nurse 260,000 hectares of young forest this year.)

Vietnam's new riches have made more evident an astoundingly impoverished societal undercarriage, which really can only be called such because there are now other hugely-rich stratas for comparison. The average Vietnamese makes $198 a year. Any trip to this strange land will open your eyes to extremes you have never encountered before, from economic to religious.

Vietnamese cities have become the destinations for the 1990s. In a word, Vietnam is hot. For instance, travel is becoming one of Vietnam's single biggest earners of foreign exchange. During the late 80s, these revenues multiplied many times over. If any two countries are truly indicative of the surge in interest in the Far East, Vietnam and Cambodia would have to be riding in the rostrum. In Cambodia, for instance, tourism has enjoyed a whopping 4500 percent increase in the last six years. In Vietnam, Americans and others are descending upon this paradisiacal nation in droves. Some to reflect on and make amends with past tragedy, others to see what Hawaii might have been like a couple of hundred years ago or so.

Whereas Europe has served as the traditional target of foreign jaunts by North Americans, travelers these days are tossing around names like Danang, Ha Long Bay, Hue and Dalat like they once spoke of Amsterdam and Paris.

And, of course the real Vietnam lies beyond the cities. It's found on the rice terraces of the Central Highlands and the coffee plantations of Dac Lak province, around the spectacular stretches of sand like China Beach, and in the incense-laced temples of Hue. It's found along the banks of the bountiful mouths of the Mekong. It's found in longhouses in the deepest jungles of northern Vietnam and aboard junks anchored in the Gulf of Tonkin. It's chronicled in the works of Somerset Maugham and Graham Greene.

Vietnam, for all its part proud, part shameful—and certainly lengthy—heritage, is just being born in many ways, and is most assuredly an embryonic host to the seasoned traveler.

Some say Vietnam has lost its lure as a frontier destination and to some extent, they're right. You see foreigners about Saigon, Hanoi, Hue and Danang these days. A bunch of them with money. Some of them are old. They either remember something and are trying to recapture it, or are looking for some fodder for their cocktail parties when they get back home. Others are young—they need no excuses, nor reasons. If you've never been somewhere, it's a frontier.

VIETNAM AT A GLANCE

The place	Square miles	Population	Languages	Religions
Vietnam	127,330	70.1 million	Vietnamese, French, Chinese, Khmer	Buddhism. Hao Hao, Cao Dai,, Christianity, Islam

Adult literacy rate	Life expectancy	Pop. growth rate	Per capita income	Mean years of schooling
88%	63 years	2.5%	US$198	4.5 years

% labor force in agriculture	Arable land as % of total	Rural pop.	Annual rate of deforestation	Growth of urban pop.
67%	17.5%	78%	0.6%	3.6% per annum

BEFORE YOU LEAVE

TRAVEL DOCUMENTS

Before you even schedule your trip, you'll need to get a passport. Check to find the closest passport agency in your area. Passport agencies are located in most large cities and selected post offices across the country. Passports cost $65 ($55 to renew). You'll need two passport photos (most photo shops can shoot them for you) and an original birth certificate. No copies. Allow about 30 days for processing. You'll need visas to visit some countries in Asia, although many nations will stamp U.S. and Canadian passports with stays from two weeks up to 90 days free of charge. Visas are necessary for Vietnam and are good for 30 days. Extensions (I've seen up to 30 days) can be applied for and are usually granted when you're in-country. At the time of this writing, the U.S. has recently lifted its nearly 30-year-old trade embargo. And although this will invariably lead to full diplomatic relations between the two countries, Vietnam and the U.S. have not opened new embassies to date, so visas still must be procured through a third party. You can contact one of the Asian tour companies listed in this chapter. They can generally provide visas for about US$160; they're so pricey because the tour operators usually arrange for them through their contacts in either Mexico or Canada. Expect a wait of up to 10 days. A more prudent and cheaper way is to get to a place such as Bangkok first. There, most of the travel agencies that line Khao San and Sukhimvit Roads like a muster of slot machines at Las Vegas McLaren Airport might get away with taking about 90 bucks from you. You'll think you got a deal—but you didn't. Instead, go right to the Vietnam Embassy at *83/1 Wireless Road, Bangkok* (☎ *251-5835* or *251-5838*, FAX: *(662) 251-7201* or *251-7203*), fill out an application and give them about US$48, a couple of passport-sized photos and five days and, presto, you're in.

Better yet, I recommend heading just a half block down Wireless to M.K. Ways (*57/11 Wireless Rd., Patumwan, Bangkok 1033*; ☎ *254-7770, 255-3390, 254-4765,* or *255-2892*; FAX: *(662) 254-5583*). If you're nice, they won't charge you a penny more than the 1200 baht you stood in the long line at the Vietnamese embassy to pay. And they'll get you as cheap a fare into either Saigon or Hanoi as you'll find anywhere along Khao San Road. (My first visa only took a couple of days to get back to me from Hanoi, but it seems the capital is being besieged with visa applications and really doesn't appear capable of handling the surging popularity of its country as it was capable of only a few short months ago.) M.K. Ways has been known to pull some hemp-taut strings in Hanoi, but even they now make you wait seven days for the visa.

INSIDER TIP

An American is permitted to rent an apartment during the first 30 day visa, but if the authorities discover that you're renting a flat rather than staying at a hotel when you apply for a visa extension, you're in trouble, pal. Tourists are expected to be lodging in Vietnam's hotels (of course because of the additional money it costs to stay in a hotel). When applying for an extension, your exit card must be stamped by a hotel showing the hotel as your lodgings in the country. If you are living in an apartment, make arrangements to stay in a hotel a few days prior to applying for your extension. The hotel will stamp your exit card and the authorities will be happy. If you don't, expect your apartment to be raided during the middle of the night by the immigration police. Not only will you have to pay an extensive fine yourself, but so will your landlord. You may even be asked (ordered, actually) to leave the country. When applying for an extension, you'll need to go through a sponsor (i.e. travel agent). Their prices for the extension will vary from between US$20-40. Shop around. If you've got a good guide, usually he'll have the contacts to get the lower fee.

SOLO AND GROUP TRAVEL

INSIDER TIP: WHO SHOULD TRAVEL TO VIETNAM?

Although Vietnam is becoming a travel destination at almost a fanatical rate, it's important to realize the country's infrastructure isn't close to having the ability of accommodating mass travel. Le Thieu Hung, Saigontourist's general manager recently said that the country has yet to "meet the needs of mass tourism for pleasure and entertainment. Vietnam is still primarily a destination of business people and culturally-minded travelers." At this time, Le Xuan Hien, manager of the operation department of Vietnamtourism said, "We're rather interested in intellectuals, educated people who come here to see the specific cultural heritage and way of life in our country. We have to be very cautious with mass tourism so that we don't spoil our beautiful country."

Solo wandering is probably the purest form of adventure travel, while group or paired travel offers its own rewards. Wandering alone in faraway places takes on a romantic and nomadic aura. Getting from point A to B can become like a pilgrimage. This type of travel courts disaster but is also the most rewarding. It's exploration at its purest, with little to curb adventure except physical stamina and funds. In only a month or two, you will meet more people, do more things and experience more of life's pitches than in a year's worth of group or paired travel. If you travel in remote regions of Asia, prepare to be arrested, detained, celebrated, attacked, seduced and tricked. It's all part of the experience. But, remember, if you are a woman traveling alone, you're setting yourself up for thieves, thugs and worse. Men certainly aren't immune but are less likely targets.

AUTHOR'S WARNING

Although major, or organized, crime in Vietnam rarely involves or has any consequences on foreign tourists, occasionally the errant tourist may become inadvertantly involved in an illegal smuggling operation. The illegal export of timber is on the rise, particularly in the Bach Binh, Tanh Linh, and Ham Tan districts, Binh Dinh province. This area has witnessed an alarmingly large scale of hardwood smuggling via freighters on the Mekong River. The Anti-Deforestation Task Force recently seized 100 cubic meters of timber in 14 cases of illegal transport. Independent travelers have been known to try to gain passage from Vietnam to Cambodia via waterway, sometimes hitching rides on freighters and other riverboats.

The next best scenario is traveling with a single friend. The big drawback is the unintended barrier you'll create between yourselves and the locals. You will use the language less, be invited into fewer homes. But this is a better way for women from a security standpoint. Additionally, you won't get as lonely traveling in a pair—and you *will* get lonely traveling solo. A good way is to split up for portions of the trip, arranging to meet at a preset time and place.

Group travel has its rewards if you've only got a week. But that's about it. Essentially, group travel is like relying on the weakest link in a chain. You can never travel faster than the slowest person; accommodations are always full; tables are too small; the prices are always higher—you name it. Group travel turns a simple pleasure into a military exercise.

PACKING

Vietnam lies in tropical latitudes. This doesn't mean a prescription of Bain de Soleil and thongs. In the highlands of south and central Vietnam, and throughout the north, temperatures can get quite cold, especially in winter. And in jungle areas so hot your brain turns to jerky, you'll want as much skin area covered as possible to ward off leeches, malarial mosquitos and the fatal bites of scared, hungry, pissed off or playful cobras, vipers, hanumans and kraits. (Lions and tigers and bears, oh my!) And, ladies, remember where you're going. The Vietnamese on the whole are a tolerant lot and Western fashion has permeated urban areas, but a show of too much skin is taboo.

Female lib hasn't gotten to Danang yet. And neither has Madonna's book. Longer dresses, pants and bras are *de rigueur* in most places other than the beach and other heavily touristed areas. And especially in religious temples—just an aside: pretty Vietnamese girls who may wear the shortest, sexiest dresses and high heels on the street wear very modest swimwear at the beach.

Both sexes should bring along light cotton clothing and not a lot of it. You'll probably—and should—get a lot of what you need where you're going. For starters, a few pairs of trousers and a couple of pairs of shorts will do. Take two or three short-sleeved shirts max, and a single dress shirt. You determine the underwear. Sandals are a good way of getting around; the Asians seem to think so. Walking or hiking boots are a must for the jungle and the mountains. Sneakers are the best all-around bet. Slip-ons will be good if you'll be seeing a lot of temples; laced shoes are not a good idea if you've got a lot of pagodas on your itinerary. A small towel will also come in handy. Other good ideas are a day pack and a fanny pack. Don't bring things you probably won't need: sleeping bag, heavy outerwear, air mattress and such. Unless, of course, the nature of your journey requires this kind of bulk.

Take along a sewing kit, electrical current adapters, and a good Swiss Army knife. Bring contraceptives and condoms. Yeah, condoms. You can get them there, but Asian condoms break like soap bubbles in a pine forest. A *great* insect repellent is essential—like Deet. Some folks swear by preparations such as Skin So Soft to keep the little buggers away. Keep a marginal supply of duty-free liquor and American cigarettes handy to pay off officials and impress your friends. Johnnie Walker Red Label whiskey is generally the East Asian poison of choice, as are 555 or Marlboro cigarettes. In-country, carry a roll or two of toilet paper. In a lot of places, you won't find it; just a bucket of water. It's why there's not a lot of social grace in the left hand.

MEDICAL/HEALTH CERTIFICATES

You should receive inoculations against **yellow fever**, **hepatitis B**, **tetanus**, **typhoid**, **cholera** and **tuberculosis**. An **influenza** shot couldn't hurt either.

Some countries will require that you have, under International Health Regulations adopted by the World Health Organization, an International Certificate of Vaccination against yellow fever. Travelers arriving from infected areas will be required to show proof of vaccination against yellow fever. The certificate will also be stamped with the other inoculations that you have received. Any general practice will be able to provide this service.

A WORD ABOUT AIDS (SIDA)

A local guide recently, on a trip in the Mekong Delta, decided he needed a rest at a truck stop (read that as whore house), where Vietnamese women obligingly take in weary travelers for some tea and a little "sympathy." Apparently, the man was not in the habit of using condoms during these little sojourns. He explained to me that, to avoid contracting the HIV virus, he had sex only with Vietnamese girls. "These girls don't have sex with foreigners," he said, his reasoning that the disease could only be spread by foreigners. Although government estimates of the spread of HIV in Vietnam are seriously lacking a firm data gathering procedure, AIDS in Vietnam is very real. At least the Vietnamese are becoming more aware of its dangers. While the general awareness of HIV/AIDS has risen from 2.9 percent of the population in 1991, now more than 40 percent of the population is aware of the danger and the spread of the disease. That using condoms prevents the spread of AIDS was known by 31 percent of the respondents in 1991, that figure jumped to 44 percent by the end of 1993.

INTERNATIONAL DRIVERS LICENSE

These can be obtained at your state's department of motor vehicles offices or through AAA and other automobile associations. The fee is approximately $7. If you're planning on driving in Asia, get one. In Vietnam, an international drivers license is required to rent a motorbike over 50 cc.

INTERNATIONAL STUDENT IDENTITY CARD

The ISIC card can help with discounts on air tickets and lodging. There's been a surge in bogus cards, which have been readily available in Thailand and Malaysia. To get a real one, contact the Council on International Educational Exchange (CIEE) at *205 E. 42nd. Street, New York, NY 10017-5706;* ☎ *(212) 661-1414.*

INTERNATIONAL YOUTH HOSTEL CARD

This'll help you in the expensive places such as Japan but may be totally unrecognized in Indochina. You can get this card through any youth hostel office. Or write *733 15th Street N.W., Suite 840, Washington, DC 20005;* ☎ *(202) 783-6161.*

AIR TRAVEL

There are now myriad airlines that call on the Pacific Rim from the U.S. and a growing number that serve both Ho Chi Minh City and Hanoi. With the lifting of the embargo, United Airlines was the first American airline to announce that it would link the U.S. and Vietnam directly. Service to both Ho Chi Minh City and Saigon may have begun by the time you read this.

Take heed that some of the airlines offer better service than the others. It's a long way around to the other side of the globe so you might want to pay the extra bucks for more comfort and better service. Not in terms of upgrading your class, but in choosing an airline. For overall service, comfort, friendliness of the flight crew, food and all the amenities, our hats are tipped to Singapore Airlines. For the feeling of entering Asia the moment you step aboard, these are the folks to fly. Not far behind is Thai Airways. Cathay Pacific and British Airways are in the next league, followed by also-rans Northwest, Korean, Air New Zealand, MAS, Garuda Indonesia, JAL, and Philippines. Delta and United also call on the Far East. But most Asia flights on these carriers are like a 24-hour trip from Des Moines to Dallas. Ugg!

When choosing an airline, comfort may be as high a priority as price. Some Asian airlines, such as Singapore, Thai and Cathay Pacific realize this and take extra pains to make the 15–25 hour flights enjoyable. Others, such as MAS and Garuda Indonesia, employ seat configurations and meal strategies designed for a maximum number of Asian travelers.

FLYING TO VIETNAM

Flights to Vietnam from the United States in economy class with advance purchase cost between $1000 and $1500 return, although you may be able to get a cheaper fare through a ticket broker.

For many travelers to the region, Vietnam is not the only stop and is part of an itinerary that may include a number of other Southeast Asian destinations. Few travelers (especially those on extended journeys) book directly to Vietnam from their original points of departure. That's why it'll help to know approximately what the fares are to Vietnam from other cities/countries in the region.

· THE STORY OF VIETNAM AIRLINES

Vietnam Airlines was formed in 1989, but its history dates back to 1954 with the takeover of Hanoi's Gia Lam Airport–now its headquarters–from the French. Then called the Civil Aviation Department, the airline went into service with a limited network of communications, meteorological information, fuel, cargo, and only five aircraft. It launched its first international service–to Beijing–in April 1956. Over the next two years, the domestic service from Hanoi was extended to Vinh, Dong Hoi and Dien Bien Phu.

Unification of the country in 1975 brought about a boom in air services due to the dramatic increase in economic, political, cultural and social activities. As a result, the airline expanded its operations under a new organization formed in February 1976–the General Department of Civil Aviation.At the time,it had a modest fleet, many say a damned dangerous modest fleet of ailing IL-14s, Antonov-24s, LI-2s, Yak-40s, dilapidated DC-3s, DC-4s and then later a couple of Boeing 707s.The aircraft were poorly maintained, and safety procedures and equipment were all but nonexistent. The airline was considered, along with China's flagship carrier, perhaps the scariest airline on the planet. Many foreigners simply refused to fly VN altogether.

The GDCA also ran a network of aviation departments and airports throughout the country. In 1977, as Vietnam Civil Aviation, the airline carried 21,000 frightened passengers, of whom 7000 were even more frightened foreigners–3000 tons of cargo was also flown during this period. How frightened the freight was flying VN isn't known.

By the time it became Vietnam Airlines in 1989, the airline and its blue and white livery, lettering, and precariously fluttering stork logo had become widely known to Vietnamese, foreign passengers, and morticians alike.

On April 20, 1993, VN became a company under the Civil Aviation Administration of Vietnam. CAAV is a state-run organization controlling the entire aviation industry of Vietnam. The establishment of the Vietnam Airlines Company is part of the reorganization of Vietnam's aviation industry to meet the growth in air services to and from the country.It marks a significant stage in the development of the airline, namely because it's been forced to purchase newer and safer aircraft as well as seriously update its safety standards.

The new VN fleet now stands at 27 aircraft, including the likes of more modern and comfortable Boeing 737-300s and 767s, the Airbus 310 and 320, and ATR-72s.The airline began utilizing the Gabriel II reservation system in 1991 and is now planning to join Abacus and other global distribution systems so as to improve its sales system worldwide. Its computer system is also being upgraded to facilitate document management (which had previously been performed by surly, disgruntled bureaucrats), ticketing and check-in services. Phone bookings are now accepted.The number of passengers has been steadily increasing since 1976 at an average of 36 percent. In 1992, VN achieved 150 percent of its passenger and cargo targets–800,000 foreign and domestic passengers and 10,000 tons of cargo. In 1993, VN began scheduled services to Taipei, Moscow and Seoul using aircraft like the 737, A-310 and 320. In October, daily service was initiated to Singapore.

THE STORY OF VIETNAM AIRLINES

VN now flies to 16 destinations overseas and operates 12 domestic routes. Not surprisingly, the domestic flights are usually aboard the aging and paint-flaked Soviet-era aircraft that dot the tarmacs of Hanoi and Ho Chi Minh airports like exhibits at a Charles Lindberg museum. But even domestic service is changing. I've flown a number of domestic flights within Vietnam and have felt relatively safe (with the aid of 20 mg of Valium) and only vomited twice.

VN's market share of passenger aircraft to and from Vietnam in 1992 was 35 percent—a significant growth from 1990's 12 percent and 1991's 27 percent. Its international passenger load grew by more than 70 percent.

VN now operates joint services with Cathay Pacific, Malaysian Airlines, Korean Air, Singapore Airlines and China Airlines—to name a few—on some international routes.

With the support of the International Civil Aviation Organization and the United Nations Development program, VN has invested tens of millions of US dollars in upgrading its services as well as ground facilities. To meet new traffic demand to and from the country, VN has inaugurated scheduled services to Japan, France, and Germany in 1994. Could the U.S. be far behind? With President Clinton's lifting of the trade embargo last February, it's a distinct possibility. What remains to be seen, of course, is how far American flyers' stomachs will lift aboard a VN flight.

Not surprisingly, the place to get the cheapest airfares into Vietnam is Bangkok. And the cheapest carrier to fly in and out of Vietnam is Vietnam Airlines (VN). At presstime, VN's one-way fare into Ho Chi Minh City was US$150, and US$160 into Hanoi. Advance purchase isn't required, and there isn't a discount for booking round-trip. To avoid the delays and hassles of running all around Khao San (or the equivelant in other Asian cities) looking for the cheapest airfares, simply contact and book through VN's representative offices charted later in this section.

AUTHOR'S NOTE: VN PRICE HIKES AND EXPANSION PLANS

Passengers departing on domestic flights from Hanoi, Hai Phong, Danang, and HCMC are now required to pay an airport service charge of 15,000 dong (about US$1.50). The fees are said to be used to improve the airports' facilities.Vietnam Airlines has plans to more than double its fleet within the next six years. The airline said it needs an additional 30 to 40 of all types of aircraft by the end of the century. Boeing and McDonnell-Douglas are considered the primary contenders for supplying the new fleet. Currently VN utilizies aging Soviet-built Tupolev and Yak-40 aircraft on domestic routes. Additionally, the airline flies nine other aircraft on international routes—five Airbus A-320s leased from Air France, two Boeing 767s leased from Ansett Airlines, and the two ATR-72s which the airline owns. Taking advantage of the growing number of travelers to Vietnam, VN will be hiking its fares on domestic routes. This increase is likely to take place before the end of the year. Currently, foreigners pay about US$150 to get between HCMC and Hanoi, an excessive amount that presumably subsidizes the current Vietnamese national fare of about US$64 each way. Pacific Airlines, a recent upstart that marginally competes with VN has announced it will match the fares. Pacific Airlines currently has two aircraft which started a daily shuttle route between HCMC and Hanoi last April. In 1993, the number of domestic passengers on VN increased by 40 percent over a year earlier.

PASSENGER SALES AGENTS FOR VIETNAM AIRLINES

VIETNAM

Cantho Tourist
☎ 88.7.21853
FAX: 84.7.122719, 21804
27 Chau Van Liem, Cantho

Cat Bi Airport
☎ 0131.48309, 01381.45217
Cat Bi Airport, Haiphong

FujiCap
☎ 84.4.260158
86 Nguyen Du, Hanoi

FPT
☎ 84.4.267312
FAX: 84.4.26706
25 Ly Thuong Kiet, Ha Noi

Nasco
☎ 84.4.266602
FAX: 84.4.266666
Noibai Int'l Airport, Hanoi

PASSENGER SALES AGENTS FOR VIETNAM AIRLINES

Trade Services Co.
☎ *84.4.264259*
FAX: 84.4.256446
79 Ba Trieu, Hanoi

Vietnamtourism
☎ *84.4.264319*
FAX: 84.4.257583
30A Ly Thuong Kiet, Hanoi

Vinatour
☎ *84.4.239190*
54 Nguyen Du, Hanoi

Vinexad
☎ *84.4.256662*
FAX: 84.4.255556
14 Ngo Quyen, Hanoi

Art Tourist Services
☎ *84.8.230234*
FAX: 84.8.298947
63 Ly Tu Trong Street, HCMC

Peace Tours
☎ *84.8.294416*
FAX: 84.8.294416
60 Vo Van Tan, 3rd Dist. HCMC

New Global Co.
☎ *84.8.292287*
108 Ly Tu Trong, 1rst Dist., HCMC

Saigontourist
☎ *84.8.298914*
FAX: 84.8.224987
49 Le Thanh Ton, 1rst Dist., HCMC

Vietlink Trading, Travel & Tour Co.
☎ *84.8.555849*
FAX: 84.8.555852
43-45 Chau Van Liem, 5th Dist., HCMC

Vietnamtourism
☎ *84.8.290776*
FAX: 84.8.290775
234 Nam Ky Khoi Nghia, 3rd Dist., HCMC

CHINA

China Int'l Travel Service Guangzhou
☎ *86.2.6671453*
FAX: 86.2.6678048
179 Huanshi Rd, 510010 Guangzhou

China Travel Service Guangzhou
☎ *86.2.3331862*
FAX: 86.2.333247
10 Qiao Guang Rd, Guangzhou 510115

PASSENGER SALES AGENTS FOR VIETNAM AIRLINES

HONG KONG

China Travel Air Service

☎ *85.2.8533888*
FAX: 85.2.5446174
5th Floor, CST House
78-83 Connaught Rd., Central

HKVN Ltd. (GSA)

☎ *85.2.8106680*
FAX: 85.2.8698915
1206A Peregrine Tower, Uppo Ctr.
89 Queensway, Admiralty

On Chit Travel Service Ltd.

☎ *85.2.5247819*
FAX: 85.2.8454713
Rm. 801, Lap Fai Bldg.
6-8, Pottinger Street C

Skyvale Ltd.

☎ *85.2.7656552*
FAX: 85.2.7657166
Twr. A, Room 603
Hunghom Commercial Centre
37-39 Ma Tau Wai Rt., Kowloon

Vietlink Int'l Co. Ltd.

☎ *85.2.3678113*
FAX: 85.2.3122735
Unit A, 13F Wardley Centre No. 9-11
Part Aver, Kowloon

Waylock Travel Ltd.

☎ *85.2.3328961*
FAX: 85.2.3859291
Rm. 1003, Tai Shing Commercial Bldg.
498-500 Nathan Rd., Kowloon

LAOS

Lao Air Booking Co. Ltd.

☎ *5351*
38-40 Setthathirath Rd., Box 3080
Vientiane

MALAYSIA

Desk Air (Malaysia) SDN BHD

☎ *60.3.248-7500*
FAX: 60.3.248-5362
MUI Plaza, Ground Floor
Japan P. Ramlee, Kuala Lumpur 50250

PASSENGER SALES AGENTS FOR VIETNAM AIRLINES

Forefrank Travel
☎ 60.3.627-7260
FAX: 60.3.621-0112
Japan Murai Dua, Batu Kompleks
Batu Tiga, Japan Ipoh
5110 Kuala Lumpur
Forefrank

Maple Travel
☎ 60.3.244-3101
FAX: 60.3.242-9392
2.46-2.49, 2nd Floor
Wisma's Stephen's 88
Japan Raja Chulan
Kuala Lumpur 50200

Pelancongan Abadisdn BHD
☎ 60.3.241-2212
FAX: 60.3. 241-2322
1rst Floor Wisma Abadi 79, Japan Bu-
kit
Bintang 55100, Kuala Lumpur

Vietlink Group
☎ 60.3.443-1972
FAX: 60.3.441-7008
34A Japan Lumut, Damaicompes
(off Japan Ipoh)
50400 Kuala Lumpur

PHILIPPINES

Imex Pan Pacific
☎ 63.2.8125.623
FAX: 63.2.8125.625
120 G/F Anson Arcade Bldg.
Pasay Rd.
Makati
Metro Manila

Sampuguita Travel Corp.
☎ 63.2.8180608
Fax:63.2.8185037
Ground Floor, Mareic Building
Tordesillas Street, Salcedo Village,
Makati
Metro Manila

Expertravel & Tours, Inc.
☎ 63.2.509360
FAX: 63.2. 5211785
1971-1973 Mabini Street
Malate, Metro Manila

PASSENGER SALES AGENTS FOR VIETNAM AIRLINES

Far Travel, Inc.

☎ 63.2.8164072
FAX: 63.2.8156203
Asian Plaza, 1 De La Costa Street
Salcedo Village
Metro Manila

Ootomo Saia Travel Service

☎ 63.2.8312441
FAX: 63.2.8334361
R. 510, Sunset View Towers
2230 Roxas Blvd. Pasay
Metro 2 Manila

Trans Pacific Air Service Corp.

☎ 879666
FAX: 8176902
Ground Floor, SGV Building
6760 Ayala Ave.
Makati, Metro Manila

SINGAPORE

Desk Air (Singapore) PTE Ltd. (GSA)

☎ 65.3888988
FAX: 65.3387810
15 Beach Rd. #03-01/11
Beach Centre, Singapore

Maple Aviation

☎ 65. 5383787
FAX: 5383183
133 New Bridge Rd. #14-04/05
Chinatown Point, Singapore

Region Air Ltd.

☎ 65.2356277
FAX: 65.7361662
50 Cuscaden Rd. #06-01 HPL House
Singapore

Vietlink International (Singapore) Ltd.

☎ 65.5382050
FAX: 65.5386202
60 Eu Tong Sen Street #01-07
Furama Hotel Shopping Centre
Singapore

Robelle Tours & Travel Corp.

☎ 63.2.5219168
FAX: 63.2.5217358
Ground Floor, L&S Building
1414 Roxas Blvd.
Ermita, Manila, Philippines

PASSENGER SALES AGENTS FOR VIETNAM AIRLINES

TAIWAN

Hong Yi Travel Service
☎ 88.6.2.5059212
FAX: 88.6.2.5023763
Rm. 602. 6-F
185 Sung Chiang Rd., Taipei

Stone International Development
☎ 88.6..2.5016521
FAX: 88.6.2.5014348
6th Floor 1. Min Sheng East Rd.
Sec 3 Taipei

Vietlink International
☎ 8662.5683828
FAX: 8662.5683820
Rm. 1401, #206
Sungchiang Rd., Taipei

Uncle Travel Service Ltd.
☎ 88.6.2.5236204
FAX: 88.6.2.5236203
3F, No. 67 Cahng Chun Rd. Taipei

Worldwide Travel Service
☎ 88.6.2.5152185
FAX: 88.6.2.5091892
No. 99 Sung Chiang Rd. Taipei

Deks Air Taiwan
☎ 88.6.2.5061388
FAX: 88.6.2.5072581
Rms. 3-1 Int'l Nanking Bldg., 3F
NO. 103, SEC 3, Nanking East Rd.
Taipei

THAILAND

Air People Tour & Travel
☎ 66.2.2543921-4
FAX: 66.2.2553750
Regent House Bldg.
183 Rajdamri Rd.
Bangkok 10330

Desk Air Thailand
☎ 66.2.2360030
FAX: 66.2.2366796
Yada Bldg. Ground Floor
56 Silom Rd.
Bangkok 10500

OnTime Co.
☎ 66.2.2520080
FAX: 66.2.2512173
564-572 Ploenchit Rd.
Bangkok 10330

PASSENGER SALES AGENTS FOR VIETNAM AIRLINES

Maple Aviation
☎ *66.2.2376145-7*
FAX: 66.2.2376148
5th Floor Chan Issara Tower
942/137
D.1 Rama 4 Rd.
Bangkok 10500

SMI Travel
☎ *66.2.2511936 or 2525435*
FAX: 66.2.2511785
578-580 Ploenchit Rd., Putumwan
Bangkok 10330

Vietlink Int'l
☎ *66.2.2214614*
FAX: 66.2.2256389
719 Mahachai Rd., Kwaeng Burapa-
pirom
Khet Pranakarn
Bangkok 10200

Vietnam Tour Services
☎ *66.2.5802632/3*
FAX: 66.2.5802631
Park Inn Hotel
30/11 Rantanathket Rd.
Nonthaburi, Bangkok 11000

UNITED STATES

Discount Travel & Tours
☎ *1-714-892-8829*
FAX: 1-714-892-0688
9191 Bolsa Ave, #129
Westminster, CA 92683

C&H International
☎ *1-213-387-2284*
FAX: 1-213-387-8442
2500 Wilshire Blvd., #1000
Los Angeles, CA 90057

Group Systems Int'l
☎ *1-310-377-5096*
FAX: 1-310-544-3532
655 Deep Valley Rd., #375
Rolling Hills Estates, CA 90274

Minh Travel & Tours
☎ *1-818-281-1088*
FAX: 1-818-281-2208
412 West Valley Blvd.
San Gabriel, CA 91766

PASSENGER SALES AGENTS FOR VIETNAM AIRLINES

Sunrise Travel Inc.
☎ *1-617-963-1840*
FAX: 1-617-963-1843
1134 N. Main Street
Randolph, MA 02368

Tokyo Travel Service
☎ *1-714-434-7136*
FAX: 1-714-434-0767
17220 New Hope Street, #114
Fountain Valley, CA 92708

Vina USA Travel Center
☎ *1-212-545-7474*
FAX: 1-212-545-7698
373 Fifth Ave.
New York, NY 10016

Vietlink Int'l Travel & Tours
☎ *1-714-531-9828*
FAX: 1-714-531-9867
9950 Bolsa Ave., Unit D
Westminster, CA 92683

IMEX Pan-Pacific Inc.
☎ *1-714-531-2255*
FAX: 1-714-775-6948
14541 Brookhurst Street, #A1
Westminster, CA 92683

The cheapest places to get to are Tokyo, Seoul, Taipei and Hong Kong (because these are typically non-stop). The more isolated the destination, the more expensive. But tickets to the Far East can be had for a lot cheaper through the proliferation of ticket brokers in major cities. Flights that typically cost in the $900 to $1000 range at airline ticket counters and through travel agents can be had for as low as $725 through some brokers upon last inspection at the end of 1993. But beware of these guys. Some of them are as fly-by-night as a red-eye to Seoul flanked by Soviet fighters. Don't give them your credit card number over the phone. Instead, try to pick up your ticket and render payment simultaneously at their offices. Many a traveler has made telephone arrangements only to watch their departure date come and go without having received their ticket in the mail. Look in the Sunday travel sections of big papers, such as the *Los Angeles Times* or the *New York Times*.

You can also obtain discounted multidestination airline tickets for about twice the usual return fare to a single destination. These tickets may permit you three or four additional destinations but, of course, restrict you to the cities where the carrier flies. Advance Purchase Excursion tickets are also discounted, but you'll be as equally limited in your choice of destinations. Cancellation penalties can also be enormous.

Another cheap source of airline tickets into Vietnam is Asia itself. One-way fares, for instance, from Bangkok–Hanoi or Kuala Lumpur–Ho Chi Minh City are much cheaper when the tickets are purchased in Bangkok or Kuala Lumpur rather than in the U.S.—even aboard the same carrier. There are hundreds of travel agencies in most East Asian cities and, if you're looking for the cheapest fares, shop around. Once in Kuala Lumpur, I was comparing one-way fares from Singapore to Bangkok and, after having called at least a dozen KL travel agents, I couldn't find anything better than Korean's US$225 offering. Finally a last call I almost didn't make gave me an agent who put me on an almost empty Air New Zealand flight for a hundred bucks. It pays to shop around.

DISCOUNT TICKET BROKERS

American Travel Ventures	☎ *(310) 274-7061*
Angels International Travel	☎ *(800) 400-4150*
Bi-Coastal Travel	☎ *(800) 9-COASTAL*
Discover Wholesale Travel	☎ *(800) 576-7770*
Eros Travel	☎ *(213) 955-9695*
Falcon Wings Travel	☎ *(310) 417-3590*
Moon Travel & Tours	☎ *(800) 352-2899*
Sky Service Travel	☎ *(800) 700-1222*
Silver Wings Travel	☎ *(800) 488-9002*
South Sea Tour & Travel	☎ *(800) 546-7890*
Supertrip Travel	☎ *(800) 338-1898*
Travel Mate	☎ *(818) 507-6283*

TOURS

Taking a tour isn't the cop-out you might think it is. Tours can actually be a better alternative to independent travel if you've got only a week or two. You won't experience the delays, language problems or other time-consuming idiosyncracies inherent in the culture you're visiting. Of course you won't be truly experiencing the culture with a few of the tours. Others, though, give you a surprising amount of freedom. And many of the "new breed" of tour operators are themselves formerly—and even currently—independent travelers themselves. Young, and perhaps only entrepreneurial by default, their tours represent not only the spirit of independent travel, but the nuances as well. These days, you can spend a couple of weeks pedaling a bicycle up the coast of Vietnam from Ho Chi Minh City to Hue (courtesy of Velo Asia), while immersing yourself in the hospitality of rural Vietnamese, Khmer and Cham villagers. It's a tour only in the sense that you're sharing your experiences with a handful of other foreigners.

Experienced travelers will tell you that bigger things come in small packages. If you have only a couple of weeks it doesn't make sense to bounce around East Asia like a good pinball shot. Limit your destinations so you can get more out of them.

Hanoi has a slew of plans for both improving and expanding tourist areas throughout the country to attract more foreign visitors. In the Mekong River Delta region, the floating markets Phuong Dien and An Binh are targeted for greater accessibility. The remarkable "Great Supermarket" of Phung Hiep (the markets distinctly dissimilar to the floating markets found in and around Bangkok), where seven of the Mekong's waterways converge, is an absolutely impressive sight; during the fruit season, hundreds of boats carrying rambutan, mango and other assorted fruit move in and out of the market areas. Visitors to the area can take an early morning coach from HCMC, eat breakfast at Tan An, and then cross the two ferries (at My Thuan and Hau Giang) to arrive at Can Tho, about 170 km from Saigon. There visitors can take a bus to Soc Trang in the afternoon, visit a Khmer museum and bat pagoda, and then return to Can Tho to view performances of "reformation" music.

The next morning, it's then off to the Ninh Kien wharf for a steamboat ride of about 25 km to reach the Phung Hiep market. There you can take a steamboat ride through the canals flanked by curious villagers, most of whom will insist that you stay at their homes for a meal of freshly-slaughtered poultry and Vietnamese whiskey the villagers usually distill under the earth in their backyards. If you're part of the tour, the steamboat ride will probably prevent you from fraternizing with the villagers, as you'll have to go back to Saigon that evening, a ride which won't be a lot of fun if you've imbibed on too much rice whiskey.

INSIDER TIP

Seven tour companies operate in conjunction with HCMC's Peace Tour, which operates land route car tours of Indochina. One tour consists of more than 400 travelers departing Bangkok via 150 privately-owned automobiles. The caravan passes through Cambodia, the Moc Bai border post, and visits the Cu Chi Tunnels and HCMC before proceeding up the coast on National Highway 1 to Danang, Hue, Quang Tri and Dong Ha before heading west on Highway 9 to the Lao border. After five days in Laos, the group then comes back to Bangkok via Cambodia.

WARNING: Because of Cambodian red tape and the potential danger caused by the fighting between Cambodian Government troops and the Khmer Rouge, the first group of the Peace Tour was stopped at the Cambodian border and not allowed to cross for more than a day. After finally entering Cambodia, the group was turned back again not more than a few kilometers inside Vietnam. Many clients abandoned the caravan, returning to Bangkok and suing their respective tour operators.

The future of these types of tours is at best nebulous at this point, but I understand tour operators are continuing their efforts to bring travelers to Vietnam by car now that the Laos border along Route 9 is open to Western travelers. (Crossing from Cambodia to Vietnam by private vehicle is still prohibited.) Crossing Cambodia seems to be the major hurdle in conducting these types of tours, as fighting continues, heavily in some areas (particularly in the west and the northwest near the Thai border). Pailin, the site of the Khmer Rouge headquarters, is now an area under constant siege. But it is my belief that these tours will become less problematic in the near future, and they'd be a hell of a lot of fun, if there's any guarantee you won't get shot in the head.

Vietnam War vets and their families can take advantage of a visit to the former battlefield at Tay Nguyen on the Central High Plateau. Currently, there are VERY FEW tourists enjoying this ecological paradise, which has environmentally recovered completely since the end of the hostilities in 1975. In addition to Khe Sanh, Dien Bien Phu and the Ho Chi Minh Trail, there are a number of barely-visited areas of the Central High Plateau. Interesting locals that see few, if any, tourists in the area include An Khe, Pleime and Dakto, as well as the mountain path to Lak Lake. A number of tourist agencies have combined their resources to make tours to the area viable.

The Central High Plateau has a number of attractions that tourists are infrequently aware of. There's the village of Bien Ho, and in the Lak district you can rent a canoe or ride on the back of an elephant. Hunting is also available for the outdoorsman.

Tourist agencies in HCMC may be able to cut out some of the more expensive portions of the tour, i.e. the airfares. You may be able to get from Da Lat to Buon Ma Thout or from Buon Ma Thuot to Nha Trang through the Phoenix Pass (Phuong Hoang)—or take Highway 19 from Qui Nhon to Pleiku via the An Khe Pass. Ask around at the travel agencies spread across HCMC. Some of the better ones are VYTA Tours at *52 Hai Ba Trung Street;* ☎ *230767; FAX: 84.8.298348,* and the Travel Agency at *110A Nguyen Hue Ave, Dist. 1;* ☎ *22511; FAX: 84.8.24205.*

There are a lot of operators out there, and a lot of new ones trying to cash in on Vietnam's growing popularity. Get to know as much as possible about a firm before selecting it. Ideally, talk to some other people who've employed the company before. And remember, there are as many different types of tour companies as there are genres of travel. To simplify your tour selection Fielding has organized package tours through a number of recommended tour operators. See "Package Tours" guide on p. 409 or call 1-800 FW-2-GUIDE for more information.

TOURS FOR VIETNAM WAR VETERANS

With improving Vietnam/U.S. relations, a few agencies now offer tours of Vietnam through areas where American soldiers fought, were based, and sent on R&R. As Saigontourist phrases it, "As understood by its appellation, war veteran tours have been set up by Vietnamese veterans for their foreign counterparts of the two Indochina Wars." These are special programs for those who served in Vietnam and would like to revisit former locations and areas of combat activities of their military units, of the Viet Cong War Zones, and especially former battlefields. There are also more extensive programs for veterans from all countries (U.S., Australia, South Korea, Thailand, France and the Philippines) to visit the sites of former bases and areas of firefights. Vietnamtourism says these programs are designed to "promote understanding and friendship, thus helping to heal war wounds." Although the tours will have special appeal to returning American soldiers, all visitors to Vietnam are welcome who share an interest in visiting former battlefields as well as experiencing "the new Vietnam." Highlights of the tours consist of visits to the DMZ, Ben Hai River, Dong Ha, Quang Tri, the former U.S. base at Khe Sanh, Ashau-Aluoi valleys, "Hamburger Hill" (south of Ashau Valley), and the Ho Chi Minh Trail.

Some of the areas visited include:

BEN HAI RIVER, THE DMZ

From 1954 to 1975, The Ben Hai River served as the demarcation between the republic of Vietnam (South Vietnam) and the Democratic Republic of North Vietnam. The Demilitarized Zone consisted of an area 5 km on each side of the river, or demarcation line.

HO CHI MINH TRAIL

Initially, this was only a small trail in the mountainous range of Truong Son only for foot soldiers. But it later developed into an intricate, intertwined road network along the majestic Truong Son range—consisting of a trail for foot messengers and guides, and a larger road for big trucks. For more than a decade, the Ho Chi Minh Trail was a special supply and communication line from North Vietnam to battle sites in South Vietnam.

For more information, see Package Tours, p. 409.

TRAVELING BY ROAD IN VIETNAM: NATIONAL HIGHWAY 1

Totaling a distance of more than 1700 km, Vietnam's National Highway 1 (in its various stretches of smooth pavement and barely negotiable, dilapidated cattle trails) is the longest and most important roadway in the country. Including Highway 1A, it links Rach Gia in the far south all the way to Hanoi. For most of the route north of HCMC it is flanked by the gorgeous Troung Son mountains on the left and by the clear waters of the South China Sea on the right.

Between villages and cities, the route deteriorates from paved scenic pavement to pothole-ridden trenches meaning that bus drivers, and others who frequent the highway, need backsides of lead to endure. Rarely can you reach speeds of more than 50 mph (78 kmph), except on a fast motorcycle where far greater speeds are possible but dangerous due to the vast amount of pedestrian, bicycle and ox cart traffic. At times the shoulder of the highway will be in better shape than the roadway itself, and you'll constantly see motorbikers using the well-worn, but relatively smooth shoulders of the road rather than the highway itself. Roadworkers can be occasionally seen throwing large rocks into the deepest trenches, but there is, amazingly enough, little work that is done to improve NH1. Some of the bridges that were destroyed during the Vietnam War have yet to be repaired, many only crossable by planks and/or railway ties that have been placed over the crumbling grid foundations.

Women line the route toting astoundingly heavy baskets supported by bamboo poles with produce going to market, perhaps many kilometers. They seem to totally ignore the speeding motorbikes and dust- and exhaust-spewing buses and freight trucks that proceed along the highway as if they were its only users. Oxen and horse carts plod the highway, pulling their loads of sugarcane and rice. Bicycles may have as many as three passengers; I've seen as many as six individuals, entire families and maybe some of their friends, astride small Honda 50 cc motorbikes. You'll come across Lambrettas, motorcycles attached with a covered cart with benches running along the sides. They're slow moving and usually packed with at least two dozen people and as many chickens or ducks. It's an unbelievably unsafe way to travel, but is the most popular form of short-distance trips.

Ornate Vietnamese pagodas flank National Highway 1 in virtually uninhabited areas.

The most useful device on your own mode of transportation is the horn. If it isn't working, it may as well be the steering that isn't functioning. You'll see hundreds of the brightly colored Ford and Desoto buses packed with passengers like sardines in oil plowing their way to places such as Danang, Hue, Quinonh, Vinh, Phan Tiet, Saigon and the likes. Water spews from small pipes in front of the vehicles near the undercarriages. The water is from the large drums attached to the roofs of the vehicles—and they must stop every 100 km or so to have these refilled, as they serve as the vehicles' cooling systems. The occupants don't seem to mind the cramped conditions aboard the buses—perhaps because most are under five feet tall. For the average Westerner, a long bus ride is intolerable and doesn't give the traveler the opportunity to really "be on the road," as the driver will stop every couple or so hours at a roadside cafe of his own choosing so the weary passengers can refill their own cooling systems. On the buses, you'll see two young men straddling straps on the stairs of the open doors, yelling at pedestrians and motorists in the bus path to move the hell out of the way.

The few cars you'll see along Highway 1 are usually hired by tourists or are government vehicles. You'll see, though, a number of microbuses of the various Vietnamese tourist agencies bouncing along the roadway usually carrying Viet Khieu (Overseas Vietnamese) tourists up and down the coast. The big trucks are usually relatively recently built Soviet heavy duty trucks, although you'll also see a number of American- and French-made trucks left over from both Indochina wars that are still quite operational, the result of primitive, but ingenious maintenance.

INSIDER TIP

Because tourism is expanding so rapidly in Vietnam, some of the sites where locals rarely laid eyes on foreigners are becoming inundated with white-skinned Anglos with funny green eyes, cameras, and Deet. Battle sites from the Vietnam War are particularly becoming popular with foreign tourists. The village of My Lai and Son My village, where American soldiers massacred hundreds of Vietnamese civilians have become hot spots to visit. Since the 25th anniversary of the massacre more than a year ago, more than 7,000 people have visited Son My. More than half the visitors were foreigners, whose number visiting the site has increased four-fold in just 12 months. The number of Vietnamese visitors has doubled. So if My Lai is on your itinerary, expect some company.

Frequently, you'll come across unhusked rice drying in the sun that may spread halfway across the highway. The larger vehicles will roll right over the grain—curiously, the farmers say it helps speed the drying process. The rice is left untended except for the occasional spreading of the path to even the terrain of the grain. Sugarcane and rice paper are also spread across the road at various points, although vehicles aren't meant to drive over the chips and (markers in the form of stones or carts are placed in front of the piles to keep drivers off them). Think of the carbon monoxide and Michelin tire ingredients in your cuisine the next time you're dining.

At various points in the villages along NH1 the road narrows to a mere fly strip as motorcycles, bicycles and heavy trucks barge through the local markets that bulge out into the road like non-ticket holders at a Grateful Dead concert. Additionally spilling out onto the highway are large groups of schoolchildren and other surrounding card games, again, totally oblivious to the traffic. NH1 is as much a social center as it is a thoroughfare.

Of course, there are accidents—many of them. Where motorists or pedestrians have died is usually marked with a buddhist-like shrine, and many drivers stop at these points to pay their respects. It is supposed to be good luck to do so. Near Ca Na, there's even a memorial where a busload of passengers died some years ago.

All along Highway 1 food stalls and cafes abound, their owners dangerously sprinting into the middle of the roadway as if there was an emergency to flag down motorists into their eateries. Usually the cafes are in clumps, so the competition for business, although friendly, is ruthless. In a way, customers at these stalls are a remedy to an emergency, as the stall owners are all quite poor. Wherever you stop, you will be swarmed by children, beggars and such, selling everything from lighter fluid to chewing gum.

Perhaps the great advantage of Highway 1, as well as other routes spread acrosss Vietnam, is the number of Honda repair shops. Every few hundred meters you are bound to see a sign saying "Honda (spelled in various configurations such as 'Hun Da, Honza, Hon Daa', etc.) Xe Dap," the latter meaning the shop also works on bicycles. At virtually any point along Highway 1 if you break down, there will be a Honda repair hootch within rolling distance. Vietnamese, mechanics or not, will instantly try to determine and remedy your bike's malady. And most are quite adept, although they tend to smoke cigarettes so close to gasoline, it's amazing the country hasn't completely defoliated itself without the aid of hostile aggressors.

You'll find that after passing several kilometers through a village or town, a team of policemen will have set up roadblocks. Their purpose is usually to stop buses and trucks for bribes. Tourists are rarely stopped by the police, although you may find yourself on a microbus whose driver doesn't possess the proper credentials to be transporting tourists. Some of these drivers employ imaginative ways of bypassing the roadblocks. One driver I met near Phan Tiet, before reaching a roadblock, unloaded his tourists and placed them on buses a kilometer before the checkpoint. He picked them back up again on the other side. Police, when they see a large motorcycle approaching, may step out into the road to flag you down with their batons—but upon realizing you're a foreigner will allow you to pass (Vietnamese are not allowed to operate motorcycles over 175 cc unless they're in "high positions," usually in the government—or they're police officers themselves).

NH1 is continually surrounded by rice fields, the workers under their conical hats stooped tending to the crop. You'll see statues of the Virgin Mary and ancient Cham towers perched on hilltops or right beside the roadway.

Near Cam Ranh, salt factories flank the roadside, and salt paddies extend out into the deep blue mountain-ringed bay.

Going north, after passing through Danang, you make a journey over one of the most spectacular passes in Vietnam, Hai Van Pass, which reaches an altitude of nearly 500 meters in the Tron Son Mountain Range. The views of both ocean and lush green mountains are unsurpassed anywhere in the world. This pass, many times shrouded in dense fog, is so dangerous and steep that steep, ascending turn-off ramps on downgrades have been constructed for trucks and buses that lose their brakes, which happens constantly on this stretch of roadway. This is the ribbon of NH1 that drivers fear the most, and perhaps the most dangerous stretch of NH1 in Vietnam. Hai Van Pass, during the 15th century, marked the border between the Kingdom of Champa and Vietnam. On top of the pass, there is an old fort that was built by the French and then later used by the Americans and the South Vietnamese Army.

And it is here, between Danang and Long Co Beach where the Vietnamese climate changes dramatically—from sunny, hot and humid to damp, gray and cloud covered—and cold. From this point to Ha Long Bay and Hanoi, you'll think you're in a different country. The fog straddling the mountainsides of Hai Van Pass creates some of the best photo opportunities in Vietnam, but you'll soon become depressed by the lack of sunlight and heat which you despised only hours earlier. Villagers and farmers are dressed in winter clothing.

The one thing to be careful about NH1 is that it forks frequently, the most confusing fingers of the road being in Quy Nhon and Phan Rang. You may travel several km before you realize you screwed up.

OTHER ROAD ROUTES BEING CONSIDERED

Now that the Friendship Bridge has been completed linking Thailand and Laos, there's a lot of talk about linking Thailand and Vietnam through Laos at other points. Some of the projects seriously being considered are Highway 8, which would link Thailand's northeastern Nakhon Phanom Province with Vietnam's Cua Lo Port, near Vinh, via Khammouan Province in central Laos. Also being considered is Highway 12, which would link Thailand's Nakhon Phanom Province with the Vietnamese port of Hon La. This route is farther south than Highway 8. Highway 9 already links Danang and Hue with Laos and Thailand.

The government is interested in all three roads but particular attention is paid to upgrading Route 9. This is to the benefit of Thailand's Mukdahan Province.There would be less investment involved, and the road traverses relatively flat terrain. Additionally a new port would not have to be built. But Nakhon Phanom has the edge in that Highway 12 through Khammouan to the Vietnamese coast is only 270 km, as opposed to the 570 km stretch along Highway 9 linking Vietnam with Laos and Thailand. One of the carrots being held out, on the part of the Thais is that construction of Highway 12 would help reduce the pressure of population growth in Bangkok, and would more evenly distribute Thai manufacturing facilities. Laos favors construction of Highway 8, because it would be the shortest way of reaching its capital, Vientiane. Whichever route is chosen, the three countries will still have a modern roadway of international standards that will eventually become a major international transportation link.

AUTHOR'S NOTE

A little advice for travelers in Vietnam: There are 10,000 km of roads, 40 percent of which are rated "poor" or "very poor." There are 8280 road bridges, 50 percent of which are considered dilapidated. There are 2600 km of railways, seven major seaports, three international airports, and 10 domestic airports.

BOOKS

The following are some of the best historical and contemporary works on Vietnam:

Browne, Malcombe, *Red Socks and Muddy Boots* (New York Times Press, 1993); this is an excellent, fast-paced accounting of the famous journalist's observations of the Vietnam War based on his 11 years in-country during the 1960s and 70s. It's a humorous and de-pressing no punches-pulled analysis of the political and military blunders both sides struggled with in justifying both their moral, po-litical and military ambitions in Indochina. Browne, journalist Peter Arnett (now at CNN) and Neil Sheehan were primarily blackballed by US and ARVN forces as traitors, so this makes for fascinating reading of life in a Huey and a suitcase.

Along the same lines is Sheehan's definitive work, *A Bright Shining Lie* (Jonathan Cape, London, 1989). This is a huge account of the war based around the life of John Paul Vann. Well researched and as eye-opening as they come. This was a pulitzer prize winner. Sheehan also wrote *Two Cities: Hanoi and Saigon* (Jonathan Cape, London, 1992).

Another colleague of Sheehan's and Browne's was David Halber-stram, whose *The Making of A Quagmire* (Ballantine Books, New York) is considered a gem in outlining U.S. participation in the war.

Also check out *The Real War* by Jonathan Shell (Pantheon Books, New York, 1987.

The Bamboo Cage by Leo Cooper (Cawthorne, Nigel, 1992). A tear-jerking account of POWs and MIAs in Vietnam during the war.

Francis Fitzgerald's *Fire in the Lake* (Vintage Books, New York, 1972) was also a Pulitzer Prize winner about U.S. involvement dur-ing the war.

Why Vietnam?, Archimedes Patti (University of California Press, Berkeley, 1980) is a compelling history of OSS (pre CIA) to funnel weapons to Ho Chi Minh at the end of WWII. Patti was with the OSS during this time and was close to Ho when he claimed North Vietnamese independence in 1945.

A Death in November by Ellen Hammer (EP Dutton & Sons, New York, 1987) is the story of Diem's overthrow and execution in 1963.

One Crowded Hour, Tim Bowden (Angus and Robertson, 1988) chonicles the work of Australian film journalist Neil Davis, who shot footage of the NVA tank crashing through the gates of the presiden-tial Palace in April 1975.

The Tunnels of Cu Chi, Tom Mangold and John Pennycate (1985). A look at the hardships the Viet Cong faced in building and living in the famed tunnels west of Saigon.

The Fall of Saigon, David Butler (Simon & Schuster, 1985) is a look at the events and the chaos surrounding takeover of the South's capital in 1975, as is *55 Days; The Fall of Saigon*, by Alan Dawson (Prentice Hall, Englewood Cliffs, NJ, 1977).

Michael Herr's *Dispatches* (Knopf, New York, 1987) is a journalist's first-hand look at the bloody conflict.

Stanley Karnow's highly respected *Vietnam: A History* (Viking Press, New York, 1983) is one of the most respected works on Vietnam in the last two decades.

Chickenhawk, by Robert Mason (Penguin, 1984) is the recollections of a chopper pilot. Fast paced, edge-of-the-seat reading.

The Pentagon Papers (Bantam Books, Toronto, 1971) were published by the *New York Times* and had the same effect, if not more, on America's sentiments toward the war as did the 1968 Tet Offensive.

Born on the Fourth of July, Ron Kovic (Pocket Books, New York, 1976). A grisly, heart-wrenching account of a soldier maimed during the war. Was made into a blockbuster movie starring Tom Cruise in an unforgettable role as the author.

The 13th Valley. It was written years before the motion picture *Platoon* hit the big screen and is easily the more horrific of the two in describing the terror of being a grunt in the jungle.

Brothers in Arms (Avon Books, New York, 1986), by William Broyles Jr. is a mildly interesting account of a former GI-turned-journalist returning to Vietnam some years after the war.

Portrait of the Vietnamese Soldier (Red River Press, Hanoi) is a provocative account of the North Vietnamese struggle against the Americans.

William Turley's *The Second Indochina War: A Short Political and Military History, 1954–1975* (Westview, Boulder, 1976), can be hard reading, but it's comprehensive and highly detailed.

Bungling military strategy is examined in *On Strategy*, by Colonel Harry Summers (Presidio Press, Navato, Calif., 1982)

Bloods: An Oral History of the Vietnam War by Black Veterans, by Wallace Terry (Ballentine Books, 1984)

Chained Eagle is a gripping account of the lives of American POWs by Everett Alverez (Dell, New York, 1989).

Viet Cong Memoir, by Troun Nhu Tang, is about the life of a former Viet Cong soldier who later rejected post-1975 Vietnamese politics. (Harcourt Brace Jovanovich, San Diego, 1985).

Ecological Consequences of the Vietnam War, SIPRI (Almqvist & Wiksell, Stockholm, 1976). An account of the environmental devastation of the war.

OTHER BOOKS OF INTEREST

The Quiet American, Graham Greene (Heinemann, London, 1954). Most of us read this highly accurate fictionalized account of the impending American involvement in the Indochinese conflict in university. As relevant today as it was then. Some say it's a masterpiece.

A Dragon Apparent: Travels in Cambodia, Laos and Vietnam, by Norman Lewis (Eland Books, 1951). A superb travelogue.

Charles Fenn's *Ho Chi Minh: A biographical Introduction* (Charles Tuttel, Rutland Vermont, 1973).

Saigon, Anthony Grey (Pan, London, 1983).

The Birth of Vietnam, Keith Taylor (University of California Press, Berkeley, 1983).

J. Helzar, *The Art of Vietnam* (Hanlyn, London, 1973).

Elizabeth Kemp, *Month of Pure Light; The Regreening of Vietnam* (The Women's Press, London, 1990).

Gerald Hickey, *Village in Vietnam* (Yale University Press, New Haven, 1964).

Vietnamese Anticolonialism: 1885–1925, by David G. Marr (University of Berkeley, Los Angeles, 1971).

The Rise of Nationalism in Vietnam: 1900–1941 (Cornell University Press, Ithica, New York, 1976).

Australia's War in Vietnam by Frank Frost (Allen and Unwin, Sydney, Boston, and London, 1987).

All the Way: Australia's Road to Vietnam by Gregory Pemberton (Allen and Unwin, Sydney, Boston, and London, 1987).

Robert F. Turner, *Vietnamese Communism: It's Origins and Development* (Hoover Institution Press, Stanford, 1975).

WHEN YOU ARRIVE

Vietnam is a surprisingly easy country to enter these days. The formalities are no more arduous than, say, entering Thailand. Frankly, it's more of a hassle entering Singapore than either Saigon or Hanoi. The infamous scams pulled by Vietnamese customs officials and policemen that were prevalent only a short time ago are all but nonexistent now. Foreigners, who are legitimate tourists of course, have little fear of being harassed or detained while an "illegal entry" fine is negotiated. Be warned, however, that a lot less English is spoken in Hanoi than in Saigon and, that if there is a problem, it probably will be both more expensive and time consuming to solve it. It appears, however, that customs officials in both cities are under instructions in no uncertain terms that each and every stamp on a foreigner's passport is synonymous with much-needed hard currency; the likelihood of you being afforded the opportunity to tell your friends and other potential visitors of the hardships you encountered entering or leaving Vietnam are these days, fortunately, minimal. And even though Vietnam is a communist country, you will be surprised at how much freedom you're afforded.

INSIDER TIP: SOME ADVICE FOR RETURNING VIET KIEU

If you're an overseas Vietnamese, or "Viet Kieu," returning to Vietnam, here's a tip: don't show your bucks. Vietnamese can instantly spot an overseas Vietnamese, usually by their behavior and attire. Many Vietnamese are wary of returning "Viet Kieu," and suspicious of their intentions. You may be only a tourist, but many Vietnamese will suspect you've returned to your home country to make a fast buck, especially if you dress flashy and exhibit the behavior and social customs you've acquired in your new home country. Curiously, although they fanatically vie for it, the Vietnamese do not trust wealth, especially the display of it. Additionally, you may face criticism from your anti-communist friends at home, who may accuse you of supporting Marxism. Don't be surprised if many at home call you a VC (Viet Cong). Although the embargo has been lifted it is still very difficult for Overseas Vietnamese to reintegrate with their people. You may feel like a stranger in your own country. The Vietnamese government will welcome your money, of course. Overseas Vietnamese send or bring into the country perhaps US$1 billion each year.

On the plane you will have filled out a customs declaration form. Those items you have declared will be inspected in all likelihood. And even though the idea of having your belongings displayed is unappealing (and downright frightening if you've got on your person anything marginally to highly suspicious, such as gems, figurines, poached animal parts, Chinese elixirs or heroin paste), remember that what you don't declare doesn't exist. Say you're traveling with a laptop computer and don't declare it upon entry. If you're searched upon leaving and it's discovered, you may end up paying a duty on it, if not worse.

LANGUAGE AND CULTURE

There are a lot of nuances that differ among the peoples of the Far East. But for every contrast, there are 10 commonalities. Asians, as tolerant as they are, will expect you to behave in ways and speak with a body language that will fluster you at first. You'll be tempted to be amused by gestures and customs that seem everything from banal to compulsive. But don't be.

AUTHOR'S OBSERVATION: DEALING WITH THE VIETNAMESE SOCIALLY AND IN BUSINESS

A few notes on how to deal with Vietnamese customs, whether you're in the country on business or pleasure. Simply reading about the "customs" in Asian nations won't be enough to learn the idiosyncrasies of Vietnamese customs and behavior. In terms of business or official meetings, get a good interpreter. That person should teach you correct pronunciation for the individuals you'll be meeting with. Learn Vietnamese greetings (the Crash Course in Speaking Vietnamese in this book will help). Learn now to recognize the individual you'll be meeting before the meeting, either through an interpreter's description or by seeing a photograph. That way, you'll immediately know who to address when entering the room. And do not greet an assistant first! When you shake hands, do so at arm's length rather than up close. Most Westerners are quite a bit taller than their Vietnamese hosts.

Sitting at a table during a business meeting, do not cross your legs or show the soles of your feet (this is really not even acceptable in social situations, although the increasing influx of naive Westerners into Vietnam has made the Vietnamese more accustomed to this—but only in social environs). Although the custom of giving and receiving with both hands is common in Southeast Asia, it is not necessary in Vietnam. When handing out business cards, start with the most important person you are with. But give cards to everyone! You never know where the mailroom clerk will be in a few years. If you're short on business cards and have to make photocopies, never mix the two when you're handing out cards. Either hand out a photocopy or the original.

One of the life threatening habits I've acquired since being in Vietnam is that I've started smoking cigarettes. This was mainly due to the fact that I was incessantly offered them as gifts. Most Vietnamese men smoke, though few women do. Simply, if you're offered a cigarette, take it. Not doing so is somewhat of an insult, even if you don't smoke. Either smoke it or place it on the table in front of you (in which case you will not be offered another).

AUTHOR'S OBSERVATION: DEALING WITH THE VIETNAMESE SOCIALLY AND IN BUSINESS

If you're employing a translator, address the person you're speaking with, not the translator. When the Vietnamese is speaking with you, look at him and acknowledge him occasionally with a nod of the head. Again, don't look at the interpreter. He is only the conduit of your conversation with the person you are meeting with.

Vietnamese love to drink. If you do, too, you've come to the right place. There are different forms of toasting in Vietnam. One of them, which is used frequently, is called "Tram Phan Tram." It means you are required to empty the entire contents of your glass. If you don't drink alcohol, a soft drink or tea will do. But if you do enjoy an occasional whiskey or beer, be prepared to enjoy your imbibement excessively. In Vietnam, you should never refuse hospitality when it's offered.

Just use good judgement. Knowing how to dress, present and compose yourself will dispel a ton of potential problems. Remember, it's better to blend in in Asia than to stand out. Dress coolly but conservatively. Shorts are okay in informal environments, but not short ones. Ladies should cover as much of their bodies as reasonably possible. You don't have to look like a nun, but it wouldn't hurt. No short dresses, except perhaps in Hong Kong. Anything you consider sexy will be taken as offensive by your Asian hosts. And try not to look like a hippie. That sarong and the beads you bought in Ko Samui are fine on Ko Samui, but now you're in a land of pith helmets, business suits and olive drab uniforms. Take heed.

Displays of emotion—from affection to anger—are considered crass and rude. Never show anger, regardless of the situation. Most Southeast Asians abhor conflict. Smile even to the man you'd rather kick than converse with. Equally as offensive, in most places, are public displays of sexual affection. Kissing and even holding hands are discouraged in most Asian communities. Save it for the hotel.

When entering an individual's home, in some cases, you'll need to remove your shoes. However, unlike other predominantly Buddhist countries in the region, the Vietnamese are generally not inclined to follow this practice, even inside temples. If you're not sure, your host will not be offended if you politely inquire. Never will you be expected to remove your shoes at hotels and public structures other than some religious temples.

Don't pat anyone on the head, including children. It's a sign of disrespect. And what you do with your hands, do with both hands or your right hand only. The left hand is considered unclean. This includes for eating and passing objects to other people. It's a pain in the rear if you're left-handed, but try and follow the rule at least when it's most appropriate, as in ceremonial occasions, toasts in your honor, etc.

The feet are considered unclean as well. When seated, don't point them in anyone's direction.

If eating with chopsticks, place them horizontally across your bowl when finished.

Finally, be especially careful of the gestures you make. Symbols that are considered innocent or even complimentary in the U.S. are construed differently abroad. However, it's only truthful to say that, as a foreigner, you won't be expected to understand proper gestures and behavior of the Vietnamese. Rather, you'll be expected not to understand. And, in most cases, violations will be dismissed with a smile, if they are even noticed. One reason the Vietnamese are more tolerant of Western idiosyncracies than other East Asian societies is the fact that 500,000 Americans and a few thousand other Westerners essentially occupied the southern half of the country for more than 10 years in the 60s and 70s. Things are changing very rapidly here.

AUTHOR'S OBSERVATION

The liberalization of the Vietnamese economy has spawned the influx of other Western influences or "extravagances" that would have been unheard of, or in this case, unseen, 10 years ago. A point in case is the rise in cosmetic sales. Just a short time a go, even lipstick was seen as a luxury for the very wealthy, models and actresses. Now Vietnamese are looking to the West for beauty aids, and companies such as Max Factor, Chanel, and Christian Dior couldn't be more ecstatic. Whereas once only Thai-made cosmetic products made poor girls even poorer, now beauty products from firms such as Chanel, Lancome and Revlon can be found in shops lining the boulevards of Hanoi and Saigon. A recent look at some of the shops found that a Suntory gift purse can be had for about US$25, while a bottle of Poison perfume fetches US$80.

Although there has existed a counterfeit market for such "brands" from Singapore, Thailand and China for years, it is dwindling quickly, as Vietnamese women are now insisting on the real McCoy. The cosmetic market though, according to most observers is still wide open, and will become increasingly lucrative as more Vietnamese women have the means to look "beautiful"—or use their meager means for beauty at the expense of food. Hopefully, we won't see the "Pepsi Generation" also become the Karen Carpenter generation.

BEHAVING IN TEMPLES

The rule of always removing your shoes before entering an Asian temple of worship is not always observed in Vietnam. It depends entirely upon the temple, the lifestyle of its hosts and local custom. As mentioned above, inquire first. At many temples, especially those frequented by tourists, a sign in English will be posted regarding the rule.

If seated before a Buddha, sit on your knees, thigh and hip, with your feet extending behind you. Do not sit in the lotus position (cross-legged). No shorts in temples, although some guides will tell you that it's okay. (They just don't want to offend you). Cameras may or may not be permitted. Usually they're not in other East Asian temples, but in many Vietnamese temples, they are permitted—especially in those with connections to the state. They charge an additional camera admission fee! And remember, customs and behavior in the south are a lot more relaxed than in the north. It's like the difference between Venice, California and Newport, Rhode Island.

A WORD ABOUT LANGUAGE

We'll admit it; the tongues of the Far East make the languages of Europe seem like dialects of English. Learning Mandarin Chinese, Japanese, Thai, Cambodian, Malay and Vietnamese virtually requires surgery. But a little effort on your part to pick up some rudimentary Vietnamese phrases will go a long way. Unlike huffy Parisians, Vietnamese people are honored when you make an attempt to speak their language, as futile and unintelligible as the resulting utterance may be.

It's an old phrase, but not without relevance. When overseas, you are an ambassador of your country. How you treat your Vietnamese hosts will be reciprocated to those who follow in your footsteps.

A WORD ABOUT ILLEGAL DRUGS

Leave them at home. Drug users and traffikers beware. A special squad formed by the Police Department's Economic Crimes Division will step up its efforts against both drug addiction and trafficking. It will become the most powerful anti-drugs force in Vietnam. In 1993, Vietnamese authorities siezed 1.4 kilos of opium and 10 kilos of heroin. During the last year, three drug smugglers have been sentenced to death, while two others were jailed for life.

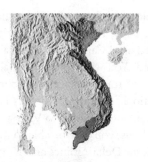

VIETNAM TODAY

Barbwire and billiards. As Vietnam's economy becomes influenced by the West, so do its artists.

Two decades after U.S. troops pulled out of Vietnam, Americans are returning to this still-battle-scarred country, only this time, they're coming as tourists.

Thanks to the U.S. government's removal of restrictions against travel to Vietnam in 1992, followed by President Clinton's lifting of the trade embargo this past February, a growing slew of tour operators now offer group and individual tour packages to Vietnam. Their numbers—and travelers' options—are expanding at a jackrabbit's pace.

Tours from the U.S. usually fly into Bangkok or Hong Kong, convenient gateways for air connections into Vietnam. Although operators say most of their inquiries are for tours that combine Vietnam with Cambodia and Laos, you probably won't see many all-Indochina tours advertised until Cambodia's on-again/off-again political problems are resolved. You will, however, be able to choose from a fairly good selection of tour packages that combine Vietnam with other Asian destinations, including China. (There are good flight connections from Nanking, China into Vietnam.) And soon, maybe by the time you read this, you may be able to fly directly to Vietnam from the U.S. (Look for Delta Airlines and United to be the companies to first offer these routes.)

Americans who have already gone to Vietnam say they're amazed by the friendliness the people show toward U.S. visitors, given the recent history of the two countries. They're also surprised to find that just about everything is priced in U.S. dollars, rather than in Vietnamese currency, the dong (about 10,800 dong equals US$1), especially in the larger population centers. Even the departure tax of $6 is paid in U.S. currency. Hotels and other businesses have started accepting U.S. issued credit cards, and Vietcom Bank has also started issuing cash advances on U.S.-issued credit cards.

VIETNAM IN A CAPSULE

One of the most overwhelmingly beautiful countries in the world...with a people to match...71-plus million of them...of the 1/2 million Americans who fought here during the Vietnam War, 58,000 died and 2,238 are still MIA...the subsequent international economic embargo of Vietnam crippled the country...it has perhaps the lowest standard of living in the world...certainly in SE Asia...however, the thawing of relations between the U.S. and Vietnam has spawned a surge in tourism...lifting of the embargo is now allowing American businesses to open offices in Vietnam...there are more than 3200 km of coastline...more than the state of California...and most of it pristine...the U.S. dollar is accepted throughout most of the country...Hanoi is moving markedly toward a market economy...it's best to visit now, before the inevitable commercialism suffocates this country's innocence.

If you're an American, even though the embargo has been lifted, it would be wise for you to make absolutely sure you have enough cash and/or traveler's checks to make it through the entirety of your stay in Vietnam. And I mean the entirety. Even though you may be able to, don't expect it as a given that you'll be able to wire cash in from abroad. Some things are changing very rapidly in Vietnam. Many other things aren't. One is the amount of red tape and paper stamping that is required for any formal transaction or document. Don't assume your American-issued credit card will be accepted in Vinh, even though you were able to take a cash advance out on it in Saigon. One American idiot, whom I won't name, started a bank account in Thailand and, knowing there were branches of the bank throughout Vietnam, brought along just enough traveler's checks to get by for "about a week or two." He just figured that if the cash ran out (it always does), he'd simply drop into the local branch of his bank for a withdrawl with a kindly Vietnamese teller. She told him he was bookoo American and was bookoo dumb for not bookooing enough bookoo to the Saigon branch from the Bangkok bank in the first place. "No biggy," my buddy said, "I'll just take an advance out on my VISA card." She said, "Yes, biggy. No can do." After only five days into a 30-day Vietnam tour, my buddy had to bookoo back to Bangkok for more buckeroos. However, it is worth starting a Thai bank account if you're going to be spending time in the region. You can even start an account and earn interest on it in Vietnam (if you do, we recommend it be with Vietcom Bank). And if you select a Thai bank (and start the account in Thailand) choose the bank carefully. For instance, an account with Bangkok Bank in Thailand won't give you access to your account at a Bangkok Bank branch of the bank in Saigon, unless you've made prior wire arrangements in Thailand. However, an account with Thai Military Bank, I'm informed, will allow you access to your money at a company branch in Vietnam.

Despite poverty and a third-world infrastructure, Vietnam—and particularly Ho Chi Minh City (which most people here still refer to as Saigon; in fact, the central part of the city is still officially called Saigon)—still retains its haughty, aggressive air. Rickshaws (called cyclos in Vietnam) buzz around town; street vendors hawk everything from lacquerware to old tires and city boulevards are graced by beautiful, newly restored colonial-era mansions built by the French.

The average hotel leaves something to be desired, although those frequented by monied tourists and business people are overall surprisingly comfortable, if not downright luxurious. The townlike squares around the Rex and the Continental have the feel of Boston or New Orleans. And there are currently about 10 or 12 hotels under construction in Ho Chi Minh City (which will be located in

Saigon, Cu Chi, which saw heavy action during the Vietnam War, and Cholon, the city's Chinatown). Among these is the 260-room Omni Saigon Hotel, which just opened at presstime, and the 600-room New World Hotel, scheduled to open in Ho Chi Minh City in 1994 (Hong Kong-based New World is also building a hotel in Pnomh Penh, Cambodia). Also, Club Med plans to build a vacation village some time soon in Vietnam, but is first testing the waters by including the country in the 1994 schedules of its cruise vessel, Club Med 2.

Of the hotels already in operation in Ho Chi Minh City, the most luxurious—and the most intriguing—is the Saigon Floating Hotel. Operated by Australia's Southern Pacific Hotel Corporation, the boat-hotel was once a fixture on the Great Barrier Reef. It has about 200 air-conditioned rooms with all the modern amenities, including hairdryers in the bathrooms and a swimming pool on the mainland. If you can't afford to stay there, few can, you can always grab an easy chair at one of the small hostess bars on the other side of the square and watch its bright lines of yellow lights twinkle in the balmy Saigon night.

Other good hotels in Ho Chi Minh City where tourists are accommodated include the century-old, but newly refurbished Continental Hotel, a favorite of W. Somerset Maugham, and the Century Saigon, which is operated by a Hong Kong firm and occupies the site of the former Oscar Hotel. In Hanoi, the capital, the lovely former Metropole Hotel has gotten a new lease on life, thanks to Pullman/ Sofitel, which restored this *grande dame* of the French colonial era. The Hotel Pullman Metropole has a superb French restaurant and a swimming pool.

FLORA AND FAUNA

Vietnam's flora and fauna are something to behold, although the forests have been extensively denuded in the last century—particularly by warfare. But compared to other regions of Southeast Asia, Vietnam is Eden. The forests contain as many as 12,000 species of plants. Just more than half of them have been identified.

AUTHOR'S OBSERVATION

Peoples' Committees throughout Vietnam have recently received documents from the Vietnamese Ministry of Forestry banning the sale of wild animals, the products of wild animals (including food), skins, stuffed birds and animals, horns, antlers, bones, claws, elephant tusks and gazelle horns, tortoise shells and the skin of leopards and tigers. Additionally, interestingly enough, the husbandry of wild animals was approved in the Forestry Ministry decree for domestic use and export.

More than 250 species of mammals trod or trapeze the topography; 770 bird species traverse its skies. Nearly 200 species of reptiles slither about, hundreds of species of fish swim in its lakes and coastal waters, and 80 species of amphibians do both. And the discoveries of new species continue. But, in sad contrast, hundreds more are expected to soon become extinct. Among those threatened are the tapir (which some believe is already extinct), the Javan rhino, and the kouprey. The Sumatran rhino is already extinct in Vietnam.

Vietnam, like virtually all Southeast Asian countries, has been mired by an abysmal record of protecting threatened wildlife species. Although there's been growing pressure by international wildlife organizations on Vietnam to get its act together—and there have been many strides made in the last few years to eradicate the poaching and/or sale for private use of endangered species—it's still a major problem here.

A little side trip I took recently to Saigon's Cho Caumung animal market on Chuong Duong Street was evidence enough. The sign was marked "Exhibition and Sales of Birds and Animals." And we're not talking about canaries, angelfish and cute little poodles. This dilapidated "pet shop" is nothing short of a concentration camp for animals. Here, nearly extinct concolor gibbons and a myriad of other exotic species live packed in cages the size of toothpaste boxes; they're stacked upon each other like pallets in a warehouse with no platforms between them to prevent the excrement of the animals lucky enough to be imprisoned on the top level from dropping their waste onto the animals interned below.

Infant rhesus maqaques monkeys, separated from their parents at birth, huddle in fear or insanely leap back and forth in their cages like screaming balls in a short racquetball court—if there is enough room. Many of the species here are protected under the Convention of International Trade of Endangered Species, Flora, and Fauna (CITES)—but obviously not at this market. There are 113 signatories to the CITES measure. Vietnam isn't one of them. The animals here all suffered from scabies, mange and a host of other maladies. Prosemian slow lores groveled in feces, their tiny heads buried into their remaining fur, in cages beside workers pounding the concrete with iron rods and hammers. A pair of CITIES-protected pangolins had been killed and stuffed, and were on display in glass counters. A magnificent 20-foot Indian python was coiled like a mammoth black firehose inside a cage the size of a suitcase. One animal, the douc langur (a monkey indigenous to Vietnam), I saw for sale even though it is officially protected in Vietnam.

Admittedly, this "pet shop" and others like it have been substantially cleaned up by the government in the last few years. Previously, the conditions at the market were even more primitive and inhumane, nothing short of a landfill. And the market offered a greater array of threatened species than it does now. But the trade in exotic animals in Vietnam is still highly lucrative. Additionally, at the market, you can purchase ivory, snake and tiger skins, and the remains of other nearly extinct creatures but don't expect to get them through customs. If you choose to take pictures here (and can get away with it), be damn careful. This isn't a sight the government would be particularly proud of having the world see, if you get my drift.

As the demise of millennia-old species proceeds unabated, on a brighter note, the discovery of new species of animals and plants continues . Apparently Dr. John MacKinnon, British-born ecologist, has discovered a fascinating new mammal species that resembles a goat, but is more closely related to the cow. DNA samples taken from the horns of the beast, believed habitating an area near Vietnam's 350-square-mile Vu Quang Nature Reserve, about 175 miles southwest of Hanoi near the border with Laos, have shown that the animal is nothing like scientists have ever seen. This is indeed the discovery of a large mammal previously unknown to science. The last time something happened of this magnitude was the 1937 discovery of the kouprey, a now nearly extinct species of wild cattle, in the forests of Cambodia.

The new creature is called *Pseudoryx nghetinhensis*, meaning the false oryx of Nghe tinh (the former name of the province where it was found). The villagers call the animal a spindlehorn. It's believed that until people began populating the region around 1950, the Pseudoryx had no natural enemies. The animal is horned and thought to weigh in excess of 200 lbs. It most likely sports a brown coat with black-and-white markings and a scent gland used to stake its territory. MacKinnon argues that its existence suggests that cows may have come from the forests, and not from grassy plains and savannahs, as is most commonly believed. A spindlehorn has yet to be captured for study. But don't hold your breath. Scientists say that perhaps 300 of the creatures exist at most.

Although the first-time visitor would hardly know it, huge parcels of Vietnamese topography were ruined during the Vietnam War. It's estimated that more than 70 million liters of defoliant were used on this country's forests during the war, resulting in a loss most experts put at close to 2.5 million hectares. Whereas nearly half the country was heavily forested during World War II, the figure has dropped to under 20% today. It is estimated that by the end of the decade, Vietnam will be virtually entirely denuded of its forests.

Traveling up National Highway 1, these estimates seem slightly exaggerated. The mountains as far as the eye can see appear immensely forested, save for areas where banana groves form columns on the hillsides. However, in the Central Highlands, one can see for miles deforested mountains and hillsides. But in the defense of the Vietnamese naturalists' doomsday prediction, I think it's accurate to say that Vietnam's banning of the exporting of raw hardwood had more impetus than simply protecting the nation's forests. The move, many environmentalists believe, was a ploy to lure foreign investment in Vietnam's ability to produce its own wood processing facilities. Quite simply, the amount of trees felled every year hasn't declined. Instead they're now processed inside Vietnam rather than Taiwan or Singapore; the exporting of processed wood from Vietnam (i.e., paper, cabinetry, furniture, etc.) is still quite legal.

VIETNAM'S GEOGRAPHY & PEOPLE

The terrain in Vietnam varies quite dramatically, from verdant mountainous edifices and dense jungle to coastal plains and delta. The climate is generally considered tropical monsoon although it can actually get get quite cool in the north, especially in the mountainous regions in Northwestern Vietnam near Laos. Its 127,000,330 square miles (329,707 square kilometers) is roughly equal to that of South Carolina, Virginia, and North Carolina together. Vietnam stretches some 1600 kilometers from tip to tip, but very little of the country is any more than 200 km at any given point. At it's narrowest, Vietnam is barely 60 km wide. But Vietnam's remarkable coastline is nearly 3000 km long, offering miles and miles of virtually deserted white sand beaches.

The largest population centers are Hanoi (pop. 3.1 million), Haiphong (pop. 1.5 million), and bustling and relatively cosmopolitan Ho Chi Minh City (pop. 5 million), which is still commonly referred to as Saigon by locals and visitors alike.

The estuary of the Mekong Delta, extremely marshy, dominates the lower quarter of the country. The area is low and flat and perfect for the cultivation of rice in this rich soil. The area around Saigon to the north and the east changes—there is low-lying tropical rainforest and the rugged yet verdant chain of the Annamite Mountains.

The climate around Saigon and in the south of the country is year-round tropical, with sometimes intense heat and unbearable humidity, although it never seems to get quite as bad as Bangkok.

TEMPERATURE AND RAINFALL

The place	Annual rainfall (mm)	Mean annual temperature (°C)	Mean annual variation (°C)
Hanoi	1680	23.5	12.4
Hue	3250	25.1	—
Danang	2130	25.4	7.8
Nha Trang	1562	26.4	4.2
Dalat	1600	19.1	3.4
Saigon	1960	26.9	3.1

Although never cold, the central highlands and the mountainous regions of the central part of Vietnam can become quite cool, with temperatures dipping as low as 50° F at night. During its northern hemispheric summer, the rainfall in the region can be quite heavy around in the delta region—whereas the central highlands experiences the crux of its precipitation during the winter.

MONTHLY AVERAGE TEMPERATURES IN SAIGON AND HANOI

CITY	Jan.	Feb.	Mar.	Apr.	May	Jun.	Jul.	Aug.	Sep.	Oct.	Nov.	Dec.
SAIGON	25	26	27	28	28	27	26	27	26	26	26	26
Rainfall (mm)	16	3	13	42	215	330	310	270	330	270	115	57
HANOI	15	17	19	23	27	29	28	28	27	24	21	18
Rainfall (mm)	22	36	45	91	215	254	335	340	275	115	48	27

With the exception of the Red River delta, northern Vietnam is heavily mountainous and not flat at all. The southwest monsoon climate means a hot, muggy period from mid-May to mid-September, while a cooler northeast monsoon from the middle of October to mid-March brings less rain. The jungle in the north is immensely thick in some areas and the canopy acts as a dome over as much as the entire northern half of the country. There are, of course, lowlands in the north (referred to commonly as the Red River Delta Plain. This is a coastal plain which extends both south and north from the delta and is seasonally flooded. There is a complex dyke and levee system that prevents serious damage to the rich dark soil.

Waves gently roll onto the rocky beaches south of Nha Trang.

Rice fields cover much of the area and the region is densely populated with rice farmers and others whom have something to do with its production and distribution.

The Vietnamese, with a three percent population growth rate, are comprised primarily of ethnic Vietnamese with a smattering of Chinese, Khmer, Thai, Cham, Muong. The major religions include Buddhism, Cao Daism, Christianity (brought in by the French and the subsequent arrival of American troops in the early 1960s), two forms of Islam (a variant of Middle Eastern Islam practiced by the Chams and the more traditional practices of ethnic Malays), and Animalism.

The Vietnamese originally began their centuries-long migration southward around the year AD 940 from what is now considered southern China. The migration was part politically forced and part economically forced. They would eventually preside over the entire area known today as the eastern seacoast of the Indochinese peninsula. Pushed on by the promises of independence, a strong national identity of the Vietnamese people formed quickly although their associations with Chinese culture weren't entirely discarded. Even today, Chinese culture plays a vast role in the identity of the typical Vietnamese. Although the 96-year French rule of the region (1858–1954) had a significant impact on Vietnamese life and culture, the Vietnamese still retain milleniums-old family and societal values that have remained unblemished by colonialism and other forays by both the East and the West.

Today, more than a million Chinese make up the total Vietnamese population, and these people are mostly concentrated in the southern half of the country, and in particular the region of Ho Chi Minh City called Cholon. The Chinese make up the largest minority in the country. Although scorned by many ethnic Vietnamese, the Chinese population is largely to be credited with Vietnam's financial success, and particularly with the economic strides made since the end of the 1980s, when the Hanoi government recognized that opening up its economy was an absolute necessity in participating and harvesting gains in world markets.

WHAT THE VIETNAMESE OWN (%)		
HOUSEHOLD WITH	HANOI	SAIGON
AT LEAST 1 CAR	1	3
AT LEAST 1 MOTORBIKE	54	73
AIR CONDITIONER	2	3
REFRIGERATOR	6	40
WASHING MACHINE	-	7
STEREO	3	64
VIDEO RECORDER	3	65
VIDEO CAMERA	-	2
COMPUTER	-	1
TELEPHONE	4	5
TELEVISION	90	80
RADIO	69	82

Source: SGR Vietnam

The Chinese are most involved with real estate, banking and rice trading in the south, and milling, shopkeeping and mining in the north. After the reunification of the country, the Chinese community was ostracized by the communist community, leaving many with little choice but to flee the country, as they did in droves as boat people—perhaps as many as half a million in the mid and late '70s.

Today, though the Chinese community in Vietnam thrives on Hanoi's reforms. Many thousands have returned to land they once fled and even officially at least are welcomed with the open arms (and no doubt profit-twinkling eyes) of their one-time adversaries.

The next largest minority in Vietnam are the two main ethnolinguistic groups of Montagnards, mountain people of the Malayo-Polynesian and Mon-Khmer groups. These people generally occupy the highlands areas and speak so many tongues, no two of which seem to be mutually intelligible, that it's a small miracle that babies grow to speak the same languages as their parents. Perhaps 30 such groups of mountain tribes occupy these highland territories.

And last but not least are the Khmers of Cambodian descent of whom perhaps half a million reside in Vietnam. As expected, most are rice farmers and they're primarily to be found in the southern half of Vietnam near its border with Cambodia as well as along the mouths of the Mekong.

One other small minority in Vietnam of note are the Chams, who once were part of the powerful Champa Kingdom which was annihilated by the Vietnamese in the 16th century.

Most Vietnamese are usually busier than this produce cart driver.

There are also the Tai who live in the extreme north of the country near the border with China. They speak a language called Tai-Kadai.

Other groups are the Nung, the Muong and Hmong, who reside generally to the south, north and west of Hanoi and have been largely assimilated into mainstream Vietnamese culture, save for the hill people of the extreme north of the country. There is also a small group of people called the Meo, who live high in the mountains and cultivate livestock, grain and profitable opium. Not surprisingly, this group of people can also be found in the opium poppy growing areas of Laos, Thailand and Myanmar—the infamous Golden Triangle area.

Amerasians—those of Vietnamese mothers and American GI fathers—are perhaps the least regarded of all the peoples of Vietnam. Generally, they're treated as scum and are often found in the streets—mostly in Saigon—looking for handouts. Many of the fortunate ones have emigrated to the United States.

Vietnamese of all ethnicities speak a surprising array of languages, helped in part by their remaining unscathed by the purges of Pol Pot in Cambodia, who effectively eliminated foreign-language speaking Khmers and ethnic Vietnamese in Cambodia during the late 1970s. Although Vietnamese remains the official language in Vietnam, don't be surprised to hear a fair amount of French being spoken, as well as Chinese and Khmer. English, however, seems to be making the biggest strides in Vietnam, as the language is universally considered the language of international business, and Vietnam is desperately seeking to align itself with the international business community. And don't be surprised to hear a 12-year-old girl speak better English than her 18-year-old brother. It's happening that quickly.

Literacy in the country stands at a remarkable 85 percent according to the latest estimates, and is at its highest among groups save for the Montagnards. Education is provided entirely free by the government, but is difficult to administer due to the continued high birth rate of Vietnamese children and a still largely undeveloped infrastructure. Vocational training is still most rigorously pursued by Vietnamese students, although with the demise of the Soviet educational style structure in Vietnam, liberal arts studies as found in the West are quickly making their way into Vietnam's educational system. No longer are Vietnamese students being sent by the thousands to school systems in the former Soviet Union and other Eastern European countries that have witnessed their own educational systems collapse. Additionally, Vietnam sends skilled laborers to parts of the world including the Middle East and North Africa.

The average male in Vietnam can expect to live to 62 years, while a woman's average life expectancy hovers around 66 years. However, despite vast improvements in medicine in Vietnam, the infant mortality rate is just a little over 50/1000.

HCMC police eye the author down during a festival celebrating the Tet New Year.

VIETNAM'S RELIGIONS

Vietnam possesses some of the most numerous and diverse religions in Asia if not all the world, including a number of different forms of Buddhism, Catholicism, Protestantism, Confucianism, numerous hilltribe hybrids of the above, Islam, Tam Giaoism, Hoa Hoa, Hinduism, Taoism and the indigenous Caodaism.

After the fall of Saigon in April 1975, the government made meticulous efforts to eliminate—or at least severely limit—the practice of most religions in the reunified country. Many outspoken clergy and their followers were sent to "reeducation camps" or simply thrown in jail. Religion had no place in the Marxist-Leninist scheme of the collective society. Those religions, Mahayana Buddhism in particular, that were permitted to function to some degree or less were strictly controlled by the state, as were those individuals permitted to become clergy.

Over the years, and especially since the latter 1980s, most doctrines have started to again become integrated into mainstram Vietnamese life, and the government has actually started to play a public relations role, albeit limited in scope, in appearing to associate itself with the importance of spirituality in Vietnam. Descriptions of the major religions practiced in Vietnam are as follows.

MAHAYANA AND THERAVADA BUDDHISM

Mahayana Buddhism is the most extensively practiced religion in Vietnam. Although Theravda Buddhism is practiced mainly in the south in the Mekong Delta area by the country's inhabitants of Khmer descent, there are some fundamental differences, and the vast majority of Vietnamese are Mahayana Buddhists.

Mahayana Buddhism means "From the North," and the largest Mahayana sect in Vietnam is Zen. Dao Trang is the second largest school.

The Chinese monk Mau Tu is usually attributed with introducing Mahayana Buddhism in the second century AD. While Indian Buddhists came in from the sea with their teachings of Theravada Buddhism, Mahayana Buddhism went to the north by way of Nepal, China, Tibet, Mongolia, Korea, Japan and Vietnam (thus it's called the Northern School). It wasn't until nearly 1000 years after Buddhism was introduced into Vietnam that it became the state religion (with the 1138–1175 reign of Emperor Ly Anh Ton). But even Buddhist teachings had become intertwined with the teachings of Confucianism, Taoism and Animism. And by the 15th century, it had become so convoluted that Confucianism emerged as the dominant religion of the state. It wasn't until the first two decades of this century that Buddhism once again found a strong foothold in Vietnam, Mahayana Buddhism particularly in the north.

There are fundamental differences between Mahayana Buddhism and Theravada Buddhism, although all Buddhists believe in rebirth, which is common with Hinduism. Buddhists believe their action in this life will determine their manifestations in the next life. Acts in this life will govern those in the next. It's what's commonly called Karma, and it's not a concept looked lightly upon even by Christians, Muslims and others the world over.

Nirvana, or the ultimate enlightenment, is the goal of all Buddhists, and a life of chastity, fasting, and minimal possessions is one of the keys to obtaining this state. Most monks own no more than three sets of clothing, a razor, a food bowl, and a needle. Food cannot be consumed after noon and can only be procured by begging.

Mahayana Buddhists, centered mainly in the north and the central part of Vietnam believe only Gautama Buddha to be the one manifestation of Buddha. The Mahayana Buddhist believes in striving to achieve perfect ideals in the form of generosity, wisdom and patience. Perhaps the fundamental difference between Mahayana and Theravada Buddhists is that the former don't simply believe in enlightenment for themselves. The goal is to reach Bodhissatvahood, the state which allows the monk to stay on earth and help others attain nirvana.

Mahayana Buddhism rose primarily for the reason of making the religion more accessible and attractive to lay people. It was a response to the vast number of followers Hinduism was attracting. Monks began becoming more accessible solely for the purpose of helping others in the quest for enlightenment. As the number of Mahayana Buddhists began to swell, so were expanded the principles of the Mahayana doctrine. However, today, most Mahayana Buddhists also consolidate the teachings of Confucius and other Chinese religions, such as Taoism.

Mahayana Buddhism is Vietnam's biggest religion.

Theravada Buddhism, which came directly from India, more closely conforms to the original doctrines as they were developed in India, and is frequently called by Mahayana Buddhists as the "Lesser Vehicle," a mainly derogatory name that is indicative of the Vietnamese presdisposal to think of the Khmer people as a lower form of humanity. Theravada Buddhism is the most prevalent religion in Cambodia, Thailand and Laos.

The historic Buddha (Sakyumuni) is the Buddha most worshipped by Theravadans. For Theravadans, in theory Buddha images represent not supernatural gods, but shrines to aid in meditation. However, recently these images have been worshipped themselves, which is indicative of the influence Mahayanas are having on Theravada practices.

However, for the most part, Theravada Buddhists consider their religion to be a less corrupt form of Buddhism.

HOA HAO BUDDHISM

Huynh Phu So, an occultist who was miraculously cured of a serious disease, founded Hoa Hao sect of Buddhism in 1939. The religion is a type of reformed Buddhism which contends that elaborate rituals are not needed to honor Buddha, but merely a private, simple and unelaborate faith. He did not believe that intermediaries were needed between human beings and God, or the Supreme Being. There are perhaps more than a million followers of the religion today in Vietnam.

The French weren't fond of Huynh—they called him the "Mad Monk"—and suppressed his activities. He was thrown into an insane asylum after jailing him did little to affect his influence (he even converted the psychiatrist who was treating him to the Hoa Hao sect !). The sect continued to grow, despite the monk's internment. During World War II, the sect formed its own army with the help of the Japanese. After the war, the sect fought the Viet Minh, and Huynh was assassinated by the Viet Minh. By this time, his army had grown rather strong in the Mekong Delta, particularly in the Chau Doc area. The Hoa Hao army disintegrated after one of its leading commanders was publicly executed by the South Vietnamese Diem regime. Much of the Hoa Hao then joined the Viet Cong.

CONFUCIANISM

Confucianism isn't really a religion in the traditional sense. The teachings of Confucius (551–479 BC) are more patterns of social behavior that have become entwined in the daily lives of most Vietnamese, more than an organized religion.

Confucius (Khong Tu in Vietnamese), born before 550 BC in China, saw human beings as both shaped by their society as well as having the ability to shape it themselves. It was social interaction that formed the basis of society. He devised a code of social interaction that specified an individual's obligation to his or her family, government, and community. Hierarchy and sense of duty are principle ingredients of Confucianism.

Confucianism arrived in Vietnam via the Chinese 1000-year rule of the country, between 111 BC and 938 AD. Its philosophy stated that only the emperor could be the intermediary between Earth and Heaven. Virtue through education gave one the right to political power. In this form, there was some degree of equality among individuals, as education rather than birth, determined hierarchy. Virtue could only be acquired through education. As a consequence, education was widespread among the "religion's" followers. Young people were taught about duty, hierarchy, and their responsibilities to both the family and the community at an early age. Each person would know his place in the community hierarchy.

A government-administered test was then given to the students to ascertain those with the greatest amount of education and virtue and it was these individuals who were selected as mandarins, members of the ruling class. Education was seen not only as a tool to acquire education but political status as well.

But only the emperor could establish this mandate between the secular and the spiritual. If virture was lost, it was believed that rebellion was just, and that until virtue was restored natural calamities in the form of floods, earthquakes and typhoons would devastate the land.

Confucianism slowly met its demise in Vietnam during the 1400s as it became more regimented, and as kings became more arrogant and recognized themselves as divine rulers rather than intermediaries between the people and the gods. The Divine Mandate crumbled.

CAO DAOISM

This is the one indigenous religion to Vietnam, and a strange one at that. It involves the worship of human beings as well as the worship of dieties. It was founded to create the perfect religion—a blend of both secular and spiritual devotion. It was founded by Ngo Minh Chieu in the early 1920s and became so popular—gaining millions of followers—areas of southern Vietnam became a virtual political state, particularly in the Mekong Delta region and Tay Ninh, the religion's headquarters nearly 100 km from Saigon. This infuriated the

South Vietnamese government to such an extent they broke up the religion and conscripted many of its followers into the South Vietnamese Army. But after reunification of the country and relaxed religious mandates on the part of the Vietnamese government, Cao Daism flourishes again, but this time as a religion only. Cao Dai temples dot the southern Vietnamese landscape from the Mekong Delta to Hue. Above Cao Dai altars is an inscription which translates into "All Religions Have the Same Reason." Today, it's believed that as many as two million Vietnamese are Cao Dai followers. (For more on Cao Daism, see the chapter on "Tay Ninh.")

TAOISM

Taoism is another religion whose origins are in China. It's based on the philosophy of Laotse, or Thai Thuong Lao Quan, who lived during the sixth century, although the formal religion of Taoism was actually started by Chang Ling around 143 BC. Although there is some question as to whether or not Laotse actually ever existed (the debate continues today), legend has it that he was consulted by Confucious and was the custodian of Chinese government's Imperial Archives. Sometime after 143 BC, the religion split into two branches: "The Way of the Heavenly Teacher" and the "Cult of the Immortals."

Taoists believe in the simplicity of life and eventually returning to what is called "The Way," the source of all things. Taoism is so complicated, few Vietnamese understand the religion—even Taoists themselves. But the essence of Taoism, namely its emphasis on contemplation and simplicity, has found its way into the various forms of Buddhism in Indochina. Taoism is a blend of superstitions, sorcery, magic and other mystical beliefs that are reflected in the architecture of Buddhist temples, which are adorned with dragons, snakes and other mythical beasts.

CHRISTIANITY AND CATHOLICISM

Missionaries from France, Spain and Portugal brought Catholicism to Vietnam in the 16th century—mainly Portuguese Dominicans and French Jesuit priests. The first bishops to be sent to Vietnam were assigned by Pope Alexander VII in 1659, and the first Vietnamese priests were ordained in 1668. There were as many as a million Catholics in Vietnam by the end of the 17th century—and today, behind the Philippines, Vietnam possesses the greatest number of Catholics in Asia. Nearly one million Catholic Vietnamese were part of the hordes of boat people who fled Vietnam after the reunification of the country in 1975. (South Vietnamese President Ngo Dinh Diem was a Catholic.)

Over the centuries, Catholics suffered a tremendous amount of persecution in Vietnam. At many times during the 17th and 18th centuries, the religion was outlawed. After 1975, the practice of Catholicism was virtually untolerated by the new government.

INSIDER TIP

Although the government has become a lot more tolerant of religious practice in Vietnam, it once in a while lets religious hierarchies know in no uncertain terms that it is the state who's boss in Vietnam—that, yes, there's a degree of religious tolerance, but any clergy who had any previous association with the varying regimes of preunification Vietnam will not be tolerated, nor will they be allowed congregations. A case in point is Hanoi's recent falling out with the Vatican over a compromise that would have permitted the appointments of priests with ties to previous South Vietnamese regimes. Hanoi insists that the government must be consulted in the selection of clergy. Vietnamese Prime Minister Vo Van Kiet has said that the issue is one of "national sovereignity," as Vietnam has not signed any agreements with the Vatican allowing them to make "unfettered" decisions in their appointments. "Each country has the right to ensure stability and order through its own rules," Vo said. Things have heated up between the Vatican and Hanoi since September 1993 when authorities in Ho Chi Minh City said "no way" to the appointment of Bishop Huynh Van Nghi as a "supervisor" of the church instead of deputy archbishop. Saigon officials charged that the appointment was part of a "Vatican plot" to place an exiled nephew of former South Vietnamese President Ngo Dinh Diem as successor to the current archbishop. Hanoi, it appears, is taking very cautious steps in permitting a potential element of dissent, the church—which the government has always viewed as a hot bed for antistate activities—to return to its previous, prewar levels of influence.

But Catholicism flourished during French rule of Vietnam—as it did with the American presence in South Vietnam during the Vietnam War. Under French rule, Catholics were given high positions in the government and preferential treatment in general. From 1954 to 1989 in the north, and from 1975 to 1989 in the south Catholic religious activities were heavily curtailed and monitored by the government. There were restrictions placed on the number of priests and the type of education Catholics could receive. Even today, the Catholic churches you see in both Hanoi and HCMC have become somewhat dilapidated, as the government still looks upon the religion as a capitalist poison.

Protestantism has flourished mainly among about a quarter of a million Montagnards in the Central Highlands. The religion first came to Vietnam in 1910 or 1911. The Montagnards have been harassed by the government for a number of years, and the introduction of Christianity into the populace didn't help matters any. After 1975, Protestant ministers, especially those trained by the Americans, were imprisoned for a number of years. Although you are free to practice the religion in Vietnam today, you're not that free.

HINDUISM

Originally, Hinduism had its roots in Vietnam with the Cham people, and its influence can be seen in many of the early Cham towers in the southern half of Vietnam, which contain the phallic symbols of Shiva. When the Champa Empire fell in Vietnam in the 15th century, so did much of Hinduism's influence on the Cham people, who then absorbed Muslim ideas into their religious practices. But evidence of Hinduism is still evident even in today's Cham Muslim religious practices.

ISLAM

If you've got to be a Muslim, become a Cham in Vietnam. Although there are small communities of Muslims (such as ethnic Malays, Indonesians and Indians) that practice Islam, the Chams aren't so strict. They're permitted to drink alcohol and don't make pilgrimages to Mecca. Rather than praying five times a day as do their traditional counterparts, Cham Muslims pray only on Friday and celebrate Ramadan for only three days. Traditional Muslims celebrate Ramadan (which requires dawn-to-dusk fasting) for an entire month.

In fact, Cham Muslims aren't entirely clear about the Islam concept. There are very few copies of the Koran in Cham villages and most of the villagers can't read it. Even the Cham Muslim religious leaders, who wear a white robe and an elaborate turban with colored tassles, can't read the Arabic script, or at least much of it. They've taken common expressions from the Koran and turned them into deities. Their religious services include only a few minutes of reading passages from the Koran, much of them decisively altered in meaning through a lack of understanding of the passages. They're also into animism and Hinduism, as they worship Hindu deities in addition to Mohammed.

The more traditional Muslims in Vietnam essentially fled the country after 1975, but there are still small pockets of Malay and Indian Muslim communities centered mainly in Saigon.

WORSHIP OF ANCESTORS

Introduced even before Confucianism in Vietnam, ancestor worship is the belief many Vietnamese have that their ancestors watch over and protect them. A person without descendants is doomed to have no home when they die. Ancestors play a role in all important events, including everything from tragedies to success in school to childbirth—and there are ancestor worship holidays on the dates of the ancestors' deaths. Sacrifices are offered to the ancestor. Ancestor worshipping families have altars in their homes devoted to their ancestors. Ancestor worship pagodas feature pictures and other items ancestors once possessed on the altars. Usually the pictures depict the ancestors as young people. Ancestor worshippers usually also have plots of land which derive income for the ancestors. The cult also designates a male as the central figure to worship when he dies.

VIETNAM'S GOVERNMENT

As you've probably guessed, the Vietnamese consider themselves a socialist peoples' republic, a somewhat cantankerous hybrid of Marxism and Leninism. What this really means, however, depends upon who you talk to. An official in Hanoi may tell you something entirely different than a prosperous Chinese merchant in Saigon's Cholon district, whose perception of "socialism" may be afternoon tea with some neighbors. However, officially, there is one political party, called the Vietnam Communist Party, which was previously referred to as the Vietnamese Workers Party, a title which remained in effect from 1951–1976. This in itself was the offshoot of the Indochinese Workers Party which was formed in the early 1930s. Vietnam's constitution was ratified December 18, 1980.

In Vietnam, there are 50 provinces which are centrally controlled under the auspices of three municipalities (Hanoi, Ho Chi Minh City, and Haiphong)—all under central government control.

In the north are Ha Bac, Cao Bang, Hoa Binh, Tuyen Quang, Lao Cai, Yen Bai, Lai Chau, Bac Thai, Son La, Quang Ninh, Vin Phu, Lang Son, Na Giang, and Lai Chau.

The Red River Delta Area has Ninh Binh, Ha Tay, Nam Ha, Thai Binh, and Hai Hung.

North Central Vietnam includes Nghe An, Thanh Hoa, Quang Tri, Thua Thien-Hue, Ha Tinh, and Quang Binh.

The Central Highlands is composed of Gia Lai, Dac Lac, Kontum, and Lam Dong.

On the South Central Coast lies Quang Nam-Danang, Binh Dinh, Phu Yen, Quang Ngai, Khanh Hoa, Binh Thuan, and Ninh Thuan.

In the South are Song Be, Tay Ninh, Dong Nai, Ba-Ria-Vung Tau, Long An, Dong Thap, An Giang, Ben Tre, Kien Giang, Soc Trang, Can Tho, Minh Hai. Tien Giang, Tra Vinh, and Vinh Long

Vietnamese independence from the French occurred in September, 1945, and the reunification of the north and the south officially took place in July of 1976. Some say the real unification took place with the temporary occcupation of the United States embassy building during the Tet Offensive of 1968. Some venture to go back even further in time to 1963 when then AP correspondent Malcolm Brown shot his historic photos of a Buddhist monk from Hue self immolating himself on a Saigon street in protest of the policies of the Thiem government, a series of pictures that ultimately found their way to Washington's Oval office and JFK's desk who, after gazing in horror at the human pyre in the street orchestrated the roots of Thiem's ouster.

Today's facets of the Vietnamese government consist of the executive branch, which is comprised of the Council of Ministers; the State Council (or the Collective Chief of State), people's committees that have jurisdiction over local affairs; the Legislative branch; which is also called the National Assembly (locally there are Peoples' Councils, and the Judicial branch, which is comprised of the Supreme People's Court).

As far as defense goes, well, these folks are into it. It's said that anywhere from 40–50% of the central government budget goes into the procurement and maintenance of defense related technology and manpower—which explains why the Vietnamese are some of the poorest souls on the planet.

VIETNAM'S LANGUAGE

As you might expect, the Vietnamese language is a pain in the backside both to speak and understand when it's heard. It can be traced to Sino-Tibetan as well as to Austro-Asiatic and Mon-Khmer origins. Under 9th-century Chinese domination, the ideograms the Chinese used were adopted for use with Vietnamese (although gratefully, a Latin-style based script was adopted during the early portion of this century, making the reading of maps and signs possible for hapless Westerners). The original *chu nho* ideograms were utilized as the only form of communication up until the 20th century.

Vietnamese seeking to sever ties with the Chinese in the 13th century further complicated matters by taking the Chinese ideograms and adapting them for their own purposes. This was called *chu nom*, considered a "vulgar" or gutter form of *chu nho*.

In the 17th century European missionary Alexandre-de-Rhodes mastered the Vietnamese language and actually created the first romanized Vietnamese dictionary.

The biggest problem in understanding the Vietnamese language is the fundamental barrier that prevents Westerners from becoming proficient with other East Asian tongues—tonal usage. The same "word" can be used with a number of different tones and possess an equally different number of meanings.

The Vietnamese alphabet has 17 consonants, 12 vowels and nearly 20 double consonants. There are no prefixes and no suffixes. There is no use of plurals with nouns and there are double negatives that must be used to accomplish what Westerners can simply do with a simple positive. In other words, if you ask someone in Vietnamese, "Will you have dinner at my house tonight?" the actual translation is something like this: "You'll have dinner at my house tonight, will you not?" Instead of simply replying, "Yes, I will," an affirmative response goes something like this: "No, I will not." If you say the former, you're telling your host that "Yes, I will not be having dinner at your house tonight."

Ay!

As anywhere you travel where the locals speak a different tongue, it can never hurt to pick up on a bit of the language. Simple greetings, phrases and requests in the local language can open a lot of doors. The Vietnamese, like the Thais, the Cambodians, and most peoples of Asia (and quite unlike the French of Paris) are impressed and even honored when even the slightest attempt by a foreigner is made to speak the host country's language, no matter how bad the result is (within parameters, of course. You don't want to tell a man that his wife looks like a swollen sow with udders for fingers when you've simply requested a glass of milk). Let the following serve as the briefest of guides to making your Vietnamese visit a little more intelligible.

A CRASH COURSE IN VIETNAMESE

GREETINGS AND FORMALITIES

Hello	*Chao*
Good morning	
Good afternoon	
Good night	*Chao* **or** *Chuc ngu ngon*
Good bye	*Tam Biet*
the above formal to older men	*Chao ong*
the above formal to older women	*Chao ba*
the above informal to men	*Chao anh*
the above informal to women	*Chao chi*
How are you?	*Có Khoe khong?*
I am doing well, thank you	*Khoe, cam on*
Thank you	*Cam on*
Yes	*Vang (in the north)*
	Co, phai (in the south)
	Da
No	*Khong*
Excuse me	*Xin loi*
I am tired	*Toi met*

PRONOUNS

I	*Toi*
You	*Cac*
to an older man	*Ong*
to an older woman	*Ba*
to a man of own age	*Anh*
to a woman of own age	*Co*
He	*Cau ay, anh ay*
She	*Co ay*
We	*Chung toi*

NUMBERS

1	*Mot*
2	*Hai*
3	*Ba*
4	*Bon*
5	*Nam*
6	*Sau*
7	*Bay*
8	*Tam*
9	*Chin*
10	*Muoi*

A CRASH COURSE IN VIETNAMESE

11	*Muoi mot*
12	*Muoi hai*
13	*Muoi ba*
14	*Muoi bon*
15	*Muoi nam*
16	*Muoi sau*
17	*Muoi bay*
18	*Muoi tam*
19	*Muoi chin*
20	*Hai muoi*
21	*Hai muoi mot*
30	*Ba muoi*
90	*Chin muoi*
100	*Mot tram*
110	*Mot tram muoi*
200	*Hai tram*
1000	*Mot nghin*
10,000	*Muoinghin*
100,000	*Mot tram nghin*
1 million	*Mot trieu*
First	*Thu Nhat*
Second	*Thu nhi*

DAYS OF THE WEEK

Sunday	*Chu nhat*
Monday	*Thu hai*
Tuesday	*Thu ba*
Wednesday	*Thu tu*
Thursday	*Thu nam*
Friday	*Thu sau*
Saturday	*Thu bay*
Today	*Ngay may*
Yesterday	*Ngay mai*
Tomorrow	*Hom qua*
Morning	*Buoi sang*
Afternoon	*Buoi chieu*
Evening	*Buoi toi*
Right now	*Bay gio*

MONTHS OF THE YEAR

January	*Thang nay*
February	*Thang hai*

A CRASH COURSE IN VIETNAMESE

March	*Thang ba*
April	*Thang tu*
May	*Thang nam*
June	*Thang sau*
July	*Thang bay*
August	*Thang tam*
September	*Thang chin*
October	*Thang nuoi*
November	*Thang mot*
December	*Thang chap*
Year	*Nam*
This year	*Nam nay*
Last year	*Nam ngoai*
Next year	*Nam sau*
Month	*Thang*

USEFUL WORDS AND PHRASES

My name is…	*Ten toi la…*
What is your name?	*Ten cac la gi?*
I would like…	*Toi muon…*
I would not like…	*Toi khong muon…*
I like…	*Toi thich…*
I do not like…	*Toi khong thich…*
I want…	*Toi can…*
I do not want…	*Toi khong can…*
I need…	*Toi can*
I understand	*Toi hieu*
I do not understand	*Toi khong hieu*
I am hungry	*Toi doi*
To eat	*An*
To drink	*Uong*
Thank you	*Cam on*
Please	*Xin*
Yes	*Da*
No	*Khong*
Come	*Toi*
Go	*Di*
Cheap	*Re*
Expensive	*Dat*
Man	*Nam*
Woman	*Nu*

A CRASH COURSE IN VIETNAMESE

Give	*Cho*
Fast	*Nhanh (in the north)*
	Mau (in the south)
Slow	*Cham*
Old	*Cu*
New	*Moi*
Clean	*Sach*
Dirty	*Ban*
Hot	*Nong*
Cold	*Lanh*
Far away	*Xa*
Close by	*Gam*
Market	*Cho*
Office	*Van phong*
Post office	*Nha buu dien*
Museum	*Bax Tang Vien*
Pagoda	*Chua*
Church	*Nha tho*
Bank	*Nha bang*
Tourism office	*Van phong du lich*
Telephone	*Dien thoai*
Mosquito net	*Man (in the north)*
	Mung (in the south)
East	*Dong*
West	*Tay*
North	*Bac*
South	*Nam*

ACCOMMODATIONS

Hotel	*Khach san*
	Nha khach
Restaurant	*Tiem an*
Room	*Phong*
Room key	*Chia khoa phong*
Bathroom	*Nha tam*
	Phong tam
Toilet	*Car tieu*
	Nha ve sinh
Toilet paper	*Giay ve sinh*
I would like an inexpensive room.	*Toi thich mot phong loai re.*
Where is there a hotel?	*O dau co khach san?*
How much does the room cost?	*Gia mot phong bao nhieu?*

A CRASH COURSE IN VIETNAMESE

Air conditioning	*May lanh*
Fan	*Quat*
Hot water	*Nuoc non*
Blanket	*Chan (in the north)*
	Men (in the south)
Laundry	*Tiem gidt quan do*
Sheet	*Ra trai guiong*
Towel	*Khan tam*

FOOD AND DRINK

Water	*Nuoc*
Beer	*Bia*
Coffee	*Ca phe*
Tea	*Nuoc che*
Sugar	*Durong*
Beef	*Bo*
Chicken	*Ga*
Pork	*Lon*
Bat	*Con doi*
Snake	*Ran ho mang (Cobra)*
	Con tran (Python)
Goat	*Con de*
Venison	*Thit Nai*
Turtle	*Con rua*
Wild pig	*Heo rung*
Noodle soup	*Pho*
Rice	*Com*
Bread	*Banh mi*
Vegetables	*Rau*
Fish	*Ca*
Shrimp	*Tom*
Crab	*Cua*
Eel	*Luon*
Frog	*Ech*
Oyster	*So*
Fish and vegetable soup	*Lau*
Vegetable soup	*Xup rau*
White rice noodles	*Banh Pho*
Eel and vermicelli soup	*Mien Luon*
Yellow wheat noodles	*Mi*
Broth	*Nuoc Leo*
Dry noodles	*Kho*

A CRASH COURSE IN VIETNAMESE

Sweet rolls	*Nem*
	Cha gio
Apple	*Bom*
	Tao
Apricot	*Le*
Avocado	*Trai bo*
Banana	*Trai chuoi*
Cherry	*Trai se ri*
Chinese date	*Trai tao ta*
Coconut	*Trai dua*
Durian	*Trai sau rieng*
Grapes	*Nho*
Grapefruit	*Trai buoi*
Green dragon fruit	*Trai thanh long*
Guava	*Trai oi*
Jackfruit	*Trai Mit*
Khaki	*Hong Xiem*
Lemon	*Chanh*
Longan	*Trai Nhan*
Lychee	*Trai vai*
Mandarin Orange	*Trai quit*
Mango	*Trai mang cut*
Orange	*Trai cam*
Papaya	*Trai du du*
	Qua du du
Peach	*Trai dao*
Pineapple	*Trai Khom*
	Trai dua
Plum	*Man*
	Mo
Pomelo	*Trai buoi*
	Trai doi
Rambutan	*Chom chom*
Starfruit	*Trai khi*
Strawberry	*Trai dau*
Tangerine	*Trai quit*
Tomato	*Ca chua*
Water apple	*Roi duong*
Watermelon	*Dua hau*

TRAVEL

Bus	*Xe buyt*

A CRASH COURSE IN VIETNAMESE

Bus station	*Ben xe*
Train	*Xe lua*
Train station	*Goi xa lua*
Airport	*San bay*
Cyclo (Trishaw)	*Xe xich lo*
Map	*Ban do*
Schedule	*Bang gio giac*
	Thoi bieu
I want to hire a car.	*Toi muon xe hoi.*
I want to go to...	*Toi muon di...*
Highway	*Xa lo*
How long does the trip take?	*Chuyen di se mat bao lau?*
How far is it to...? (kilometers)	*...Cach xa day bao nhieu kilomet?*
What time does the bus leave?	*Xe buyt se chay luc may gio?*
What time does the train leave?	*Xe lua se chay luc may gio?*
What time does it arrive?	*Xe se den luc may gio?*
What time does the first bus leave?	*Chuyen xe buyt som nhat se chay luc may gio?*
What times does the last bus leave?	*Chuyen xe buyt cuoi cung se chay luc may gio?*
What time does the first train leave?	*Chuyen xe lua som nhat se chay luc may gio?*
What time does the last train leave?	*Chuyen xe lua cuoi cung ce chay luc may goi?*
I would like a receipt.	*Toi muon bien lai.*
I would like a sleeping berth.	*Toi muon giuong ngu.*

GEOGRAPHY

Mountain	*Nui*
River	*Song*
Island	*Hon dao*
Boulevard	*Dai lo*
Street	*Duong*
	Pho
National Highway	*Quoc Lo*
City square	*Cong truong*
Bridge	*Cau*

AT THE MARKET

Expensive	*Dat tien*
Cheap	*Re tien*
Buy	*Mua*
Sell	*Ban*

A CRASH COURSE IN VIETNAMESE

Market	*Cho*
How much does this cost?	*Cai nay gia bao nhieu?*

EMERGENCIES

Help	*Cuu toi voi*
Police	*Cong an*
Thief	*Cuop*
	Cap
Pickpocket	*Moc tu*

MEDICAL

Doctor	*Bac si*
Dentist	*Nha si*
Hospital	*Benh vien*
Pharmacy	*Nha thuoc tay.*
I am sick.	*Toi bi benh. (in the north)*
	Toi bi om. (in he south)
Please call me a doctor.	*Lam on goi bac si.*
Please get me to a hospital.	*Lam on dua toi den benh vien.*
Diarrhoea	*Ia chay*
Stomach ache	*Dau bung*
Malaria	*Sot ret*
Feverish	*Cam*
	Cum
Vomiting	*Oi*
	Mua
Toothache	*Nhuc rang*
Headache	*Nhuc dau*
Backache	*Dao lung*

SOME OTHER USEFUL PHRASES IN VIETNAMESE

Where do I collect my visa?	*Toi nhan visa o dau?*
One of my bags is missing. Where do I make a report?	*Toi bi mat moy tui. Toi phai bao o dau?*
I bought this camera/video camera in ...	*Toi mua may anh/may quay phim nay o...*
I have had this camera/video camera for ...years.	*Toi mua may anh/may quay phim nay...nam roi.*
My flight number is...	*So chuyen bay cua toi la...*
What is your flight number?	*Chuyen bay cua ong/ba so bao nhieu?*
Have they called my flight?	*Ho da thong bao chuyen bay cua toi chura?*
Can I carry this as hand luggage?	*Toi co the xach tay tui nay duroc khong?*

A CRASH COURSE IN VIETNAMESE

Where do I pay the airport tax?	*Toi phai dong le phi san bay o dau?*
Over there, to the right/left.	*O dang kia, ben Phai/trai.*
How much is the airport tax?	*Le phi san bay la bao nhieu?*
Where is the transit lounge?	*Phong cho di noi chuyen o dau?*
Where can I get a taxi?	*Toi co the don taxi o dau?*

Cham brick columns at the Po Nagar Cham Towers in Nhe Trang.

HISTORY OF VIETNAM

As Americans, we're all too aware of the recent history of Vietnam. For the last 30 years, its past has been entwined with our own. As Vietnam crippled the U.S. spiritually, we ravaged Vietnam economically. As Vietnam reshaped our own awareness of the world by repelling and finally bursting the bubble of the infallibility of American intervention abroad, we regrouped as a nation, only to witness the crumbling of an impotent strain of Southeast Asian Marxism. Nearly 60,000 young Americans paid for this social rebirth—both America's and Vietnam's—with their lives, along with perhaps hundreds of thousands of Vietnamese.

Of course, Vietnamese history predates this conflict by centuries, if not milleniums. And, perhaps not surprisingly, much of the country's culturally rich history has been marred by conflicts.

The early Ly Dynasty seemed to be at war with everyone, and at the same time. There were the Chinese. And there were the Chams. And the Khmers. The list goes on. However, the ancient Vietnamese were a resilient lot. They pushed south toward the Gulf of Thailand and virtually annihilated the retreating Chams.

The Tran Dynasty ruled Vietnam in 1225 and faced its most potent threat from the north. The 300,000-plus Mongol soldiers of Kublai Khan attacked the nation and were repelled. But the dynasty would eventually crumble by 1400, when the Chinese again attempted to gain control. After a largely successful 20-year effort to eradicate Vietnamese culture, Le Loi emerged as the new leader of a free Vietnam. He was phenomenally wealthy and used his riches to help the poor, which made him extraordinarily popular. His family rule included the annexing of Laos and basically ended in 1524, but not until after a significant amount of reforms had been initiated, including civil rights for women. But it was also a time when China culturally dominated Vietnam.

THE SPLIT BETWEEN NORTH & SOUTH

Soon after Le's demise, conflict again interceded. Vietnam was split between north and south, under the rule of two factions, the Nguyen and the Trinh. Fortified by Portuguese arms, the Nguyen lords prevailed and eventually conquered all of what is present-day Cambodia.

Various factions continued to battle each other and they intermittently ruled Vietnam. Finally, a rebellion in 1771 spread to the south and Nguyen Lu became king of the south, while Nguyen Nhac became king of the central part of the country and Nguyen Hue became king in the north. The Chinese, again seeking to take advantage of the internal turmoil in Vietnam, attacked in the north, but were defeated in 1789.

DYNASTIES IN VIETNAM		
DYNASTY	**DATES**	**CAPITAL**
Hong Bang Dynasty	*2876–258 BC*	*Phong Chau*
Thuc Dynasty	*257–208 BC*	*Loa Thanh*
Trieu Dynasty	*207–111 BC*	*Phien Ngung*
Trung Sisters	*AD 40–43*	*Me Linh*
Early Ly Dynasty	*544–602*	*Around Hanoi*
Ngo Dynasty	*939–965*	*Co Loa*
Dinh Dynasty	*968–990*	*Hoa Lu*
Early Le Dynasty	*980–1009*	*Hoa Lu*
Ly Dynasty	*1010–1225*	*Thang Long*
Tran Dynasty	*1225–1400*	*Thang Long*
Ho Dynasty	*1400–1407*	*Dong Do*
Post Tran Dynasty	*1407–1413*	
Le Dynasty	*1427–1788*	*Thang Long*
Mac Dynasty	*1527–1592*	
Northern Trinh	*1539–1787*	*Hanoi*
Southern Nguyen	*1558–1778*	*Hue*
Quang Trung	*1787–1797*	
Nguyen of Tay Son	*1788–1802*	*Saigon*
Nguyen Dynasty	*1802–1945*	*Hue*

Nguyen Anh, an exiled prince, managed to gain the support of French traders in India and, with the help of French mercenaries, captured Vietnam in 1802. The Nguyen Dynasty lasted until 1945, at least on paper. But the Vietnamese, on the whole, began rejecting Western influences in the 19th century, in particular those transplanted via religious missionaries. Many of these missionaries' converts were executed by the Vietnamese, prompting the French to capture and control three southern provinces in 1862.

After a French merchant was killed in 1872 by pirates, French retaliation sent the north into anarchy. The emperor, Tu Doc, sought Chinese, English, as well as American assistance in repelling the French, to no avail. Soon, the French were in control of all of what is known today as Indochina. The Indochinese Union was formed in 1887.

The French are generally thought to have controlled the region poorly. There were heavy taxes. Bandits prospered. The opium trade flourished. A growing sense of Vietnamese nationalism then helped fuel the emergence of the Communist Party, led by Ho Chi Minh. After World War II had severely exhausted France's colonial resources and influence, the communists began emerging as the strongest political party in Vietnam. Incidentally, this group, which became known as the Viet Minh during WWII, were supported by both the Chinese and the Americans when they fought the Japanese.

The Japanese overthrew the French government in Vietnam in 1945. During their short reign, an estimated 10 million people starved to death due to Japanese requisitions of rice that year.

After the atomic bombs had been dropped on Japan by the Americans later that year, the Viet Minh assumed full control of the north. Other non-communist groups wrestled for power in the south. The Democratic Republic of Vietnam was formed in Hanoi on September 2, 1945.

RETURN OF THE FRENCH

Because of further Chinese incursions in the North and a volatile situation in the South (which, incidentally, the British sought to control with both French and Japanese support), the North was forced to bargain with the French to purge Vietnam of the pesky Chinese. French rule of Vietnam was the price Ho Chi Minh had to pay.

But less than a year later, Vietnamese opposition to the French had risen again. With France foundering in Indochina on American aid, Vietnam again became independent, but still divided north and south. The government in South Vietnam, bolstered by Western support, lost support among the Buddhists as it sought to implement pro-Catholic policies. Protesters hit the streets and a U.S. backed coup in 1963 installed the first of a number of puppet military regimes.

THE WAR IN VIETNAM

Meanwhile, minds in the north were thinking unification. The Viet Cong was formed in 1960 to force the withdrawal of all foreign troops on Vietnamese soil. In 1964, North Vietnamese troops were making forays into the south. The rickety regime in Saigon was becoming weaker through mass desertions and disillusioned peasants.

The Americans, who had actually had troops inside Vietnam as early as 1955, made a full-scale military commitment to the preservation of the South Vietnamese government.

The turning point in the war came with the Tet (Chinese New Year) Offensive of 1968. Saigon was attacked by the Viet Cong. Mass devastation took place in the countryside. In one three-week period, more than 165,000 civilians were killed in the fighting.

Growing resistance to the war by Americans helped form the American policy of "Vietnamization," which marked the first efforts toward sending American troops home. But shortly afterwards, the U.S. began its massive carpet bombing of Cambodia. The public outcry in the U.S., combined with the phenomenal and unexpected perseverance and resiliency of the communist troops, ultimately forced the U.S. to negotiate with Hanoi. The withdrawal of all U.S. troops from Vietnam was ceded for Hanoi's recognition of the South's independence. But in 1975, North Vietnamese troops rolled into Saigon after a massive offensive and Saigon fell.

In April 1975, a North Vietnamese Army tank smashed through this gate to Saigon's Presidential Palace, symbolizing the fall of South Vietnam.

POST-WAR VIETNAM

The country then began the painful process of reunification and "reeducation." Hundreds of thousands of Vietnamese fled their country for the U.S. and Europe. Cut off from the West economically, Vietnam has suffered greatly.

In 1977, Vietnam entered the United Nations. At the end of the following year, the army invaded Cambodia and deposed Pol Pot's murderous Khmer Rouge regime in January of 1979, installing a pro-Hanoi government. The Vietnamese government began withdrawing their troops from Cambodia in 1989 and agreed in October, 1991 to the Paris Peace Agreement that paved the way to the first free elections in Cambodia.

The Bill Clinton administration in the U.S. dropped the trade embargo on February 4, 1994 and is moving closer and closer to establishing full diplomatic relations with Hanoi. Many in both politics and the business world expect relations to become normalized by the end of 1994.

INSIDER TIP

At presstime, U.S. and Vietnamese negotiators have agreed in principle to establish liaison offices in Washington, the first steps toward establishing full diplomatic relations. These negotiations were the first major talks between the two countries since the Paris Peace Agreement in 1973 that technically ended U.S. involvement in the Vietnam War. These liaison offices will ultimately become full-fledged embassies should relations between the two countries improve. The U.S. office in Hanoi will primarily function to assess and aid trade improvements between the two countries and also to continue to monitor human rights issues and American MIA cases. America already maintains an office in Hanoi solely for the purpose of locating MIAs. Vietnam's only official presence in the U.S. consists of its delegation to the United Nations in New York. The two pending liaison offices will also deal with financial claims made by the two countries following the seizure of American assets by the Communists after the fall of South Vietnam in 1975, and Hanoi's claims of some US$290 million in frozen assets in the United States. American claims are approximately US$230,000, the crux of that being U.S. investments in the south, including seized properties and buildings and enormous assets in South Vietnam once held by Occidental Petroleum Corp (see below). What this all means to you, the traveler, is that even though the embargo has been dropped, the U.S. and Hanoi have still yet to fully normalize relations. In other words, there is no embassy of the United States as of yet in Vietnam. So don't travel under the illusion that you'll have access to embassy support and services should you get in trouble in Vietnam, lose your passport, etc.. The healing process is not quite yet complete, and neither will your privileges as an American citizen be fully realized until such an embassy exists. So be warned.

THE PROCESS IS ACCELERATING

Settling financial and MIA claims will be the keys to achieving normalization. Talks between key Vietnameese and American officials occur frequently in Hanoi and other venues. Part of the disagreement that remains between the two nations revolves around U.S.

and Vietnamese assets left behind in Vietnam after the war. Some estimates put the number of U.S. assets lost after the fall of Saigon in 1975 at $230 million. U.S. government claims include the former U.S. Embassy in Saigon, which is currently being used by a Vietnamese oil company. The Vietnamese, in their behalf, claim that the U.S. maintains frozen Vietnamese assets totalling more than $290 million. U.S. oil companies were big losers with the U.S. withdrawl from Vietnam in 1973. Simply, American companies would prefer to have their old real estate back once they move back into Vietnam rather than having to be forced to procure new land and offices. Merely the fact that these talks are occurring is a sure sign that normalized relations are imminent.

The MIA probe will imminently end in 1994, and well may have by the time this edition hits the stores. Vietnam is opening up its borders and military bases to the Americans to expedite the determination of the fate of the 1647 Americans still unaccounted for in Vietnam. Additionally, 505 Americans are still missing in Laos, 78 in Cambodia, and eight in China. The largest joint search with Vietnamese since the end of the war in 1975 was completed last January. Five more operations, even larger in scope, are occurring as we go to press. U.S. guidelines for a full accounting of all U.S. war dead includes bringing back those who are still alive, which is unilaterally agreed as highly unlikely, as well as all remains. If the remains cannot be brought home, it must be demonstrated by the Vietnamese why this isn't possible. Groups, including families of missing veterans charge that Hanoi "calculatedly withholds" MIA information.

But what is certainly not being "calculatedly withheld" in Vietnam today is the people's reverence for Americans and things American. North American rock singer Bryan Adams played a Saigon show last January which marked the first performance by a North American musician in Vietnam since the end of the war. The *Bangkok Post* reported that manic Saigon concertgoers payed as much as US$100 for the privilege of watching Adams, here in a country where the annual per capita income barely reaches $200. After the show, when the lights came back on, "some fans remained in their seats, almost in tears, staring at the ceiling, as if to (forever) imprint the experience," according to the report. American singer/songwriter John Denver appeared in Ho Chi Minh City in May. Although a has-been in the States, the performer was able to sell out the Hoa Binh Theatre in HCMC with ticket prices in the US$35 range.

Soon the people of Vietnam will have many more positive experiences with Americans that will most surely be equally as imprinted as those created by the burgeoning number of American cultural artists now beginning to perform in Vietnam.

VIETNAM IN A NUTSHELL	
Ho Chi Minh City (Saigon)	*Although at one time on par with Bangkok, but now eclipsed by the Thai capital, Saigon is still one of the most thriving cities in all of Southeast Asia, certainly the most bustling in Indochina. Vibrant. Entrepreneurial. With the exception of the revolutionary posters and hammer and sickle flags swirling about, you'd never know you were in a communist country. Population about 5 million. Natural attractions include the nearby Mekong Delta. Man-made wonders include the nearby Cu Chi tunnel Viet Cong network.*
Nha Trang	*This coastal area features beautiful beaches which are popular with both locals and tourists.. There's great snorkeling and scuba diving as well as fishing and great seafood..*
Danang	*This is a historic city and one of Vietnam's major seaports. And although it bustles with shipping activity, the water is remarkably clean and the area boasts some good beaches. Some of the attractions include the local Cham architecture.*
The Central Highlands	*Generally known for the great scenery and cooler climate. Also the Montegnard tribespeople. The verdant mountain scenery is unmatched in Vietnam save perhaps for some areas in the northern part of the country. There are waterfalls and many beautiful, clear lakes.*
Hue	*This city, although devastated during the war, retains a great deal of its historical charm. Hue is really the traditional cultural, art, educational, and religious capital of Vietnam. There are all kinds of pagodas, palaces and museums to visit here. The royal tombs are just south of the city.*

VIETNAM IN A NUTSHELL

Halong Bay	*Beautiful beach area with thousands of islands and spectacular grottos rising from the Gulf of Tonkin southeast of Hanoi. The area is targeted by the government to become a major tourist area it says will rival those of Thailand and the Eastern peninsula of Malaysia. Visit this area now, while it is still absolutely pristine.*
Hanoi	*The charming capital of Vietnam but not nearly as colorful as its onetime rival in the south–Saigon. The people here are more reserved than their neighbors to the south. But it is a charming colonial city if charm is your thing. The Old Quarter, although rapidly becoming transformed by weird-looking add-on building additions and satellite dishes, the "gingerbread" style architecture and tree-lined boulevards make the capital worth a visit of moderate length.*

PLANNING AHEAD

VIETNAMTOURISM AND SAIGONTOURIST

VT, Vietnam's official tourist information office, doesn't yet maintain an office in the U.S. (although this is bound to change shortly with the dropping of the trade embargo), but you can obtain informative brochures from the U.S. representative, (Ms.) Hont Nguyen, *200 Waterside Plaza, New York, NY 10010* (☎ *212-685-8001*). In Saigon, check out SAIGONTOURIST Travel Service at *49 Le Thanh Ton Street*; ☎ *298-914* or *295-834*. Or fax them at *84-8-224987*. In all frankness, though, I didn't find these people particularly helpful save for all but the usual tourist package trips like three-hour expensive (US$15) city tours aboard buses that have to fight off thousands of bicycles and cyclos that swarm Saigon streets like bees in search of tulips to pollinate. Some of their offerings weren't so bad, though. For instance, I recommend the day trip to Bien Hoa, an area in the Mekong River Delta with green rolling hills, for about $35. But you gotta like those buses. If you're simply not into buses, forget it.

INSIDER TIP: A NOTE ON TOURIST OFFICES, MAPS AND ROADS

Although tourist offices exist in most major Vietnamese destinations (and even some minor ones–although I couldn't locate one in Tay Ninh), they are often of little use to the independent traveler–this includes especially the major offices of Saigontourist and Vietnamtourism in HCMC. Rather they cater more toward organized tours, providing guides (usually individuals with limited English capabilities at exorbitant prices), renting vehicles (also often at ridiculous rates) and providing little if any information on sites that aren't regularly visited by tourists–sights, regardless of their lack of scenic or cultural appeal, that independent travelers intuitively seek out. Their primary function is to procure dollars, and tour packages comprise the best means of doing so. Even obtaining local maps at the tourist offices can be difficult if not impossible.

Saigon is the best place to obtain reasonably detailed maps of areas in soputhern Vietnam. And the best map stalls line Le Loi Blvd, generally across from the Rex Hotel. Maps cost usually between US$1-2, depending on the area. Hanoi is the best place to find maps to areas in the north. Curiously enough, the least detailed maps seem to fetch the higher prices, and some of them seem virtually useless for ground travel. Many maps depict road routes but do not number them. If you're traveling by surface, before you depart, find someone who knows the numerical identifications of major Vietnamese roads and mark the maps at intervals, as route numbers have a tendency to change at times. In many cities, towns and villages where major routes pass through, the route numbers will become names, such as Le Loi Street, Nguyen Hue Blvd., etc. If you're not bringing a guide with you on independent travel along Vietnamese roadways, have someone mark on the map(s) where road conditions are particularly dismal. This is particularly important if you are drafting an itinerary and expect to reach specific locations at the end of the day.

A 150-km trek say between Nha Trang and Danang is going to take a considerably shorter period of time than the same distance between Ben Tre and Soc Trang in the south. And the roads in the north, traditionally known for their resemblance to cratered cattle paths rather than vehicle highways, are improving. Tourists traveling north in Vietnam from HCMC to Hanoi have traditionally gone only as far as Hue, at which point they opt to take the train or fly to points north. This still seems to be the case, even though the roads in the north are now in acceptable enough shape to be negotiated by means more sophisticated than a sow.

VISAS

Tour operators obtain visas for travelers, and the processing period doesn't take as long as a month as a lot of other guides claim. Although the visas obtained by the tour operators are currently procured from outside the U.S. (usually at Vietnam's Mexican embassy), usually it's just a matter of a week or 10 days before it's in your hands.

INSIDER TIP

Tour companies and travel agencies are extremely competitive and part of any particular company's lure is its ability to get you a visa quickly. With some companies, it might just take a couple of days, others as long as 10. But remember, that in order for a tour company to get your visa quickly it has to press Vietnamese immigration officials to push the paper like a used-car salesman, some of whom don't like to be shoved around, even when tourist dollars are involved. A travel or tour agency known for its expediency in delivering your visa may ironically not be in such good favor with the Vietnamese authorities because they're such a pain in the rear to the Vietnamese. If you've got the time, settle for the longer visa processing time if your tour operator can compensate in other areas–and believe me, they can. Even so, never wait until the last minute to book.

The best way to get a visa, as it is with all of the restricted countries in the region, is to get to Bangkok first. There you can pick up a visa in just a few days for around US$60–90 at the travel agencies or for US$48 at the Vietnamese Embassy at *83/1 Wireless Rd.*, directly across from the U.S. Embassy. They're usually open from 9–11 or 11:30 in the morning and 1–4 or so in the afternoon. Show up with a couple of passport photos. If you do use a travel agency, SHOP AROUND! In fact rather than stand on line at the embassy for my visa, I just walked half a block down Wireless Rd. to M.K. Ways. They didn't charge me a penny more than the embassy for the visa (almost unheard of in travel agency circles). They also specialize in Indochina tours and bookings and, frankly, they'll probably save you a lot of time prowling around Khao San Road for an airline bargain.

One of the increasingly popular ways of getting to Vietnam is through Cambodia. Again, arrange for your Vietnamese visa in Bangkok, not Phnom Penh. If you do it this way, you can expect to pay as little as US$40 for the single-entry tourist visa. Making Vietnamese visa arrangements in Cambodia is both expensive and time consuming, as it is in Vientiane. In Bangkok, you'll need to get three passport-type photos.

INOCULATIONS AND MEDICAL ADVICE

Arrival within six days after leaving or transiting a yellow fever zone requires an inoculation. But you should have all the proper vaccinations before coming to Vietnam. Disease is rife here. One source told me that Vietnam is the only country in the world where you can still get bubonic plague. Even if it isn't true, just the rumor itself is an indication that you would no more walk around Vietnam without inoculations than you would the surface of the moon without a space suit.

There is pneumonia here of every variety, malaria, diarrhoeal diseases, tetanus, tuberculosis, cholera, hepatitis, polio, rabies, leprosy, diptheria, dysentery, typhoid and rickets. You should be vaccinated for meningitis, hepatitis A and B, tuberculosis, typhoid, tetenus and diphtheria. Remember to have these performed well in advance of your trip as some will require boosters before you begin your journey. Also note that the period of efficacy differs by vaccination. Some will give you protection longer than others. And all of your vaccinations should be recorded in an International Health Certificate that you should carry with your passport.

Malaria is another story. Of course, you should obtain a larium prescription which you should begin taking about seven days before entering malarial zones. But the problem with this little monster of a disease is that it has this nasty tendency to become immune to virtually every medicine developed to fight it. Malaria mutates like Wolfgang Puck restaurants.

Also essential is a good first-aid kit with all the trimmings. And add to your booty when you get to Asia. A lot of the drugs you need a prescription for in North America, you can get over the counter in East Asia. And if you're going remote, painkillers are a great idea. You'll be thankful if you take a fall. We don't know too many docs Stateside who will write a downer "scrip" simply because you've said you'll be running in a road rally in Borneo for a month. But bring with you anti-diarrhoeal drugs such as codeine, Imodium or Lomotil. Also antiseptic and a laxative.

ENTRY BY AIR

Entry by air is by regularly scheduled flights into Hanoi and Ho Chi Minh City. Both cities are served by a variety of airlines, including Thai, Cathay Pacific, JAL, Korean Air, Garuda Indonesia, Philippine Airlines, MAS, Air France, and others depending on your departure point. There's also, of course, the infamous Vietnam Airlines, which has been likened by more than a few travelers to a fleet of coffins with wings. But I'll be honest, I've survived a number of bumpy trips aboard a Vietnam Airlines Boeing 767 and Airbus 320, as well as the Aerospatiale ATR-72, and I figure any British pilot working for a Vietnamese airline had to have done something to get canned at British Airways, such as planting a 747 on a German autobahn. But we made it each time, and he sounded as if he was having a jolly good time of it. I've got to admit it, though, it's a little unnerving to board a plain with absolutely no markings. The international fleet is painted white. A couple of numbers on the fantails, that's it. No logo or anything. I can think of a bunch of airspace in areas of the world where that would go over real well.

There have been reports by Westerners of having to bribe Vietnamese immigration officials both in Hanoi and Ho Chi Minh City after arrival, even with all documentation in order. And it can be expensive—upwards of US$100. But these instances are becoming fewer and fewer as officials realize just how important tourism is to the country.

INSIDER TIP

Vietnam Airlines ("Hang Khong" in Vietnamese and nicknamed "Hang On Vietnam" by those who have survived a VN flight), and its ancient fleet of Soviet-built Tupolev and Antonov aircraft, has had a miserable reputation over the years, both for service and safety. In the past, the advice had always been to avoid VN whenever possible. However, the airline is beginning to realize that most travelers' first goal when flying is getting to their destinations alive, the second being that their luggage arrives sometime within a year or two later. VN seems to be answering the call. The airline has purchased a new fleet of French-built Airbuses as well as Boeing 737s and 767s (I've heard even a 747) for use on international routes. And the Vietnamese start-up Pacific Airlines may give VN a run for its money and kick-start some good old-fashioned competition into the friendly Marxist skies. The attention to safety at VN seems to be improving, but don't expect filet mignon and headphones to catch Jurassic Park *just yet.*

ENTRY BY LAND

From Cambodia, the border crossing at Moc Bai is currently open to Westerners, who usually are on a bus from Phnom Penh to Ho Chi Minh City. There have been reports of Westerners being detained by Vietnamese border guards trying to solicit bribes. Be cool. The best bet is to pick up your visa (a 15-day transit visa has recently been lowered from US$20 to US$10) at the Cambodian consulate in Saigon (see Ho Chi Minh City "Directory" for the address and phone number).

The border between Vietnam and Laos has recently been opened to foreign tourists at Lao Ebbao. There's a little confusion about the costs of these visas. There is a free 3–5 day transit visa which can be issued at the border at Lao Ebbao, I was told. Another official at the Lao consulate in HCMC said that transit visas lasting a week cost US$25 and can be picked up at the Laos embassy in Hanoi and at both the Laos consulates in Ho Chi Minh City and Danang (Danang, I was told by the Lao consulate in HCMC is your best bet). From north of Danang, National Highway 9 crosses Vietnam into Laos and finally into Thailand. This route can be traversed by foreign tourists by land. But the road in Laos is in dismal condition, and officials at the consulate said that foreigners should attempt a crossing into and through Laos from Vietnam in the dry season only—which runs from November through April. The roads in Laos west of Vietnam are not navigable during the rainy season between May and October. If you really want to get stuck somewhere for an extended period of time, say six months, in an area where there is virtually nothing that allows human beings to survive, I'd strongly suggest traveling into Laos from Vietnam by road during the rainy season.

The Chinese border to the north is becoming increasingly easier to cross for both Vietnamese and Westerners alike. Many travelers now say it's a piece of cake.

ENTRY BY SEA

Entering Vietnam by sea is legal only by freighter or cruise ship. It would be dangerous to attempt a landing in Vietnam by any other means. It could mean months in jail. Keep your yacht and jet skis in Singapore.

CURRENCY

The official currency in Vietnam is the dong, although U.S. dollars are accepted, even preferred, in the population centers. Bank notes come in the denominations of 200d, 500d, 1000d, 2000d, 5000d, and 10,000d. Most travelers today are using the dollars over the dong, and many upscale hotels require payment in dollars. Carry a good amount of U.S. money in small denominations. You may be using dollars entirely while you're in Vietnam.But if you must know, 10,800 dong is equal to a buck.

INSIDER TIP

Under U.S. Treasury restrictions, American travelers may spend up to US$200 per day in Vietnam (transportation and communication excluded) to purchase items related to travel. The use of U.S. credit cards has been prohibited in Vietnam (although by the time you read this, the ban will probably have been dropped, as will spending limits). And a $100 value limit is set on merchandise Americans bring back from the country. This doesn't include maps, books and other educational material. But receipts are required. Vietnamese officials stringently restrict the exporting of antiques.

TIPPING

Tipping is becoming increasingly expected in Vietnam, although it certainly isn't required. Some establishments add a 10% surcharge. Keeping some duty-free booze and foreign cigarettes on you is always a good idea. Marlboros and 555s are the best bets for the butts, Johnnie Walker Black Label whiskey for the booze. And remember, most waitresses in Vietnam make a salary of US$20 per month. Nearly all help support their families on this amount.

OFFICIAL LANGUAGE

The official language is Vietnamese, which is a combination of Chinese, Tai, Cham and Mon-Khmer. English is spoken by the many Vietnamese who worked with Americans during the Vietnam War as well as a number of schoolchildren and students. There's been an escalating interest in English since the country began opening itself to tourism in 1989. Many in the older set can speak French, and there are a lot of French tourists to practice with.

BUSINESS HOURS

Most businesses open between 7 and 8 in the morning, shut down for a couple of hours around 11–12 noon, and open again until 4 or 5 p.m. Government offices are generally open a half-day on Saturday. Museums are generally closed Mondays.

TELEPHONE, TELEX AND FAX

These services are actually quite good, especially in Ho Chi Minh City. They used to be outrageously expensive, but prices are coming down. Faxing is your best bet. In fact, faxing from many places in Vietnam is cheaper than doing so from Thailand, Malaysia and Singapore, even from hotels. Most institutions with faxes in Vietnam charge by the page rather than by a three-minute minimum. It's a better deal if you're only faxing a single page. Expect to pay anywhere from US$6.75 to US$8.50 per page (compared to the 3-minute minimum prices of around US$9 in Thailand). And beware. If you're faxing overseas from a hotel, ask to see the hotel's rate chart in print. Opportunistic clerks frequently pad the costs by a dollar or two per page. I've caught a few of them at it. International faxing and phoning is generally cheaper at post offices than at hotels.

AUTHOR'S NOTE: TELECOMMUNICATIONS

The official line is this: Calls to Singapore cost US$3.80 for the first minute and $2.95 for each subsequent minute. Calls to France cost US$4.60/ $3.82 for each subsequent minute. To Indonesia, the rates are US$4.55/$3.50, and to the US, US$4.50/US$3.82. In practice, I found these rates to be higher, not significantly, but high enough so that a business call that might take a certain amount of time adds up. Hotels are generally more expensive than going though a GPO, but don't count on it. Ironically, I've found it cheaper to fax the US from small hotels in the middle of the boonies than to make the "less expensive" calls though the general post offices in the major urban centers. Who knows, you may be getting ripped off. But what the hell are you going to do about it? Interestingly enough, I've heard that it's a lot cheaper to call places like Hanoi from Singapore, than vice versa (about US$2 a minute) but I have yet to verify this.

A phone call to the U.S. usually runs around US$5.50 for the first minute and a few pennies less than that for each minute thereafter. It's not cheap. Faxing is a better deal. The influx of foreign business into both Hanoi and Ho Chi Minh City should soon bring these costs down as the country's communications infrastructure develops. Telexes aren't of much use any longer as the West has mostly discarded them in favor of the fax.

INSIDER TIP

Vietnam is a communist country. When faxing, avoid including information and/or opinions of a political nature. In some hotels, especially in the provinces, you can fax internationally direct–from hotel fax to destination fax–so there's little to be concerned about. This might be a little paranoid, but beware. In places like Saigon, your fax is first transmitted to the general post office or other communications center before it is refaxed onto your destination. Usually, there's no hassle with this–and I have yet to experience a problem–i.e., state police battering down my hotel door at three in the morning. But just know that other eyes will see your communication before it's sent out of the country. Before you fax overseas, ask the fax operator (i.e. hotel clerk) if your message will be transmitted directly rather than through a middle source. As a rule of thumb, avoid sending anything even remotely controversial that could potentially raise a red flag. Literally.

INSIDER TIP

Soon you'll find it a lot easier to make a phone call in Vietnam. The number of telephone lines in the country will increase by 200,000 to a total of more than 460,000 lines by the end of 1994–40,000 lines will be installed in Hanoi, 60,000 in HCMC and the remaining 100,000 in the provinces around the country. The total project is expected to cost in the US$275 million region. Most of the investment will come from overseas. Vietnam currently (at presstime) has only three lines for each 1000 people in this country with a population of more than 71 million. The government expects to have 750,000 lines in operation by the end of 1995, bringing the rate to about 10 lines per 1000 people.

Most major cities provide relatively easy access to IDD (International Direct Dial) lines, most of them in the better hotels. Most budget travelers make overseas calls from GPOs in Vietnam's cities, and virtually all clerks at these post offices will tell you (seeing that you're a foreigner) that making collect calls overseas cannot be done. However, there is a way to make a collect call overseas. Get to know a Vietnamese local and have him do it for you. In some areas it's more difficult than in others, but generally it can be done.

INSIDER TIP

Have an English-speaking Vietnamese friend explain to the clerk that he wants to make an overseas call, say to the U.S. (Vietnamese are given vast preferences over foreigners whenever trying to conduct any type of communications, accommodations, restaurant or utility-related business.) The Vietnamese person will have to give the operator his or her name, of course. Tell the Vietnamese friend to add your name to his when giving his own name to the operator. For instance, if you're calling your parents in Georgia and the Vietnamese's name is Nguyen Tu, tell him to add your name to his. You can use your first name or surname depending upon whom you're calling (and the name the party will recognize you by).

If your name is Franklin Beethoven, have the Vietnamese say to the operator that his name is Nguyen Beethoven Tu. Your party in the States will probably recognize the situation and accept the charges. The operator may ask the Vietnamese how the hell he got the name Beethoven, but he simply needs to say it's a nickname. (In this case he might say his music teacher gave it to him, that it's a stupid one, but one that stuck.) There is no guarantee that this will work, but it has worked for me on a number of occasions. A tip should be in order for the Vietnamese helping you. (It'll be a hell of a lot cheaper than paying for the call yourself.)

WHAT TO WEAR

Vietnam has a sticky, tropical climate. Light cotton clothing is a must, particularly in the south. In the north (especially the mountainous north), it can become quite cool on winter evenings. A sweater or wrap would be appropriate. And places like Halong Bay can get darn cold in January. Bring a coat. Jackets and ties for doing business only.

LOCAL TIME

Vietnam is seven hours ahead of Greenwich mean time. It's in the same time zone as Bangkok and Phnom Penh.

NEWSPAPERS AND MAGAZINES

English-language periodicals in Vietnam include *Vietnam Weekly,* *Vietnam Economic News, Saigon Times* and *New Vietnam*—all geared toward foreign business travelers, but most contain useful travel information on interesting destinations, some off the trodden path. Best bet in Ho Chi Minh City is the *Bangkok Post, The Asian Wall Street Journal, USA Today* and the *International Herald Tribune* for newspapers and *Time* or *Newsweek* for magazines. In addition, since the lifting of the American embargo, you can pick up even current issues of *People* magazine. Things are *really* changing here.

Both the newspapers and the magazines are current. In fact, the *Bangkok Post* is that day's issue.

INSIDER TIP

Obtaining periodicals and newspapers dealing with the outside world used to, frankly, be a hassle in Saigon—and an expensive one at that. This seems to be changing. American publications such as the Wall Street Journal, USA Today, TIME, People *and* Newsweek *are readily available, especially around the Rex and Continental Hotels. Swarms of children scour the streets hawking English-language rags to foreigners, but still, unfortunately, at inflated prices. Be aware that you may be able to bargain for many of the magazines and newspapers the kids are touting, namely because they've been pilfered from the hotels after the guests have finished with them. The bookstore across the square from the Rex is an especially well-endowed newsstand, selling current newspapers and magazines from all over the world. The biggest disappointment is that the best locally produced periodicals, including the* Saigon Times, *the* Vietnam Investment Review *(highly recommended for business travelers) and* Vietnam Today—*all extremely useful and remarkably well-done publications—still fetch exorbitantly high prices. US$4-5 is the norm. For many travelers, though, the publications are an investment rather than a way to pass time in the toilet.*

ELECTRICAL CURRENT

Since Vietnam's infrastructure is still rudimentary, and power outages occur without warning, be sure to bring a flashlight. The electric current is 220V/50 cycles in most places. Take along adapter plugs and a converter.

AUTHOR'S NOTE

Vietnam's 500 kilovolt north-south power transmission line has started operation from Hoa Binh, about 75 km west of Hanoi, to Ho Chi Minh City. The line will supply 2.5 billion kwh for the southern cities and is currently the country's biggest infrastructure project. The goal is to provide power to southern cities that chronically suffer from seasonal shortages of power.

CLIMATE

Dress comfortably, and pack clothes that are easy to launder and a comfy pair of soft-soled shoes. Bring plenty of film. The climate in Ho Chi Minh City, and elsewhere in the south, is hottest (in the 80s and 90sF.) and most humid in March and April, with the dry season running from November to April and the rainy season from May to October. In Hanoi, and elsewhere in the north, although the seasons occur at about the same time, temperatures are much cooler, and there is less rain, except in coastal areas during the summer.

LOCAL TRANSPORTATION

Buses are one of the best ways to get around because they're so cheap and they get to so many places within the country. And they're even better if you've got a lot of time—because they take a lot of time. Oh, yeah—they break down a lot, too. There are more runs during the night now that curfew restrictions have been relaxed.

Cars are a better way to get around than buses but are usually quite expensive, at least 25 cents a km on top of a day charge. And you can't rent them yourself yet, at least to drive. Alas, yours will have to come with a driver. It's better that way anyhow. There's right-side-drive in Vietnam and, although the cops are tough, one of the most common infractions is driving on the left. There are a lot of companies that hire out cars and drivers in Ho Chi Minh City.

You can rent a **moped** (under 50 cc) without a special license in Vietnam, or hire a moped driver. You can even now rent a **motorcycle** in Ho Chi Minh City for about US$10 per day. You will need an international drivers license with a motorcycle certificate.

Trains are also a great way of getting around along the coast. They're slower than the buses, but are a helluva lot more comfy if you shell out enough dollars (you'll be required to pay in dollars) for anything more than a hard seat. The only problem is that the government slaps a surcharge on rail travel that makes it virtually as expensive as flying the same route (at least between Ho Chi Minh City and Hanoi).

Hitchhiking is a piece of cake in Vietnam and not nearly as risky as in Cambodia, but expect to pay for your ride.Other travelers, however, report waiting hours for rides. It pays to look neat.

Cyclos are also a cheap way to get around, especially the cities. And they're everywhere where tourists hang out.

Bicycles are perhaps the best and cheapest way to get around in the towns and cities. They rent for no more than a dollar per day and they can be had many places, including hotels, restaurants and sidewalk stalls. Some operators will ask for a deposit sometimes as high as US$20. Outside Saigon and Hanoi, most don't require any.

INSIDER TIP: TAXIS AND CAR HIRE IN VIETNAM

A service is available from Tan Son Nhat airport to Saigon. The 20 or so minute ride costs about US$8-15 depending on your negotiating abilities. Taxis are also available from Noi Bai Airport in Hanoi, costing anywhere from US$20-25. The trip is a long one, sometimes taking up to an hour. Within the cities, taxis don't normally cruise the streets looking for a fare. Instead they can be found at taxi stalls, or they can be arranged through hotels or by simply calling them. Some officials say that you can arrange for a car and a driver for about $35 in both major cities a day, but I haven't found this to be true. Usually the rate, especially if you're considering excursions to the Mekong Delta and Cu Chi Tunnels in Saigon, or Ha Long Bay in Hanoi, can be considerably more expensive. In Saigon, for instance, expect to pay upwards of US$70-90 a day (for a car and a driver in Saigon) and even more in Hanoi. Travel agents will do their best to make you think you're getting the deal of the century. But remember, the only deal of the century that can be found in Vietnam is drinking fresh beer (Bia Hoi). Metered taxis in Saigon and Hanoi are expensive, about US$2 just to get into the car and another US70 cents for every kilometer. And availability depends upon the bookings, so plan your excursions from your hotel well in advance.

TOUR OPERATORS

(Note: Local numbers are for information; toll-free numbers are for reservations). In the U.S., you can contact:

Absolute Asia
155 W. 68 St., Suite 525
New York, NY 10023
☎ *212-595-5782; 800-736-8187*

EastQuest
1 Beekman St., #607
New York, NY 10038
☎ *212-406-2224; 800-638-3449*

IPI/InterPacific Tours International
111 E. 15th St.
New York, NY 10003
☎ *212-953-6010; 800-221-3594*

Here Today, There Tomorrow
1901 Pennsylvania Ave., N.W., #204
Washington, D.C. 20006
☎ *202-296-6373; 800-368-5965*

Sino-American Tours

37 Bowery
New York, N.Y. 10002
☎ *212-966-5866; 800-221-7982*

South Sea Tour & Travel

210 Post St. Ste 910,
San Francisco, CA 94108
☎ *415-397-4644; 800-546-7890*

Velo Asia

1412 MLK Jr. Way
Berkeley, CA 94709
☎ *800-884-ASIA*

Abercrombie & Kent International

1520 Kensington Rd.
Oak Brook, IL 60521-2106
☎ *708-954-2944; 800-323-7308*

Or in Bangkok, Thailand, you can contact:

Exotissimo Travel

21/17 Sukhumvit Soi 4, Bangkok 10110
☎ *253-5240/1, 255-2747; FAX: 254-7683.*

Lam Son International Ltd.

23/1 Sukhumvit Soi 4, Bangkok 10110
☎ *255-6692/3/4/5; FAX: 255-8859*

Red Carpet Service & Tour

459 New Rama 6 Rd., Phayathai, Bangkok 10400
☎ *215-9951, 215-3331; FAX: 662-215-3331*

Viet Tour Holidays

1717 Lard Prao Rd., Samsennok, Huay- Kwang, Bangkok 10310
☎ *511-3272; FAX: 511-3357*

Vikamla Tours

Room 401 Nana Condo, 23/11 Sukhumvit Soi 4, Bangkok 10110
☎ *252-2340, 255-8859*

FESTIVALS AND HOLIDAYS

Like the rest of Southeast Asia, Vietnam enjoys its holidays and festivals.

January 1	New Year's Day	*Public Holiday*
February (moveable)	Tet (Traditional New Year)	*This is the big celebration of the year. It's the time that people forget their grievances; they pay off debts, kiss and make up–that sort of thing. Interestingly enough, Tet also marks everyone's birthday. The Vietnamese don't celebrate individual birthdays. On Tet, everyone's a full year older! The celebration is marked with a tremendous amount of eating. It's believed that the first full week of the year determines how the rest of it will go.*
February 3	Founding of the Communist Party Day	*Public holiday.*
March (moveable)	Hai Ba Trung Day	*Marks the revolt the Trung sisters led against the Chinese in A.D. 41.*
April 30	Liberation Day of South Vietnam	*Public Holiday. Marks the toppling of the Saigon government in 1975.*
April (moveable)	Thanh Minh, Holiday of the Dead	*Feast of the Pure Light. Vietnamese walk outdoors to contact spirits of the dead. Shrines and tombs are cleaned.*
May 1	May Day	*Public holiday.*
May 19	Birthday of Ho Chi Minh	*Public holiday.*
May 28	Celebration of the birth, death and enlightenment of Buddha	*Public holiday.*
August (moveable)	Wandering Souls Day	*After Tet, this is the second most important festival. By praying for the dead, their sins can be absolved. They can leave hell hungry and naked to their loved ones. Celebrations in temples and homes. Money is burned.*
September 2	National Day	*Public holiday.*
September 3	President Ho's Anniversary	*Public holiday.*

FESTIVALS AND HOLIDAYS

September (moveable)	Mid-Autumn Festival	*A children's holiday that features parades.*
November (moveable)	Confucious' Birthday	

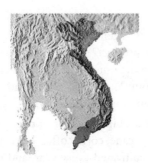

VIETNAM'S ECONOMY AND DOING BUSINESS IN VIETNAM

Vietnam's markets are crammed with vendors and buyers alike during the early morning hours.

Back in the 1980s, the real growth rate in the Vietnamese economy was estimated to be in the six percent range, but that would hardly be accurate today, as the country is courting foreign investment like a queen bee in heat. And the drones of Japan, South Korea, Taiwan, Singapore, Malaysia, Indonesia, Canada, France and Australia are more than happy to pollinate Vietnam's fertile embryo. It is unlikely the country will ever experience proverbial menstruation again.

Vietnam enjoys an abundance of natural resources, including coal, phosphates, hardwoods, gems, manganese, chromate, boxite, rubber, palm oil, marine products and—of particular interest to American oil interests—vast deposits of offshore oil reserves just waiting to heat every home from Anchorage and Albany—and perhaps even more important, from Quito to Asunscion.

Although Vietnam is a big producer of rice, rubber, fruit and vegetables, as well as sugarcane, corn, coffee and manioc, less than seven million hectares are cultivated every year, and only perhaps 20% of the country's land is arable (estimates range from as low as 17.5 % to as high as 30%). Food processing, chemical fertilizers, cement, textiles, steel and electric power make up the crux of the country's exports, as does a $900 million trade involving primarily agriculture, seafood, rubber, wood flooring, coffee and coal. But, of course, these exports have been traditionally shipped to places that don't even exist anymore.

You wouldn't guess it, but the owner of this hootch is considered prosperous by his peers.

In short, Vietnam is poor, perhaps the most impoverished nation on earth—certainly one of the 10 poorest. We've already mentioned the typical American can spend on a pair of mediocre shoes what the average Vietnamese makes in a year. And Vietnam owes the International Monetary Fund some $1.5 billion in debts that its creditors are not likely to recoup. Perhaps the only plus in the whole scenario is that a lot of the cash is owed to the former Soviet Union, whose own crumbling monetary system makes the Vietnamese dong seem as solid as a Michael Milken junk bond investment of the mid 1980s.

And this perhaps reveals one of the most ironic economic paradoxes of the nation—Vietnam as a single unique country sharing the same economic woes and monetary cemeterial plots. This simply is without foundation. The two halves of the nation have evolved independently of each other, for all intents and purposes, for more than 40 years—and even the fall of Saigon to the north has done little to imperil the entrepreneurialism of the residents of the southern half of the country. Although the party virtually retains a brutal Stalin-like grip on its people, it also covertly encourages perhaps the most liberal of all economic principles in Asia to function unabated. Some call the ideology schizophrenic, others believe it's just plain economic sense in dealing with a communist world that is collapsing around the last bastions of Marxist-Leninism like a ficus in an ice storm. Despite the loss of more than 50,000 American soldiers during the Vietnam War, Vietnam clearly remains two distinct countries.

The south is aggressive, outspoken, even pompous. The north, although tolerant—apparently for the gains it stands to realize—is more suspicious of the wave of Westerners (although first-time American tourists may be stunned on how warmly they're received). Hanoi, although charming enough, is void of the filigree of dissent, of muted protest—of diversity, in other words. It lacks an "edge," where youth and the free-spirited are thwarted from pushing the envelope of thought and art. Ho Chi Minh City makes no such pretense of Marxist piety. A curb may be built for keeping pedestrians from traffic, but they're also a lot of fun for bounding with skateboards and strolling on while donning headsets pounding with the likes of Metallica and Guns 'N Roses.

AUTHOR'S OBSERVATION: FYI FOR 'VIET KIEU'

Overseas Vietnamese, or "Viet Kieu" may or may not become a major component of foreign investment in Vietnam. Many analysts think their impact on the economy will be relatively marginal. Others are far more optimistic. FDI (Foreign Direct Investment) in Vietnam in 1994 is anticipated to be in the US$4 billion range. There hasn't been a lot of overseas Vietnamese foreign investment to date, but the government is implementing incentive programs for overseas Vietnamese investors. A corporate income tax reduction of 20 percent may be the carrot overseas Vietnamese are looking for but, to date, only 10 overseas companies have made any formal contact or inquiries with Vietnam's SCCI (State Committee for Cooperation and Investment).

Both the north and the south can be considered hard working, and it's one of the reasons Cambodians are so resentful of the ethnic Vietnamese that reside in their country, simply for their work ethic. The Vietnamese are educated, as mentioned earlier, but are beset with the problems of centralized government that continually results in grave shortages of staples and spare parts for machinery. Unemployment is rampant. Some put the estimates as high as 50%.

Why? Well, for once, it seems there are some easy answers. In fact, it's only one answer and it's twofold: the U.S. trade embargo and Hanoi's insistence that so much of its budget go into military spending. There is China to the north, of course, relatively bitter foes. Cambodia to the west, hardly a cohesive and formidable foe, even against its own internal insurgents—and there is Thailand, whose real threat to the stability of Vietnam in the '90s is nonexistent.

AUTHOR'S OBSERVATION

Contrary to popular opinion, it has become less evident that Vietnam can attribute the US economic embargo as the single greatest hinderence to the nation's prosperity. But it still had impact. Although the embargo in all likelihood had little effect for the first decade following the end of the Vietnam War, the breakup of the Eastern Bloc and the collapse of the Soviet Union was a devastating blow to Vietnam's recovery from the war. The embargo prevented loans to Vietnam from the International Monetary Fund, and essentially cut off aid from the West. Although there were moves during the Jimmy Carter administration in 1977 to begin to normalize relations with Hanoi, the U.S embargo wasn't dropped until February 4, 1994. Only a day before, three large block letters were taped over and disguised against the white cement facade of a large computer retailer on Saigon's Ly Tu Trong Street. The day after President Clinton lifted the embargo, workers on scaffolding had unmasked the big logo and were busy painting the letters in a familiar deep blue. They read "IBM," of course.

But, despite the hardships created by war and international isolation, Vietnam has been a strongly resilient country. Despite the loss of massive economic aid from the former Soviet Union, Vietnam has stayed on its feet. It's dealing with new trading partners, and the relationships have been mutually profitable. Singapore has emerged as Vietnam's largest trading partner—a far cry from Moscow in every sense of the word. Foreign investment has been growing at rates unparalleled outside Asia. By the first quarter of 1993, total foreign investments in the Vietnamese economy totaled more than US$3 billion, more than double the figure of only two years previously. Mid-1994 estimates put the figure at US$5 billion. Money is pouring into Vietnam from Japan, Taiwan, Australia (even though it still steadfastly refuses to "Asianize" itself), Hong Kong, France, Great Britain, and Germany. The rewards for Vietnam's trading partners can be astronomical. For instance, Vietnam's Foreign Investment Code, at the time of this writing, permits 100% foreign business ownership—astounding for a "communist" country. Foreign businesses are allowed up to 99% equity participation in joint ventures.

But if it all seems too good to be true, maybe it is. Foreign businesses are confronted in Vietnam with an essentially nonexistent infrastructure. Many charge that corruption runs rampant in the government, and accountings of how the pies of foreign investment are sliced and where the crumbs fall can be ambiguous if not downright purposefully deceptive.

Beer trucks have yet to make their debut in Vietnam.

But the money into Vietnam continues to flow like an aqueduct sourced at a deep snowpack. Tourism, of course, has skyrocketed. In 1989, about 60,000 tourists visited Vietnam, most of whom were overseas Vietnamese living in foreign countries taking advantage of Hanoi's increasingly liberal policies dealing with repatriation and the visiting of relatives inside Vietnam by political and "economic" refugees. Another significant chunk of that figure was the flow of tourists from Communist countries, who have more access to Communist-controlled tourist destinations than to places like Miami or Rio.

But the figure jumped to nearly 190,000 tourists just one year later, in 1990. Optimistic government officials then predicted that by 1995, the 1991 figure would double. It turned out to be a pessimistic forecast at best. The figure authorities in Hanoi now openly speak of hovers at around one million. No wonder it's easier to declare a camcorder at customs.

AUTHOR'S NOTE

By the year 2000, Vietnam will need between 12,800 to 17,300 tourist cars and between 47,000 and 63,000 commercial vehicles. If the country decides not to build its own plants, it will have to spend nearly US$1.5 billion to import them. If Vietnam decides to build its own plants, government officials will be looking primarily at the United States, Western Europe and Japan for the necessary technology.

The problem is a lack of facilities to accommodate all these people. Maybe "facilities" isn't the word. Change that to quality hotel rooms. The number of hotel rooms in Bangkok alone today stands around 30,000. Compare that with less than 10,000 in the entire country of Vietnam, whose population exceeds that of Thailand's by nearly 20 million.

But these rooms, and thousands more, will come—if for no other reason than there is so much money to be made here. It's estimated that northern Vietnam possesses some of Asia's greatest coal deposits. Offshore oil reserves make your head spin. A recent survey estimated that Vietnam's oil reserves are somewhere between two and three billion barrels—more than half a million barrels could be output in a single day in about 10 years from now. With the lifting of the U.S. trade embargo, Vietnam is poised to become a huge exporter of oil in the near future.

AUTHOR'S OBSERVATION

Besides the high-profile measures the government of Vietnam has made in recent years to lure foreign investors, many of its fledgling and more subtle, recent decrees to placate potential investors tend not to make the headlines. But they're being noticed by companies that stand to make a lot of money in the consumer products sector. For instance, the government has begun a serious crackdown on counterfeit consumer products, including locally-produced and bottled fake Coca-Cola, fake Johnnie Walker Black and Red Label whiskey, Marlboro cigarettes, and counterfeit Lacoste shirts. Around Hanoi, and especially Saigon, it's been commonplace to find electronics outlets peddling cassette players with names suggestive of the real McCoys, brands called "Pensonic," "Sonv," and "Toshida." It's called intellectual property rights and, for years, they've been virtually entirely unprotected in major metropolitan areas throughout Southeast Asia. At least in Hanoi, it seems to be changing. The government has promised to be in a position to effectively enforce these rights within the next four years. Granted they have a tough task before them. Hanoi has even established an economics police unit to deal with the problem solely.

Vietnam's Patent and Trademark Bureau of the Chamber of Commerce and Industry, along with other state-owned enterprises, acts as the patent attorney for foreign businesses that have registered their invention rights and industrial property in Vietnam. Much of the counterfeit products are available in Vietnam for a fraction of the cost of the originals. Because the Vietnamese have enjoyed greater buying powers over the last few years, there's been a tremendous surge in patent and trademark applications by foreign firms doing or planning to do business in Vietnam. More than 50,000 trademarks have been registered in Vietnam—eighty of them by foreign companies. It's turned out to be an overwhelming amount for the government to process. Last year, the Ministry of Science, Technology and Environment received nearly 8,500 applications to register service trademarks, patents, and industrial designs. This was up from 6617 from the previous year. The system has become bottlenecked, a system which has always been marred in red tape.

Much of the counterfeit merchandise comes from abroad. "Pensonic" products come from China. And other counterfeits, such as bogus Henessey cognac smack so much of the original, right down to the seal, it would be impossible to make this product in Vietnam, whose own domestically-produced liquor caps virtually disintegrate after the seal is broken. (If you purchase Vietnamese spirits, be prepared to consume them in one sitting). Additionally, imitation and substandard medications are rampant in Vietnam.

AUTHOR'S OBSERVATION

To its credit, Vietnam became a member of the Geneva-based World Intellectual Property Organization, and arm of the UN. The country also became affiliated with the International Patent Corporation Treaty. Vietnam was also a participant at the Paris Convention on patents, trademarks and other forms of industrial property protection. After the U.S. embargo was dropped, another 200 U.S. companies applied for patent protection, bringing the number of American applications to nearly 1500. So far, there is no copyright protection for film or literary works in Vietnam. These are areas that will have to be addressed in attracting hundreds of foreign cultural imports.

THE NEW WAVE OF AMERICAN INVESTMENT IN VIETNAM AND SOME TIPS FOR ENTREPRENEURS

The recent lifting of the trade embargo, although some expected that few American companies would jump into the country's burgeoning economic environment like banshees, has spawned a wave of American business people seeking opportunities in the country. (Although Vietnamese here have the impression that Americans have a "take the bull by the horns" attitude and inititate and execute ideas at phenomenal speed, the going will be slow until there is full normalization of relations between the two countries.)

The Asia Pacific Chamber of Commerce (APCC) based in Seattle, Washington sent a commission to Vietnam last April called the "Business Opportunity Mission to Vietnam." Its purpose was to help American entrepreneurs learn Vietnamese business and social customs and how to do business in perhaps the world's fastest growing economy. According to APCC execs, American companies attending the mission included Caterpillar, Clark, Microsoft, Sun Micro Systems, US West and McCaw Cellular (both telecommunications companies), Crate & Barrel, Advanced Technology Labs, and Space Labs (a hospital monitor company).

Official members of the delegation included Senator Patty Murray of Washington, Adlai Stevenson and Paul Cleveland (The U.S. Trade Ambassador).

There were also participants from the American Grocer's Association, the Washington Apple Commission, and officials from Washington State's Department of Agriculture.

Among the many American companies rushing into Vietnam to sign deals are the Texas-based WG Ripley Group (assembly lines for cotton production, a US$2.5 million deal), DuPont (which has opened an office in Ho Chi Minh City and said that Vietnam is now a focal point for its efforts to quadruple sales—to move global sales from 7 to 20 percent—in the region by the turn of the century). (Incidentally, DuPont was one of the first U.S. businesses to open shop in Vietnam after the lifting of the embargo.) DuPont's energy subsidiary, Conoco, has been seeking to obtain offshore oil exploration rights. The company, like a slew of others, is forecasting increasingly sophisticated consumer and industrial markets for electronics, automotive products, electrical goods, construction materials, clothing and crop protection.

Vietnam may become a major importer of U.S. farm products, perhaps procuring as much as US$300 million annually. Vietnam purchased US$213 million worth of food in 1992, the last year statistics are available. About a quarter of the products were purchased from the European Union, Singapore, Japan and Hong Kong.

Because Vietnam is looking at moving toward an economic strategy that would increase its growth rate between 8 and 10 percent annually, agricultural imports are likely to skyrocket in coming years, according to a U.S. State Department report. Total agricultural purchases in Vietnam could reach U.S.$1.7 billion annually. Vietnam's interest in American agricultural products include wheat, wheat flour, feed grains, poultry, pork and processed meats, vegetable oils and oil seeds, cotton, and processed fresh fruits.

Businesspeople considering doing business in Vietnam may want to consider that there may be only limited demand for branded consumer products. But assistance with the country's agricultural industry should provide self-starters with boundless opportunities. But remember, you've got a lot of catching up to do. The U.S. currently ranks 33rd in foreign investment in Vietnam. But investment opportunities still flourish. Nearly all of the country's 52 provinces and cities are openly vying for overseas investment.

AUTHOR'S NOTE

Hollywood, not one to miss scouting a good location, is also jumping in on the post-embargo feeding fray in Vietnam. The American film "Fields of Fire" will be the first post-embargo American film shot in Vietnam. The film, of course, will be a Vietnam War film, and more than likely feature the rising Vietnamese-American actress Kieu Chinh in the lead role. Production began in May. The film was adopted from the novel of the same name written by the film's director James Webb, who was a lieutenant in the U.S. Army during the war stationed at Quang Nam-Da Nang. Webb also served as secretary of the Navy under the George Bush administration. Fields of Fire chronicles the fates of soldiers on both sides of the conflict. The film's primary locations are set in the district's of Duy Xuyen and Dai Loc. Up until now, most movies depicting the war, including Francis Ford Coppola's epic Apocalypse Now and Platoon used the Philippines, Thailand, Malaysia, and other Southeast Asia locations for shooting.

In addition, aviation will undoubtedly provide a slew of opportunities for American firms. American aviation companies jumping on the Vietnam bandwagon include United and Delta Airlines, Boeing, McDonnell-Douglas, Continental Airlines and Northwest. Delta, in particular, is working with Vietnam Airlines to establish direct links between the United States and Vietnam. Up until this point, travelers have had to endure long layovers in places like Bangkok, Singapore, Hong Kong, or Seoul before boarding flights on different carriers to Vietnam.

U.S. INVESTMENT IN VIETNAM (IN US$ MILLIONS)		
SECTORS	*1994-1995.*	*1998*
ENERGY & TRANSPORTATION	1062.0	2493.0
ROAD CONSTRUCTION	100.0	210.0
TELECOMMUNICATIONS	223.5	457,5
OIL & GAS EQUIPMENT	113.3	11375.5
AVIATION CONTROL EQUIPMENT	87.0	195.0
OIL EXPLORATION	25.7	41.3
REFRIGERATION	4.5	24.0
COMPUTERS	24.5	118.8
AIRPLANE ENGINES	200.7	750..0
HOTEL CONSTRUCTION & MANAGEMENT	36.1	54.8

U.S. INVESTMENT IN VIETNAM (IN US$ MILLIONS)		
SECTORS	1994-1995.	1998
AUTOMATIC PRODUCTS	33.3	65.8
PHARMACEUTICALS	13.3	54.0
AIR SERVICES	44.8	68.2
MEDICAL EQUIPMENT	3.0	9.8
CHEMICALS	25.5	110.1
CONSTRUCTION MATERIALS	20.0	73.0
PETRO-CHEMICAL PRODUCTS	45.0	10.0
OTHER INDUSTRIAL PRODUCTS	60.3	138.2
CONSUMER GOODS	390.6	1303.3
AUTOMOBILES	30.6	57.4
BANKS & STOCKS	21.9	68.8
SHIPPING	100.0	438.0

Source: U.S.-ASEAN Council

In the areas of construction, major U.S. companies either seeking to establish contracts in Vietnam or those whose ink has already dried include Fluor Daniel (66th among the largest diversified service companies in the world, according to *Forbes* magazine), and Indochina Partners.

In the north, conditions for conducting and initiating business transactions are far more problematic than in the south. American businesspeople are now jamming airliners headed to Hanoi, and officials in Vietnam are having a difficult time accommodating all the interest American companies are developing in the country's economy. As one observer noted, "The Vietnamese economy still lacks the fundamental preconditions for high, sustainable growth."

In a way, Vietnam is going through a potentially dangerous phase. Central planning has been all but eliminated entirely. But the country has yet to establish a free market system that works within any predictable or regulatory network. And the budget defect continues to widen, currently about 7 percent (see AUTHOR'S NOTE below).

But some of the other numbers sure look good: The gross domestic product expanded by 8 percent last year, without any measurable degree of inflation.(Prices rose slightly more than 5 percent.) Nearly one million new jobs were created in the country during the past 12 months (although countless millions of Vietnamese still remain under- or unemployed). These new workers are helping to construct houses and produce durable goods, efforts that have yielded more progress in the country in the last five years than in the previous half century.

In 1994, projects that have been capitalized comprised more than US$300 million, and experts suggest that foreign investment in Vietnam may have doubled to nearly US$4 billion in 1994.

AUTHOR'S NOTE

Although the business rush into Vietnam is making people a lot of money and improving the lives of the Vietnamese people, not everyone is happy about it : the communist hardliners in Hanoi. If the pages of the Army's daily newspaper **Quan Doi Nhan Don** *are any indication, the trend toward a free market system in Vietnam has a number of high ranking Hanoi officials becoming just a little paranoid. Hanoi's Defense Minister Doan Khue has called for "increased revolutionary vigilance" against those who want to move toward a market economy in order to end communist rule of the country. "Hostile forces are attempting to wipe out socialism and the revolutionary gains of our people," he said. Party ideologues are calling for creating a stable political front where the party's leading role "will hold forever the irreversible gains of the Vietnamese Revolution."*

The officials claim that those calling for the improvement of Vietnam's human rights efforts are doing so "under the cover of democracy...They are trying to denigrate the Socialist regime," said Doan, who is the fifth ranking member of Hanoi's Politburo. He is perhaps the leading conservative in Vietnam and he fears that the opening of the economy will bring with it corruption, poverty (if there's not enough already) and other "social ills." "The cause of renovation is going well and achieving many advantages," he said, "but the scheming tricks of the enemy against our country, against socialism, remain unchanged. Inside the country there are destabilizing elements which we must not underestimate...We must increase revolutionary vigilance, patriotism and self reliance."

AUTHOR'S NOTE

Both the police and the military have already voiced their concerns regarding the U.S.-based opposition umbrella movement called the Movement for National Reconciliation and the Construction of Democracy, which is attempting to organize human rights forums in HCMC. Hanoi steadfastly rejects the notions of a multi-party system in Vietnam, and insists on the Party's "democratic" control of the state. According to Vietnamese Prime Minister Vo Van Kiet, in Vietnam, "There are five economic elements, but only one political thought." Of Vietnam's more than 71 million people, only 2.5 million belong to the Communist Party, and even many of those have joined the party simply in the hopes that they will be the first to benefit from Vietnam's expanding economic opportunities.

Taxation law in Vietnam remains a problem and is generally considered to still be administered mainly by corrupt party officials. The "savings rate," a prime indicator that gleans the mobilization of capital by commercial banks, has risen slightly (to 11% of the gross national product) but needs to double, according to the experts, in order for Vietnam to move up to par with the economies of Thailand and Singapore. Additionally, Vietnam's economic growth must be more concurrent with progress in social change, according to government officials. Economic management must match social efforts to reduce or eliminate entirely corruption, drug abuse, prostitution, and especially smuggling, officials say. This disparity could possibly dissuade foreign investors in utilizing the country's vast work force. One has to remember that Vietnam is starting from Ground Zero.

AUTHOR'S OBSERVATION

Vietnamese will not be the only beneficiaries of the lifting of the American embargo. American shoppers will soon start seeing some of the amazing products that this exotic nation has to offer. Soon Vietnamese rattan and other Vietnamese handicrafts will be finding their way into the homes of Americans. For instance, a trial shipment of more than US$20,000 worth of antiques, miniature bicycles and other decorative items recently left Saigon bound for Houston. Look for a lot more.

U.S. FIRMS DOING BUSINESS IN VIETNAM

American International Group	Insurance
Ashta International, Inc.	Consultancy
Baker Hughes	Oil and Gas
Coca Cola	Soft Drinks
Pepsico	Soft Drinks
Baker McKenzie	Lawyers

U.S. FIRMS DOING BUSINESS IN VIETNAM

Carrier	Air Conditioning Equipment
Caterpillar	Heavy Equipment Supplies
DeMatteis Development Corp.	Construction
Connell Bros.	Commodities
General Electric	Electrical Equipment
Gemrusa	Gems/Mining
L.A. Land Resources	Property
Manolis Co. Asia	Development and Architecture
Esso/Exxon	Petroleum
Otis Elevator	Lifts
Philip Morris	Tobacco and Food
Spivey International	Medical Supplies
Vatico	Consultancy
VIIC	Consultancy
VINA-USA	Financial Services for Overseas Vietnamese
South Sea Tours	Tourism
Vietours Holidays	Tourism
Bank of America	Banking
Citibank	Banking
Russin Vecchi	Lawyers
American Trading Co.	Trading
Deloitte Touche Tohmatsu	Accountants
Digital Equipment Co.	Computer Technology
Apple Computer	Computer Technology
American President Lines	Shipping
Du Pont Far East Inc.	Chemicals
International Direct Marketing, Inc.	Marketing
Technomic Consultants	Consultancy
American Service Co.	Consultancy
Eastman Kodak	Photographic Materials & Equipment
IBM	Computer Technology
Motorola	Telecommunications
Leo Burnett Co.	Advertising
White & Case	Lawyers

AUTHOR'S OBSERVATION

Interestingly enough, although it was not technically in violation of the U.S. trade embargo against Vietnam at the time, Ted Turner's CNN television news network signed a 1989 draft agreement on cooperation in Vietnam. The agreement is that TBS (Turner Broadcasting Systems) would offer a VTV satellite reception station to receive CNN programs and allow Vietnam the right to record and use CNN programs in return for the ridiculously low fee of 50 dong (about US$.5 cents). No word on what's going on since the lifting of the trade sanctions.

WHAT THE BUSINESSPERSON SHOULD KNOW

Investors in Vietnam should be prepared to expect a lot more red tape than they're used to at home, but also considerably more concessions. The economy is hovering around a double-digit growth rate. Labor is phenomenally cheap, especially compared to labor costs in the U.S. The taxes are low. And there are options for 100 percent foreign ownership of your business.

But remember, Vietnam is a Socialist state. Private enterprise in Vietnam is hardly fully developed. The move toward a free-market economy is still embryonic and is, at best, an experiment. Private businesses are operating under a Socialist political umbrella, deflecting all types of influences that may compromise its integrity. You'll want to grab for the country's economic opportunities, but be prepared for long delays.

You cannot, at the time of this writing, own land in Vietnam. You can lease but can't own. And the land you lease from the government may be claimed at some point in the future by its former owner(s). It could become a sticky litigation problem lasting years. And you need to acquire licenses from the Vietnamese State Committee for Cooperation and Investment (SCCI) as well as local and other authorities, a process that can take months, even years, depending on the nature of your business. The structuring of joint ventures can be difficult and time consuming as well.

But there are routes through the yarn ball, many of them.

The most important element is to establish trust with the Vietnamese you contact. The only way you'll get business transacted relatively smoothly is by networking with as many people as possible in Vietnam, both Vietnamese and foreigners who have already established businesses and/or contacts in Vietnam. The better you treat your hosts, the better you will be treated in return. It also pays to know what does and doesn't offend the Vietnamese during formal discussions. Here are some tips.

1) If you've made an appointment with a Vietnamese official—government or otherwise—know as much about the person as possible before your first meeting. If possible, get a snapshot of the principal individual before the meeting through a local guide, or other source, so you'll immediately recognize the person you're meeting with.

2) If the meeting involves more than one person, go directly to the principal participant upon being introduced and offer your business card. Presenting yourself to a report first is considered an insult. Present your cards based upon the chain of command.

3) Vietnamese men smoke like a train climbing Pike's Peak. Virtually all men in Vietnam smoke. You will undoubtedly be offered a cigarette. It is important to accept the cigarette, even if you don't smoke. (Many a self-righteous anti-smoker has taken up the habit after spending significant time in Vietnam.) If you don't smoke, simply place the cigarette on the table in front of you. You won't be offered another—not in contempt, but in respect.

4) Try not to cross your legs during the meeting, as, in Buddhism, pointing the sole of your foot at someone is a sign of disrespect. However, I've seen an increasing number of men cross their legs in both casual and business environments.

The key to getting things done rapidly in Vietnam is by developing trust and friendship with your Vietnamese contacts. Favors and gifts are also highly appreciated by Vietnamese businesspeople, and will more than likely be reciprocated by means of a smoother and swifter transaction of business.

INSIDER TIP

*If you're considering doing business in Vietnam, Fielding suggests you subscribe to **Fielding's Vietnam Quarterly Insider** newsletter for the latest in business news and trends in Vietnam's burgeoning economy. Unlike most other guidebooks, the author of Fielding's Vietnam lives in Vietnam, and is available to help businesses and entrepreneurs get their feet planted in Vietnam. For more information, or to reach Wink Dulles, contact Fielding Worldwide, 308 S. Catalina Ave., Redondo Beach, CA 90277. ☎ (800) FW2-GUIDE. Other helpful publications for businesspeople considering Vietnam include The 1994 U.S.-Vietnam Business Guide—which offers investment, travel and contact information—and The Vietnam Business Briefing Book—which offers updates on Vietnamese policy and regulation changes, news clippings, economic trends and statistics, as well the entire text of Vietnam's Foreign Investment Law. For more info, contact Global Business Inc., 2000 L Street NW, Ste. 200, Washington DC 20036. ☎ (800) 260-2090.*

LIST OF GOODS PROHIBITED TO EXPORT AND IMPORT

The import of used electronics, electrical equipment, motorcycles and automobiles is prohibited by the government.

1) Prohibited Exports: Weapons, ammunition, explosive materials, military equipment, antiques, kinds of drugs, toxic chemicals, round timber, sawed-up timber, kinds of semi-processed wood products, rattan material, wild and rare animals and plants.

2) Prohibited Imports: Weapons, ammunition, explosive materials, military equipment, kinds of drugs, toxic chemicals, reactionary and debauched cultural products, firecrackers, "toys harmful to children's personalities or social order" (I wonder if this includes Barbie dolls and squirt guns), cigarettes (except quantity fixed in personal luggage), used consumer goods (including sewn or weaved goods), under 12-seat automobiles, motorcycles and motor and non-motor tricycles, family-used electronics and electric equipment (except quantity fixed in personal luggage), material that may cause environmental harm or "other inconvenience" (such as used accessories, used tires, abolished products—abolished materials are also classified as prohibited imports—automobiles and vehicles with steering wheels on the right side (including accessories and dismantlemants)—except some special vehicles and automobiles having narrow circulation.

AUTHOR'S NOTE

In special cases, the import of goods belonging to the above list can be permitted by the Prime Minister with a written statement. The prohibition of export of wild animals to protect the environment is guided by a written statement from both the Ministry of Forestry and the Ministry of Science, Technology and Environment. The government also says that to avoid being "backward" about industry, complete equipment as well as separate machines being used and valued from US\$100,000 or more must be checked by the leading offices (Provincial People Committees or Ministries) of the business and the Quality Standard Measurement Office; a license to import will be issued by the Ministry of Commerce. The Ministry of Commerce, the Ministry of Home Affairs and the Customs Office will together approve a concrete list of special vehicles and automobiles addressed under Article 11.8. After making an agreement with the Ministry of Commerce and the Ministry of Foreign Affairs, the Customs Office will apply guidelines for the article "Property." It all sounds pretty complicated.

Ho Chi
Minh City

HO CHI MINH CITY

Rush hour in central Saigon makes traffic in Los Angeles seem like a Utah interstate highway.

HO CHI MINH CITY IN A CAPSULE

Formerly known as Saigon...Still called Saigon by most...Renamed after the Americans left in 1975...but central district is still called Saigon...population of about 5 million...Once called Paris of the East because of its French colonial architecture and sidewalk cafes...Much more open than conservative Hanoi to the north...Free enterprise abounds on the streets...City is about 70 km from the South China Sea...Vietnam's economic reforms are most evident in Ho Chi Minh City...Tourism here is booming...Compared with other SE Asian cities, there is very little crime.

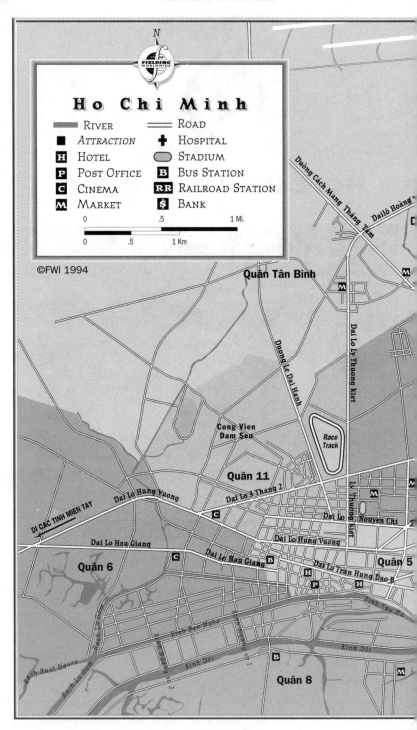

Ho Chi Minh

RIVER
ROAD
■ ATTRACTION
✚ HOSPITAL
Ⓗ HOTEL
STADIUM
Ⓟ POST OFFICE
Ⓑ BUS STATION
Ⓒ CINEMA
RR RAILROAD STATION
Ⓜ MARKET
Ⓢ BANK

0   .5   1 Mi.
0   .5   1 Km

©FWI 1994

Quận Tân Bình

Dương Cách Mạng Tháng Tám

Dailô Hoàng

Dai Lo Ly Thuong Kiet

Duong Le Dai Hanh

Cong Vien
Dam Sen

Race
Track

Quận 11

Dai Lo Hung Vuong

Dai Lo 3 Thang 2

Ly Thuong Kiet

DI CAC TINH MIEN TAY

Dai Lo   Nguyen Chi

Dai Lo Hau Giang

Dai Lo Hung Vuong

Quận 6

Dai Lo Hau Giang

Dai Lo Tran Hung Dao B

Quận 5

Rach Ruot Ngua

Kinh Ben Nghe

Kinh Tau Hu

Kinh Doi

Kinh Doi

Quận 8

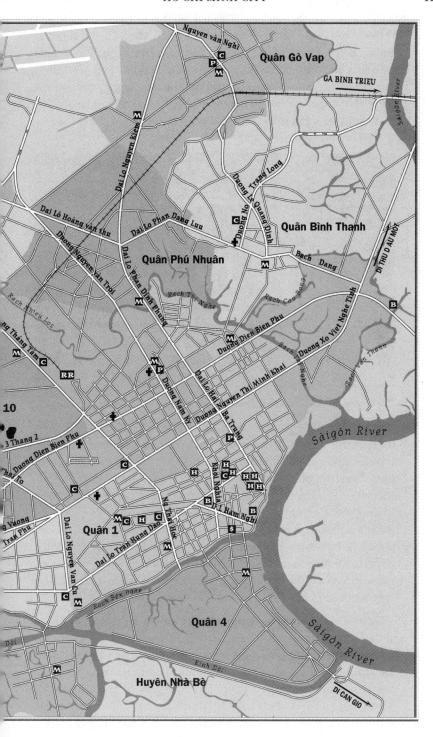

This is a city that has been called no fewer than seven names through the years, and the latest one, Ho Chi Minh City, is about as embraced by its population as the Marxism that tagged it. People who live here call it Saigon, and people who don't live here call it Saigon. In fact, so many people still call the city Saigon, the government allows the central district to be officially called Saigon. And in that spirit, *we'll* call it Saigon—except in the headings.

The Opera House in central Saigon is the district's social hub on Sunday.

Like its neighbor to the west, Phnom Penh in Cambodia (although for different reasons), Saigon swelled with refugees from the countryside during the height of the Vietnam War as North Vietnamese forces were toppling the South and closing in on the capital. After the fall of Saigon, the city actually started to resemble Hanoi for a while—with its glum-faced citizenry looking over their shoulders for someone to tout, but instead catching the narrow gaze of the secret police. But all that's changed and it's "Happy Days Again" in some respects for Saigonese, who are starting to come out of the woodwork to service the burgeoning number of Western tourists who have descended upon the city in relative swarms in recent years.

There is no doubt that bustling Saigon is the industrial, business, and—many argue—the cultural heart of Vietnam. There are thriving markets, discos and eateries. The ethnic Chinese of Cholon (Hoa) are again exerting their economic might. Before the fall of Saigon, the Hoa controlled more than three quarters of the industry of South Vietnam and nearly half the banks. After 1975, they were persecuted as opportunists by the Vietnamese—but now they're accepted, even encouraged to invest by the government. In fact, Hanoi sees Hoa prosperity as integral in its efforts at moving toward a free market system. Of course, the move toward free enterprise has its inevitable victims. It's estimated that hundreds of thousands of Vietnamese in Saigon alone are unemployed.

In terms of lifestyle, Saigon is like the Southern California of Vietnam. And, if you're real lucky (or unlucky, depending upon your viewpoint) you might catch a glimpse of a young Saigonese skateboarding along a rutted sidewalk boogying to an old American rock anthem blasting in his headset.

THE POLLUTION HAZARDS IN HCMC

Pollution in Ho Chi Minh City is becoming a problem. Respiratory diseases due to pollution are on a marked increase. Asthma cases have risen more than 62 percent since 1988; bronchitis has jumped more than 45 percent; sinusitis more than 40 percent. Pollution in HCMC is primarily caused by industrial waste and motor vehicle exhaust. Thu Duc district is considered the most polluted part of the city. And pollution levels in HCMC are almost twice as high in the dry season than during the rainy season. If you are really sensitive to pollutants, avoid visiting Saigon during the Tet New Year (late January-early February), when the ceaseless detonation of firecrackers causes even the perfectly healthy to want to seek an oxygen tent. On New Year's Eve last February, lead density in the air was 3.5 times higher than the minimum safety limits.

It's also worthy to note that sewage and rotting garbage in the city poses a semi-serious hazard. Of the 16,000 cubic meters of garbage and the 2500 tons of manure that are disposed of daily, only about 27 percent of the garbage and less tham 10 percent of the latter are properly treated. A lot of the trash ends up in the rivers, canals and lakes.

The people of Saigon are remarkably friendly to Americans, considering the horrific experiences most had to endure just a short generation ago. In fact, once it's gleaned you're not a Russian, you're still likely to be followed down the street by a posse of curious children.

AUTHOR'S OBSERVATION:
BACKPACKING IN SAIGON

Tay ba lo. That's the local Vietnamese name for the increasing number of Western backpackers plodding HCMC streets. The Vietnamese know the backpackers have few dong and are mainly interested in Vietnamese culture and sights on a tight budget. Tay ba lo range from students to teachers to unemployed sheet metal workers. But the one thing in common they all have in HCMC is where they eat and sleep. Most eat at small food stalls for around 5000 dong and stay in guesthouses in District 1 on Le Lai, Calmette, Pham Ngu Lao and Bui Vien Streets. Guesthouses on these avenues cost in the US$5-15 range. If you're lucky, you may be able to get by for as little as US$2-3 a day for accommodations in HCMC.

Getting around by cyclo is cheap, although you must be a shrewd negotiator. Agree on the price beforehand, and make sure that both you and the cyclo driver understand the amount. There is an increasing problem in cities such as HCMC, Hanoi, Danang, Hue, etc., with drivers demanding additional payment after they've dropped you at your destination, saying it was the agreed price. They will not accept the money you give them, nor will they leave, but will instead stand around like a cheated card player, sulking and complaining while a crowd gathers. The point here is to gain sympathy from the bystanders, some of whom may insist you cough up the additional cash. More than likely, though, among the crowd will be an English-speaking Vietnamese who knows precisely the scam the cyclo driver is up to. In all probability, you will find the Vietnamese on your side, and the cyclo driver will end up "losing face." And the loss of his face is preferable to the loss of your cash.

Renting a bicycle is also cheap. Many rental shops are on or near the above-mentioned streets. Many bike rental firms will ask for 10,000 dong a day (about US$1), but you can usually get this price down, sometimes to as low as 5000 dong per day. But you should never have to pay more than 8000 dong per day for a bicycle. Make sure the tires are full before you depart. If you want a motorbike (50cc or under), check out the shops on Dong Khoi Street as well as Lam Son Square. (I recommend Kolo Rentals at 7 Lam Son Square. The service is extremely friendly, the equipment reliable. Plus if you break down, simply call the shop and they'll arrange for the repair—as well as pay for it.) Remember that renting a motorbike over 50cc requires an international drivers license. In most cases, you will be asked to leave your passport for the duration of your rental. No sweat, GI. Just have a photocopy made to keep on yourself as well as your original visa. This will be appropriate documentation should you be stopped by the police or get into an accident.

Many foreigners can get by in Vietnam for as little as US$500 per month. In HCMC, most backpackers frequent the Sinh Cafe Pham Ngu Lao Street, where meals can be had for as little as 3000 dong. Drink will cost you another 2000 dong. Around the area of De Tham and Pham Ngu Lao Streets there are maybe a dozen restaurants or food stalls with similar prices. Included here are the Lotus Cafe, Kim's Cafe, Long Phi, Thang Com Binh Dan and the Saigon Cafe.

A WORD ABOUT SHOPPING IN HCMC

Souvenir stores and kiosks abound in Saigon. If you're looking for simple souvenirs for your friends and relatives back home, it's best to find them on the street rather than in the fancy, ornamental and expensive shops that line Le Loi Blvd. and Dong Khoi streets in District 1. Although the souvenirs aren't as finely crafted as those found in the shops, they are incredibly cheap. Printed T-shirts go for as little as US$1. And small wooden boats run from between US$5–50 dollars. These are incredible bargains. A lot of it, of course depends upon your ability to bargain. You can also purchase collections of ancient stamps, coins and silk paintings at astoundingly low prices. But remember something: Never pay anything more than 50 percent of the asking price.

But remember the bargains are becoming fewer in HCMC, as the number of tourists continues to escalate. Prices for local art and sculpture in both HCMC and Saigon are spiraling. One artist in Hanoi, Nguyen Quan, who only just two short years ago was peddling his art to diplomats and businesspeople looking for cheap souvenirs to bring home, has witnessed his art double and even triple in price—and it continues to ascend at a remarkable rate. "The artists in Vietnam now have the freedom to paint subjects other than peasants, workers and soldiers," he said.

Art in Saigon and Hanoi has taken on distinct Western influences, mostly in the European abstract style. The ban on painting nudes has also been lifted. Paintings that sold for as little as US$300 a year ago are now fetching US$1000 or more. And this is in a country where the per capita annual income hovers around US$200. Private galleries in both HCMC and Hanoi are proliferating to capitalize on the demands of foreign tourists and businesspeople.

WHAT TO SEE AND DO IN HO CHI MINH CITY

Places that are must-see in the city generally include the Reunification Palace, formerly the Presidential Palace; the War Museum, which is filled with photographs and memorabilia, including exhibits that depict the horrors of the Vietnam War; the Historical Museum, containing some noteworthy archaeological artifacts and a beautiful bronze Buddha that dates from about the 5th century A.D., and the Cu Chi tunnels, which were originally built during Vietnam's battle for independence from the French. The tunnels were greatly enlarged during the war with the U.S. to accommodate the Viet Cong, and contain living quarters, kitchens and surgical areas for the wounded.

American War Crimes Museum ★ ★

Located on Vo Van Tan Street near the intersection of Le Qui Don Street.
This may be the most popular attraction in Saigon. Built on the site of
the former Information Service Office of Saigon University, the
museum exhibits a slew of photos depicting events of the Vietnam
War in general, and alleged and real American atrocities in particular.
Many of the shots are absolutely gruesome. Some of the events covered here are the My Lai massacre and the effects of Napalm, Agent
Orange, and phosphorous bombs on the Vietnamese people. Particularly nauseating are the jars of deformed human fetuses. Outside the
museum is a collection of war materiel, U.S. choppers, and tanks.
Here you can see a bunch of downed trainer fighters, light aerial and
slow bombers that would hit their targets accurately, but they weren't
very fast, which probably explains why I'm looking at one in Ho Chi
Minh right now. There's an array of machine guns from both sides of
the war; weapons in poor condition. It's all just a testament to a war
that, if one didn't know any better, looks like it may have taken place
during the last century.

Americans are depicted as murderers, without any real perspective that
war itself is hell, only Americans. You won't see photos here of U.S.
GIs giving candy bars to VC children while they sit in Bob Hope's lap.
There are a lot of photos depicting carnage all over the place here and
weapons mounted on pods. Some of the stuff looks pretty bizarre, like
microwaves at one of the first Burger Kings. In another room there are
lot of aerial photos, depicting bombardment from B-52s—also some
evidence here that looks like animal experiments being performed by
U.S. scientists, DNA stuff that was conducted by Americans, geneti-
cally altering animals to be Robocops trained to destroy the VC.

The worst sight are the photos of babies hideously deformed, the
alleged consequences of exposure to Agent Orange. Jars contain
fully-formed fetuses that are fully deformed. Most of the material here
is pure propaganda, but there's a lot to be said for the proportion of
it which is correct. Also here are prison and torture cells where VC
prisoners were held—cement torture chambers. Scrawled words cover
the walls. Above the cells are grid-like floors where the captures could
observe the torture below. The Huey helicopter in the courtyard is in
good shape. All in all, despite the fetuses, this is not an unnerving
sight. Worth the visit.

Botanical Gardens

At the end of Le Duan Blvd., there were once thousands of species of
beautiful orchids and other flowers here, although the war did a lot to
dilapidate the place. It's still worth a visit though, if for nothing other
than the small zoo on the grounds.

Central Market ★ ★

Here's where you'll feel the economic pulse of the "new" Vietnam.
This is Saigon's Ben Thanh, and its definitely a must-see if you're

going to hit the market scene—there are maybe 40 or so sprinkled about Saigon. Here you'll find an incredible array of imported goods, including the usual assault of Japanese electronic goods. VCRs are becoming popular—as are the peripherals that come along with them, namely Hong Kong skin flicks.

Cholon ★★

Talk about the economic pulse of the new Vietnam. This is Saigon's Chinatown, where nearly 400,000 ethnic Chinese are helping to breathe new fire into the Vietnamese economy. There are also pagodas here. The beautiful **Thien Hau Temple** was built in 1825 and is dedicated to the cult of Thien Hau, the goddess of the sea and protector of fishermen. The **Quan Am Pagoda**, built in 1816, has some incredible ceramic illustrations of traditional legends. The **Phuoc An Hoi Quan Pagoda** may be the most elaborately decorated in the city. There's also **Cha Tam Church**, where South Vietnamese President Ngo Dinh Diem fled during his escape in 1963, and the Taoist shrine **Khanh Van Nam Vien Pagoda**. Also check out the produce market of **Binh Tay**.

Historical Museum ★

This was formerly called the National Museum and is the best place to step back into Vietnam's 4000-year-old history. In addition to the art of the early Chinese and Indonesians, the museum houses artifacts from the Bronze Age and the Dongson period (3500 B.C.–A.D.100). The building was built in 1928 and now also contains items related to the early communist presence in Vietnam. There's a bronze standing Buddha from the 5th century and artifacts from the country's various hilltribes. Also look for Khmer and pre-Angkorean statuary of the Funan period. See if you can get a guide. At last check, none of the labeling was in English. Open 8–11:30 a.m. and 1–4 p.m. Tues.–Fri. Small admission fee.

Notre Dame Cathedral

Built in 1883 and designed by the French architect Bouvard, this Catholic church (near Tu Do Street) is constructed of granite and red brick. It's quite a magnificent sight in contrast with its surroundings.Tu Do Street was the old red-light district in Saigon.

Reunification Hall (Presidential Palace)

This is the modern administrative center, located to the southeast of Xo Viet Nghe Tinh Street, where, in a famous photograph, an NVA tank slammed through the gates in April 1975, which symbolically marked the South Vietnamese defeat in the war. The President and the entire South Vietnam cabinet were in the palace at the time and were arrested shortly afterwards. You can tour the former palace in a group. Open 7:30–10:30 a.m. and 1–4:30 p.m. Mon.–Sun. There is an admission charge.

Ho Chi Minh City's Reunification Hall was formerly called the Presidential Palace before Saigon fell to the North Vietnamese in 1975.

The Rex Hotel

Located at the intersection of Nguyen Hué and Le Loi Blvds This was the famous hangout of American officers during the war. It has regained some of its previous glory and now features a number of almost luxurious amenities (at least by Vietnam standards). There's a beauty parlor and an on-site tailor. There are also some respectable business services, such as photocopiers and a fax machine. The place is always packed, so if you're planning a stay, reserve early. Europeans cover the place like bees in a jar of jelly. Rex Regal splendor. If Vietnam is communist you'd never know it. Mahogany and marble all over the place. The breezy roof-top bar's a good place for expensive drinks.

Military Museum

Across Nguyen Binh Khiem Street at The corner of Le Duan Blvd Here's an array of Vietnam War-era Soviet and Chinese weapons such as a 57 anti-aircraft gun which supported the Army Corp 4 in the Xuan Loc battle; it was laboriously moved along with the unit to Vien Hoa to liberate that city. There's also an 85 mm gun which was one of the guns of Division 5, Engineering Unit 232, that was used to support the unit as it crossed the Van Co River to attack Phulam Radar station, a strategic outpost near the capital. Next to that is a 105 mm gun which was one of the guns that was used to stun the ARVN military position northeast of Saigon to support the unit that was attacking the Dong Hu base. Right next to this is a 130 mm gun which was one of the guns of the Nhon Trach battle used to attack Tan Son Nhat on April 29, 1975, which marked the beginning of the victory of the Ho Chi Minh campaign. There's also a 37 mm anti-aircraft gun which belonged to the 7th Anti-Aircraft Regiment of the 7th military zone, which took part in the liberation of Loc Linh, and later in the liberation of Vien Hoa. There's also an American aircraft, a Cessna A-37, used by the South Vietnamese Air Force. Under Nguyen Thanh Trung's command, five planes left Thanh Son to bomb Tan San Nhat airport on April 28, 1975. There's also an engineerimg vehicle and vehicles belonging to various information/propaganda regiments, which don't really bring back a lot of memories other than the truck used by the Beverly Hillbillies. These information units were primarily propaganda units that supported the army units as they moved south. There's also an ARVN armored personnel carrier here, which was captured at Phuoc Long in Janauary 1975. There are also some bulldozers that are only worthy of note because they were supplied by the Cubans, as was engineering aid by Castro advisors. There's an area of destroyed U.S. and South Vietnamese aircraft that clutters some of the grounds of the compound, and it seems nobody had been able to identify the wrecks. Perhaps the most interesting attraction of the museum is the F-5 fighter plane which was flown by the renegade pilot Nguyen Than Trung. According to the description, this was the aircraft that bombed the "Puppet President's Palace" and then landed in a liberated area. It took off with South Vietnamese markings. The plane bombed the palace and then fled the capital. There is also the interesting T-54 tank, Number 848, which was the tank that attacked the Independence Palace at 10:30 a.m., April 1975. Inside, the museum chronicles the history of Vietnamese campaigns ranging from the first Indochina War through the American war. There's an assortment of photos as well as a number of small arms that were used during the wars. The guides here speak relatively decent English, and the photos and maps have English descriptions, although the English is a bit shoddy and not nearly as descriptive as the Vietnamese captions to the museum's artifacts. There's also a large VC and tactical map showing troop movements and firefight sites at American military positions.

Vinh Nghiem Pagoda

This is one of the largest pagodas in Saigon. It was built in 1967 in the modern Japanese style. It's an impressive sight; at seven stories, it's one of the largest pagodas in Vietnam.

Xa Loi Pagoda

Located near the War Crimes Museum, this temple was built in 1956 and features a multistory tower which houses a sacred relic of the Lord Buddha. There's a huge bronze-guilded Buddha in the main sanctuary. The pagoda was the site where monks self-immolated themselves in opposition to President Ngo Dinh Diem in the mid–1960s.

HO CHI MINH CITY ENVIRONS

Entrances to the Cu Chi Tunnels were remarkably well hidden during the Vietnam War.

★ *CU CHI TUNNELS*

This is a vast network of more than 200 km of underground tunnels in Tay Ninh, a little under 40 km northwest of Saigon. These tunnels were constructed and used by the Viet Cong to conduct operations, sometimes within the perimeters of U.S. military bases, and hide from the enemy. These are thoroughly fascinating subterranean vestibules, where the VC lived, slept, and ate. There are underground hospitals, kitchens and communications centers. There are living areas, sleeping quarters and munitions storage centers. There are even "street" signs under the earth to help guide errant guerrillas and newcomers. When operational, these tunnels amazingly stretched all the way from Saigon to the Cambodian border. What you'll crawl through today are actually widened versions of the originals. Getting access to tunnel areas other than the touristed ones is problematic. You may even get a chance to fire an AK-47 or an M-16 for a U.S. buck a bullet. Full automatic can be pricey.

THE IRON TRIANGLE

This is an area, not far from the Cu Chi Tunnels, that was named by American troops during the war because of their inability to penetrate this Viet Cong stronghold. Although the area isn't far from Saigon, in the forests between Ben Cat, Cu Chi, and Dau Tieng, the region was impenetrable. The "Triangle" served as the base for attacks by the VC on Saigon, in particular the battles during the 1968 Tet lunar New Year as well as bloody battles at Binh Long and Dong Xoai. Now that a greater number of visitors are coming out to the tunnels at Cu Chi, there has developed an interest on the part of tourists to see the Iron Triangle area. To get there, take Highway 13 about 17 km, crossing the Binh Trieu Bridge. You'll arrive at Lai Thieu, a small village known for its handicrafts and lacquerware. You'll also pass Binh Nham and Suoi Don before reaching the town of Thu Dau Mot. From there, on the road to Dau Tieng, you'll see a trail on the left, which is the path to the Iron Triangle. Although altogether void of any cultural, natural or topographical attractions, the region is bound to become popular with returning American veterans of the war. Tours of the area can be arranged through Vietnamtourism. You'll visit former battlefields, military bases and villages heavily damaged in the war.

MY THO

In the Mekong Delta, about 70 km southwest of Saigon, this is the capital of Dinh Tuong Province. This fertile area is home to several interesting temples—including **Vinh Trang Pagoda** and **My Thoo Church**. There's also a bustling central market. This area is often included on tours outside of Saigon. (See a more complete description of the area under the My Tho section.)

VUNG TAU BEACH

This is a popular beach resort a couple of hours or more south of Saigon at the mouth of the Saigon River. The front and back beaches are the choice of Vietnamese surf frollickers, while secluded Pineapple Beach features villas and a large statue of Christ overlooking the South China Sea. There are several decent temples here, including the largest one in Vietnam: Niet Bau Tinh Xa. (See a more complete description of the area under Vung Tau.)

TAY NINH

Usually combined with a visit to the Cu Chi tunnels, Tay Ninh is a town about 100 km northwest of Saigon. This is the capital of the Tay Ninh Province, which borders the Cambodian border. Back in the 1970s, Cambodian Khmer Rouge guerrillas, in their campaign of terror against anyone Vietnamese, attacked villages in the province frequently and relentlessly. These attacks were part of the reason the Vietnamese Army invaded Cambodia in late 1978. A few weeks later, in January 1979, Pol Pot's Phnom Penh government collapsed and the Khmer Rouge fled into western Cambodia. Tay Ninh is primarily known for the indigenous religion of Cao Daoism and the **Cao Dai Great Temple.** Set inside a complex of schools and other buildings and built between 1933 and 1955, the temple is distinctive for the European influences in its Oriental architecture. It's one of the most intriguing temples in Vietnam, if not all of Southeast Asia. Tay Ninh Province was also the strategic end of the Ho Chi Minh trail during the Vietnam War. (See a more complete description under the Tay Ninh section.)

WHERE TO STAY IN HO CHI MINH CITY

Asian Hotel

146/150 Dong Koi Street. ☎ *296-979. FAX: 84-8-297-433* • One restaurant; no charge for children under 12. Service charge and breakfast are included in the tariff. Moderate to expensive.

Reservations: Direct.

Bat Dat Hotel

238-244 Tran Hung Dao B Blvd. ☎ *555-817* • *117 rooms.* Recommended by the backpack set. Cheap rooms with air conditioning; cheaper still with fan; Chinese restaurant. Inexpensive.

Reservations: Direct.

Kim Do Hotel

133 Nguyen Hue Blvd., Quan 1 • *133 rooms.* Newly opened by Saigon-tourist. Mucho dinero. US$119–449 (the high end for executive suites). Business center, in-house movies, health club, orchid and rose garden, satellite TV. Expensive as hell.   *Reservations: Direct*

Caravelle Hotel

17-23 Lam Son Square. ☎ *293-704/5/6/7/8. FAX: 84-8-299-746* • *115 rooms.* Not as well kept up on the outside and more run down than its French neighbor the Continental across the square. Very, very French, to a fault. Once owned by the Catholic Church. Recently renovated; 9th floor continental restaurant; conference facilities; foreign exchange counter; Japanese restaurant; disco; coffee shop; air conditioning; IDD; gift shop; gym; sauna; tailor in-house; massage; excellent location. Friendly. Moderate.   *Reservations: Direct.*

Chains First Hotel

Khach San De Nhat. ☎ *441-199. FAX: 84-8-444-282* • *132 rooms.* Near the airport; tennis courts; business services; airport shuttle; gift shop; coffee shop; three restaurants; sauna; air-conditioned; refrigerator. Has separate area with rooms with fans. Moderate–expensive.
Reservations: Direct.

Cholon Hotel

Su Van Hanh Street. ☎ *357-058* • Popular with visiting Taiwanese; clean rooms; restaurant. Inexpensive. **Reservations: Direct**

Century Saigon Hotel

68a Nguyen Hue Blvd. ☎ *293168; FAX: 84.8.292732* • Sort of *nouveau* colonial; big bucks in the first district. Mainly for business travelers. Business center, health club, visa extension assistance service, in-room movies, restaurants and lounges plural. With what the Big Bens people shell out here, this is the definition of "Marksism."
Reservations: Utell, Delton, Century Hotels, Aviation & Tourism Int'l.

Continental Hotel ★★★★

132-134 Dong Khoi Street. ☎ *299-201, 299-255. FAX: 84-8-290-936* • *87 rooms.* This was the setting of Graham Greene's novel *The Quiet American.* Built in 1880, this French colonial building is kept in exquisite shape. It was renovated in 1989. Large, open courtyard. Large rooms with air conditioning; Bamboo Bar; Azur Bar; La Dolce Vita Bar; expensive Italian restaurant; Continental Palace Restaurant serves great Vietnamese faregood service. Business services. Expensive.
Reservations: Direct.

Dong Khoi Hotel

12 Ngo Duc Ke Street. ☎ *294-046* • *34 rooms.* Old French colonial building. Air-conditioned suites with high ceilings. Friendly proprietors; good security. Inexpensive. **Reservations: Direct.**

Hai Van Hotel

69 Huynh Thuc Khang-Quan 1. ☎ *291-274, 230-400. FAX: 84-8-291-275* • For under US$25, this is the best place in town, and no one seems to know about it. The staff couldn't be friendlier, perhaps more so than in hotels twice as expensive. Ground floor restaurant serves great Vietnamese fare. There's a karaoke-type club on the second floor. Hot water. Strong water pressure in the showers. Mattresses a little firm for my tastes. Helps if you share it with one of the friendly locals.No TVs in the rooms. Big deal. If you're in Vietnam to watch the tube, you're not here for the right reason. Moderate.
Reservations: Direct

Hotel Bongsen

117-119-121-123 Dong Koi Street. ☎ *291-516. FAX: 84-8-298-076* • *130 rooms.* This is actually two hotels: Bongsen I and II, the first being the pricier of the two. Breakfast included and children under six stay free at both. Air conditioning, mini-bar; private baths with hot water; VCRs; IDD and other business services; sauna; shopping arcade; laundry and valet; photo lab on site; medical staff; travel reservations. Bongsen I is moderate to expensive, Bongsen II inexpensive to moderate.   ***Reservations: Direct***

Omni Saigon Hotel   ★★★★
215 Nguyen Van Troi Street; Phu Nhuan District. ☎ *84.8.449222; FAX: 84.8.449200* • *250 rooms.* US$108 plus. This is a brand new (Feb. '94), extravagant facility near the airport with rooms, suites and longer term apartments. The business services here are outstanding, including fully-serviced satellite offices. Also a ballroom, health club, outdoor swimming pool, IDD, color TV, air-conditioned rooms, minibar, etc., and the full array of capitalist running-dog amenities that would have V.I. Lenin spinning in his formaldehyde. Expensive as hell.   ***Reservations: Omni Hotels.***

Huong Sen Hotel
66-70 Dong Khoi Street. ☎ *290-259 (290-916 to make a reservation). FAX: 84-8-298-076* • *50 rooms.* Air-conditioned; IDD telephone; TV; hot water; refrigerator; minibar; sauna; coffee shops and restaurants; laundry and valet; cars for hire; express photo services; travel reservations and services. Good location. Friendly staff. Moderate.
                          Reservations: Direct.

Majestic Hotel
1 Dong Khoi Street. ☎ *295-515. FAX: 84-8-291-470* • *100 plus rooms.* Once the city's best hotel, a fire ravaged it. Now passable. Some of the rooms have a river view; two restaurants; postal and some business services. Moderate.   ***Reservations: Direct.***

Mondial Hotel
109 Dong Khoi Street. ☎ *296-291 or 296-296. FAX: 84.8.296324* • *40 rooms.* Some rooms with balconies; most have private baths, bar and lounge. Elegant and expensively decorated. Great location in Saigon's 1st District. French restaurant with Continental cuisine.Orchid Lounge; quiet, comfortable. Ornate lobby. Exotic place. There are traditional Vietnamese cultural shows here three times a week. Moderate.   ***Reservations: Direct.***

New Hotel
14 Ho Huan Nghiep St. ☎ *230-656, 231-343. FAX: 84-8-241-812* • Located just off Me Linh Square, this really is a new hotel. The best way to describe it is to say quaint. It's tight and tall, five stories, but it has one of Saigon's only B&B atmospheres. The suites facing the street are impressive and run only about US$65 a night. Cheaper singles run around $25. Friendly staff; fax; laundry, cafe. This is one of the quietest hostelries in the 1st district, yet you're right next to all the action. Moderate–Expensive.   ***Reservations: Direct***

Norfolk Hotel

117 Le Thanh. ☎ *295-368. FAX: 84-8-293-415* • *45 rooms.* Located in central Saigon.Usually booked solid. Australian owners/managers. Attached bathroom; air-conditioned; well-furnished; elegant lobby; hot water; color TV with Star satellite network; wetbar; business center with secretarial services; fax; meeting facilities; restaurant; bar; rooftop BBQ. Moderate. ***Reservations: Direct***

Orchid Hotel

29A Don Dat Street. ☎ *231-809. FAX: 84-8-231-811* • *30 rooms.* Air-conditioned rooms; bathroom; telephones; refrigerators; bar; restaurant; coffee shop. Moderate. ***Reservations: Direct.***

Palace Hotel

56-64 Nguyen Hue Blvd. ☎ *297-284. FAX: 84-8-299-872* • Rooms have bathrooms and hot water; swimming pool; bar; restaurant; great location. Moderate. ***Reservations: Direct***

Regent Hotel

700 Tran Hung Dao Blvd. ☎ *353-548. FAX: 84-8-357-094* • Also called the Hotel 700. Located in Cholon. Joint Vietnam/Thai venture. Moderate. ***Reservations: Direct.***

Rex Hotel ★★★★

14 Nguyen Hue Blvd. ☎ *296-042. FAX: 84-8-291-269* • *120-plus rooms.* A favorite of American officers during the war. Enjoying a new life with the opening of tourist and business frontiers in the city. Air-conditioned; color TV; refrigerators with wet bars; three restaurants; IDD telephones; hot water; cassette players; large statuary and topiary; art gallery; dance area; business center; cinema; tailor in-house; large gift shop; tennis court; swimming pool. Expensive as hell. Get there for a drink if nothing else. See description under "What to See and Do in Saigon." ***Reservations: Direct.***

Riverside Hotel

19 Ton Duc Thang Street. ☎ *224-038. FAX: 84-8-298-070* • *34 rooms.* Rooms have TV; telephone; refrigerator; self-contained bathrooms; business center; bar; restaurant. Moderate. ***Reservations: Direct.***

Saigon Floating Hotel ★★★★★

Saigon River at Hero Square on the edge of the central city. ☎ *290783. FAX: 84.8.290784* • *200 rooms.* Towed from Australia's Great Barrier Reef in 1989. The best hotel in Saigon. Floats on the Saigon River; swimming pool; tennis court; ice machines; 24-hour room service; two restaurants; business center; fitness center; saunas; conference room; disco; two bars; cafe; meeting rooms for up to 200 people; gift shop. Rooms have color TV; radio; refrigerator/wet bar; valet service; laundry service; IDD calling. Very Expensive.If it's out of your league, you can watch its lights at night from across the square on the porch of one of the hostess bars while sipping a Tiger Beer with a charming hostess. ***Reservations: Direct.***

Duc Huy Hotel

422 Hai Ba Trung Street, District 1. ☎ *442937; FAX: 84.8.230132 •*
US$12. This is one of the best bargains in town, for businesspeople as
well as for backpackers and other tourists. Just opened in April. The
rooms are immense and lavishly appointed. Attached bath with hot
water. Refrigerator, karaoke and video facilities, meeting rooms,
air-conditioned, color TV. Car, motorbike and bicycle rentals. Organized sightseeing tours throughout the country. There are even backpacker tours at "backpacker rates." Hotel, airline and rail bookings.
The staff, all English speaking, are extremely friendly. Highly recommended. Moderate.   ***Reservations: Direct***

Saigon Hotel

41-47 Đông Du Street (District 1). ☎ *230-231/2, 241-078, or 299-734.*
FAX: 84-8-291466 • 105 rooms. 16 deluxe suites. Room rates include
breakfast, and fruit baskets and newspapers come with the deluxe
suites. Children under six stay free. Satellite color TV in the deluxe
rooms and suites; IDD; 24-hour service.Minibar; hot water; air conditioning; conference center; bar on the 9th floor and restaurant in the
lobby. Also will do air ticket booking. Moderate.
Reservations: Direct.

WHERE TO EAT IN HO CHI MINH CITY

Probably the heartiest places to eat in Saigon are at the hundreds of
street stalls on the streets. For the most part they're safe, excellent, and extremely inexpensive—with prices usually less than a dollar. But if you want
more ambiance, there are a number of decent establishments in town. The
best, and also the most expensive, are found at the better hotels. Here's a
look at some of the eateries around Saigon.

INSIDER TIP

As might be expected, Saigon is experiencing a degree of the "Bangkok Syndrome," an Asian City homogenizing Eastern and Western infleuences with the pâte of the Chao Phraya River and 30-weight motor oil. Western food is invading the palates of Saigonites like a mozzarella revolution. Case in point, four new pizza joints have opened in HCMC, in just the past few months, a couple of them not half bad. Ristorante Pizzeria Capuccino is a case in point. Swiss-born Danny Koeppel, sort of the Wolfgang Puck of Indochina, whose credits include more than a year at the internationally-famous Chez Guido at the Continental Hotel, has become something of a consultant to the increasingly popular pizzerias springing up around the city. His new "consultancy" venture is with the new Pizzeria Capuccino, 11 Ho Huan Nghiep (off Dong Koi Street, ☎ 291051). Because the competitiion is getting stiffer in Saigon, Koeppel has decided to broaden the offerings. The specialty of the house is pasta, of course. Mozzarella, as well as the anchovies, are shipped from Italy. Koeppel claims to be the first to create "spaghettata," an "island" of pasta surrounded by sauces prepared in minutes for businesspeople on the run. The homemade bread with a dish of chopped chilies in sauce is delicious. Ho Huan Nghiep Street is known for its bars, and a lot of people come into the eatery without the intention of investing the time in a full sit-down dinner. So try the cheeseburgers if you've got the dong (they run nearly US$4), or even a hot dog; the sausage is imported from Germany. There's also ice cream and, of course, coffee.

Cafe Brodard

131 Dong Khoi Street. ☎ *225-837* • A hangout for expats, backpackers, and hipsters.

Chez Guido   ★

Continental Hotel • Expensive Italian cuisine; good portions.

Givral Cafe

169 Dong Khoi Street • Like the Brodard, mostly expats and journalists, but better food.

Harbor View Restaurant

At the curve where Ton Duc Thang and Ben Chuong Duong Streets meet • Lavish eatery right on the riverfront overlooking the harbor. The food (Asian, Vietnamese, and Western) is superb but expensive. This place is frequently rented out for wedding receptions.

La Bibliotheque

84 Nguyen Du • Very good Vietnamese fare and excellent beef.

Le Mekong   ★

32 Vo Van Tan St., ☎ *291-277* • French fare at great prices.

Marina Cafe ★

Saigon Floating Hotel • Great lunchtime buffet; the prices aren't too bad. Menu features U.S. steak (during the embargo, the meat was cowjacked, so I was told) and seafood. Probably the best Western food in-country.

Maxim's

13 Dong Khoi Street. ☎ *299-820* • Live music, decent food, high prices.

Nha Hang 5 Me Linh ★

Near the statue of Tran Hung Dao • Great Vietnamese fare. Even Cobra!

Nha Hang 51 Nguyen Hue

51 Nguyen Hue Blvd. • Ditto.

Nhon Bashi Japanese Restaurant

On the ground floor of the Rex Hotel • Run-of-the-mill Japanese fare but expensive.

Oriental Court

Saigon Floating Hotel • Good Asian cuisine for Western palates.

Palace Hotel

15th floor restaurant • The best view of Saigon in town.

Rex Garden Restaurant

86 bis Le Thanh St., ☎ *292-186* • The only place in town with both a tennis court and a tank as a setting for dining. In back of the Rex. A little pricey and curiously nearly always close to empty.

Sinh Cafe

6 Pham Ngu Lao Street • A good mingling place for travelers.

Veranda

Saigon Floating Hotel • International cuisine.

Vietnam House ★

93-95 Dong Khoi Street. ☎ *291-623* • Posh. Expensive Vietnamese cuisine. Attentive and friendly service.

Restaurant Huong Rung ★★

462 Pham The Hien Street, District 8. ☎ *55323* • This is one of the most bizarre dining experiences in HCMC. Eccentric owner Tran Van Kien has created a setting where live pythons, cobras, iguanas, lizards, and all assortments of other reptiles and birds roam the environs of this posh and expensive restaurant freely. While eating such exotic delicacies as cream of goat testicles soup, you may suddenly find a snake slithering into your pants pocket or a turtle traversing your beef satay. This seems to be a popular place with noisy Russian expats drinking vats of Tiger beer. It's a lot of fun until they start singing. Then leave.

DIRECTORY

INSIDER TIP: VIETNAM'S BURGEONING MOTORBIKE PROBLEM

Saigon is one of the most dangerous cities in the world to travel through via car, bicycle, motorbike and motorcycle. To the uninitiated, two-wheeled traffic here is so overwhelmingly intimidating that few Westerners venture into traffic through their own means. And the motorcycle problem in HCMC is only going to get worse. In 1993, there were nearly two and a half million motorbikes on the streets of Vietnam, compared to only 600,000 in 1990. Honda accounts for about 70% of these machines. And more than 400,000 motorbikes and motorcycles are imported into the country each year. Most come from Japan, Taiwan, Korea, Indonesia, Singapore, Thailand, Russia and Germany. But an increasing number of the machines are being smuggled into Vietnam through the Cambodian border. Last year alone, 200,000 motorcycles were registered in HCMC alone, bringing the total number of motorbikes in the city to 1,060,000. This is making congestion virtually unbearable. The number of motorbikes—many dangerously traversing Vietnamese streets—has seriously hampered HCMC's mass transit's capabilities. Quite simply, the Vietnamese' increasing ability to purchase motorbikes has far outpaced the government's ability to improve the traffic network. If you have the insane inclination to rent a motorbike in Saigon, remember this important regulation: For any bike you rent over 50cc, you must possess an international driver's license. Vietnamese themselves are not permitted to own or operate a motorcycle more than 175cc, although foreigners are permitted to rent bikes with far greater power (which you'll greatly appreciate on good roads out in the provinces on long journeys). A Vietnamese spotted by the police on a big motorcycle will invariably be pulled over, although foreigners rarely are. (I have been pulled over by the police, however, without violating any Vietnamese law.)

TRANSPORTATION

Ho Chi Minh City is 1710 km from Hanoi, 1071 km from Hue, 965 km from Danang, 445 km from Nha Trang, 340 km from Ha Tien, 300 km from Dalat, 250 from Rach Gia, 165 km from Can Tho, 115 from Vung Tau, 147 from Vinh Long and 72 km from My Tho.

By air: Ho Chi Minh City is about half an hour's ride from the airport (Tan Son Nhat Airport). It's a relatively modern airport by Southeast Asian standards, but still is far from the likes of Bangkok's Don Muang or Singapore's Changi Airports. But the facilities here are quite a bit better than at Hanoi's Noi Bai Airport. Do not let your film, computerized camera, laptop computers, etc., go through the airport's primitive X-Ray machines although they display signs in English saying they are "film safe," which simply means that your equipment won't actually melt or come out the other side as an Egg McMuffin.

There is a branch of the Vietcom Bank here for changing money, as well as Vietnamtourism, Saigontourist and Cuu Long Tourist offices. There is also a post office here. Don't rely on any of the tourist organizations for hotel suggestions if you're on a budget. Instead, just outside the airport, you will find at the taxi stand an acceptable list of accommodations in Saigon with their prices posted. Many backpackers arrive at the airport without any idea as to where they'll be staying, but instead rely on travel guides that often list accommodations that simply don't exist anymore. Remember, hotels in Saigon are generally quite expensive, and if you're only planning on spending US$3–5 a night here, be prepared to share your "room" with various other manifestations of Southeast Asian life forms.

Use the list at the taxi stand to determine where you'll spend at least your first night in HCMC. You should choose a hotel in the US$10–20 range, and one preferably close to District 1 (Downtown Saigon).Get a feel for the city and where other travelers are staying, but the place not to do this is at the bar atop the Rex Hotel. Be sure that all your paperwork is in order, and carry additional passport photos than the required three. Any lapse in presenting the correct documents will send you back to the end of the customs lines, which have become massive waits in recent months with the armies of tourists arriving in Vietnam. If you're an American, at the time of this writing, your visa will not be stamped into your passport, but instead will be a separate document with your picture attached. You'll also need additional photos for your declaration forms. If you don't have the necessary photos, there is a desk behind the customs area where you can have the photos taken. But this can take as long as customs processing itself.

Upon arrival at HCMC Airport, assuming everything is kosher, it'll take more than an hour before you're on the street. Outside the airport are numerous touts with license badges attached to their shirts signifying they are official taxi drivers. They will swarm upon you like bees on new lotus blossoms. By taxi, you shouldn't pay any more than US$8 to get to your destination. There are regular international connections to Jakarta, Bangkok, Manila, Kuala Lumpur, Singapore, Vientiane, Moscow, Paris, Frankfurt, and Amsterdam (to list a few) on airlines including Vietnam Airlines, Air France, Philippine Airlines, Garuda Indonesia, Thai, Lao Aviation, SK Air, MAS, Singapore Airlines—and soon on Delta and United.

By bus: The Mien Tay terminal (in An Lac, about 10 km west of HCMC. To get there, take Hau Giang or Hung Vuong Blvds. west from Cholon. ☎ 255955). It is quite a distance southwest of town on Hung Vuong Blvd., and serves the Mekong Delta area, including My Tho, Vinh Long, Can Tho, Chau Doc, Rach Gia, Long Xuyen, An Long, Ca Mau, and other delta locations. Buses to points north, including Phan Tiet (6 hours), Vung Tau 3 hours), Da Lat (8 hours), Nha Trang

(11 hours), Qui Nhon (17 hours), Danang (25 hours) and Hue (29 hours)—as well as other locations—depart from HCMC's Mien Dong terminal, which is on the north side of the city on Xo Viet Nghe Tinh Street off National Highway 13 near the Saigon River.

(Note: Express buses receive priority treatment at ferry crossings and, although I've heard horror stories of tourists waiting an hour or more to cross the two rivers by ferry from HCMC to Can Tho, I've never had to wait more than just a few moments. Automobiles and motorcycles also receive priority treatment at the ferry crossings.) Book your tickets in advance—although, in many instances, you won't need to, as they depart when they are full (first come, first serve). You can also take a bus to Cambodia's Phnom Penh, which leaves from the Phnom Penh Bus Garage at *155 Nguyen Hue Blvd.* You'll need a Cambodian visa; tickets are cheap (about US$5 one way) and the trip takes from 10–12 hours, although I've heard of some taking as few as 8 hours due to a lack of delays at the border.

By microbus: You can also travel by microbus (or minibus), which has become an increasingly popular form of travel for Overseas Vietnamese, Vietnamese, and foreign tourists. However, there never seem to be any permannent departure points for these vehicles. Hotels are the best places to ask about microbus service. There is a microbus office at *39 Nguyen Hue Blvd.* Buses here leave for Dalat, Vung Tau, Nha Trang, Hue, Danang and Qui Nhon. Another office, I was told, is at *89-91 Nguyen Du Street.*

By train: The Saigon Railway station (Nha ga) is about 2 km from District 1 and has regular daily connections with all points north of Saigon. If you're going anywhere by train for more than eight hours, get a sleeping berth. The trip to Hanoi can take from between 40–50 hours. Ouch! Foreigners are charged extraordinarily more for tickets than are Vietnamese. To get to the dilapidated station, take Cach Mang Thang Tam Street to the turn-off at *132/9.* Or take the roundabout at *Cach Mang Tam Street* and *3 Thang 2 Blvd.* A cyclo ride from the city center should cost between US$.50–1. Train schedules change, so it's nearly pointless to list them here.

By ferry: To get down to the Mekong Delta, go to the ferry landing on Ton Duc Thang Street at the end of Ham Ngi Blvd. To get to Can Tho takes about a day and costs US$1. To Chau Doc, count on another 12 hours and additional 2000 dong. There are also high speed river **hydrofoils** that make the trip to Vung Tau down the Saigon River from near the Harbor restaurant on Ton Duc Thang and Ham Nghi Streets. It's an exhilarating and fast ride (about 1.5 hours) but expensive (US$10).

By car: Cars with drivers rent for anywhere between US$40–70 a day from HCMC travel agents. However, there are many private operators who hang out in the square next to Reunification Hall and will undercut the tourist and travel agents. To the Cu Chi tunnels, a car can be had for about US$20; although this is only a half-day trip, most of the tourist companies will insist that the minimum car rental period is a full day. Also, some of the larger hotels can provide autos, but filled with five passengers, for as low as US$30 a day. Check around.

Getting around Saigon is easy and cheap. **Cyclos** are the slowest but cheapest form of transportation (the drivers that hang out at the more expensive hotels usually charge more), but you can also rent **bicycles** from numerous hotels and bike rental shops throughout the city for 8000–10,000 dong per day. Negotiate. You can also rent small **motorbikes** such as Honda Cubs and Dreams for as little as US$6 per day. I recommend Kolo Rentals at *7 Lam Son Square* (across from the Continental Hotel). ☎ *296499*. They'll rent even larger bikes if you've got the proper international drivers license.If you break down within a 100 km radius, they will provide the necessary repairs free of charge.

TAXI SERVICES

Saigon Taxi: ☎ *297545*

Tourist Car: ☎ *290600*

Saigon Tourist Car: ☎ *295925* (Keep your eye on the price)

Phnom Penh Bus: ☎ *230754*

BANKS AND MONEYCHANGERS

Vietcom Bank is located across the city, at Nguyen Hue Blvd. across from the Rex, at *123 Dong Khoi Street*, and a large main branch on Ben Chuong Duong and Nam Ky Khoi Nghia Streets. **The Foreign Exchange** bank is located at *101 Nam Ky Khoi Nghia Street* (Vietcom as mentioned above). There is also a Vietcom bank at the airport's international terminal.

Many foreign banks have now opened offices in Saigon. **Bangkok Bank Ltd.** has a branch on Nguyen Hue Blvd about halfway from the Rex to the River. The **Thai Military Bank** is also in Saigon, and banking with them you have the advantage of withdrawing funds directly from the office in Saigon even though your account may be in Thailand. Bangkok Bank offers no such service. And remember, at many banks, you will not be permitted to convert dong into dollars.

You can also change money at hotels, although the rate you're likely to receive is 10,000 for every dollar, whereas the official exchange rate is 10,800 dong to the dollar. Some hotels will offer rates as high as 10,700 dong to the dollar—not bad considering the hotels aren't banks. You can also change money in jewelry and gold shops at favorable rates, but don't change money on the street. At the various markets around HCMC you will be approached by black marketers offering to exchange money. Keep in mind that now 50 or so foreign banks have recently opened offices in HCMC, and the number rises daily.

A portait of Ho Chi Minh dominates Saigon's General Post Office.

GENERAL POST OFFICE

2 Cong Xa Paris, next to the Notre Dame cathedral, open from 7:30 a.m.–10:00 p.m. every day. There are international telephone and fax connections here, although you won't be able to make a collect call overseas without getting a Vietnamese to do it for you.

TNT INTERNATIONAL EXPRESS

406 Nguyen Tat Thanh Street. ☎ *222886* or *225520.*

DHL WORLDWIDE EXPRESS

At the GPO. The major hotels such as the Rex and the Saigon Floating Hotel offer all types of international business services.

FOREIGN AFFAIRS OFFICE

6 Thai Van Lung Street. ☎ *223032* or *224124.*

IMMIGRATION OFFICE

161 Nguyen Du Street. ☎ *299398.*

HOSPITALS

Choray Hospital. *Nguyen Chi Thanh Blvd.*

AIRLINES

Vietnam Airlines
(International Office) *116-118 Nguyen Hue Blvd.* ☎ *292118.* Across from the Rex next to City Hall. (Domestic Office) *15 Dinh Tien Hoang Street.* ☎ *299980.*

Air France
130 Dong Khoi Street. ☎ *230746.*

Pacific Airlines
27B Nguyen Dinh Chieu Street. ☎ *20930*

MAS
116 Nguyen Hue Blvd, just above the VN office. ☎ *292118.*

Singapore Airlines
6 Le Loi Street. ☎ *231583*

Cathay Pacific
49 Le Thanh Ton Street. ☎ *223272.*

KLM Royal Dutch Airlines
244 Pasteur Street, Quan 3. ☎ *231990, 231991; FAX: 231989*

EVA Air
129 Dong Khoi Street. ☎ *22488; FAX: 223567*

China Airlines
132-134 Dong Khoi Street. ☎ *251387/9: FAX: 251390*

Quantas
311 Dien Bien Phu Street. ☎ *396194; FAX: 396199*

Philippine Airlines
☎ *292200*

Thai Airways
116 Nguyen Hue Blvd. ☎ *223365.*

TOURIST OFFICES

Saigontourist
49 Le Thanh Ton Street. ☎ *295834; FAX: 224987.*

Vietnamtourism
69-71 Nguyen He Blvd. ☎ *290772; FAX: 290775.*

CONSULATES IN HO CHI MINH CITY

Cambodia
41 Phung Khac Hoian Street, District 1. ☎ *294498.*

China
261 Huang Van Thu Street Phu Nhuan District. ☎ *441024.*

Cuba
23 Phung Khac Hoan Street, District 1 . ☎ *295818.*

Czech and Slovakia
176 Tu Duc Street, District 1. ☎ *291475.*

France
27 Xo Viet Nghe Tinh Street, District 1. ☎ *297231.*

Germany
126 Nguyen Dinh Chieu Street, District 3. ☎ *291967.*

Hungary
> *22 Phung Khac Hoan Street, District 1.* ☎ *290130.*

Laos
> *181 Hai Ba Trung Street, District 1.* ☎ *299262.*

Malaysia
> *53 Nguyen Dinh Chieu Street, District 3.* ☎ *299023.*

Poland
> *2b Tran Cao Van Street, District 1.* ☎ *292215.*

Russia
> *40 Ba Huyen Tahnh Quan Street, District 3.* ☎ *292936.*

Singapore
> *5 Phung Khac Hoan Street, District 1.* ☎ *225173.*

IMPORTANT PHONE NUMBERS

Ambulance. ☎ *15*

Emergencies. ☎ *296485*

Fire. ☎ *14*

Police. ☎ *13*

Traffic Police. ☎ *296449*

MAPS

The best and perhaps the only places to get maps of areas and cities of Vietnam are sidewalk stalls on Le Loi Blvd. opposite the Rex Hotel. Do not rely on obtaining maps on the road, as you will be severely disappointed—even in the major cities. Saigon is the only place in the south where you can obtain maps of various destinations. Don't say we didn't tell you.

PHOTOGRAPHY

There are dozens of film shops along Nguyen Hue Blvd. between the Rex and the Saigon River. Kodak (an American company) recently opened its first lab on the northeastern side of Nguyen Hue Blvd. about halfway between the Rex and the river. But remember, the overwhelming amount of shops develop and sell Fuji film only. Kodak has a long way to go to catch up.

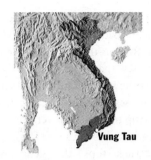

Vung Tau

VUNG TAU

VUNG TAU IN A CAPSULE

An average beach town about a three-hour drive from Saigon...Mostly frequented by weekending Saigonese...The beach sees few foreign tourists...Kiosks and restaurants line the beachfront, but face the road rather than the water...Perhaps that's because it's so windy here all the time...The drive out from Saigon is over flat terrain and not particularly scenic...But there are a number of decent hotels in town.

This is the closest beach of any note to Saigon, about 130 km, and where most Saigonese head on out to when the heat becomes too much and they don't mind the 2-1/2 to 3 hour ride along generally good roads. Frankly, I found the beaches a disappointment. Even the drive out is mainly lacking in any natural beauty. If you're on a tour bus, this would be a good time to catch a few z's. If you're driving or riding a motorcycle yourself, as I did, you'll die, maybe even if you don't fall asleep. In fact, I'd avoid this place altogether unless you have a desk job in Saigon and can only get away from the city for a day or two at a time.

Vung Tau used to be called Cap Saint Jacques, in honor of the Portuguese patron saint. Before the 17th century, the city was under Khmer rule and the town began to develop as a seaside resort near the beginning of the 20th century. It is a triangular shaped peninsula that juts out into the South China Sea near the mouth of the Saigon River. Subsequently, the sea is gray and silty, and certainly that of the tropical white-sand variety the travel agents will show you when you're looking for a place to munch on shellfish and suck on pina coladas for a few days while intermittently basking in azure lagoons.

The Thanh Truck Cafe is at about km marker 62 from Vung Tau and makes an excellent road-side rest area for a cool drink about halfway from Saigon. Rubber trees dot the side of the roadway. You pass a former military base that looks just like the former U.S. installations you see all over the south. The strip at Vung Tau is lined with small cafes and bath houses. Not surprisingly, prostitution has spread from one side of the strip to the other, yet the hookers are low keyed and generally, the beach makes for a safe family environment. There aren't the roadside "truck stops" that generally characterize many other coastal areas of southern Vietnam beaches, although this is bound to change as tourism increases in the area. Presently one doesn't see a lot of Westerners here, primarily because the beaches aren't particularly good; the surf is rough and unpredictable. Even surfers would want a 9-hp outboard attached to their boards just to get far enough out to a break, which might be, say, the Philippines. There are only a few decent hotels in the area (and those that are decent are quite decent). They are primarily frequented by Vietnamese and other Asian tourists, although Westerners are warmly welcomed in most places. You just don't see a lot of them. The beachfront itself is fairly dilapidated, the structures weather beaten. And, unusually, most cafes and beachside eateries have seating areas that face the road rather than the beach, which makes for sort of a ridiculous view of nothing really—a couple of hills. The only reason I can figure for this is that the onshore winds are quite brisk and strong. And many a sweltering city dweller, awaiting the ecstasy of a dip in a cool sea may find themselves disappointed that by the time they reach the beach at Vung Tau, they're about as eager for a swim as they are for a sauna.

There are two "mountains" in the city (a giant statue of Jesus looks down upon the ocean from one) and they make for good bike riding. In fact, this may be the best activity here, both for the view and the fact that the beach is usually so windy that it feels like being pelted by small weapons fire due to the blowing sand. The big Jesus gives sort of that Rio De Janeiro look with its outstretched arms overlooking the sea. The statue was built in 1974. The best way to get up to it is by a rocky path.

Vung Tau was an area that was very popular with the Russians back during the period when Russians had a great degree of influence here. Here was the headquarters of VIETSOVPETRO, and many Soviet expats used to live in villas around Front Beach, most of which have been razed for the building of hotels for tourists. Many villas also look over Back Beach; they're very attractive and almost Mediterranean in appearance.

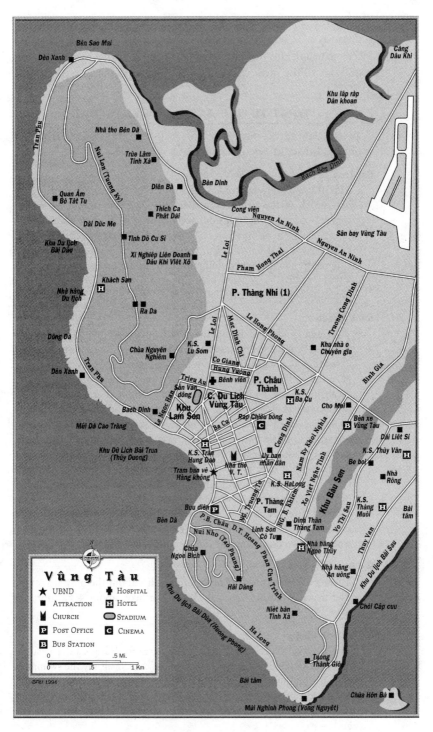

Vung Tau is also famous as a departure point for the hundreds of thousands of Vietnamese who fled the country during the latter 1970s through the mid 80s. This may explain why Vung Tau possessed one of the most vast secret police networks after reunification in 1975.

WHAT TO SEE AND DO IN VUNG TAU

As you might expect there's not a lot to do here other than swim or look at the rapids-like surf and contemplate it.

Bai Troc

This is commonly referred to as Front Beach, and it's probably the best beach in town, but even then, the standards are hardly what a western tourist would consider acceptable as a resort or even as a day beach. If you're on vacation on a tropical land, you want your beaches to be a little more exotic than Coney Island with a bunch of beggars and touts hawking everything from snails (actually quite tasty) to kites. It's dirty, rocky, and only acceptable if you close your eyes and dream of being somewhere else.

Back Beach

This area is about 2 kilometers south of town and is the area that attracts the most tourists, most of them Saigonese and visiting Asians. You can rent a beach chair and tent for a couple of thousand dong and gaze out at the dangerous surf, which is usually only frequented with locals in inner tubes pilfered most likely from old army trucks. What the beach has going for it is that it is the only beach in the area with actual beach. Vendors, kiosk proprietors, and a bunch of people carrying strings of dried squid provide the culinary delights. Soda pop and beer are readily available. If you can, get a Vietnamese to do the buying for you; it'll be cheaper. Like other areas in the town, the water can be dangerous for swimming. Sometimes flags will be posted warning of the conditions. A white flag means the water is safe (from what I'm not sure). A red flag means the conditions are unsafe. But take solace in the fact that only a couple of years ago, a red flag flying anywhere in the country meant the conditions were unsafe.

Bai Dau Beach

There's a pagoda on a hill near here and it's about the only attraction. The beach is nothing special. And it's a hike, about 4 km north of town.

Bai Nghinh Phong

This is actually a relatively nice bathing area for Vung Tau. The surf is more predictable (at least during my visit) but locals say the swimming can still be quite dangerous. And the few people you do see in the water are rarely swimming but just standing around in the surf getting their street clothes sopping wet, for reasons only Asians truly appreciate.

Hon Ba

This is an impressive looking pagoda on an island only a few hundred yards off the headland, accessible by foot at low tide.

The Lighthouse

This offers the best view of the area. It was built just after the turn of the century and rises some 200 km above sea level and can be reached by bicycle, although by foot may be the more attractive alternative. You can also get up to the top from Back Beach, but the roads can be muddy, especially during the wet season.

Pagodas

There's the island pagoda of **Han Ba**, of course, but there are others in Vung Tau worthy of a visit only if pagodas run like heroin through your veins. **Niet Ban Tinh Xa** is easily the most impressive pagoda in Han Ba. It features a giant bronze bell. There is the 1000 year old **Linh Son Co Tu Pagoda** at *61 Huang Hoa Tham Street*. Also you might want to see the **Whale Dedication Temple**, again not spectacular, but if you've come this far, well... **Thich Ca Phat Dai Park** is where the locals hang out. There's a huge Buddha that sits on the side of a hill. There are also a lot of animal and people figurines. There are restaurants here as well as a number of souvenir kiosks. The park is on the eastern side of Large Mountain.

Vung Tau Market

The market is on seaside Phan Tru Street north of town and was "built" in the beginning of the century. The gardens are pleasant.

WHERE TO STAY IN VUNG TAU

Hai Au Hotel 9

100 Halong Street, ☎ *2178 • 64 rooms.* This is a small clean place that was only opened about four years ago. Pool, air-conditioned. Inexpensive. ***Reservations: Direct***

Thang Moi Hotel

4-6 Thuy Van Street. ☎ *452665 • 90 rooms.* About US$15. This is an old place on Back Beach and one of the nicer places in the area despite its age. It's a quiet place with a pool, air-conditioned, restaurant and an open courtyard-type area surrounded by the single-story guest units. Moderate. ***Reservations: Direct***

The Seabreeze Hotel

11 Hguyen Trai Street, ☎ *6.452.392; 84.6.459856 •* The hotel was opened in 1992 and is Australian-owned and managed. The rooms are expensive by Vietnamese standards but appear to be worth it. Air-conditioned, TV, refrigerator, telephone, fans and clean bathrooms. The more expensive rooms are three room suites. Also a swimming pool and restaurant. Moderate–expensive. ***Reservartions: Direct.***

Canadian Hotel

48 Quang Trung Street. ☎ *6.459.852; FAX: 84.6.459851* • This is also a new hotel, having opened in 1991. It's well-managed and clean—you'd expect it for the prices. Rooms have views of the sea. Restaurant, tennis court, business center, air-conditioned, minibar, disco and a bar. Expensive.   ***Reservations: Direct***

Rex Hotel

1 Duy Tan Street. ☎ *91766; FAX: 84.6.97561* • This is a huge structure by Vung Tau standards, nine stories. Restaurant, tennis courts, air-conditioned, disco.Moderate.   ***Reservations: Direct***

Hoa Hong La Rose Mini Hotel

39 Durong Thuy Van. ☎ *59455* • About US$20. A service oriented inn on the beach with a dining room. Comfortably and tastefully furnished with secure parking. Staff, although their English is limited to non-existent is extraordinarily friendly. Moderate.
                                              Reservations: Direct

New Hotel

Next door to the Rex at Duy Tan and Quang Trung Streets • Just like the New Hotel in Saigon, this is also a new hotel, completed just a couple of years ago. On Front Beach. Good views of the sea. Moderate.
                                              Reserevations: Direct

International Hotel Hai Dau

242 Ba Cu Street. ☎ *452178, 2571* • About US$20.Only five years old, this place looks like it could have been used as a fire base by American troops during the war. The amenities, though, belie the trashiness of the place. There's a swimming pool, business center and two restaurants. I'd stay away. Moderate.   ***Reservations: Direct***

Pacific Hotel

4 Le Loi Blvd. ☎ *452279. US$16-30* • The more expensive rooms have a view of the sea. This is a large, drab complex with air-conditioned rooms, refrigerators, hot water, a disco/nightclub, and a decent massage. Moderate.   ***Reservations: Direct***

Palace Hotel

Nguyen Trai Stret near Quang Trung Street. ☎ *452411* • *105 rooms.* About US$40. This is also a sprawling but stale and plain place that at least offers all its rooms with air conditioning, TV, and a refrigerator. It can be tough getting up in the morning in some of the rooms as they have no windows; they almost create a prison-like feel. But there are a couple of restaurants, a "nightclub," a massage parlor and a tennis court. If these can be called redeeming characteristics, you know you're in Vung Tau. Moderate–expensive.   ***Reservations: Direct***

Phoung Dong Hotel

02 Thuy Van Street-VT. ☎ *52158, 525983* • US$50-plus. This is a new and impressive hotel in Vung Tau, perhaps the town's finest. It sits on the hillside overlooking Back Beach and just above a complex of some of the architecturally attractive Mediterranean style villas in Vung Tau. Service is extremely considerate and the grounds are immaculately kept. Kareoke, massage, and a host of other amenities. It is frequented primarily by visiting Asian businessmen apparently, but the manager, Dinh Van Ha, made it clear in no uncertain terms that Westerners are welcome here. Expensive. ***Reservations: Direct***

Diamond Hotel

8 Tran Nguyen Han Street. ☎ *95930; FAX: 95930* • US$15–20.Not much here but a restaurant and a room to watch videos. Rooms with air conditioning. Moderate. ***Reservations: Direct***

INSIDER TIP

In Bai Dau, there are dozens of guest houses catering to budget tourists, but many of them only accept Vietnamese. And these are sometimes nothing more than short-time hooker stops. (If you must, these "ladies" can be had for as little as 40,000 dong, or about US$4. Don't expect a wake-up call.) Although the area itself is not particularly unappealing, the beach along Bai Dau is. Some of the "cement-floor" types might want to try the Nha Nghi My Tho at 47 Tran Phu Street, the Nha Nghi 29 on the beach, the Nha Hang 96 (not on the beach), or the Nha Nghi DK 142, although it's a bit pricier. One thing to remember is that places come and go virtually overnight in this part of the country. Construction of new dwellings is rampant around here, albeit slow. A lot of the older hotels and kiosks appear to be changing their names, or at least recreating their marquees in a grandiose manner to attract customers. Sometimes the addresses of the establishments will be displayed with far more prominence than the actual hotel or restaurant name. So it pays more to know where you are than where you want to be going.

WHERE TO EAT IN VUNG TAU

There are literally dozens of eateries lining the beach along Ha Long, Quang Thung and Thuy Van Streets. Of note on Thuy Van Street along the Back Beach: Thuy Van Cafe, Quan An Binhean Cafe, Don Qui 59, Quai Quan Thuy Tien,Lam Thon Thung, Dai Dung, Nha Hang and Qua Hang. Also try: Thanh Nien, 55 Quang Trung Street.

DIRECTORY

BANKS AND MONEY CHANGERS

Vietcom Bank, *27 Tran Hung Dao Blvd.* They will exchange travelers checks and, at last report, issue advances on American issued credit cards.

GENERAL POST OFFICE

4 Ha Long Street, near the Hai Au Hotel.

TOURIST OFFICE

Vung Tau Tourism, *59 Tran Hung Doa Blvd.*

TRANSPORTATION

The bus station is on Van Cu Street. There are minibuses that depart from Trang Hung Dao Blvd. and Ly Tu Trong Street. The minibuses depart for Saigon as soon as they're filled, usually around every 40 minutes or so and cost about 8000 dong (US80 cents). They usually take about three hours, but frequently longer. The regular non-express buses take a lot longer (maybe four hours), but cost only about 2000 dong (US$20 cents). It may not be necessary, but it's probably a good idea to buy your tickets to Saigon in advance, even as much as a day. Buses from Saigon for Vang Tau from the Mien Dong Bus Station also leave when they're filled. You can also take a bus to Vang Tau from the station at Nguyen Hue Blvd. These are express buses and usually take about three hours and cost about US$5 return fare. If you want to go by car, ask around, but feel lucky if you can get a ride for less than US$70 round trip for a day excursion. Getting around Vang Tau is best by bicycle, and there are plenty for rent, despite what people might say. Most of the hotels now rent bikes, as do a number of beachside cafes.

NIGHTLIFE IN VUNG TAU

Listening to the surf seems to be the most pleasant way of spending the waking darkness hours here. This way you don't actually need to see the beach and you can fantasize about being somewhere else. Otherwise, there has been a proliferation of nightclubs and karaoke clubs springing up. Most of the good hotels have some form of nightlife.

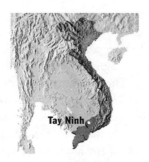

TAY NINH

TAY NINH IN A CAPSULE

Headquarters to the Cao Dai Sect, one of the most intriguing religions in Asia, if not the world...features some of the most ornate and intricate religious symbolism in the world...there are elements to the temple that are unique in the world...Coa Daoism is an odd blend of both Eastern and Western faiths that were somehow coagulated to form the "perfect religion"...There are elements of Christianity, Buddhism, Confucianism, Hinduism, Taoism, Islam and God knows what else...There was a major conflict between Cao Daoism and the South Vietnamese government back in the mid-1950s which ultimately led to the reannexation of Cao Dai territory to the Vietnamese...Tay Ninh itself is nothing special and not worthy of a journey simply for the town itself...It's a typical Vietnamese village with avenues flanked by food stalls, electronics shops, etc....There seems to be emerging an increasing number of petrol stations, though...Before the 17th century, this province, close to the Cambodian border, was under Khmer rule.

Tay Ninh, the capital of Tay Ninh Province and about 100 km from the capital, is home to the famous and magnificent, if not bizarre, Cao Dai headquarters, a complex of temples and fields that features the Cao Dai Great Temple. The excursion is an easy day trip from Saigon and can be done by rented car, bus, or motorcycle. By motorcycle (you can rent one in Saigon with the proper international driving permit for about US$10 per day), the ride is an exhilarating experience, although the countryside isn't all that magnificent. And unless you plan on being at the temple for noon prayer (there are also prayer services at 6 a.m. and 6 p.m.), just getting there might be the highlight of the day, as the roads are well paved and suited for touring by motorcycle (be careful).

Once you get out of Saigon(from District 1, take Cach Mang Thang Tam to Huong Lo and follow the highway past Co Chi to Go

Dau, then take a right), which can take a very long time (the locals insist the entire trip to Tay Ninh takes two hours by car or fast motorbike). It can easily take as long as 3-1/2 hours from central Saigon even at speeds as high as 70 or 80 mph and drain your nervous system entirely. The highway becomes relatively free of heavy-vehicle traffic outside the sprawling metropolis and you soon become surrounded by rice fields and then, amazingly enough, a few more after that. There are a number of small, pastel yellow pagodas along the route, but few, if any are worth a detour, unless the road starts to become a little too much and you want to prime yourself for the sights of Tay Ninh.

Between 1975 and 1979, Tay Ninh Province was increasingly encroached upon by Cambodian Pol Pot's Khmer Rouge, who invaded villages and reportedly raped women and killed men and children indiscriminately. It was these deeds that gave the Vietnamese government the impetus (or at least a damn good excuse) to invade Cambodia in December of 1978.

The best reasons to visit Tay Ninh, of course, are the Cao Dai temples, particularly the Great Temple. Cao Daoism's roots stem from the 1920s in southern Vietnam after the religion's founder, a civil servant named Ngo Van Chieu, received a "visit" from "God," or Cao Dai. Similar to Moses, who descended Mount Sinai with God's gifts of the tablets of the 10 Commandments (not ironically, Cao Dai means "high tower"), Ngo received a message from Cao Dai that the religion was to be based on the "Giant Eye." (The Giant Eye is above each altar in a Cao Dai temple.) In fact, the religion subscribes to five commandments: don't kill anything living, don't practice excessive or extravagant living, do not slander, do not be tempted, and do not covet. This Giant Eye was apparently the manifestation of the vision of a number of lay people, from politicians to poets. Included as saints in the Cao Dai religion are such illustrious, yet many hardly saintly, luminaries as Winston Churchill, Moses, Joan of Arc, the French writer Victor Hugo, Sun Yat Sen, and Brahma. This helps explains Cao Daoism's attempt to merge secular and scientific principles with religious or spiritual devotion. Followers of Cao Daoism interpret the "scriptures" through meditation and sort of a séance that contacts the saints utilizing a corbeille-a-bac, an odd wooden planchette.

Their religion became formalized in 1926 and soon developed an almost nationalistic fervor. Within a short time, Cao Daoism had tens of thousands of followers.

A year later, Cao Dai convert Le Van Trung staged a religious coup and assumed leadership of the fledgling faith. He built a temple in the village of Long Hoa, near Tay Ninh. Ten years later, the following of Cao Daoism had become massive; there were an estimated 4–5 million followers of the sect. It essentially became a political state which, of course, didn't amuse the government. In 1955, when as many as 15 percent of southern Vietnamese were Cao Dais, there was a major confrontation between the religion and the state that ultimately gave the government back control of territory that it had "lost" to the Cao Dais. The South Vietnamese government then conscripted tens of thousands of Cao Dai ahherents as soldiers.

After the fall of the south in 1975, Cao Daoism all but ceased to exist. And because they refused to support both the Viet Cong and the South Vietnamese forces during the protracted war, they faced especially intense scrutiny and hardship after the Saigon leadership collapsed. Since the relaxation of tensions between the peoples of the north and the south, Cao Daoism has reemerged and nearly 1000 Cao Dai temples can be found throughout Vietnam, primarily in the south, receiving the worship of an estimated 2 million adherents to the religion.

Cao Daosim has the strongest influence in the province of Tay Ninh and in the Mekong Delta region.

Cao Dais aim to break the cycle of reincarnation by following the five commandments. The principle dieties are the Mother Goddess and God. Men and women equally share positions of supreme authority; both men and women become clergy, except at the highest levels. If men and women clergy of the same status are based in the same temple area, the men are bestowed greater authority. Male priests are called "Thanh," while female clergy are referred to as "Huong." Cao Dai temples are built in a fashion where male clergy enter the structures from the right, while the women enter from the left. The same goes for worship; men worship on the left side of the temple while the women do their praying on the right side of the temple.

INSIDER TIP

Visitors to the temples should remove both hats and shoes. Similar to Cao Dai clergy, women enter the temple through an entrance on the left, while the men do so on the right–similar to how Cao Dai clergy enter and exit their temples. You'll usually be accompanied by a Cao Dai priest (man or woman), and you will be expected to provide a small donation–the amount entirely up to you. Curiously enough, my guide barely spoke a word of English, and I found that other clergy at the Cao Dai Great Temple weren't exactly fluent in anything but what they seemed to be muttering either. So be prepared. Read the section on Cao Daoism in this book (or other more extensive selections, such as Cao Dai Spiritism: A Study of Religion in Vietnamese Society, by Victor Oliver (EL Brill, Leiden, 1976) before visiting the temple. Without doing so, your visit may be virtually meaningless, save for a few snapshots. You will understand none of the artistic depiction of three periods of history that hang on the walls. In the main temple two rows of pink pillars line the aisle, inscribed with dragon figures. These aisles lead up to the main altar, above which is the Giant Eye. Visitors watch the service from a balcony overlooking the cathedral. Plan on staying for the entire service, which lasts about an hour. It would be a disruption as well as an insult to depart earlier. At no time should you walk down the center portion of the nave, although when I inadvertently did I was met with a kindly but "you stupid Hoa Ky" smile from my guide. You will be allowed to take pictures, at least, I believe I was told. However, another tourist said that taking photos of clergy members is forbidden unless they grant you permission, which may mean a small "donation."

Prayer services—conducted four times daily (6 a.m., 12 noon, 6 p.m., and midnight)—are the best time to visit the temples. Clergy and dignitaries wear ornate red, blue and yellow ceremonial robes and hats, and there are offerings of fruit, flowers, alcohol and tea. During the normal prayer sessions on weekdays, perhaps hundreds of clergy members may be present. But there are special Cao Dai holidays where you may actually find yourself amidst thousands of Cao Dai priests.

Cao Dai priests practice celibacy and vegetarianism. The Cao Dai separate history into three distinct periods or revelations: the first was when the existence of God was revealed to human beings through Laotze and the influences of Taoism, Buddhism, and Confucianism. The second phase involved Sakyamuni Buddha, Jesus Christ, Mohammed, Moses, and Confucious. During the second period, the Cao Dai came to believe that the conduits carrying the divine messages from these individuals had become convoluted and impure.

The new, or third phase, of Cao Daoism has its followers believing that the convoluted previous messages have been eliminated through their communication with the spirits. These "spirits" include former Cao Dai leaders as well as an eclectic blend of both lay people and clergy. Many Westerners are spirits the Cao Dai contact frequently. Among them are Shakespeare, Louis Pasteur, and V.I. Lenin (who, curiously enough, didn't appear to inspire the Cao Dai to align themselves with Marxist Viet Cong forces during the war, even though Cao Dai members sided with the French against the Japanese, the Americans against The Viet Minh, and the Viet Minh against the South Vietnamese government). The spirits are communicated with in a number of languages, including French, English, Vietnamese and English. In one ceremony, the priest seals a blank piece of paper in an envelope and places it above the altar. When he takes it down, a message is contained in the envelope.

Although formal Cao Dai seances have been held in temples across the country since 1925, the only "legitimate" seances that reveal divine truth can be conducted at Tay Ninh.

WHAT TO SEE AND DO IN TAY NINH

Cao Dai Great Temple ★★

This is the principal temple of the Cao Dai religion and the focal point of the Cao Dai complex called Holy See. Its colorful pastel yellow architecture (which seems to get a new coat of paint hourly by the hordes of workers one sees on scaffolds all the time) is set among a large complex of schools, dormitories, and a "hospital," which utilizes traditional Vietnamese herbal medicine. The main temple consists of an intriguing complex of architectural styles, ranging from Oriental to European. The large front facade features reliefs with depictions of Cao Dai saints. Some have called the building the most impressive structure in the Orient, while others have compared it with Disneyland. If you're impressed with Disneyland, though, you may be disappointed by the lack of rollercoasters at the temple.

The temple is constructed on nine levels, which represent the nine steps to heaven. On each level you will find a pair of columns. There are impressive columns in the nave decorated with dragons. Above the altar, of course, looms the Giant Eye with an eternal flame. The domed ceiling that the columns support represents the heavens.

There is a mural in the entry area displaying the three signatories of the "Third Alliance Between God and Man." There are seven large chairs at the far end of the temple in front of the globe, the largest of which is supposedly "reserved" for the Cao Dai pope, a position that hasn't been filled since the early 1930s. Three of the chairs are for the use of those Cao Dai responsible for the religion's law books. The remaining three chairs represent the seating areas for the religion's leaders of its three branches.

Cham Temples

About a kilometer to the east of Tay Ninh are a number of Cham temples.

Long Hoa Market

In the middle of Tay Ninh, about a kilometer or two from the Cao Dai complex. Nothing really worth writing home about here; just the basic staples bought by the basic crowds you see in marketplaces all over rural Vietnam. Foodstuffs, fake designer clothes, etc.

WHERE TO STAY AND EAT IN TAY NINH

Near the bridge there are a few places to stay in the US$10-20 range, but Tay Ninh is not an area worth more than just a few hours' visit, which can easily be arranged from Saigon by tour group or rented car. Most visitors combine day tours of Tay Ninh with a visit to the Cu Chi Tunnels, which lie along the route (National Highway 22) to Tay Ninh from Saigon.

For food, your best bets are the numerous food stalls that surround the Long Hoa market. Two restaurants of note are the **Nha Hang So 1**, which is on the western side of the river near the bridge and **Nha Hang Diem Thuy**, located at 30/4 Street. Both restaurants, as are all in Tay Ninh, are extraordinarily cheap, with most meals costing as little as 5000 dong (about US$.50).

TAY NINH ENVIRONS

BLACK LADY MOUNTAIN

This is also called Nui Ba Den, and it's located about 15 km from Tay Ninh. I've heard this is the highest peak in southern Vietnam. There are a number of temples on the mountain (the main temple which can be reached in about 45 minutes via a relatively simple hike from the base of the hill), the result of centuries of Khmer, Cham, Vietnamese and Chinese domination of and influence in the area. The term Black Lady Mountain is based on the legend of a young woman named Ly Thi Huong who, despite being wooed by a rich Chinese Mandarin, ended up marrying the man of her dreams. (Another version of the tale has Huong leaping off the side of the mountain in protest of the wealthy Chinese' romantic pursuits.) While the husband was away fighting wars, Huong would make pilgramages to the summit of Nui Ba Den to visit a magical Buddha statue. One day, as legend has it, there was an attempt by bandits to rape the woman, who, believing death was the more virtuous alternative, threw herself off the face of the ediface. The story became known through her communication with a local monk.

The mountain, which reaches about 900 meters or more above the rice fields was also the setting of intense firefights between the Viet Minh and the French during the first Indochina War, and between the Americans and the Viet Cong during the Vietnam War. Americans heavily defoliated the region during the war, though one can hardly tell today. (If your grandchildren are born resembling cauliflowers, you'll realize that the American defoliation of Vietnam is a lot like AIDS—you may look verdant on the outside, but something inside is ripping you apart.)

The principal temples of pilgramage on the mountain are Lang Chang Pagoda and Chua Linh Son Pagoda. Some of the fortune tellers in and around the pagodas speak English.

DIRECTORY

TRAVEL

The best way to get to Tay Ninh is by minibus or car, the latter which can be had for the US$70–90 range a day, although some private entrepreneurs will offer cars and drivers for as little as $40 a day ($20 per day if you're going only as far as Cu Chi.) Buses leave for Tay Ninh regularly from Saigon via Cu Chi from the Mien Tay Station and the Mien Tay bus station in An Loc. They take about three hours, sometimes longer. The other alternative is to rent a motorcycle. Make sure you leave Tay Ninh (if you're not spending the night) by 3 p.m. to avoid the extremely dangerous nighttime traffic, both on treacherous Route 22 and in Saigon, where nighttime motoring is something akin to a circus bumper car ride without electricity. Unless you know what the hell you're doing, it's better to get out to this area with a guide or in a group. Buses back to Saigon leave from the Tay Ninh bus station regularly to the same stations.

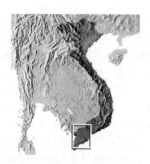

THE MEKONG DELTA

THE MEKONG DELTA IN A CAPSULE

My Thanh *(60 km south of Can Tho) was one of the first "strategic hamlets," a largely unsuccessful attempt by the South Vietnamese government to create artificial urban centers for farming that would be safe from Viet Cong infiltration...***Thot Not** *(40 km upriver from Can Tho on the Bassac River) was where the Trotskyite revolutionary Ta Tu Thau was born...***Thap Moi**, *or The Plain of Reeds, at the junction Long An and Dong Thap provinces, is a former Viet Minh and Viet Cong base that neither the French nor the Americans were able to occupy..***Ca Mau** *(348 km from Ho Chi Minh City, 210 from Vinh Long.) is the biggest city in the Ca Mau peninsula on the Gonh Hoa River. Ca Mau is famous for the U Minh forest, the second largest mangrove swamp in the world. There are many precious and endangered birds and animals...***Ha Tien** *(340 km from Saigon, 250 km from Vinh Long.) is a small town of Kien Giang Province in the Gulf of Thailand, 8 km from the Cambodian border. It has many beautiful beaches, caves and romantic settings. Phu Tu Islet (Father-Son Isle), with its panoramic views, looks like Ha Long Bay in miniature...Stone Cavern...Dong Ho Lake...Cape Nai...Offshore island of Phu Quoc.*

This is the richest and the most prolific agricultural region of Vietnam. In fact the majority of all Vietnamese are fed with agricultural products from the Mekong Delta. It's an extremely rural area covering some 67,000 sq. km but, surprisingly it is one of the most densely populated areas of Vietnam, and more than half of the entire region is under cultivation. The only regions of the delta that are to date sparsely cultivated or not cultivated at all are the areas around Minh Hai Province.

The Mekong Delta was formed primarily by mud from the Mekong River spreading in fork-like directions out to the South

China Sea. The area itself was sparsely populated until the 19th century, when Vietnamese settlers moved slowly down south to take advantage of the newly-formed region's rich agricultural potential. They called the area "Mien-tay," or the "West." Most of the area's geographical, cultural and architectural attractions are, by Vietnamese standards, brand new. Temples that may appear to be hundreds of years old may in fact have been built as recently as the 1930s and 40s. The oldest area of the Delta is Ha Tien, on the southwestern coast at the border of present-day Cambodia. Ha Tien was settled and highly prosperous as early as the start of the 17th century.

Crops grown in the delta include mango, mangosteen, jackfruit, oranges (believe it or not), guava, pepper, durian and pineapple, among others. Also under cultivation are coconut, sugarcane and seafood. In fact, although the rice yields are lower in the delta than in the north of Vietnam, there is nearly three times as much rice acreage per person as there is in the north. The region is entirely flat and contains a vast network of rivers and waterways that comprise the tributaries of the Mekong River—locally called Song Cuu Long (or the River of the Nine Dragons).

The Mekong's source is high on the Tibetan Plateau, making the river perhaps the mightiest and longest in Asia. It flows nearly 4500 km through China, Laos, Cambodia and Myanmar before finally splitting into both wide and thin branches of waterway in Vietnam's southern region.

In Vietnam, the Mekong splits into two major channels. The river itself moves through Hang Ngu and Vinh Long, where several fingers then branch out on their journeys to the South China Sea.

INSIDER TIP

The Vietnamese government will spend US$9.2 billion each year on improvement of the country's waterways. Investments are also expected to be made to develop modern passenger ships as well as domestic touring vessels.

The Bassac River, which runs through Long Xuyen and Can Tho is the other main branch. The best time of the year to see the Mekong is in the fall, when the run-off from upriver all through Southeast Asia makes the waterways an incredible sight, as the flow of the river reaches nearly 40,000 cubic meters (compared to 2000 during other times of the year).

INSIDER TIP

There has been increasing interest among independent travelers to creatively find their own ways of exploring the Mekong River. Beware, though, that pirate attacks are not infrequent along this vast stretch of interior waterway. Pirates recently boarded a Cambodian freighter bound for Phnom Penh and beheaded 18 people, including children, and dumped their bodies into the river. Armed with AK-47 rifles and grenade launchers, the pirates escaped before being apprehended by Vietnamese authorities.

Not surprisingly, because the mighty river's force continues to extend the shoreline of southern Vietnam by as many as 15 meters a year and extend the shorelines at the mouths of the river by about as much as 80 meters a year, the Mekong Delta region is geologically relatively recent in origin. As mentioned, the land of the delta was formed by the silt being pushed down the river from the highlands of China, Myanmar and Laos, and the area—save for the Ha Tien region which was settled in the 17th century—remained virtually unpopulated until the 19th century. Vietnamese settlers moved south into the "Mien-ty." Consequently there is very little of any deep historical significance in the delta. The temples are new, although some appear to be centuries old.

Perhaps the amazing oddity of the Mekong occurs not in Vietnam, but in Cambodia, where, when the river is at flood stage, it drains up the Tonle Sap River, which prevents flooding in the Mekong Delta region and brings Cambodia's Tonle Sap Lake to enormously high levels.

Originally, the delta region belonged to the Cambodians and wasn't settled by the Vietnamese until centuries later (see the Ha Tien chapter). Although most of the region's population is comprised of ethnic Vietnamese, you'll find a number of Khmer descendents living particularly in the lower end of the delta.

AUTHOR'S OBSERVATION

The Irrawaddy dolphins of the Mekong River are getting blown out of the water. Literally. The increasing use of explosives by Khmer fishermen to more easily harvest fish from the waters of the Mekong is including in its carnage the slaughter of the Irrawaddy, a rare dolphin that inhabits the waterways of the Mekong in Laos, Cambodia and Vietnam. This is the report from the Bangkok-based Project for Ecological Recovery. According to the report, and travelers visiting the region, the blasting of fish out of the river is on the rise, and has increased steadily in the last 10 years (and even to a greater extent since the signing of the Cambodian Peace Accords in October 1991) occasionally during the high-water rainy season but much more frequently during times of the year when the water levels go down. Many visitors to the region report hearing 10–20 explosions per day in the river.

The Mekong Delta is a fascinating area to tour, but it is also a monotonous glut of real estate, the topography changing very little, if at all, for thousands of square kilometers. I toured the area by motorcycle and boat, and, frankly, would not have done it any other way simply for the reason that the numerous rest stops I took were the most enjoyable part of my adventure. The people of the delta are truly its attraction, not the topography nor the historical sights. Being invited into families' homes for meals, falling in love with the locals and trading love messages that have to be translated by relatives, these are the real attractions of the delta. At one cafe in the tiny southern delta village of Soc Xoai, I was grilled by a young lady's parents over Vietnamese whiskey and BGI beer about my background and profession in order to gain permission to marry the young woman (which was essentially granted) even though my only request was that myself and the young lady exchange addresses for correspondence purposes.

There are unknown ferry trips across the Bassac and Hau Giang rivers to villages whose inhabitants have never before laid eyes on a Westerner.

This is the Mekong Delta, not a 10-hour bus ride to Rach Gia to see a couple of fishing boats leave port.

But keep in mind that traveling the delta below Can Tho isn't easy, and can be quite dangerous. The roads are in dismal shape. I had two flat tires, a broken clutch cable—and both tail lights fell off due to the harshness of the terrain. At the end of the day, you will be covered in dust, vehicle exhaust and mud if you travel by any other means than a tour group in a car or microbus. And the water at many hotels in the region may turn out to be nothing more than motivation to remain as dirty as you'll get. Travel by regular bus in the delta below Can Tho is *excruciatingly* uncomfortable for taller Westerners, and that's why I mention some of the available tours below. Because nowhere else in Vietnam, especially the southern half of the country, will you have to "rough it" like you will in the Mekong Delta

For information on Mekong Delta tours, see "Package Tours" on p. 409.

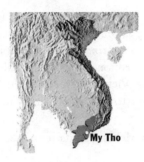
My Tho

MY THO

MY THO IN A CAPULE

Just 2 hours from Saigon...Capital of Dinh Tuong Province...Under Khmer rule until the 17th century...The French colonized the area in the mid-1800s...A strategic American military base was here in the mid-1960s...Considered the site of the Viet Cong's first major military victory...Makes for an easy day trip from Saigon.

My Tho, one of the first stops in the Mekong Delta, is only about a two-hour drive from Saigon (about 76 km) and is the capital of Dinh Tuoung Province (also known as Tien Giang Province), with a population of about 100,000. It sits on the banks of the My Tho River, one of the many Mekong River tributaries near the mouths of the Mekong. It was under Cambodian rule until the 17th century and was settled mainly by Chinese after Nguyen Lords took control of the area later that century. Thai forces subsequently invaded the area but were forced out in 1784. The French took control of the region in the mid-19th century. In the mid-1960s, an important American military base was here.

My Tho is often considered the site of the first Viet Cong victory over ARVN forces, but the fight actually took place in nearby Ap Bac.

Today, My Tho is a relatively prosperous city known for its rice production and fruit orchards. The city itself isn't as drab as Vinh Long, but that's not saying a lot. My Tho can easily be seen in a day visit from HCMC, but if you take this kind of excursion, get the most out of it. I especially recommend visiting the nearby islands of Ben Tre and Phung Island, former home of the Coconut Monk—although don't expect a lot of truly magnificent scenery at either. It's the history of the area that makes it worth seeing.

WHAT TO SEE AND DO IN MY THO AND ENVIRONS

Trung Trac Central Market

Located on Trung Trac Street, of course, near the Bao Dinh channel on the eastern edge of town. If you've seen one market, you've seen them all. At least the streets are closed to traffic here. A lot of produce here, and fruit. I mean a lot. Most of it I'm sure ends up in HCMC. You'll also see a lot more tobacco sold here than in other delta markets. However, this is the best place to get a sample of life in My Tho, as it is the city's most bustling area in an otherwise laid-back environment.

My Tho Church

32 Hung Vuong Street. This is a big pastel yellow church with twin towers that was built about 100 years ago, making it ancient by Mekong Delta standards. The church serves the city's 8000 or so Catholics, but it's open only about 6 hours a day: very early in the morning (you'll still be in bed), and in the afternoon for about 4 hours. Masses are held twice every day and at least three times on Sunday. The plaques on the wall inside the church are dedicated to Fatima.

Vinh Trang Pagoda

This is an unimpressive little pagoda that's a little tough to get to without asking for directions. Well, here they are: Cross the bridge at Nguyen Trai Street and then turn left down Nguyen An Ninh Street to the end. Then walk down a dirt path to Nguyen Trung Truc Street. You'll come across a painted bamboo gate on the right. This is the entrance. The actual entrance to the pagoda is through a porcelain gate. Architectural styles range from Chinese to Vietnamese to French colonial (the temple was built in the mid-1800s). I'd simply avoid this place altogether if only for the fact that the animals kept here in the "zoo" live in dismal conditions. It seems the pagoda's lure is not spiritual or architectural, but purely capitalistic. It's sickening to watch the microbus loads of Asian tourists gawk at the animals and behave as if they were at Disneyland. The only thing worth seeing here is the portrait of Ho Chi Minh with real beard hairs. I'm not sure they were actually his or some drunk Australian tourist's. It's open from 9 a.m.–12 noon and from 2 to 5 in the afternoon.

Quan Than Pagoda

3-9 Nguyen Trung Truc Street. This is a nice restored temple with plaster figures. Otherwise not a lot to see here.

Con Phuong

This is the island of the Coconut Monk, about 3 km from My Tho. After World War II, the Ong Dao Dua (the Coconut Monk) built a small village on Con Phuong and started a new religion, which was a mish-mash of Christianity and Buddhism. In its early years it might have reminded you of singer Michael Jackson's ranch in California, with park-like attractions in an attractive setting (although Disneyland's influence seems all too apparent in and around My Tho). The grounds used to contain ornate structures: dragon-wrapped columns and the likes, but today, they're run down and musty. The Ong Dao Dua, who was born Nguyen Thanh Nam, was given his moniker because he reputedly ate nothing but coconuts for three years on a stone slab where he also meditated both day and night. Before his monastic life, he was educated in France, married and had a daughter. Later, during his coconut diet, he was persecuted and imprisoned by the various South Vietnamese governments as he sought to reunify Vietnam though a peaceful process. To get out to the island, you can hire a boat at the south end of Trung Trac Street. Prices vary depending on the size of the boat, ranging anywhere from US$3 an hour to US$20 for a round trip and "tour." Try not to be disappointed. Many tourists return from the island in that very state of mind.

Tan Long Island

This is worth seeing only because it's a cheap five-minute boat trip from My Tho. Fishing boats cover the palm-lined shores. Take some pictures and then come back.

Snake Farm   ★

This is about 8 km from My Tho toward Vinh Long. Many varieties of snakes, all indigenous to Vietnam, are raised here, from pythons to deadly cobras. The military runs the place and raises the animals for their medicinal qualities. I assure you these snakes have not had the lethal venom removed and the ability of the soldier/snake handlers in dealing with these vicious creatures is a sight in itself. The belief is that the snakes have healing powers in their flesh and glands. These medicines are then bottled and sold to the hordes of French tourists who've climbed off the microbuses.

WHERE TO STAY IN MY THO

Hotel 43

43 Ngo Quyen Street. ☎ *73126, 72126 • 24 rooms.* US$6–8. The expensive rooms are the doubles with air conditioning, while the cheaper rooms can sleep three and have an attached bath. Service here is some of the friendliest in My Tho. Great value. Inexpensive.

Reservations: Direct

Song Tien Hotel (formerly the Grand Hotel)

101 Trung Trac Street. ☎ *712009 • 35 rooms.* About US$20. This is an expensive place that used to have a better reputation as the eight-story Grand Hotel. The staff has been reported to be dishonest. And honestly, the place is overpriced. The upper end-rooms have refrigerators and air conditioning. Moderate.   *Reservations: Direct*

Thanh Binh Hotel

44 Nguyen Binh Khiem Street • *4 rooms.* US$3. Forget it. Like spend-
ing the night in a janitor's closet. I wouldn't let them pay me to stay
here. In fact, I'm not even sure they still allow foreigners. No fans; no
bath. Very inexpensive. **Reservations: Direct**

Rach Gam

33 Trung Tac Street • US$3–6. This is one of the cheapest acccommo-
dations in town and it shows. Backpackers only. Very Inexpensive.
Reservations: Direct

Lao Dong Hotel

Le Loi and 34 Thang 4 Streets • About US$6. This is a relatively new
hotel that hasn't yet gotten the opportunity to descend into unclean-
liness. And it's cheap. Again, for the backpacker set. Very Inexpensive.
Reservations: Direct

WHERE TO EAT IN MY THO

My Tho is known for a couple of specialty dishes, the best being *hu tieu
my tho*, a spicy and garnished soup packed with herbs, shrimp, vermicelli,
pork and chicken. Find it, or in its various forms at:

Restaurant 43

43 Ngo Quyen Street • Vietnamese, Asian. Inexpensive and good.

Nha Hang 54

54 Trung Trac Street • Vietnamese, Asia fare. Ice Cream.

Nha Hang 52

52 Trung Trac Street • Vietnamese, Asian. One of the best in town.

DIRECTORY

TRANSPORTATION

By **bus** or **car**, My Tho is about 76 km from HCMC and another 70 km
from Vinh Long. It's about 180 km to both Rach Gia and Chau Doc, and
275 km fom Ha Tien. You can get to My Tho in only a couple of hours
from Saigon's Nien Tay Bus Station. The bus station at My Tho is 4 km
back on the road toward Saigon and Vinh Long. The station is open from
about 4 a.m. to 5 p.m. Take Ap Bac Street to Naional Highway 1 to get
there. There are also buses to Vinh Long, Can Tho, Rach Gia, Chau Doc
and other destinations in the delta. Buses generally leave when they are
full.

By **boat**, ferries leave to My Tho in the afternoon from Saigon and take
about 3–4 hours, sometimes quite a bit longer. They leave from the wharf
on Ton Duc Thang Street at the end of Ham Nghi Street. Price about
US$1. Transportation around My Tho is by cyclo or by small motorized
boats which can be rented from the ferry landing on Trung Trac Street.
You can hire a car at Thuan Hung, *130-156 Le Loi.* Note: if you're traveling by car from Saigon to My Tho, remember the road (NH1) splits about
68 kilometers from HCMC. Proceed straight (which is a fork off NH1) to

get to My Tho, or turn right to proceed on to Vinh Long. Signs are well marked.

TOURIST OFFICE

Tien Giang Tourism, *66 Hung Vuong Street.*

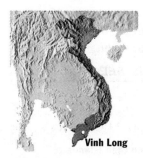

Vinh Long

VINH LONG

VINH LONG IN A CAPSULE

Vinh Long, *(about 135 km southwest of Saigon) is the site of a major temple dedicated to Tong Phuc Hiep, general of the Nguyen Dynasty. It was also the home of Petrus Ky (Truong Vinh Ky), the 19th century spirit who sought to modernize Vietnam.*

About 145 kilometers from Ho Chi Minh City on the Hau River, Vinh Long Province occupies a core area of the Mekong Delta. It may be regarded as a microcosm of the entire Mekong Delta due to its primordial prosperity. An Binh Island and Binh Hoa Phuoc Islands dot the huge networks of meandering rivers, bisected by countless arroyos under the dense tropical delta foliage. When you pay a visit to the orchards you can taste ripe fruits you pick from the trees yourself or have friendly conversations with the local people.

Vinh Long (the capital of Vinh Long province) is not the kind of place you'll really want to spend a lot of time in, however, save for taking boat trips along the Co Chien River to visit the orchid-covered islands. There are some decent hotels that have gone up in recent years that make the town a more attractive resting spot for areas further south and to the west such as Can Tho, Long Xuyen, Rach Gia and Ha Tien. Vinh Long is also the nucleus of the spread of Catholicism in the Mekong Delta region, so you'll come a cross a couple of cathedrals and a seminary. There's also a Cao Dai church near the second bridge into town coming from both Saigon and My Tho. Vinh Long is about 140 km south of HCMC. The city was also the home of Truong Vinh Ky (Petrus Ky), a legendary figure of the 19th century who sought to bring Vietnam into the "modern" age.

If you visit the islands around Vinh Long, you'll have to hire a boat, the smallest of which can be had for around 10,000–20,000 dong per hour (about US$1–2). The best islands to see are unquestionably An Binh Island and Binh Hoa Phuoc. The town of Vinh Long itself is rather dreary, but is becoming an increasingly comfortable place to spend the night.

WHAT TO DO AND SEE IN VINH LONG AND ENVIRONS

The Tong Phuc Hiep Temple
This temple was dedicated to Tong, who was considered a great general during the Nguyen Dynasty. It's worth a few minutes visit.

Binh Hoa Phuoca and An Binh Islands
Just a short ride across the Mekong (this finger called the Co Chien here) are islands teeming with tropical fruit plantations, fruit that's eventually trucked or shipped up to HCMC. You could actually spend a few hours out on the river as there are other islands dotting the river, many having never been visited by tourists. Again, though, there are not a lot sights out here, and the boat ride may be worth it just for the ride itself and the breeze to break up the intense delta heat. For boat info check with the Long Chau Hotel or the Vinh Tra Hotel (addresses below).

WHERE TO STAY IN VINH LONG

An Vinh Hotel
3 Hoang Thai Hieu Street.

Vinh Tra Hotel
1 Thang 5 Street; ☎ *23656* • *20 rooms.* US$12–35. Cheapest rooms get you a fan, the more expensive hot water, air conditioning and refrigerator. Hotel offers Mekong River tours, car and microbus rentals, restaurant with Asian and European cuisine and dancing. Hotel overlooks the Mekong. Moderate.   ***Reservations: Direct***

Hotel Long Chau
Next door to the Cuu Long Restaurant. 50' Duong 1 Thang 5; ☎ *22488.*   ***Reservations: Direct.***

Long Chau Hotel
*#1 * 1-5 Street;* ☎ *23611* • US$6–8. $6 rooms with public toilet. $8 rooms have private bath. The pricier rooms also have air conditioning. Hotel offers river tours, car and microbus rentals. Restaurant featuring Asian and European cuisine. Dancing hall, orchestra and entrtainment nightly. This is a hell of a good deal. Inexpensive.
          Reservations: Direct

WHERE TO EAT IN VINH LONG

Phuong Thui Restaurant
Thang 5 Street, across the street from the Vinh Tra Hotel. Excellent seafood at some of the cheapest prices in the delta. There are a number of restaurants serving river fish and seafood specialties along Thang 5 Street. However, the Phuong Thui may well be the best.

DIRECTORY
TOURIST OFFICE

Cuu Long Tourism
   1 Thang 5 Street, ☎ *23616.*

POST OFFICE

Just behind the bus station on Doan Thi Diem Street.

TRANSPORTATION

Hired motor car or motorcycle is the best way to move between Saigon and Vinh Long, and many tourists will combine a day trip with a visit to nearby My Tho or even Can Tho (about US$70 for the car and another $20 a day for the guide). (Frankly, I don't think a day trip to Vinh Long is worth it. The stop is only reasonable if you're planning an extended trip into the delta.) But if you must travel by bus, buses from HCMC's Mien Tay Station to Vinh Long take between 3-1/2 and 4 hours, as does the return trip from Vinh Long's bus station next to the post office and central market. Buses leave when they're full. There is also bus transport from Vinh Long to other areas in the delta, including My Tho, Can Tho, Rach Gia, Ha Tien and Long Xuyen.

SA DEC

SA DEC IN A CAPSULE

Sa Dec, *about 135 km southwest of Saigon, is the site of the tomb of Nguyen Van Nhon. Two important people, a French military general and the governor of Cochinchina, were assassinated here by a Viet Minh Cao Daoist.*

Sa Dec, halfway between Vinh Long and Long Xuyen, is about 135 km from Saigon and is probably most famous for the many flower nurseries that transport fresh flowers daily to Saigon. Ho Chi Minh's father used to spend time here and his grave is located in Sa Dec. Here is also the tomb of Nguyen Van Nhon, the mandarin who helped Emperor Gia Long defeat the Tay Son. Also, the commander of the French Forces in Cochinchina, General Chanson, was assassinated here, as was Thay Lap Then, the governor of Cochinchina, in July 1951. The killings were the work of a dissident Viet Minh Cao Daoist.

Sa Dec is really only worth a visit for the beautiful nurseries. Photographs are permitted, but don't pick any of the flowers yourself unless you'd like to see them on your grave.

WHERE TO STAY AND EAT IN SA DEC

Sa Dec isn't worthy of an overnight stop. The few food stalls offer standard Vietnamese fare, but watch where the proprietors crack the ice. If they're doing it on a sidewalk or in the street, avoid it.

DIRECTORY

TOURIST OFFICE

The tourist office for Dong Thap Province is located at *108 5/A Hung Vuong Street* in Sa Dec. It's called Dong Thap Tourist. ☎ *61430* or *61432.*

Can Tho

CAN THO

*This skipper carefully negotiates a narrow canal in the Mekong Delta near
Can Tho.*

CAN THO IN A CAPSULE

Can Tho *(170 km southwest of Saigon) is considered the capital of the
delta. Since the colonial days, it has been the delta's major center of rice
cultivation. There's an important rice research institute here, as well as
a university.*

Can Tho (about 170 km south of Saigon), capital of Hau Giang (or
Can Tho) Province on the Bassac—or Hau River—is considered to
be the Mekong Delta's Capital of the West and is the largest population center in the delta, with more than 200,000 inhabitants. It's
probably the cleanest and nicest city to visit in the delta if staying in
Mekong Delta cities is your thing. Frankly, I think each population
center in the delta isn't worthy of being much more than a base to

explore the surrounding villages and islands. Canals and rice fields surround this intermittently picturesque city. It also serves as the delta's most important transportation center. Roads and ribbon-thin river tributaries lead to surrounding towns and villages, many of whose inhabitants have rarely seen foreigners.

Can Tho is certainly the political, cultural and economic hub of the Mekong Delta, and many farmers in the surrounding villages possess vast parcels of land (recently given back to the farmers after the communist government seized most private land after 1975) used for agriculture, including tropical fruit, cotton and pepper. Along the canals (that rise to great heights and drop like a flushing toilet with the tides) outside Can Tho, visitors will be surprised at the increasing number of tall, modern deco-like structures being erected along the waterways' banks, the result of local prosperity and the money sent back to families by wealthy Overseas Vietnamese (Viet Khieu).

In the city's center, along Hai Ba Trung Street on the Can Tho River, is a bustling market and a huge, silver painted statue of Ho Chi Minh in the riverside park that looks like a carved brewery vat. City dwellers and tourists get around by a unique motorcycle cyclo that—although found elsewhere in the delta—is unique in Vietnam's local transportation methods.

Can Tho is also the site where Nguyen Khoa Nam, commanding general of the 4th Military Region, and his deputy Le Van Hung committed suicide in May 1975 after the fall of South Vietnam to the communists.

WHAT TO SEE AND DO IN CAN THO AND ENVIRONS

Binh Thuy Temple

Just a few kilometers west of Can Tho, this structure was built in 1852 by Bin Ton and features shrines to the king of longevity. There are some beautiful portraits—and others that are rather amateurish and less flattering—of Vietnamese and Chinese leaders such as Phan Boi Chau, Bui Huu Nghia and Nguyen Hue. Perhaps the most striking features of the temple are the numerous cranes that are built near dragon-wrapped columns. Other figures of cranes and dragons are built of brass that frankly, could use a bit of polishing. There is also a large 150-year-old stuffed tiger. The symbol of the giant cranes reflects the large white birds' visits to the area to be fed marijuana by the locals (as legend has it). Others from Can Tho to Long Xuyen will attest to the birds feeding on the illegal crop each day near sunset on the river's islands. The temple was designated a cultural and historical area by the Hanoi government in 1989. Maybe it was for the brass or the grass.

Munirangsysram Pagoda

Here, at *36 Hoa Binh Blvd*, is a Khmer Hinayana Buddhist temple that features a 1-1/2-meter tall figure of Siddhartha Gautama, the original Buddha, sitting beneath a bodhi tree. It was built in 1946, at which time more than 200 monks lived at the pagoda. An extremely elderly monk lives here as well as a few much younger monks, youths really. They are extremely friendly and will invite you into their quarters for tea before viewing the inside of the relatively small pagoda. The temple serves the several thousand Khmer Theravada Buddhists who live in the Can Tho area. I felt guilty neglecting to leave a donation, but if the monks were displeased, they didn't show it. Prayers are held early in the morning and in the evening.

Quan Thanh De Pagoda

Also known as Minh Huong Hoi Quan, Le Minh Ngu On Street. Built by a Cantonese contingent nearly 75 years ago, this small Chinese pagoda was the house of worship for Can Tho's enormous ethnic Chinese population, who mainly evacuated the city—and Vietnam—in the late 1970s during the Communist government's anti-Chinese persecution program. Quan Cong as well as administrative mandarin Quan Binh and General Chau Xuong are in the main dias, while Ong Bon, the Guardian Spirit of Happiness and Virtue are situated to the left of the dias. The Goddess of the Sea (Thien Hau) is on the other side.

Can Tho University

This small university was founded in 1966 and isn't really worth a stop unless you have nothing better to do.

Central Market

Just down the river on Hai Ba Trung street from ths statue of Ho, is a busy, cluttered market lined by numerous food stalls.

The Villages Surrounding Can Tho   ★★★

These are the real attractions of the city, and if you can get a guide with relatives in the area, the US$20 expense will be more than worth it. All along the main highway to Long Xuyen, are rutted paths that lead deep into the delta's heartland. Small villages line the canals and motorized and oar-propelled boats navigate the sometimes dangerously shallow canals with amazing ingenuity. The best reason for the guide is the opportunity to be invited into his relatives' homes for meals and Vietnamese whiskey, whose distillers have no qualms of beginning their imbibing as early as 10 in the morning. In many of these areas, villagers have never set eyes on foreigners, and wherever you stop you'll be surrounded by dozens of children and women offering coconut milk. If you can go by boat it's better, especially one that can be arranged through a relative of your guide. In one day I had no fewer than five chickens slaughtered in my honor by families scattered along the banks of the canals. I was shown grave sites of family members killed by the VC during the war, as well as rich, vast parcels of deep black, rich soil covered with fruit and eucalyptus trees. If you must make the journey along the canals yourself, there are boats for hire in Can Tho that usually rent for around US$2 an hour. They can be found along the river front. You won't have to look hard.

WHERE TO STAY IN CAN THO

Hotel Song Huong

101 Nguyen Trai; ☎ *25074* • *12 rooms.* US$10–12 for rooms with double or multiple beds. US$6 for a small room with a fan. Restaurant, private toilet. Foreigners accepted and management are quite proficient in English. Inexpensive. ***Reservations: Direct***

Tay Ho Hotel

36 Hai Ba Trung Street; ☎ *23392* • *12 rooms.* US$7. Rooms have two beds with fan and private bath. Foreigners encouraged. Next door is the Mekong Restaurant.Great Vietnamese cuisine at shamefully low prices. Inexpensive. ***Reservations: Direct***

Tay Do Hotel

61 Chau Van Liem Street; ☎ *21009* • *27 rooms (14 double, 13 single).* US$4–5. This place seemed active with French and German backpackers. Private bath with the doubles, public toilet for the singles. Fan in all rooms. Inexpensive. ***Reservations: Direct***

Phong Nha Hotel

75 Chau Van Liem (Nguyen An Ninh Old); ☎ *21615* • *24 rooms.* US$4–5. Singles and doubles both have private baths. Reception friendly. For the price, it's well furnished. Worth the price. Inexpensive. ***Reservations: Direct***

Hotel Phong Phu

79 Chau Van Liem; ☎ *20149* • *14 rooms.* US$4–5. One of the best bargains in town for the price. Private rooms with bath. No hot water, of course, but hot water in Vietnam is for tea, not bathing in. Electric fan. Currently the hotel is adding more rooms and adding air conditioning. Inexpensive. ***Reservations: Direct.***

Viet Hong Hotel

55 Phan Dinh Phung Street; ☎ *25831* • *68 rooms.* US$8–12. Here's another bargain. 54 of the rooms have electric fans; the balance have air conditioning. Restaurant. The hotel provides tourist services from Can Tho Tourism. They'll also book flights to Phu Quoc Island, which leave on Mondays. For foreigners the cost is US$30 (the cost from Can Tho to Saigon to Can Tho is the same) Inexpensive. ***Reservations: Direct.***

Khach San Khai

83 Chau Van Lien • At presstime, this place wasn't accepting foreigners, although I expect that to change in the coming months. I don't know if it'll help their business any, though.. ***Reservations: About staying here, I'd have some.***

Hotel Hoa Binh
5 Hoa Binh Street. ☎ *20530, 20536* • *22 rooms.* US$6–18. The single rooms at six bucks aren't much, but there is a fan. Rooms with three beds can be had for US$11, and non-air-conditioned doubles for US$8. Check around here at the different rooms. There are a lot of configurations. For instance, 13 of the rooms offer only a public toilette. There is air conditioning offered in nine of the twin bed rooms, which run US$18. Foreigners are welcome and the price includes breakfast. Inexpensive–Moderate.   ***Reservations: Direct***

Hao Hoa Hotel
8 Hai Thuong Lang Ong Street • I know nothing of this place other than they've had problems accepting foreigners in the past.

International Hotel
12 Hai Ba Trung Street; ☎ *35973* • US$25–40. This is the classiest place in Can Tho without a doubt. You might even be tempted to say that it's up to international standards which, in my opinion, it is. Its well-maintained, modern exterior and interior stand out like a diamond amid the typically Vietnamese environment surrounding it. Right on the waterfront. Air conditioning, restaurant, friendly service. Moderate.   ***Reservations: Direct.***

Hau Giang Hotel
34 Nam Ky Khoi Nghia Street (Can Tho center city); ☎ *21851, 21806* • *35 rooms.* US$23–36. Nicely appointed and friendly staff who know English well. Rooms have private bath, air conditioning, refrigerator, telephone (IDD in the lobby), radio cassette and TV. Hot and cold water systems. Photocopy services, foreign exchange services, car rental service and river tours to orchid-covered islands. Air-conditioned restaurant with 200 seats; Vietnamese, Asian, seafood, Chinese and European dishes. Open from 6 a.m. to 11 p.m. 7 days. Price includes both breakfast and lunch. Dancing hall and karaoke room. Moderate.   ***Reservations: Direct***

WHERE TO EAT IN CAN THO

Restaurant Can Tho
52 Nguyen Trai Street. ☎ *22186* • Vietnamese, Asian, Chinese.

Restaurant Can Tho
27 Chau Van Liem Street • Vietnamese, Chinese, European. Romantic setting, nice ambiance.

Restaurant Hoang Huy
65 Phan Dinh Phuong, 1st floor • Vietnamese.

Restaurant Rain-Bow
54 Nam Ky Kitui Nghia • Vietnamese, Asian.

A Chau Restaurant
> *91 Chau Van Liem Street.* ☎ *22129, 22130* • Vietnamese, Asian. Prepare for your meal to be served quickly.

Vin Loi Restaurant
> *42 Hai Ba Trung Street* • Soups are the tastiest here. The Vietnamese cuisine is both delicious and cheap as hell.

DIRECTORY

CAN THO POLICE DEPT
☎ *270281.*

FIRE DEPARTMENT
☎ *20170* (An Hoi Quarter, ☎ *21286*).

POST OFFICE
25 Hoa Binh Street.

EMERGENCY MEDICAL SERVICES (EMS)
213 Hoa Binh; ☎ *6l: 24644, 24244.*

CAN THO TOURIST CO. (HEADQUARTERS)
27 Chau Van Liem Street, ☎ *21804,21853; FAX: 84.71.22719.*

CAN THO SERVICE CENTER
18 Hai Ba Trung Street, ☎ *21852; FAX: 84.71.22719*
(In Ho Chi Minh City) *01 Nguyen Tat Thanh Street-4th District,* ☎ *291053.*

THOT NOT (CAN THO SUBDISTRICT)

There's not much here, unless you're moving at night east to Can Tho (about 40 km away) and are extremely tired and want to spend the night at one of the cheapest hotels in Vietnam. The one attraction in this area is **Tan Lap Island**, another area *very rarely* seen by foreigners. You can hire a boat in Thot Not and cross the Hau River for a visit to the orchid-covered island.

WHERE TO STAY AND EAT IN THOT NOT

Thot Not Hotel
> *No address, across the bustling main drag from Thanh Binh Restaurant;* ☎ *51309* • *10 rooms.* US$2.50–3. This lies on a busy main street lined with cafes, food stalls and small restaurants. The hotel itself is a converted office building that's dirty and musty and sees few foreign travelers. The rooms are relatively clean, but if you've gotten a room with two single beds attached, don't move them apart. The floor will reveal a putrid display of dead cockroaches, rat excrement and used condoms. The public toilet is abhorrent. Don't use it unless you've got a good, high pair of trout fisherman's boots. The water in the

showers is like grape vinegar. The manager, though, is eager for business, and is eager to please Westerners, especially Americans. Very inexpensive. **Reservations: Direct**

There are numerous food stalls up and down the "strip" in Thot Not with surprisingly great sea and river food. Most of the proprietors are relatively old and speak both French and English—i.e. they fought or were associated with the South Vietnamese/American efforts to win the Vietnam War. They'll want to practice their English with you and will often trade conversation for libations, and even food. You can have a night on the town here without even having a town to have a night with.

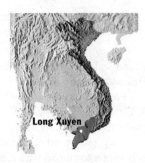

LONG XUYEN

LONG XUYEN IN A CAPSULE

Capital of An Giang Province...A grimy city...But marvelous scenery on the other side of the river...The Hoa Hao sect was once very powerful here and had its own army based here...Home to the Hoa Hao University.

Long Xuyen (about 182 km southwest from Saigon) is the capital of An Giang Province with a population of about 100,000 situated on the west bank of the Bassac River. It's a rather shabby city, as are many in the delta, and seems virtually indistinguishable from Can Tho save for the riverside parks and cafes, of which I couldn't find any in Long Xuyen. It was once a major area of the Hoa Hao sect, an interesting religion without temples nor priests that act as the bond between man and God. But the Hoa Hao people were extremely influential in the area and even possessed their own surprisingly strong and disciplined military force. Today the city is the home of the Hoa Hao University, which was founded in 1970.

My impressions of the provincial capital were redundant with some of the other city centers of the delta: bustling markets, shabby hotels, a confusing river transportation system that takes a lot of asking around of numerous people to get pointed in the right direction, and small temples and pagodas that are only really worth seeing if you haven't seen some finer examples in other areas of the delta.

There's not a lot to see and do here, and perhaps its greatest attractions are the locations on the other side of the river, many of which have not been seen by foreigners (see next INSIDER TIP).

WHAT TO SEE AND DO IN LONG XUYEN

Tong Duc Thang Museum

This museum features some fine architectural findings from the Oc Ceo.

Dinh Than My Phuoc Pagoda

Le Minh Nguy On Street, near the intersection of Huynh Thi Huong Street. There's an impressive roof here and the walls near the altar are covered with murals. Worth a quick stop.

Quan Thanh Pagoda

8 Le Minh Nguy On Street. This isn't far from Dinh Than My Phuoc Pagoda and is probably more worth the visit. The entrance wall is covered by beautiful murals, and the altar features a figure of Mandarin General Quan Cong as well as other Mandarin leaders including Quan Binh and General Chau Xuong.

Cao Dai Church

Near the end of Long Xuyen toward Chau Doc on Tran Hung Dao street is a small Cao Dai temple that, again, is really only worth a visit if you haven't already been to Tay Ninh.

Long Xuyen Catholic Church

This is a huge Catholic church in the center of the triangle formed by Nguyen Hue A, Tran Hung Dao and Nung Vuong Streets that's an easy landmark in the city and can be seen from several km from outside Long Xuyen. It was finished just prior to reunification of the country in 1975. There'a a 50-meter high bell tower and two giant hands clasped together form the spire of the church. This church is reputedly one of the biggest in the delta, if indeed not the largest. Masses are conducted here quite early in the morning (around 4:30 a.m.) and in the evening from 6 to 7 daily. On Sunday, there are three masses.

Protestant Church of Long Xuyen

At *4 Hung Vuong Street.* This is much smaller than its Catholic cousin close by and is only really worth a visit unless you have some guilt pangs passing it by. Services are held every Sunday.

Cho Moi ★

This is the verdant agricultural district on the other side of the Bassac River reached by ferry from the ferry terminal at the base of Nguyen Hue Street. It features bountiful tropical fruit groves of mango, banana, jackfruit, guava, durian and longan. It's worth a few hours' visit.

My Hoa Hung Memorial House

(See the following INSIDER TIP)

INSIDER TIP

Do you want to visit a fascinating island across the Basac River from Long Xuyen where giant, brilliant white flamingo-like storks arrive by the thousands each evening to munch on marijuana? Do it. As of my visit, according to both guides and the local villagers, no independent travelers had ever visited the My Hoa Hung Village, and this incredible sight of perhaps thousands of snow-white cranes getting trashed on pot. The island is also home to the My Hoa Hung Memorial House, which is where Ton Duc Thang, one of the most well known architects of Vietnamese communism and the Vietnamese labor movement lived from 1888-1906. The memorial house, across the road from Ton's magnificent tropical and eerie hardwood home, features photos of the Viet Minh's—and North Vietnam's—eventual leader at the usual state and formal functions. More interesting are the letters he wrote which are on display in glass cases, as well as his shoes, uniforms, suitcases, spectacles and other clothing items. The memorial house is visited seldomly, and the only Westerners to have seen the area (which have been very few indeed) have arrived via the fledgling Anziang Tourist Agency in Long Xuyen as part of small tour groups crossing the ferry at An Hoa.

The place was deserted when I got there. There is no admission fee, but small donations (say 2000 dong) are appreciated. As far as getting out there, forget the tourist agency. (They'll tell you that the storks don't feed on marijuana because it's illegal to grow or possess marijuana in Vietnam. I guess someone's gotta tell that to the storks.) Nothing's marked, so read carefully. If you're coming west from Can Tho continue to Long Xuyen via Lien Tinh Street. Go around the first round-about in Long Xuyen and continue straight on Lien Tinh. At this point stop and ask someone where Binh Duc Bridge is (it's located along the same route, but you'll need to know EXACTLY where it is!). Just before reaching Binh Duc Bridge, at the last possible meter, there will be a dirt turnoff to the right. Keep going on this path, which flanks the Dra On canal, for about 500 meters to an extremely small ferry landing.

On the other side (only bicycles and motorcycles permitted on the ferry) of the river, you'll pass through My Hoa Hung village. You'll then see a bridge off to the right after about 3 km. Make a right over the bridge. The Memory House isn't much farther. Plan your visit to see the stoned storks between 5 and 6 p.m. The ferry to My Hoa Hung village is 700 dong; tack on another 600 dong for a bicycle, or 800 dong for a motorbike. Instead of returning the way you came, continue straight along the dirt road to the An Hoa ferry which runs across the river into downtown Long Xuyen.

WHERE TO STAY IN LONG XUYEN

Long Xuyen Hotel

17 Nguyen Van Cung Street. ☎ *52927* • *37 Rooms.* US$10–20. Newly renovated, at least to an extent, within the last year. Hot water, air conditioning. Cheaper rooms have a fan, no air conditioning. It's run by Angiang Tourism. Moderate. ***Reservations: Direct***

Cuu Long (also called The Mekong Hotel)

21 Nguyen Van Cung Street. ☎ *52365* • *24 rooms.* About US$20. Huge rooms here with private bath. Perhaps the best hotel in town. Hot water, air conditioning. Restaurant. Moderate.

Reservations: Direct

Tien Thanh Hotel

240 Tran Hung Dao Street. • On the road east to Can Tho, several km out of town. Haven't stayed here, so I can't say much about it. Inexpensive. ***Reservations: Direct***

Thai Binh

12 Nguyen Hue Street. ☎ *52184* • *24 rooms.* US$6–12. A good value for the price. The more expensive rooms have air conditioning. Restaurant. Public and private toilet. Inexpensive. ***Reservations: Direct***

Xuan Phuong Hotel

68 Nguyen Trai Street. ☎ *52041* • US$10–15. This is also not a bad deal. It's a clean hotel, and the more expensive rooms can accommodate four people. Air conditioning. Inexpensive–moderate.

Reservations: Direct.

Song Hau

243 Nguyen Luong Duyet Street. ☎ *52308* • 26 rooms. US$6–10. The cheaper rooms come with fan, while there's air conditioning in the others. Inexpensive. ***Reservations: Direct***

WHERE TO EAT IN LONG XUYEN

As in other Mekong Delta destinations, food stalls abound in Long Xuyen, and they're understandably the cheapest places to eat. Most of the small restaurant/cafes can be found along Hai Ba Trung Street, as can the **Long Xuyen Restaurant**, perhaps the best eatery in town, on Hai Ba Trung and Nguyen Trai Streets. Cuisine is Vietnamese, Chinese, and European.

DIRECTORY

TRANSPORTATION

Long Xuyen is about 65 km from Can Tho and 126 km from My Tho. The distance to HCMC is about 190 km. **Buses** leave from Saigon's Mien Tay Bus Station. The express bus to HCMC leaves Long Xuyn at 4 a.m. every day. The Long Xuyen bus station is about 1.5 km east of town on Tran Hung Dao Street, not far from the Catholic cathedral. The ride to Saigon takes about 7 hours along generally good roads. Bus connections from Long Xuyen can also be made to Can Tho, Vinh Long, Chau Doc,

Rach Gia. It's important to note there are other bus stations around town that can provide more comfortable express bus service to HCMC. An express microbus leaves from near the GPO about 2 a.m. There's also a tourist express bus service at *93 Nguyen Trai Street* to HCMC at 4 a.m. each day. It can be confusing to figure out what the best situation is for your own needs, so ask the folks at **Angiang Tourist Office** (*6 Ngo Gia Tu Street*). There are a few private bus companies that offer faster and more comfortable solutions to your transportation needs. Transportation around town is generally via the type of **"cyclo"** which is unique to this part of Vietnam. They are in effect wagons that are pulled by either motorcycle or bicycle. They are the easiest way to get around town.

POST OFFICE

101 Tran Hung Dao Street.

BANKS AND MONEYCHANGERS

Vietcom Bank is located *1 Hung Vuong* near the intersection of Hung Vuong and Nguyen Thi Minh Khai Streets. Money can also be changed at reasonable rates at gold and jewelry shps about town, usually about 10,700 dong to the dollar. Many hotels, if the they do change money, tend render 10,000 dong per dollar.

TOURIST OFFICE

Angiang Tourist Office is at *6 Ngo Gia Tu Street.* ☎ *52036.*

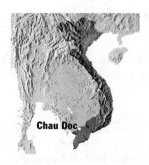

CHAU DOC

CHAU DOC IN A CAPSULE

300 km from Saigon, 150 km from Vinh Long...Chau Doc is a part of An Giang Province near the Cambodian border...There are many ranges of spectacular mountains, beautiful landscapes and a lot of historical relics...Mount Sam...Ba Chua Xu Temple...Yay An Pagoda...Thoai Ngoc Hau Mausoleum.Breeding fish rafts on the rivers.

As is Can Tho, Chau Doc (population about 80,000), is a relatively attractive and clean city for the Mekong Delta and a major commercial center in the western delta—it attracts a lot of French, Vietnamese and particularly Chinese, Taiwanese and Hong Kong tourists. It sits on the west bank of the Bassac River near the Cambodian border and possesses perhaps both the largest Khmer and Cham populations in Vietnam. Until the middle of the 18th century, Chau Doc was under Cambodian rule but was ceded to Nguyen Lord Nguyen Phuc Khoat after his help in suppressing an uprising in the area. You'll notice that many of the women here, rather than the traditional Vietnamese conical hats, wear Khmer scarves on their heads. The area is also home to the Hoa Hao religion, which was founded by Huynh Phu So in 1939 and claims more than a million members, most of whom live in the Chau Doc region.

An interesting and curious feature of Chau Doc are the floating houses in the river. They're not built on stilts, but rather float directly on the river. Fish are raised in nets under the houses and are fed whatever the owners want to feed them. Of course, raising fish this way makes them easier to catch. And, perhaps of greater benefit, fishermen don't have to drop explosives into the river to reap their bounty.

WHAT TO SEE AND DO IN CHAU DOC AND ENVIRONS

Chau Doc Church

459 Lien Tinh Lo 10. This is a tiny church that really isn't worth a stop unless, of course, you're Catholic and it's Sunday at 7 a.m.

Chau Doc Market

This large market stretches along the riverfront on Chi Lang, Le Cong Thanh Doc, Bang Dang and Phu Thu Streets. In addition to an array of fresh produce, you can also find an abundance of goods smuggled into Chau Doc from Thailand via Cambodia.

Chau Phu Temple

Gia Long and Boa Ho Thoai Streets. This temple was erected in the mid 1920s in honor of Thoai Ngoc Hau. There are both Vietnamese and Chinese influences here, and funeral markers commemorating deceased dignitaries.

Chau Giang Mosque

Take the ferry from the Chau Giang ferry terminal and proceed about 25 meters before taking a left and going another 50 meters. This attractive mosque features a large dome and arches and is where Chau Doc's Cham Islamic population comes to worship.

Sam Mountain

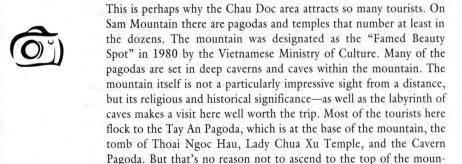

This is perhaps why the Chau Doc area attracts so many tourists. On Sam Mountain there are pagodas and temples that number at least in the dozens. The mountain was designated as the "Famed Beauty Spot" in 1980 by the Vietnamese Ministry of Culture. Many of the pagodas are set in deep caverns and caves within the mountain. The mountain itself is not a particularly impressive sight from a distance, but its religious and historical significance—as well as the labyrinth of caves makes a visit here well worth the trip. Most of the tourists here flock to the Tay An Pagoda, which is at the base of the mountain, the tomb of Thoai Ngoc Hau, Lady Chua Xu Temple, and the Cavern Pagoda. But that's no reason not to ascend to the top of the mountain, where vistas of the vast countryside give testimony to the area's agricultural bountifulness.

Tay An Pagoda

Here there are hundreds of wooden carvings of religious figures. There are both Islamic and Hindu elements in the architecture of the pagoda, which was built in the mid 1800s. It was rebuilt in 1958. Tombs of various monks surround the temple, and close to the temple is the statue of Quan Am Thi Kinh (the Guardian Spirit of Mother and Child). Carvings of dragons and lions can be seen above the bi-level roof of Tay An Pagoda as they fight for possession of lotus blossoms, pearls and apricot trees. There's also a statue in front of the pagoda of a black elephant with two tusks and another, a white elephant with six tusks.

The Tomb of Thoai Ngoc Hau

Thoai was once a powerful Nguyen lord who served the Nguyen Dynasty. He ordered that his own tomb be built at the base of Sam Mountain and isn't far from Tay An Pagoda. The steps leading to the platform where the tomb is (and those of his two wives) are made of red stone imported from the eastern and southern portions of Vietnam. There are other less impressive tombs in the area of some of the men who served under Thoai Ngoc Hau.

Temple of Lady Chau Xu

This inauspicious temple faces Sam Mountain and is also not far from both the tomb of Thoai Ngoc Hau and Tay An Pagoda. It was built in the early 19th centruy from bamboo and shrubbery but was later reconstructed in the 1970s. Legend has it that the statue of Lady Chau Xu, which now stands at the base of Sam Mountain, was originally at the peak of the hill, but was brought on its way back to Thailand by Siamese warriors in the early part of the 19th century. But they never made it. It was so burdensome, they dumped it by the side of some path. Local villagers then brought the statue back to their town to build a temple for the statue. A young woman in the village, who pronounced herself Lady Chau Xu, instructed 40 virgins to bring the statue down to the base of the hill. After they reached the plain, the statue became too heavy for the women as well, and it was believed by the locals that because the women had stopped carrying the statue out of pure exhaustion, that this was the site where Lady Chau Xu had chosen for a temple to be constructed around it. And that's where it remains today. There's an important festival surrounding the temple from the 23rd to the 26th of each lunar month.

Cavern Pagoda ★

The upper section of this pagoda, which lies about a third to halfway up the western slope of Sam Mountain, is comprised of two areas: the main sanctuary, where there are statues of Thich Ca Buddha and A Di Da (Buddha of the past). In the back of the cave is a shrine dedicated to the Goddess of Mercy (Quan The Am Bo Tat). The lower area of the pagoda houses the pagoda's monks and also contains two tombs where Thich Hue Then and a lady named Le Thi Tho are buried.

WHERE TO STAY IN CHAU DOC

Hang Chau Hotel ★

On the river on Le Loi Street near the ferry terminal. ☎ *66196* • US$20–25. This is the best and most expensive hotel in Chau Doc. There's a swimming pool, restaurant and a busy night club. All the rooms come with air conditioning. The more expensive rooms have a great view of the river. Moderate. ***Reservations: Direct***

Thai Binh Hotel

37 Nguyen Van Thoai Street. ☎ *66221 • 15 rooms.* Foreigners were previously not allowed to stay here, but this may change by the time you read this.

Hotel 777

47 Doc Phu Thu Street. ☎ *66409 •* US$6. This a small hotel popular with backpackers. Very Inexpensive.   ***Reservations: Direct***

My Loc Hotel

51 Nguyen Van Thoai Street. ☎ *66455 • 20 rooms.* About US$10–15.Double rooms with ceiling fans. Some of the rooms have air conditioning. The more expensive rooms sleep up to four guests. Moderate.   ***Reservations: Direct***

Chau Doc Hotel

17 Doc Phu Thu Street. ☎ *66484 • 42 rooms.* About US$6–10. Dismal but appropriate enough for backpackers, who seem to fill the place. Very Inexpensive.   ***Reservations: Direct***

Nha Khach 44

44 Doc Phu Thu Street. ☎ *66540 •* About US$6.Another popular backpacker's stop. There are doubles and triples here. Inexpensive.
                                                       Reservations: Direct

WHERE TO EAT IN CHAU DOC

The best place undoubtedly is the restaurant at the **Hang Chau Hotel**. There's live entertainment offered here. There's also the **Tourist Restaurant** at the corner of Doc Phu Thu and Phan Ding Phung Streets. Also try **Lam Hung Ky** (*71 Chi Lang Street*).

The cheapest places to eat are at the food stalls that are in and surrounding the Chau Doc market. The river-caught fish is particularly tasty.

DIRECTORY

TRANSPORTATION

Chau Doc is about 245 km from HCMC, 118 km from Can Tho, 180 from My Tho, and 96 from Ha Tien. The Chau Doc bus station is on the southeast side of the city on the south side of Le Loi Street, about 1.5 km out of town. Buses to Saigon take about 7 hours and arrive at HCMC's Mien Tay bus station. There is supposedly an express bus that leaves for HCMC from in front of Chau Doc Hotel. Buses to Long Xuyen take about 2 hours. There are also connections to other destinations in the delta area, but remember, there is no direct road from Chau Doc to Ha Tien. You'll have to go east nearly to Can Tho before Highway 1A heads south to Rach Gia. Ferries to Saigon often take over 24 hours and leave daily from the wharf at Ton Duc Thang Street (about US$1.20). Ferries, I am told, also ply their way down a series of canals to Ha Tien. Buses to Chau Doc leave from HCMC's Mien Tay station. The principal form of transport around Chau Doc is by motorized cyclo.

POST OFFICE

On the corner of Bao Ho Thoai Street opposite Chau Phu Pagoda. ☎ *94550.*

RACH GIA

RACH GIA IN CAPSULE

Unattractive coastal city on the Gulf of Thailand...But the seafood is great...Considered to be in one of the most, if not the most, prosperous province in Vietnam...One of the two gateways to Phu Quoc Island...Large numbers of ethnic Khmer and Chinese live here.

Rach Gia, the capital of Kien Giang Province with a population approaching 125,000 people, is a major port city on the Gulf of Thailand at the very bottom of Highway 1A. The flies here outnumber the residents by about five to one (and the prostitutes outnumber the flies). Yet despite its appearance, it's considered to be the center of Vietnam's most prosperous province. Many of the hotels allow prostitutes into guests' rooms, and it is very unlikely one, or perhaps more, won't knock on your door after you've checked into your hotel, some of which are the cheapest in all of Vietnam (both the hotels and the hookers). You'll frequently see men about town with large red circles on their backs and chests. This usually means they've recently been in the company of a hooker, who will perform a flaming alcohol massage by placing the bases of hot glasses on your skin in addition to employing their more traditional sexual duties.

The population contains a large number of ethnic Chinese and Khmers. This is one of the oldest population centers in the Mekong Delta, so some pagodas and temples that can be found are relatively old (if you consider the 18th and 19th centuries relatively old). The city center itself lies on an island between two branches of the Cai Lan River. This is where you'll find most of the hotels, restaurants and shops. Rach Gia is also one of two ports with ferries bound for Phu Quoc Island (Ha Tien being the other).

Rach Gia is a delta boom town—with many goods entering Vietnam here from Thailand and other points in Southeast Asia (many of them smuggled)—and is expected to become even more prosperous in the future as the Vietnamese government continues to loosen its economy.

> ### INSIDER TIP
>
> *The ferry from Rach Gia to Phu Quoc Island (about a 9 hour ride), although it is supposed to leave at about 9 a.m. and around 10 p.m., usually leaves when it is filled with passengers. The round trip costs approximately US$8 (about 80,000 dong) and you can bring a bicycle or motorcycle aboard the ferry for an added surcharge (for a motorcycle, 80,000 dong round-trip). Warning: If you are traveling in this part of the Mekong Delta by motorcycle and want to bring the machine with you out to Phu Quoc Island, only depart from Rach Gia, and not from Ha Tien (which is much closer to the island with lower fares to match). The boat trip to the island from Ha Tien is aboard a much smaller craft, and even the locals consider the ride a dangerous one. Do not bring a motorcycle from Ha Tien to Phu Quoc by ferry. If you plan on bringing your bike to Phu Quoc, you won't be able to go with it. It will leave on the night ferry. You yourself will then be required to leave by the ferry the next morning. The gamble's yours.*

Despite being directly on the Gulf of Thailand coast, there are no beaches in Rach Gia. There's a dirt road (Than Hung Dao Street) that leads from the harbor to a small waterside "park" called Hoa Bien Park, which is nothing more than a big dirt patch where you can rent a chair, watch the sea, drink beer (there are a couple of food stalls here) and swat away at the flies.

WHAT TO SEE AND DO IN RACH GIA AND ENVIRONS

Phat Lon Pagoda

Just off Quang Trung Street. The name means Big Buddha. It's a big Khmer Hinayana Buddhist temple that features figures of the historical buddha Sakyamuni. Eight small altars are scattered around the exterior of the pagoda. You'll see two curious-looking towers that are used to cremate dead monks. Tombs of other monks surround the temple. The pagoda was constructed 200 years ago. Although the monks that live here at the pagoda are ethnic Khmer, you'll also see ethnic Chinese worshipers. Prayers are held in the wee hours of the morning and in the early evening.

Nguyen Trung Truc Temple

18 Nguyen Cong Tru Street. Nguyen Trung Truc was the fellow who led the Vietnamese resistance forces against the French colonists in the mid 1800s. He was responsible, at least for the most part, in the destruction of the French warship Espérance, after which he fled to Phu Quoc Island and eluded French capture for a number of years. This infuriated the French so much that they kidnapped his family and took hostage a number of other civilians in 1868. Nguyen gave himself up to the French authorities and then was executed in the Rach Gia marketplace in October of the same year.. Although the first temple bearing his name was primitive in structure it has been rebuilt a number of times over the years. On the altar in the main hall is a portrait of Ngyuen.

Pho Minh Pagoda

At the corner of Nguyen Van Cu and Co Bac Streets. There's a Thai-style Sakyamuni buddha here that was a gift to the Pagoda by Thai buddhists in 1971. The small pagoda itself was built in 1967. Close by is the Thich Ca buddha in the Vietnamese style. There are nuns here that live behind the pagoda. Prayers are held at the practical hours of 3:30 in the morning and also at 6:30 in the evening.

Ong Bac De Pagoda

14 Nguyen Du Street. This pagoda has on its main altar a statue of Ong Bac De, a reincarnation of the Emperor of Jade. To the left of the statue is Ong Bon (the Guardian Spirit iof Happiness and Vitue), and to the right is the likeness of Quan Cong. The pagoda was built about a hundred years ago by Chinese living in Rach Gia.

Tam Bao Pagoda

The corner of Thich Thien An and Tran Phu Streets. Although rebuilt in the early 20th century, the pagoda was originally constucted in the early 1800s. The garden of sculpted trees and bushes depicting dragons and other creatures is quite beautiful. The pagoda is open from 6 a.m. to 8 p.m.

Rach Gia Museum

21 Nguyen Van Troi Street. Not a lot here.

Rach Gia Catholic Church

Vinh Thanh Van subdistrict, across the channel from the Vinh Than Van Market. This is an unimpressive Catholic church built of red bricks in 1918. It's worth a visit if you're Catholic and don't want to miss mass, which is conducted at 5 a.m. and 5 p.m. on weekdays and at 5 and 7 in the morning and 4 and 5 in the afternoon on Sundays.

Vinh Thanh Van Market

Sprawled along at Bach Dang, Thu Khoa Nghia and Trinh Hoai Streets. There's an imported products market close by between Pham Hong Thai and Hoang Hoa Tham Streets.

Oc Eo

Oc Eo is an ancient city near Vong. The village, about 10 km from Rach Gia, was in its prime during the 1st through 6th centuries and was a major commerce center when the area was ruled the empire of Funan. Many archeological discoveries have been made here with relics found representing ancient Malay, Thai, Indonesian and even Roman Empire artifacts. Many of these artifacts can be seen in

HCMC's History and Art Museum and the History Museum in Hanoi. There used to be travel restrictions to Oc Eo but, at the time of this writing, they have been lifted.

Soc Xoai

There is absolutely nothing to do in this small village about 16 km west of Rach Gia on the dilapidated, rutted and chokingly musty highway 9 to Ha Tien (about 90 km to the west) except make a pit stop at the Phuong Mai Cafe on the right side of the highway about halfway through town.

WHERE TO TO STAY IN RACH GIA

Ha Tro Dormitory

No addresss nor phone, but it's located right at the wharf on the gulf where the ferries leave for Phu Quoc Island. This may be the best deal in town at US$3 for a double room with fan. Popular with Dutch and French tourists I was told, although the only Westerner I saw was Clint Eastwood on a nearby video screen. Fan; no hot water. Public toilet and shower; the water seemed a little dirty and was another reason it's best to visit this part of the world with a crew cut. But if you're going to take the ferry, this is a good place to be, because there really isn't a schedule out to the island. Some leave at 9 at night. Others early in the morning. Stay at this hotel and you'll know at a moment's notice. And you can't beat the price. I stayed in only one hotel in the Mekong Delta that was cheaper. Here is also the Caphe Hung (it closes early) for libation and the Xuat Hai Restaurant next door. Very Inexpensive. ***Reservations: Direct***

Nha Kach 77.77

77.77 Tran Phu Street. ☎ *63375* • Not much here. Dumpy rooms with public water closest. Inexpensive. ***Reservations: Direct***

1-5 Hotel (Khach San 1-5)

38 Nguyen Hung Son Street; ☎ *62103* • US$5–15. The biggest problem in what seems to be a nicely decorated hotel is that I couldn't find anyone who could speak English. Rooms have air conditioning, telephone. There's a large parking area if you've come by car. Restaurant with European and Asian dishes. The manager was able to somehow explain that both the receptionists and waitresses were "young." Whether this was for my benefit or yours, I couldn't tell. The business card says the waitresses are "warn careful." Hmmm. Sounds like a government SIDA (AIDS) brochure. Souvenir shop, tourist cars, barber and beauty shop. Massage available. Inexpensive–Moderate.
Reservations: Direct

Hoa Binh Hotel

5A Minh Mang Street; ☎ *63115* • US$3.50. Another cheapie popular with the backpacker set. There are double rooms with a private bath and single rooms with no air conditioning nor hot water. Bargain basement. Very inexpensive. ***Reservations: Direct***

WHERE TO EAT IN RACH GIA

Thien Nga

4A Le Loi Street • Vietnamese, Asian, and some hybrid European food. Cheap.

Rach Gia Restaurant

Intersection of Ly Tu Trong and Tran Hung Dao Streets on the water • Delicious seafood.

Hai Van Restaurant

Khu 16 ha. ☎ *6305* • On the rutted dirt road leading to Hoa Bien Park near the harbor. Shrimp, lobster, squid, frog, chicken and fish. Overlooks the water.

In addition, there are numerous food stalls all across the city.

DIRECTORY

TRANSPORTATION

Rach Gia is about 250 km from Saigon, 115 km from Can Tho, 180 km from My Tho and 90 km fro Ha Tien. The bus station is on Trung Truc Street south of town. Buses leave regularly for Saigon's Mien Tay station when full. The trip takes about 8 hours. Express buses leave for HCMC from *33/40 Thang 4* street. There are also buses to Can Tho, Long Xuyen, Ha Tien. Buses to other local areas including Soc Xoai, Tan Hiep, Vinh Thuan, Tri Ton, Duong Xuong, Hong Chong, Go Quao and Giong Rieng usually leave the station very early in the morning, between 4 and 5 a.m. Buses leave Saigon's Mien Tay station for Rach Gia regularly. At present there is no air service into Rach Gia. Cyclos are best way to get around town.

POST OFFICE

The general Post office is on Tu Duc Street, near the corner of 207 and Duy Tan Streets.

TOURIST OFFICE

Kien Giang Tourism is at *12 Ly Tu Trong Street.*

BANKS AND MONEYCHANGERS

Vietcom Bank is next to the post office at *2 Duy Tan Street.*

HA TIEN

HA TIEN IN A CAPSULE

The southwesternmost town in Vietnam...Sits on the Cambodian border...The road leading to the city is in dismal shape...The springboard to Phu Quoc Island...The sight of mass killings by Cambodia's Khmer Rouge in the late 1970s...Has perhaps the most intriguing history of any area in Vietnam...Was once the best link for sea traffic crossing the South China Sea for India.

Situated in the far southwestern corner of Vietnam on the Cambodian border, Ha Tien, with a population of about 90–100,000) is a seaside anomoly, a mish mash of Khmer, Chinese and Vietnamese (many from the north and other sections of the Mekong Delta working to construct something reminiscent of roads along the dilapidated dirt paths that connect Ha Tien with the rest of the Mekong Delta.(Most of the road workers say that the roadwork will be completed by the end of 1994 and that they expect to return to their home towns; don't count on it. Completing the paving of roadways in the southern Mekong will take at least two years in my opinion. These workers' assignments in the Rach Gia/Ha Tien area are going to take a damn long time.

Although most tourists use Ha Tien as a springboard to nearby Phu Quoc Island, the city of Ha Tien has perhaps the most interesting history of all the regions of southern Vietnam. In 1671, a young Cantonese named Mac Cuu left Fukien Province at the age of 17 for the capital of Cambodia, Oudong. There, he impressed the current Cambodian monarch King Chey Chettha IV so much, that he was indoctrinated into royal service. He was an aggressive individual capable of attracting vast commerce and exploiting the far away, completely undeveloped reaches of Cambodia. Most of his efforts were in the far southeastern edge of Cambodia in the Ha Tien area, the southern coast of the Cambodian state. Through his vast successes in developing agriculture in the region, the King granted him governorship (Oc Nha) of the region.

Soon, the area that is currently known as Ha Tien became a huge commercial success. Chinese settlers were offered free land. Agriculture flourished in the region, as did the trade in fishing and the distribution of agricultural tools.

Soon, Mac Cuu's "kingdom" without defined borders took on a more formal state-like structure. It became an essentially autonomous state maintaining a precarious existance between neighboring Cambodia, Thailand and Vietnam.

Because of Ha Tien's location as Cambodia's only important port of entry (and the best harbor on Indochina's western peninsula), it attracted the Siamese, who invaded the area in 1708 and essentially ruined the area's prosperity. (Ha Tien had become the strongest link for sea traffic traversing the South China Sea from India.)

Mac Cuu understood that the only way to maintain his "kingdom" was to enlist the aid of more powerful neighbors. So, in 1708, he sent a delegation to the then Vietnamese capital of Hue for a visit with Minh Vuong, southern Vietnam's leader at the time and one of the Nguyen Dynasty's most effective and dynamic Lords, chiefly responsible for expanding Vietnam's empire in the south. Minh liked the idea of essentially annexing territory from the Siamese and Cambodians at virtually no expense without concessions.

When the Siamese invaded the Ha Tien area a short time later, Vietnamese forces quickly drove the aggressors away. Ha Tien was then transformed from a colony of refugees to a full-fledged state, and it once again regained its prosperity, this time as a southern Vietnamese political state on the southern coast, that remarkably retained a separate identity, even as a province of the Nguyen empire.

Ma Cuu died at 80 in 1735 and is today considered the father of the southern peninsula. His grave, along with those of his family, is located outside the city center and are ornately looked after by the descendents of his family.

Prince Mac Tu Kham, the seventh generation of the family of Ma Cuu, was the last Vietnamese ruler of province—until 1857, when the French decided to annex Ha Tien with the rest of the Mekong Delta. Under French control, pepper plantations were established, but little was done to improve the lives of the region's people.

Much of the recent history of Ha Tien surrounds Khmer Rouge military raids of the city during the savage Cambodian leader Pol

Pot's reign of terror, where hundreds of Vietnamese men, women and children were slaughtered by unspeakable means by Khmer Rouge guerrillas. The graves of the Vietnamese victims are scattered at different sites across the town and, by chance, I came across a remote site near the memorial tomb of Ma Cuu, where a sweat-soaked lone man surrounded by a score of children was digging into the clay-like earth beside a dirt path. At first I thought he might be digging a latrine or well. I stopped and found out that he was exhuming the remains of his mother and three sisters who had been buried at the site in a single plastic bag 15 years earlier. It is customary for the inhabitants of Ha Tien who had relatives murdered by the Cambodians to exhume the remains of their relatives and have the remains burned and then sealed in a large lacquer pot. I watched in near horror as the man dug and picked his way through four feet of earth, finally reaching a tattered black plastic bag, which he then unceremoniously pulled from the ground as if he were simply removing the roots of a tree. Opening the bag, he sifted through the bones and the still intact clothing his relatives had been wearing the day they were executed. The children, he told me, had been ripped apart alive limb by limb by the guerillas' own hands. On a decayed, crumbling finger of his mother, he pulled off a gold ring, stained brown by the years of its clay earthen environment. The bones of the corpses had become part of the soil and he meticulously separated bone from the earth. The clothes of the woman and the children were then placed back into the grave and set on fire.

Ha Tien's topographical setting in the Mekong Delta is unlike the rest of the region, and might remind you to a degree of northern Vietnam's Ha Long Bay, with its huge rock formations and caves towering above the seascape.

You'll be disappointed to discover that Ha Tien is one of the more expensive areas to stay and eat in the Mekong Delta. Even Vietnamese nationals are overcharged in many places, and it isn't unusual to pay US$2.50 or so for a meal, about three times the rate you'll pay in most places in the delta. Hotels tend to be expensive because fresh water has to be hand carried to each establishment from the city's water tower. Throughout the city, one sees sun-withered men stoically hauling giant drums of fresh water on the back of dilapidated carts. Even in the few hotels that are marginally habitable, the water is often brown and silty, water that you'll eventually be required to bathe in if you decide to spend a few days here. Although it's expensive, I recommend bathing and brushing your teeth with bottled water only.

WHAT TO SEE AND DO IN HA TIEN AND ENVIRONS

Thach Dong

This is a massive, cavernous stone temple just a stone's throw from the Cambodian border, where you can watch farmers and other merchants pedal their wares through the border gate from a few locations high in the cave. It's an odd sight, because just on the Vietnamese side of the frontier, formations of Vietnamese police officers can be seen lined up in the style of 18th-century British combat techniques, training in the use of mortars, automatic rifles and small arms—all the weapons pointed toward Cambodia and the flat Khmer countryside (although, admittedly, I didn't see any rounds fired).

It was at Thach Dong where the Khmer Rouge massacred at least 130 people (some of the locals say the number was higher, 162 exactly). Chambers in the grotto feature altars to the Emperor of Jade (Ngoc Hoang) and the Goddess of Mercy (Quan The Am Bo Tat. Some of the more adventurous types might be tempted to make an ascent to the summit of the cave/mountain, but the only route is up a slippery, vertical tunnel which serves as the home to hundreds of bats and, consequently, their droppings. Don't try it.

Dong Ho

Granite hills surround this inlet from the Gulf of Thailand. It's just east of Ha Tien. The other side of the inlet is flanked by the To Chan hills.

Ha Tien Market

Right in the center of town, left after you cross the floating bridge. It's a bustling place that's worth noting mainly for the smuggled goods you can purchase there from Thailand and Cambodia. And it may be the only market south of HCMC where some of the goods (probably smuggled) can probably be had for cheaper than in Saigon.

Tam Bao Pagoda

328 Phuong Thanh Street. Mac Cuu founded this temple in 1730. A statue of the Goddess of Mercy (Quan The Am Bo Tat) can be found in front of the pagoda standing in the middle of a pond surrounded by lotus blossoms. The area surrounding the temple contains the tombs of 16 monks. The bronze statue of the Buddha of the Past (A Di Da Buddha) is inside the temple. Prayers are held in the morning and the afternoon.

Phu Dung Pagoda

Off Phuong Thanh Street. Founded just a short time after Tam Bao Pagoda by Mac Cuu's second wife, this temple features a statue of nine intricately carved dragons surrrounding the newly-born Siddhartha Gautama (Thich Ca Buddha). The bronze statue of the pagoda came from China and is encased in glass. There's hillside beside the pagoda where the tombs of Nguyen Thi Xuan and other monks are carved into the hillside. (Supposedly Mac Cuu was killed in battle in Thailand and is buried there, although some locals who claim to be of the 8th generation of the family say that his tomb is not in Thailand but on the hillside, as well. The history books indicate there are no longer any living descendents of Mac Cuu.) From the hillside you can look across the bay at the mountain the locals call the "Sleeping Elephant." (They must be smoking something.)

Behind the temple is a smaller structure, Dien Ngoc Hoang based on the Taoist Emperor of Jade. Figures beside the emperor include Nam Tao on the right (Taoist God of Happiness and of the Southern Polar Star) and Bac Dao (God of the Northern Polar Star and Longevity) on the left. It is in this area where other unmarked graves contain the victims of Khmer Rouge massacres in the area.

The Beaches of Ha Tien

Don't expect the crystal clear waters of Ca Na, Nha Trang or those found further down the Gulf of Thailand coast, but the water here is calm and extremely warm—hardly refreshing. Bai No Beach, one of the best, is about three km west of Ha Tien. It's clean, there's decent snorkeling and it usually isn't as crowded as Mui Nai Beach, which is about 3 km west of town. Mui Nai is usually where the tour microbuses stop for the afternoon after reaching Ha Tien from Saigon. The beach is small and the sand dark. Women are frequently seen here trying to peddle their recent crab catches. There are two restaurants here, the **Sea Star** and the Sao **Bien** (which also means Sea Star), which are in fact one and the same, but in two different structures. I was disappointed with this beach.

Phu Quoc Island

This is a verdant mountainous island with a population of about 50,000 about 45 km in the Gulf of Thailand west of Ha Tien. It's exquisite beaches are quite popular with French tourists (as is the balance of Vietnam). It's about 50 km long with an area of 576 sq. km to 1325 sq. km depending upon the source you get your info from (the former figure I feel is more accurate). It provides fantastic fishing for the locals and the water is clear and calm. It's great for swimming and snorkeling and features some of the finest coconut tree-lined beaches in Vietnam, especially in the southern portion of the island. The island lies only about 15 km off the Cambodian coast and, although there's a lot of nasty, verbose talk about sovereignty of the island, it seems that it will remain in Vietnamese control for some time. There are a few ways of getting there, flying in from HCMC the easiest and the most expensive (about US$140 round trip). Or you can take a ferry from either Rach Gia (about 10 hours) or from Ha Tien (about 4 hours, but the locals say it takes up to 6). The trip from Rach Gia costs 40,000 dong one way per person, and another 40,000 if you bring a motorcycle. Do not attempt to take the ferry from Ha Tien to Phu Quoc with a motorcycle. The police in Ha Tien, as well some of the locals, say the trip on the small ferry is dangerous enough in itself. The ferries leaving Rach Gia are considerably larger. Also, do not plan on a day trip to the island from Ha Tien. Theoretically, you might board a 9 a.m. ferry (that supposedly only takes 4 hours) and return on the afternoon ferry. But don't try it. You'll have to spend at least one night on the island, and in expensive accommodations.

THE INDUSTRIALIZATION OF PHU QUOC

Phu Quoc has an area of 576 square km and is roughly the size of Singapore. There are more than 100 km of beach and thousands of square km of fishing areas. 305,000 tons of sea products are pulled from the Gulf of Thailand each year. By 1995, that figure is expected to climb to 500,000 tons. The island's fish sauce is very popular in Vietnam. There are 80 such fish sauce processing plants on the island which have a capacity of producing 5 million liters of the sauce each year. Pepper is also grown here, but production is down in recent years. However, cashew nut growing areas are increasing rapidly. But to Phu Quoc's credit, the island is investing billions of dong into reforesting 300 hectares that have been denuded within the 370 square km area of forests the island possesses. There is also a boom in industrial products and handicrafts on Phu Quoc. The island now makes some 100 billion dong a year from food processing, building materials and forest products. The Vietnamese government has now permitted Phu Quoc (Kien Giang Province) to directly work with foreign companies to build roads, a sea harbor, an export-processing zone, and to install electrical and water supply systems. A total investment of more than US$500 million is planned for such projects. This island is going to change very quickly.

WHERE TO STAY IN HA TIEN

INSIDER TIP

Although Ha Tien has accommodations that are ridiculously inexpensive, most of the hotels (and the food they serve if they have a restaurant) come with price tags that are the highest in the Mekong Delta. The primary reason is the water, which through the city's water lines is more akin to used radiator antifreeze than anything potable. Fresh water has to be hand carted to the hotels, restaurants, homes, etc., from a storage tank on the edge of town. Most of the water you will find yourself bathing in in Ha Tien hostelries is the color of Jamaican Rum. The point is to be careful in Ha Tien. This is not a clean city, and many Vietnamese were surprised that I didn't contract viruses related to the water. Be careful of both what you eat and drink in Ha Tien. A good guide is your best source of where to eat and drink in Ha Tien. The following is a list of hotels and eateries I personally experienced, although it is no guarantee that you won't become sick in any of the following places.

To Chau Hotel

299 Ben Tran Hau; ☎ *52148 • 7 rooms.* US$5–6. There are singles and a couple of classes of doubles here. Fans and public water closet.

Dirty, but acceptable for Ha Tien, where prices are traditionally higher than in all other areas of the delta. Inexpensive.

Reservations: Direct

Don Ho Hotel

Thu Tran Hau Street; ☎ *52141* • *19 rooms.* US$4–6. Run of the mill but cheap with a pleasant staff. Fan, public water closet. Very inexpensive. *Reservations: Direct*

Phuoc Thanh Guesthouse

This place costs only 5000 dong for Vietnamese for a room and 1500 dong for a dormitory setting. Conditionals are dismal here, and the water is as black as Central Highlands coffee. Public toilet and "shower" that guests also frequently use to urinate in. Don't brush your teeth here or wash yourself unless it's with bottled water. In fact, I'd avoid the place altogether, despite the fact that you can get a room for as little as US$.50. Cheap, cheap, cheap.

Reservations: Don't bother, but direct if you must when you get to town.

Binh Minh Guesthouse

Duong Neac Du Street; ☎ *52035* • *8 rooms.* US$5. Standard guest house fare but better than the Phuoc Thanh, and more expensive. Public toilet, no hot water, no air conditioning. Accepts foreigners but staff English is limited. Inexpensive. *Reservations: Direct*

Kach San Du Lich

Cong Ty pu Lich, Kien Giang; ☎ *52169* • *18 rooms.* US$10. Ceiling fan, no hot water, but has private Western-style toilets; cafe. Moderate, and probably worth the added cash because they spend more money purifying their water. Inexpensive–Moderate.

Reservations: Direct

WHERE TO EAT IN HA TIEN

There are a number of places to eat in Ha Tien, and you'll find that they're relatively more expensive than elsewhere in the Mekong Delta. After crossing the floating bridge, immediately to your left and right will be a number of semi-outdoor cafes and restaurants. If possible eat at sidewalk stalls, as they tend to be about half as expensive as anything indoors, with or without air conditioning. It is not uncommon to spend US$2.50 a meal at an indoor restaurant, and about half that for food just as palatable as that served in the indoor eateries. Be careful what you ask for at an outdoor stall. They'll promise to serve it but may have to run across the street to have the meal prepared at another restaurant. You'll end up paying more. Eat only what you know the stall or cafe can prepare itself.

Ha Tien reputedly grows coconuts not found elsewhere in the country. Many places serve the exotic coconut milk. If you must eat indoors, perhaps the only place I can recommend is **Xuan Thanh Restaurant** across from the market on Ben Tran Hau street. The food seemed to be prepared in soiled surroundings, but I found it quite good, although Johnny Tu, my guide, was appalled at both the prices and the food, and swore never to return. I guess that means I won't be coming back either.

DIRECTORY

TRANSPORTATION

Ha Tien is about 92 km from Rach Gia, 96 from Chau Doc, 205 km from Can Tho, and 340 from Saigon. The bus station at Ha Tien is on the south side of town, just across the floating bridge on the right hand side of the road. The trip to Saigon takes about 10 hours over some amazingly dismal roadways. Buses arrive at HCMC's Mien Tay Station. They usually leave for Saigon in the wee hours of the morning, so don't plan on sleeping. Buses for Rach Gia leave at least four times daily I was told, the trip taking about 4–5 hours or more depending on the roadwork being done. By fast motorcycle, the trip is much quicker, by at least an hour, as it is by car. But again, the roads in the southern Mekong Delta area are in such disrepair it is unlikely Lewis and Clark would have ventured across them. Currently there is no air service between HCMC and Ha Tien, although you can fly to the island of Phu Quoc from HCMC. Travel into Cambodia, which is terribly tempting, is not permitted. Border police at Ha Tien, although mostly friendly, will turn nasty if you ask too many questions. They say that Khmer Rouge units still operate regularly on the Cambodian side of the border. You can try to get authorization at Ha Tien's immigration police office, but they'll turn you down as well.

Soc Trang

SOC TRANG

Rather than taking the highway southeast toward the South China Sea, most tourists in the Mekong Delta head northwest to Long Xuyen and Chau Doc or south to Rach Gia and Ha Tien. Soc Trang is an infrequently-visited city by foreigners, mainly because it has few attractions. It is also quite far from the sea, and there is no access to the South China Sea from Soc Trang, at least by road.

The only real reason to come here, besides bypassing the city altogether to get to the far southern town of Ca Mau, is to see the bizarre Vietnamese Pagoda which is covered with swastikas, Buddha figures (mainly heads) and the statues of animals that cover the grounds. There's also another pagoda here, a Khmer monastery called the Bat Temple, where fruit bats live in the trees. They make for good photo opportunities. There are a number of murals here that were supposedly paid for by wealthy Viet Kieu (Overseas Vietnamese).

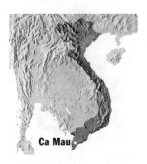

Ca Mau

CA MAU

CÀ MAU IN A CAPSULE

On the southern edge of the U Minh Forest...Considered the largest mangrove swamps outside the Amazon Basin...Few Westerners visit here...American defoliation during the Vietnam War obliterated the area...Possesses a zoo that's more like a leper colony...Take medical precautions while visiting this vast swamp.

180 km from Can Tho and 350 km from Saigon, Ca Mau is on the banks of the Ganh Hao River. It is the largest settlement on the Ca Mau peninsula and is at the southern edge of the U Minh Forest, a giant cajeput swamp that covers approximately 1000 sq. km of Minh Hai and Kien Giang provinces.

Apart from the Amazon basin in South America, the U Minh forest is considered by most to be the largest cajeput (or mangrove) swamp in the world. Aerial defoliation by the Americans during the Vietnam war practically ruined the area. However, nature has its incredible resilience and, today, much of the swamp has regained its beauty (although nearly a quarter of the swamp remains a dank wasteland). Much of the waterfowl have returned to the area, and bees pollinate the mangrove blossoms. However, the area is still being depleted of its natural resources today via shrimp breeding ponds. Locals also use the cajeput in a number of different ways: as charcoal, as a source of timber, and thatch for dwellings.

Ca Mau also features a "zoo," which is a dilapidated, inhumane environment designed for tourism that houses diseased, dismally treated animals that survive (barely) here for the benefit (or the nausea) of the few foreign tourists that visit this area. I'd stay away from it. It will do nothing but enhance your already negative attitudes regarding how the Vietnamese treat their animals, from domesticated dogs and cats to farm animals and wild, exotic creatures that are only marginally protected under vague and often ignored Vietnamese animal protection laws.

And bring your deet and malaria pills (although they might not be effective). Mosquitos in the mangrove swamps and the town abound. They're especially bothersome at night, and eating at outdoor food stalls can be a miserable experience for this reason alone.

WHERE TO STAY AND EAT IN CA MAU

The **Khach San Sao Mai** on the corner of Duong Ly Bon and Phan Ngoc Hien Streets appears to be nothing more than a whorehouse, as are most of the hotels in Ca Mau. Most of Ca Mau's hotels are on Phan Ngoc Hien Street, as is probably the best hotel in town, **Phuong Nam Hotel** (About US$50). Everything else ranges from around US$7–20, and most of the places are filthy and run down. It's one of the many reasons so few Westerners make it down this far. There is little if any tourism infrastructure in Ca Mau.

On Ly Bon Street can be found a number of roadside food stalls. You'll need nourishment, so eat at them, although the food is nothing to write home about. You should only travel to this area after having spent enough time in Vietnam to become accustomed to eating food stall fare, drinking boiling water, and bathing in rancid water. This is an easy place to get sick, and if your immune system hasn't yet adjusted to rural Vietnam, I'd avoid this area until it has.

DIRECTORY

TRANSPORTATION

Ca Mau is about 350 km from Saigon and 180 km from Can Tho. Buses leave for Ca Mau from HCMC's Mien Tay Bus Station and the trip usually takes between 10 and 11 hours by express bus and up to 13 by other buses. The road from Can Tho to Ca Mau is like other roads in the southern delta; they can only peripherally be classified as "roads." Potholes the size of B-52 bomb craters make the trip a roller coaster ride. The long trip by bus from HCMC is unendurable. If you want to go by boat from Saigon, the trip takes well over a day; boats leave for Ca Mau about every other day. Local transport is by water taxi, motorbike, or cyclo. You cannot reach Ca Mau by air.

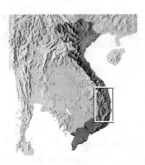

THE CENTRAL HIGHLANDS

Vietnam's Central Highlands offer some of the best vistas in the south.

THE CENTRAL HIGHLANDS IN A CAPSULE

Some of the most spectacular mountainous scenery in Vietnam...The hillsides are dotted with hill people villages...The southern region of the highlands possesses Vietnam's best climate, warm days, cool nights...Dalat has become a Disneylandlike tourist mecca...Many of the natural attractions have been totally spoiled by overcommercialism...Tourists are fewer and the accommodations less in the northern areas such as Pleiku...There was considerable military action in the highlands during the Vietnam War...Remarkably, Dalat was left unscathed...

THE CENTRAL HIGHLANDS
IN A CAPSULE

Areas north of Dalat are barely accessible because you first have to drive to the coast, then north along NHl, and then west again for hundreds of kilometers before reaching points a crow could reach within a hundred kilometers.

The lush Central Highlands are the home of many ethic groups and famous for spectacular scenery. The area is part of the southern chain of the Truong Song Mountain Range, with a cool climate, beautiful lakes and waterfalls. Although not many people live in the Highlands, the area was considered strategically important during the Vietnam War, and travel restrictions to some areas of the Central Highlands exist even today—although they are becoming fewer and fewer.

A giant rooster crows toward Dalat from the small village of Duc Trong.

Independent travelers can reach (if they are physically able to) many areas that were once prohibited. Provinces in the Central Highlands consist of Dac Lac, Kon Tum, Lam Dong, and Gia Lai. During the war, a lot of fighting took place around Pleiku, Kontum and Buon Na Thuot. However, Dalat was remarkably spared from the fighting. Supposedly top military brass on both sides of the conflict used Dalat as a summer retreat, and it's said that officers from both opposing armies spent R&R time in villas only a few kilometers from each other.

Although Americans were recently prohibited from visiting the Central Highlands with the exception of touristy Dalat due to the continuing conflict between government forces and FULRO (the United Front for the Struggle of the Oppressed Races. There were even rumors of Reeducation Camps still existing in the area), these restrictions have been almost entirely removed. And where there are the few remaining restricted sites, you know longer need to be guided by Vietnamese Army soldiers. Instead tourism permits can be arranged at provincial tourist offices for a nominal fee of about US$5 (although you'll still have to hire one of their guides and perhaps a vehicle, even if you have your own).

The road leading from Saigon to Dalat is a generally good one (excellent by Vietnamese standards) and scenery is spectacular, particularly between Bao Loc and Dalat. You'll want to stop and take pictures in numerous places, across verdant mountainous vistas as well as the bridge spanning a small section of the lake between Bien Hoa and Bao Loc, where floating hootches dot the marshes and lake. The final 20 km to Dalat are almost straight up and, although it's a treacherous ride, the road winds deep through some of the greenest mountainsides you'll ever have a chance to see.

The highland areas of Vietnam are considered by most as the most culturally and linguistically numerous and diverse in the entire world. In the southern Central Highlands, there are as many as 35 different tribes, and as many as 50 throughout the country. Some of the ethnic groups possess as few as 500 individuals; the largest may number in the millions. Here's a look at some of the hill people, including those that are in the north:

BAHNAR

Mostly concentrated in the central highland provinces of Gia Lai and Kontum, the Bahnar are an ethnic minority group that speak Mon-Khmer. Their population is estimated at about 100,000. After enjoying nearly four centuries of power in the region (15th–18th centuries), the group was nearly wiped out in the 19th century by the Harai and Dedang people. The Bahnar became close with the French, and Christianity (particularly Catholicism) became widespread among the Bahnar. Men and women are considered as equals. Wealth is evenly distributed among a Bahnar family, and marriages can be arranged by the parents of either the man or the woman.

KOHO

These matrilineal people, also called the Kohor, inhabit Lam Dong Province near Dalat on the Lam Dong Plateau. Today's population of around 100,000 live in longhouses in extended family groups. These houses can reach 30 meters in length. Men who marry often live with the family of the wife. Settled agriculture provides the Kohos' subsistence.

RHADE

This is another matrilineal group that primarily inhabits the central highlands. They're also known as the Edeh, and their population is believed to be approximately 170,000. They also befriended the French and Christianity is prevalent in their communities. They are considered to be among the most "modern" of the ethnic hill people. Extended families, like the Koho, also live in longhouses. Inheritance is usually given to the highest ranking female member of the family. Wet rice agriculture is the Rhades' primary form of subsistence, although some communities still practice the more traditional forms of shifting cultivation.

GIA RAI

Found primarily in the hills in and around Pleiku in the provinces of Gia Lai and Kontum, these 260,000 matrilineal people represent the largest ethnic minority in the Central Highlands. They are also known as the Zrai people.

SEDANG

Another Central Highlands tribe, the Sedang (or Xo-dang) number about 100,000 people who live in longhouses in the Gia Lai and Kontum province areas. Subsistence is by wet rice cultivation and shifting agriculture. These are a violent people; they have fought both the French and the Viets, and was the group that nearly made the Bahnar extinct in the 19th century.

MUONG

As we move north, we find the Muong who are, numbering at nearly 600,000 one of the largest ethnic minorities in Vietnam. They inhabit the central and northern provinces of Hoa Binh, Son La, Thanh Hoa, Ha Tay, and Nghia Lo provinces. There are many similarities between the Muong and ethnic Vietnamese, both in culture and language. Wealth is inherited through the male line, and their subsistence is through the cultivation of both wet and dry rice. However, unlike the ethnic Vietnamese, the Muong were not confronted with the Chinese and Christian influences that permeated Vietnamese culture. Some Muong still apply a black lacquer to their teeth in the their mid-teens to symbolize entry into adulthood.

HMONG

The Hmong, who can be found in highland areas throughout Vietnam, have a population of about 750,000 people, making them one of the largest group of ethnic hill people in the country. Originally settling in Vietnam in the 19th century from China, most Hmong can be found near the Chinese border and to the south to about the 18th parallel. The Hmong are a very isolated people, choosing to live at altitudes far higher than those inhabited by other ethnic hill people. Usually they live some 1500 meters higher then their lower neighbors. Warlike like the Sedang, they fought both the French and the Vietnamese. They use slash-and-burn agricultural techniques. There are different groups of the Hmong: the White Hmong, the Flowered Hmong, the Red Hmong and the Black Hmong.

NUNG

These mostly Buddhist people, centered primarily north of Hanoi in the provinces of Ha Bac and Bac Thai, number more than a million people. They subsist on settled agriculture and are known for their bravery in battle. They have been strongly influenced by both the Chinese and the Vietnamese.

ZAO

There are perhaps 400,000 Zao (also called Yao, Dao or Man) people living in the highland areas of northern Vietnam. Most are Buddhists, although some Zao are into Taoism and Confucianism. Theyy usually live in the mountains at between 700-1000 meters high.

THAI

This is the largest ethnic minority in Vietnam, inhabiting primarily northwest Vietnam, whose numbers exceed 1.4 million. They first came to Vietnam from China during the 4th century. The Thai consist of three groups; the Red Thai (*Thai Do*), the Back Thai (*Thai Den*) and the White Thai (*Thai Trang*). The names are based on the color of the tunics worn by the women of each group. They live in the provinces of Lai Chau, Son La, Thanh Hoa, Nghia Lo, Nghe An and Hoa Binh. They use Chinese ideograms for their writing and subsist on the cultivation of wet rice.

Other ethnic minority hill people with significant populations include the **Hre**, who number about 80,000 in the provinces of Gia Lai and Kontum; the **Mnong**, who number about 65,000 in the provinces of Lam Dong and Dac Lac, and the **Stieng**, who number about 50,000 in the provinces of Dac Lac, Song Be and Lam Dong.

THE BIGFEET OF VIETNAM

Legend has it that a group of Vietnamese living in Hue were cast under a spell by a "witch doctor," which forced them into the mountains of the Central Highlands in western Quang Binh Province. This "spell" made these people grow hair all over their bodies, similar to apes, and took away their ability to speak. After first establishing settlements in this rugged, mountainous region, they were forced further into the highlands as Vietnamese and other ethnicities migrated into these areas. They made no contact with anyone, but at night would surround the new villages established by the migrating Vietnamese and howl from deep in the forest in remorseful memory of who they once were, and the human capabilities they formerly possessed. Many believe these "monkey people" still exist and torment villages, without being seen, late at night with their howling. In reality, this isn't far from the truth, although it's doubtful they metamorphosized as the result of magic. They're called the Ruc ethnic group and they do indeed inhabit the high jungles of western Quang Binh Province in north-central Vietnam, living by hunting and gathering. By the best estimate, there are only about 200 surviving members of this primitive animallike tribe. They live in highly remote and mountainous stone caves that are entirely inaccessible. Earlier, the Ruc people had civilized knowledge as well as their own language. They also possessed a concept of the sun and earth and of different species of living animals. But due to scientifically unknown historical events, they were forced to retreat higher and higher into the western mountains near Laos, where they lived totally cut off from the rest of Vietnam's population. The untamed forests, wild animals and severe environment made their lives quite primitive. At night they creep into their caves or primitive huts. In the daytime, the men stalk through the forest and boulders in search of monkeys, deer and bees for food. The men wear only tree bark loin cloths, while the women wear loin cloths of the same material, but covering the lower parts of their bodies only. The children do not wear clothes. Fire is created by rubbing black stones together. The fires are kept burning for months and even years. When women give birth, the woman will go deep into the forest and dig a hole where she will bear the child alone. The husband is not allowed to be with his wife, but passes food to her with a long stick. After the birth of the child it is the husband's duty to search the forests for seven white monkeys. Only after the wife has eaten all the monkeys can she return home. This is an important rite for the Ruc, as they believe the practice of giving birth in the forest prepares the newborn child immediately for the severe climate. God decides whether the child will live or die, and the Ruc pray to God by rubbing two bamboo pipes together. The Ruc people are a deeply attached community. For instance, when a water hole is discovered, the person making the find gathers the entire community together to drink at the site. If a man discovers a tree called *nhuc*, he will summon the women and the girls of the community to get the heart wood for food. When a group of men returns to the "village" after a hunt, they share their catch with everyone—and the man who killed the beast severs the head himself. The rest of the meat is shared by the tribe. There are Ruc festivals, where tribespeople gather around fires to listen to primitive *K Teng* and *T Lenh* songs. These people have been more exposed to the outside "world" in recent years and their customs are changing quickly. Regrettably, the "Bigfeet" of the remote Vietnamese forests will soon start donning Nikes.

A floating village off National Highway 20 near Tan Phu.

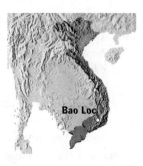

BAO LOC

Spectacular Dam Ri Waterfalls outside Bao Loc cascade 40 meters.

BAO LOC IN A CAPSULE

Gateway to the Central Highlands...A good stopover from Saigon to Dalat...Site of some of the most spectacular waterfalls in southern Vietnam...110 km south of Dalat on Highway 20...Surrounded by lush, rolling hillsides supporting coffee and tea plantations...A major center of silk production...Dam Ri waterfalls rarely seen by tourists...Brand new elegant hotel called the Seri.

Bao Loc (or B'Lao) is 110 km south from Dalat on Highway 20, or Tran Phu Street as it passes through town. It makes for a convenient stopover between Saigon and Dalat. The area consists of lush rolling green hills that support a number of coffee, mulberry leaf and tea plantations. Silk production is big in this area. There are also a number of small waterfalls, and one massive one that only a handful of foreigners have ever discovered, the falls at Dam Ri. Listed in none of the guidebooks, these falls make the waterfalls in Dalat seem like bathroom showers, and they well may be the most spectacular falls in Vietnam. The vast majority of travelers bypass Bao Loc completely. Unfortunately, this will change after this edition is published.

WHAT TO SEE AND DO IN BAO LOC AND ENVIRONS

Dam Ri Waterfalls

Located about 17 km west of Bao Loc are perhaps the most magnificent waterfalls in Vietnam, in southern Vietnam for sure. More than 40 meters high, the rushing water cascades down a solid rock edifice in a fury cloud of mist and multi-hued spray. Wonderful photos can be taken from both the summit and the base of the falls. But down below, you'll get wet, so keep your camera dry. The best times of the day to see the falls are in the early morning, where the spray creates spectacular rainbows, or late in the afternoon, when the low sun spills angles of light directly on the rushing water. The best thing about the falls is that no one knows about them. I saw not a single tourist. Nor are there the floating duck boats and cowboys on ponies with plastic pistols—the blatant, gawdy commercialism—that have taken all of the delight out of visiting the falls in the Dalat area. From Bao Loc, you turn west at the post office and then have to make a number of turns on side streets before reaching the road toward the falls, which is flanked by silk, tea and coffee farms. Ask for specific directions at The Bao Loc Hotel or the Seri Hotel. There's the big, but usually empty Dam Ri Restaurant at the admission area. Admission: 10,000 dong for foreigners. Frightful but worth it. Not to be missed.

Bay Tung Falls

Take Highway 20 seven km south from the Bao Loc Hotel. Then take a trail, 3 km after crossing the Dai Binh River, to the hamlet of Ap Dai Lao in the village of Xa Loc Chau. The trail starts on the right side of the road. You'll walk about 400 meters through tea bushes and coffee trees as well as banana and pineapple groves to reach Suoi Mo, the Stream of Dreaming. There the path goes left through thickets of bamboo. Soon you'll see the Bay Tung falls and the pools of the stream of Dreaming. Worth a visit only if you're planning on spending a day or two in Bao Loc—few people do. The falls pale in comparison to the Dam Ri Falls.

Bao Loc Church

Nothing spectacular, but if you're Catholic, you may want to pay a visit. It's located about three hundred meters on Highway 20 north of the Bao Loc Hotel.

Tea, Silk and Coffee Factories

Get a local to show you around to some of the factories that produce coffee, tea and silkworms. You can find the factories on Highway 20 south of Bao Loc and also on the well paved road leading to the Dam Ri Falls.

WHERE TO STAY IN BAO LOC

Bao Loc Hotel & Restaurant

So 11 A Tran Phu-B'ao (National Highway 1). ☎ *4107 or 4268; FAX: 01.63.4167 • 12 rooms.* US$5–20. There are only two "hotels" in Bao Loc, this one and the more upscale Seri, but I'd suggest, if you're on a budget and only planning to spend the night in Bao Loc, you stay here. It's a pretty big place considering the number of rooms, but the rooms are clean and comfortable—and I didn't see another guest during either visit. Yet the relatively big building, constructed in 1940, has two large, empty restaurants. Everything here seems spacious and empty, even the staff. But it's clean enough and the staff is kind. It's one of those hotels you wonder how it remains in business because of such a small occupancy rate. At the entrance to the hotel, there's a taxidermist's shop—stuffed threatened wildlife cover the driveway to the hotel, another sad testament to Vietnam's continuing ecological naivete. Inexpensive–expensive.   ***Reservations: Direct***

Seri Hotel   ★★

Baoloc-Lamdoc Province, just off Highway 20 in the center part of town. ☎ *4150, 4430 or 4065. FAX: 2183 • 57 rooms.* US$20–40. This is a strikingly elegant hotel in a strikingly inelegant city that's a cross between Saigon's Floating Hotel and the Pentagon, and why it would expect to fill its spacious, tastefully decorated rooms is well beyond my comprehension given the lack of attractions in the Bao Loc area. The higher priced rooms are luxurious suites. Singles and doubles, all with TV, hot water, telephone. Restaurant, snack bar, dance hall and Karaoke. It's the kind of place where you'd want to spend at least a few nights here, but there's no reason to. The staff is especially friendly, well-dressed and surprisingly fluent in English. A shop sells beautiful locally produced silk clothing, but at relatively exorbitant rates. Hotel also offers minibus transportation to tea and coffee plantations, as well as to the area's waterfalls, including the Dam Ri Falls. The falls alone make this hotel worth the visit. Moderate–expensive.

Reservations: Direct or through HCMC, 28 Mac Dinh Chi.
☎ *298438 or 231375. FAX: 84.8.294086.*

WHERE TO EAT IN BAO LOC

There are a number of food stalls and cafes that line NHI (Tran Phu Street) through Bao Loc.

Restaurant Dang Nguyen

02b Tran Phu Street • Vietnamese, cheap.

Tram Anh Tra Cafe

5 Tran Phu • Comfortable, shaded and popular.

Restaurant Hung Phat and the Hung Phat Cafe

Tran Phu Street, across from the Bao Loc Hotel, 20 meters south • One of the best restaurants in town with friendly service. There's an outdoor dining area which consists of one-table gazebolike booths. If you happen to get a date in Bao Loc, bring your friend here.

Dream Cafe

Across Thran Phu Street from the Restaurant Hung Phat • Nothing to write home about.

Bao Loc Hotel

So 11a Tran Phu Street • Usually empty, but vegetable dishes are great. Also Western food.

Seri Hotel Restaurant

Seri Hotel • Better then average Vietnamese and Western fare for the area.

Dam Ri Restaurant

Dam Ri Waterfalls • New, big and modern establishment; average food.

A rainbow cuts through the mist created by Bao Loc's 40-meter high Dam Ri Waterfalls.

Dalat

DALAT

Dalat's railway station used to serve Saigon via Phan Rang until continuous Viet Cong attacks ruined the track and made the journey impossible.

DALAT IN A CAPSULE

Founded by French scientist Andre Yersin as a French hill resort in 1897...Possesses perhaps the best climate in Vietnam...a primarily temperate zone with huge tea and coffee plantations as well as silk production facilities...A favorite honeymooning spot for Vietnamese newlyweds...Much of the mountainsides have been heavily deforested in recent years...Very little fighting took place here during the Vietnam War...Montagnard, Da Hoa and Lat hillpeople live in the region...Attractive waterfalls and lakes surround this mountainous area...The area has become heavily commercialized and attracts many more Vietnamese than foreign tourists.

What can you say about Dalat (population about 130,000)? It's certainly one of the most beautiful cities in all of Vietnam and sits atop a mighty plateau at nearly 1500 meters. It features the best climate in Vietnam (warm days and cool nights all year round). Temperatures average here 24 degrees C in the day and 15 degrees at night. There is a rainy season from April through November, although even during these months it still rains infrequently and only for a short duration.

The Lang Biang Mountains to the north rise to nearly 2500 meters. They're inhabited by a number of ethnic minorities, including Montegnards, Lat and Da Hoa tribespeople.In the center of the city is pristine Xuan Huong Lake. Around town there are waterfalls, beautiful gardens of temperate flora, deep pine forested valleys, a man-made reservoir, lakes and even a golf course.

Dalat was founded by Frenchman Andre Yersin, who convinced the French government to establish a hill station here in the late 1890s. There was a railway station here that linked Dalat with Phan Rang and Saigon (although it is defunct now). During colonial times, the Frenchmen of Saigon used Dalat as a summer resort to escape the intense heat of Saigon. Much of the architecture is French.

Dalat is still a popular resort destination with more than 2500 villas surrounding the region. But rather than with Europeans and other Westerners, Dalat is a more popular resort with the Vietnamese, and the area is a favorite for newlyweds. Caravans of ballooned and streamer-covered cars and minivans traverse the hilly area, and honeymooning couples can be found at practically every attraction site dressed elegantly for photos.

Although Dalat was once well known as a big game hunting resort as late as the 1950s, the wild animals—bears, rhinos, tigers, elephants, and deer—that once roamed these once dense forests have disappeared.

I found Dalat disappointing in a number of ways. Massive deforestation in the area has created bare mountainsides in every direction. This wasn't a result of the war, but instead the result of relentless commercial timber activities.

There was actually very little fighting in and around Dalat during the Vietnam War. In fact, high ranking officers on both sides of the conflict used Dalat villas as retreats not more than a few kilometers apart. But comparatively little remains of the lush environment of the highlands surrounding Dalat.

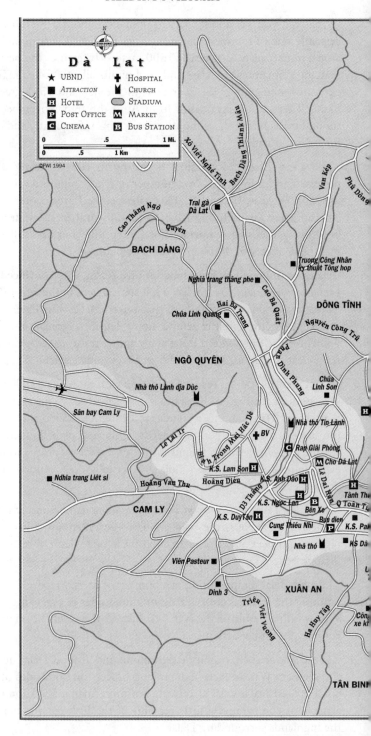

Dà Lat

★ UBND   ✚ HOSPITAL
■ ATTRACTION   ✟ CHURCH
H HOTEL   ⬭ STADIUM
P POST OFFICE   M MARKET
C CINEMA   B BUS STATION

0   .5   1 Mi.
0   .5   1 Km

©FWI 1994

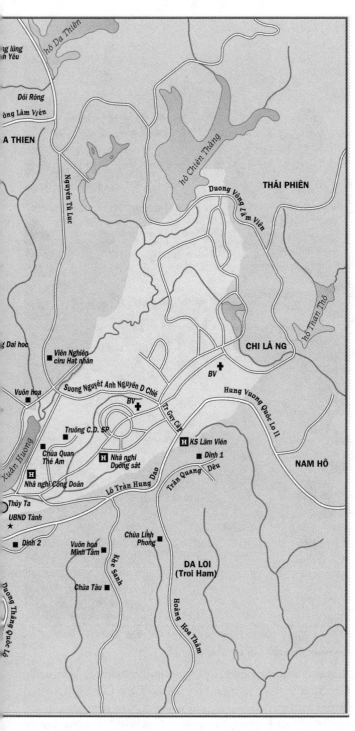

Dalat's Hang Nga's Guest Home and Art Garden features some of the most bizarre architecture in the country.

Dalat has also become extremely over-commercialized. At virtually every attraction in and surrounding the area are these dilapidated paddle boats with duck heads that look like a cross between old Soviet submarines and floating bathtubs. "Cowboys" in attire out of the "Wild,Wild West" lead tourists around on ponies in these circus-like environments. There are "zoos" with poorly treated animals, and those unlucky enough to be alive have been stuffed by omni-present Vietnamese taxidermists and glued to trees and rocks. The sight of these rare and sometimes endangered species is sickening. And these poor creatures are everywhere. In shops, at the parks, at the waterfalls, etc. If you care about this stuff (forgive the pun), your visit to Dalat will be dampened by these sights.

Thousands of Dalat dwellers were resettled by the new government after 1975 to areas down the plateau outside the city. One such Lat village is 20 km south out of town along Highway 20.

In previous years, you needed a police permit to visit many areas outside of Dalat—and the horror stories abound of corruption and bribery. But when I visited the immigration police station, I was po-litely told that a permit was only needed to visit Lat Village, about 12 km northwest of town. The permit costs US$5 and could be ob-tained through Lam Dong Tourism. You'll have to hire a guide through the tourism agency, however. At least it won't be a police-man or soldier.

There also used to be problems with foreigners checking into the few foreigner-permitted hotels. You'd have to file a phenomenal amount of information with the police. This is no longer the case. As in most of Vietnam, travel by foreigners is basically unrestricted in Lam Dong Province.

WHAT TO SEE AND DO IN DALAT AND ENVIRONS

Xuan Huong Lake

This is an artificial lake that was created in central Dalat by a dam on the west end of the valley in 1919. The lake itself isn't particularly spectacular but it's surrounded by kiosks and cafes. Rent a bike and take the road that runs around the perimeter of the lake. Many locals swim here, but I'd avoid it, seeing what they toss into it. The lake was named after a controversial 17th-century Vietnamese poet. Unfortu-nately, this is one of the many water sites in Dalat where you can rent one of those Bozo bathtubs and look like a fool for an hour or two.

Dalat Flower Garden

These are beautiful gardens set on the northeast end of the lake. They were established in 1966 by the South Vietnamese Agricultural Ser-vice. After becoming nothing more than a weed patch, the entire gar-dens were renovated in 1985. Here you can see both tropical and temperate flora, including hydrangeas, orchids, roses, fuchsias, lilies and camellias. How some of the flowers are grown is interesting. Orchids are grown inside coconut palm trunks. Admission: 2000 dong.

Dalat Cathedral

Yersin and Tran Phu Streets, next to the Dalat Hotel. Built in the early 30s and not finished until 1945, the impressive 48-meter high spire can be seen from all over town. The medieval-style stained glass windows were imported from France and were crafted by Louis Balmet. There are wood carvings of Jesus lining the nave. Masses are conducted everyday at 5:15 a.m. and 5:15 p.m., and on Sundays at the ungodly hour of 4:00 a.m. as well as 5:15 a.m., 7 a.m., 8:30 a.m. and 4 p.m. This might be why the pastor seemed a little exhausted during our brief conversation.

Quan Am Tu Pagoda

2 Chien My Street. Not a lot here, except for the Buddha with the electric halo around its head. The gardens are nice here, too. Worth a brief stop if you keep stealth from the nice monk, who'll want to keep you there for hours.

Linh Son Pagoda

120 Nguyen Van Troi Street. There's a huge gold and bronze bell here. I did not see any women here and was told women weren't allowed by an old man trying to sell me incense. There are two dragons in front of the sanctuary with small ponds on each side of them.

Su Nu Pagoda

1 km south of Le Thai To at 72 Hoang Hoa Than Street. This pagoda is strictly for nuns, although men are allowed to visit. Don't visit here during the lunch hours, you'll offend the praying women, who are all bald headed and wear grey or brown robes. It was built in 1952.

Domaine de Marie Convent

6 Ngo Quyen Street. Built in the erly 1940s, This convent once housed more than 300 nuns. The few nuns still around today make fruit and spice candies as well as the fruit they grow in an orchard out in back.

Minh Nguyet Cu Sy Lam Pagoda

Built in 1962, this is a Chinese Pagoda just across from the Thien Vuong Pagoda (see below). It is a round structure representing a lotus blossom. The sanctuary is to the right of the main gates after entering the path. Inside the pagoda is a statue of Quan The Am Bo Tat (the Goddess of Mercy). Lotus flowers can be seen all over the gates and the bars on the windows. The pagoda, as is Thien Vuong Pagoda, is very popular with Chinese and Hong Kong visitors. Take off your shoes before entering the pagoda after passing the few stalls that sell vegetable and fruit concoctions.

A giant white Buddha at Dalat's Thien Vuong Pagoda overlooks the pine-covered Central Highlands.

Thien Vuong Pagoda

At the end of Khe Sanh Street, this is Chinese and one of the more interesting pagodas in Dalat. At the end of Khe Sanh Street a dirt path rises up a pine covered hill leading up the pagoda. Souvenir stalls line the path up to the pagoda where there are two large yellow wood-built buildings. In the first building you will not be required to remove your shoes. In this structure is a statue of one of Buddha's protectors, Ho Phap and another statue of Pho Hien, an aide to the A Di Da Buddha (Buddha of the past). In the next building, where you'll be required to remove your shoes, are three huge Buddhas brought over from Hong Kong. These Buddhas are thought to be the largest sandalwood Buddhas in Vietnam. They represent Quan The Am Bo Tat on the right, Sakyamuni (the historical Buddha) in the center, and Dai The Bo Tat on the right. Behind the second building further up on the hill is a giant white Buddha overlooking the valley. The pagoda was built in 1958.

The Tomb of Nguyen Huu Hao

Nguyen Huu Hao was the father of Bao Dai's wife, Nam Phuong. Nguyen died in 1939. The tomb is atop a 400-meter high hill northwest of Cam Ly Falls.

Cam Ly Falls

A ton of Vietnamese tourists—that's what you'll find here along with cowboys, plastic guns, and a lot of kids who are convinced your breath is so foul that Wrigley's chewing gum is the only cure. Or your breath is so sweet, the only solution is a pack of Jet cigarettes. A guide here costs US$1 an hour and it ain't worth it, folks. You can adequately tour the small falls in under half an hour on your own quite well, thank you. Animal lovers will cringe at the stuffed jungle animals.

Valley of Love

Five km north of Dalat. Given the name by students in the early 1970s who used to hang out here with their lovers, the original name was the Valley of Peace after Emperor Bao Dai decided *that's* what it should be called. Obviously, he was happy by himself. Now the place is a circus, with cowboys and people running around in bunny suits. You can rent those damn floating bathtubs here as well as buy everything from lottery tickets to straw hats. The cowboys are the most annoying aspects of a visit here as well as the chewing gum hawkers. Refreshment stalls abound, as do Vietnamese tourists. A new name should be given to the place: The Valley of the Love of Dong.

Dalat (or Crèmailllère) Railway Station   ★

Five hundred meters east of Xuan Huong Lake and off Quang Trun Street, is a sight not to be missed. About a half dozen ancient train cars and a black, steam engine that has to be at least a century old lie on the track next to the pastel yellow railway station. Opened in 1938, the station used to serve Saigon through Phan Rang until continuous Viet Cong attacks on the track made the journey impossible, and the routes were shut down in 1964. However, tourists can now take the "train" about 7 km out of town to Trai Met Village for the ridiculous price of US$10 round trip (why would you want to stay in Trai Met?). The journey's a novelty and pleasant—you pass well-tended, dense vegetable fields—but 10 bucks? Instead, I'd get some good shots of the train cars and the station itself.

Central Market

Located at the end of Nguyen Thi Minh Khai Street, this is one of the most interesting markets in Vietnam and certainly the best for getting produce and fruit such as strawberries, carrots, plums, avocados, cherries, potatoes, loganberries and apples. Friends in the south will be highly appreciative if you bring back a gift of some of these foods.

The French District

This is the area around Rap 3/4 cinema that looks as if you were in the middle of France, except for the amount of Asians you'll see on the street, of course.

Dalat University

1 Phu Dong Thien Vuong Street. With the aid of New York's Cardinal Spelman, Dalat University opened its doors in 1957 as a Catholic learning institution by Hue Archbishop Ngo Dinh Thuc, who was the older brother of President Diem, assassinated in 1963. When Dalat was "liberated" in 1975, the university shut down but was reopened a couple of years later. Now more than a thousand students study here, from English to agriculture.

Dalat's Quang Trung Reservoir was created by a dam in 1980.

Quang Trung Reservoir

Head down Highway 20 toward Bao Loc. About 5 km from town, turn right down a rutted, dangerous rock and dirt path to the reservoir. It was created by a dam in 1980 and, today, about 30 poor people live on floating houses in the reservoir. It was named after Quang Trang, one of the Tay Son rebellion's great leaders, who was responsible for repressing a vicious Chinese attack in 1789. The reservoir is situated in a deforested valley (there are some recently planted pine trees) beneath a spectacular new Vietnamese pagoda. There's not much to see here and there are only a few visitors, so the child gum and cigarette hawkers are at a minimum. There is one cafe and supposedly small power boats for rent, but I didn't see one on the entire lake.

Truc Lam Thien Vien (Thuyen Nen Tuyen Lam) Pagoda

Also called the Bamboo Forest Meditation Center, this is a spectacular new Vietnamese pagoda of 24 hectares high on the bamboo forest hillside overlooking Quang Trung Reservoir. But it's a hike to get up there (150 steps). The brand new domiciles are now home to 52 monks and 45 nuns. The chief monk, Thong Triet (who will not leave the hillside pagoda for at least 3 years) will be more than happy to show you the giant sand and cement Buddha trucked up from Saigon at the altar as well as the one-ton bell that's rung twice a day (at 3 a.m. and 6 p.m.) brought over from Hue. This is a magnificent new structure (built in 1994) with beautiful temperate flora landscaping. Inside the pagoda "giang huong" hardwood covers the ceiling and altar archways. There's also a brand new guesthouse for visiting monks alongside the pagoda. If you're out of shape, a trek up to this pagoda is a day trip.

Vietnamese cowboys toting plastic six-shooters are typical of Dalat's commercialism.

Lake of Sighs

About 5 km on Phan Chu Trinh Street northeast of Dalat. This lake, a natural one that was enlarged by a French-built dam, is supposedly named after girls who were brought here by students at Dalat's military academy. Another story says that it was named after the lovers Hoang Tung and Mai Nuong, who met and fell in love here during the 18th century. Hoang Tung then joined the army to help fight the Chinese, but left Mai Nuong unaware of his new duties and travels. When he left to fight the Chinese, Mai felt that she had been abandoned and drowned herself in the lake. The lake itself is nothing spectacular and largely denuded of its once dense vegetation. There are a few souvenir stands here and the usual stuffed animals. Again, you'll find those damned cowboys and their plastic guns looking to bring you around the lake on horseback.

Datanla Falls

These falls are about 200 meters or so farther down Highway 20 from Quang Trung Reservoir. The falls themselves aren't as impressive as some of Dalat's other waterfalls (and pale in comparison with Bao Loc's Dam Ri Falls) but the pleasant thing about them is that they lack the county fairlike environments of other Dalat attractions. There is only a small viewing area, which is usually full of tourists picnicking. The down side to these falls (again, forgive the pun) is that you've got to be a decathlete to reach them. The walk down the path is steep and long. If you're not in shape, forget it. Halfway down the rugged path I saw a pregnant Western woman stopped alongside gasping for air. And I could've sworn I saw the six-month old fetus huffing and puffing in her pelvic region as well. What the hell she was thinking I don't know. But I don't advise pregnant women to visit Datanla unless it's by helicopter.

Prenn Falls

At the base of Dalat on Highway 20 at the Prenn Restaurant, these are perhaps the nicest falls in Dalat, but they're packed with tourists, souvenir touts, mini-sailboats and Vietnamese on horseback dressed like Red Skeleton on the set of Mel Brooks' *Blazing Saddles*. At an altitude of 1125 meters, water cascades off a 15 meter edifice into a brown-colored pool the size of a backyard swimming pool in Lubbock where you can rent these tiny toy ships for a "voyage" that's more like an ant crossing a cup of coffee. Kiosks and food stalls abound. The parking area is packed with minibuses. The park around the falls, sprinkled with palm-thatched gazebos was dedicated to Thailand's Queen in 1959. Admission: 5000 dong.

Prenn Pass ★★

This is the steep stretch of roadway on Highway 20 that leads down from Dalat past Quang Trang Reservoir, Datanla Falls toward Prenn Falls. This is a beautiful, but sometimes narrow and dangerous road that's surrounded by tall palms and thick vegetation. Some of the scenery is magnificent. By motorcycle, you'll be tempted to do a Pike's Peak climb in record time. Don't try. The veering minibuses treat the road as if it was their own and use both sides of the road. A collision here and you're in for dalat of trouble.

Duc Trong Village (Quang Hiep)

My guide insisted that this small village 20 km south of Dalat down Highway 20 was Lat Village. To my knowledge, he was wrong. Instead this small agricultural community on the right side of the road is where displaced ethnic Da Hoa were forced to move into the valley by the government after 1975. There's not much but a bunch of hootches and chickens and a giant statue of a chicken that must have taken an addicted drumstick lover years to build from cement. Here, you'll want to visit Mrs. Nguyen Thi Kim Phung, an English teacher whose knowledge of the relocation of Dalat residents after 1975 is vast and interesting. She'll also want to guide you to the summit of Elephant Mountain, a four-hour, round-trip hike up the heavily deforested peak. Worth a brief visit unless you want to do the hike, which offers spectacular scenery at the summit.

Lat Village

Here, about 12 km north of Dalat, is the only area around Dalat you'll need a permit to visit, which can be obtained through the Lam Dong Tourist Office for US$5. You'll have to use one of their guides and that'll cost you more. Why you need to obtain a permit to visit these nine small hamlets is a mystery to me. The ethnic Lat, Koho, Ma and Chill tribes that inhabit the area really don't seem like the insurgent types, although many Lat and Montagnard people worked for the Americans during the war. Here, the houses are constructed of thatched-roof dwelling built on piles. There are about 300 hectares where the villagers grow rice and produce charcoal. Lat Village also has two Christian churches. It's worth a visit, but the US$30 or so you'll have to spend to make the trip may create some reservations about doing it.

Lang Bian Mountain

These are five volcanic peaks, heavily deforested, and about a four-hour hike from Lat Village. The two highest peaks are called K'Biang and K'Lang. Not so many years ago, tigers, bears, elephants, boars and rhinos roamed the peaks. But not anymore. The hike is worth it for the spectacular views.

Ankroët Lakes & Falls

About 20 km northwest of Dalat, the lakes are actually part of a hydroelectric project. Many hilltribes in the area. The falls aren't spectacular, reaching a height of about 15 meters.

INSIDER TIP

There are a number of falls in the Dalat area that require a considerably long and steep hike to reach. Although most tourists in third-world countries are in generally good shape, others aren't. If you have a heart condition, are pregnant, or just can't plain blow out a candle from three feet, I recommend staying at the top, purchasing a souvenir or two and a postcard, and telling your friends at home how beautiful the falls were.

Dalat's Cathedral, with its 48-meter-high spire, began construction in the early 1930s but wasn't completed until 1945.

WHERE TO STAY IN DALAT

INSIDER TIP

Even though tourism in Dalat is exploding it still seems that two of every three hotels in the city will not allow foreigners. If you find yourself in the center of Dalat and are not sure where to stay, it will be a waste of time to roam the streets–which are packed with hotels and mini-hotels (guest houses)–looking for a suitable hotel. You'll get frustrated. Even though the number of foreigners that visit Dalat is increasing rapidly, the overwhelming majority of visitors to Dalat are Vietnamese on holiday.However, on the plus side, the cheaper hotels that once didn't provide hot water now usually do. And you'll want hot water in Dalat, even during the warmer months.

Thanh The Hotel

118 Phan Dinh Phung Street. ☎ *22180* • *42 rooms.* US$5–12. Friendly English speaking staff; comfortable singles and doubles. Private bath, clean rooms. Hot water. Restaurant, cafe. Incredible value for the price, and one of the few hotels on Phan Dinh Phung Street that accepts (and welcomes) foreigners. A similar room in Saigon would go for twice as much money. This makes the Thanh The one of the best values in Dalat. Also, it is enhanced by its central location in the middle of town. Inexpensive.   ***Reservations: Direct***

Thanh Van Hotel

9/1 Phu Dong Thien Vuong Street. ☎ *22818; FAX: 22782* • *21 rooms.* US$20–25. Clean, comfortable rooms, but a little pricey. Price includes breakfast. Restaurant. Private bath. Centrally located. Large, comfortable rooms. Car hire for local tours of the Dalat area. Moderate.   ***Reservations: Direct***

Palace 2 Hotel   ★

12 Tran Hung Dao Street. ☎ *22092; Will have fax number by the end of summer 1994* • *28 rooms.* US$30–50. Hotel has been open for about 6 years. This place, an elegant structure and built in 1933, was formerly the Governor-General's Residence, and then was used as a guesthouse for dignitaries and official receptions. Now anyone can stay if you're willing to pay the price, which includes breakfast. The pricier rooms are deluxe suites. There are 19 first-class rooms, seven second class rooms. Rooms are large, almost palatial. Attached bathroom, restaurant, telephone and television in all the rooms as well as IDD services. Organizes area tours via vans, coaches and microbuses. I found the service here a little too stuffy, although friendly enough. I think the French will be more at home here than American visitors. The friendly, businesslike manager dresses like Art Carney at a county fair. If you need to spend much time with him, wear sunglasses.Moderate–expensive.   ***Reservations: Direct.***

Hang Nga's Guest Home and Art Garden

3 Huynh Thuc Khang. ☎ *22070* • *12 rooms.* US$15. This is the most bizarre-looking hotel in the Milky Way, a towering, dripping, sculpted building designed by Dang Viet Nga (who may be the Southeast Asian reincarnation of Salvador Dali) that resembles an outcropping on Uranus. Something right out of a Steven Spielberg flick. Even if you don't stay here, if you're in Dalat, make sure you give this place a visit. They even charge 2000 dong just to go in and see the place. It's right out of Disneyland. However, the rooms are spacious and adorned in a bear cavelike motif with carved dragons and stuffed bears. Big baths. Sitting areas. The lighting is romantic and the place would make a good honeymooners' spot, with the emphasis being on "moon." A giant sculpted giraffe sits next to the complex—it's gotta be 20 meters high. Why it's there and what it has to do with the rest of the hotel's motif is a total mystery. Moderate. ***Reservations: Direct***

The Palace Hotel

2 Tran Phu. ☎ *23496* • This hotel is being thoroughly renovated, and it's taken 4 years—although they expect to reopen in July or August of 1994. The building was originally erected in the early 1920s. The renovation has been taking years and the staff keeps pushing back the opening date. But when it's finally done, it will be a magnificent big building with great views of the Xuan Huong Lake. The grounds themselves should be beautifully landscaped once all the cement blocks are on the structure and not on the grounds. No one seemed to have any idea what the prices of the rooms will be, however, I expect they'll be in the US$50 range. During my visit, workers were sitting around smoking cigarettes, a number of the Jet butts in succession, so a July opening may be a little optimistic.

Bao Dai's Summer Palace ★

Biet Dien Quoc Truong • This is a beautiful 25-room villa that was constructed for Emperor Bao Dai in 1933. This is now actually a hotel with prices ranging in the US$30–40, but the place is a little ambiguous because it closes for "lunch" for a couple of hours during the day and you simply can't get into the place. Even the reception area is closed. I'm not sure what you'll want to do while you wait for the office to reopen about 1:30 p.m. You can also tour the palace/hotel when it is open whether you're staying there or not. Even if you're already a guest, I'm still not sure you can get into the structure between 11:30 a.m. and 1:30 p.m. The attractions here are many. There's an engraved glass map of Vietnam that was given to the Emperor during the early 40s by Vietnamese studying in Paris before World War II began really taking its toll on the French people (and others studying there). The palace also features an ornate dining room and Bao Dai's office, which contains some of his books and other personal effects as well as his desk. The "palace" doesn't look really either like a palace or a hotel. Bao Dai spent his enormous amount of money on airplanes while stashing the rest in Swiss and U.S. bank accounts in anticipation of his political demise.

Savimex Guest House

11b 34 Street. ☎ *22640* • US$25. This is one of the first hotels you'll run into after cresting the mountain and heading down toward Dalat. Its hillside location offers good views of the mountains and the valleys. Relatively new building. English speaking staff. Hot water, restaurant. Moderate.   ***Reservations: Direct***

Cam Do Hotel & Restaurant   ★

81Phan Dinh Phung Street. ☎ *22732* • US$7–20. Run by Dalat Tourist, this is one of the classier hotels in Dalat and quite a bargain. Price includes breakfast. Friendly, English speaking staff. Elegant lobby. Quite popular with foreigners in the fall. Rooms have private bath and hot water. Restaurant. There are also microbus tours of the Dalat area run by the hotel. Other tourist services. The hotel also provides one-way minibus service to Nha Trang, Phan Rang, and HCMC. Inexpensive–moderate.

Reservations: Direct and through Dalattourist

Mimosa Hotel

170 Phan Dinh Pung Street. ☎ *22656* or *22180* • *31 rooms.* US$7–12. This is a friendly, centrally located hotel located in the heart of Dalat that looks more expensive than it is. Private bath, restaurant in the lobby. You can rent cars here for sight-seeing and the hotel will arrange bus and travel tickets. Mr. Long is the man to talk to about Dalat, especially if you're planning an itinerary within a tight schedule. Popular with backpackers, but I also saw a couple of families here as well. Inexpensive.   ***Reservations: Direct***

Hha Hang Huong Son

27 Duong 3 Thang 4. ☎ *22124* • *10 rooms.* US$25. Pricey but comfortable. Hot water. Restaurant. Check to see whether they'll allow foreigners. For some reason, there's a disproportionate amount of hotels in Dalat that do not accept foreigners. One employee said yes, the other no. Moderate.   ***Reservations: Direct.***

Buu Tram Hotel

138B Phan Dinh Phung Street. ☎ *22887* • *15 rooms.* US$20–30. A mostly non-English speaking staff here which at present, doesn't accept foreigners, however, the mamasan said this may change soon. 8 rooms with private bath, 7 with public toilet. Room service. Moderate.   ***Reservations: Direct.***

Thang Long Mini Hotel and Restaurant

154 Phan Dinh Phung Street. ☎ *22690* • Prices appear to be in the US$10–20 range. This is another one of those places that currently doesn't accept foreigners but may in the near future as the increase of foreigners in Dalat continues. Call in advance. ***Reservations: Direct.***

Ngoc Lan Hotel

42 Nguyen Chi Thanh Street. ☎ *22136* • *25 rooms.* About US$10. This is near the southern entrance to Dalat on a hill that overlooks the lake and the bus station. You can decide which is the better view. Inexpensive. ***Reservations: Direct***

Dalat Hotel

7 Phan Tru Street. ☎ *22863* • *65 rooms.* About US$25. A bit run down and the rooms are large, but I think it's too expensive, even though the views are nice. Hot water. Moderate.

Reservations: Direct

Anh Dao Hotel

50 Hoa Binh Square, up the hill from the Central Market. ☎ *22384* • About US$25–45. This is a renovated, spotless place with good service. Private bath. Hot water. Restaurant. Moderate.

Reservations: Direct

Minh Tam Hotel

20A Khe Sanh Street (about 3 km out of town). ☎ *22447* • *17 rooms.* About US$30–50. A bit out of the way but the views of the surrounding forests and valleys are nice. It was built in 1936 as the palace of South Vietnamese President Ngo Dinh Diem's infamous sister-in-law Madame Nhu. It was renovated in the mid 1980s and is especially popular with domestic tourists. All the amenities one would expect for 50 bucks. Moderate–expensive. ***Reservations: Direct.***

Thuy Tien Hotel

73 Thang 2 Street. ☎ *22444* • About US$12. This hotel is close to both the market and the bus station. A little run down for the price. Hot water, restaurant. Inexpensive. ***Reservations: Direct.***

Nha Khach Com

48 Phan Ding Phung Street • US$6. Out of the way, but cheap. Reasonable rooms. Inexpensive. ***Reservations: Direct.***

Lang Bian Hotel

6B Nhuyen Thi Minh Khai Street. ☎ *22419.* It's in the other guides but locals told me it was shut down.

Than Binh Hotel

40 Nguyen Thi Minh Khai Street. ☎ *22394* or *22909* • *42 rooms.* About US$10-20. Near the Central Market and a decent value. Hot water. Attached bath. Restaurant. Inexpensive–moderate.

Reservations: Direct.

Hai Son Hotel

1 Nguyen Thi Minh Khai Street. ☎ *22379, FAX: 84.8.92889* • About US$15–20. This is a musty, dirty and overpriced place, but the price includes breakfast. Hot water, attached bath. Not worth it. Moderate.

Reservations: Direct or through HCMC office.

VYC Hoa Hung Hotel

Lu Gia Street. ☎ *22653.* About US$15–20. This is away from town but relatively new, clean and friendly. Attached bath, hot water; restaurant. Moderate.
Reservations: Direct or VYC Tourism in HCMC, 180 Nguyen Cu Trinh. ☎ *298707.*

Duy Tan Hotel

83-3 Thang 2 Street. ☎ *22216* • About US$20. Too expensive. Dormitory setting as well as nondescript, private rooms with attached bath. Hot water. Moderate.   *Reservations: Direct.*

Triaxco Hotel

7 Nguyen Thai Hoc Street. ☎ *22789* • *8 rooms.* About US$30. This overlooks Xuan Huong Lake and some of the rooms have a great view of the lake. But others don't. The rooms vary considerably, so look at a few before deciding (granted the place isn't full, of course). Hot water. Moderate.   *Reservations: Direct.*

WHERE TO EAT IN DALAT

Dalat has a reputation throughout Vietnam of offering only mediocre food. Of course these are Vietnamese comparing the Vietnamese food of Dalat with that available in other locations. However, most foreign travelers won't be disappointed by the food (particularly vegetarians), especially the Vietnamese food available in Dalat. Most of the hotels have their own restaurants and they are often empty, with a bevy of uniformed waitresses sitting around and not doing much. One reason for this is that food in restaurants is generally more expensive than dishes found in private restaurants or food stalls. One exception would be the Hoang Restaurant at the Thanh The Hotel listed above. The food is good and cheap. Because of Dalat's somewhat temperate climate, it is an excellent source of vegetables and is a vegetarian's paradise. There are a number of small restaurants and cafes along Nguyen Thi Minh Khai street that offer an excellent variety of Vietnamese dishes. Just pick the one that looks the cleanest. And something to remember about eating in Dalat: Restaurants where the prices are included in the menu are generally more expensive than eateries that don't list prices on menus. If the menu has been professionally printed, the same is true. If the menu is handwritten in Vietnamese only (with poor English translations, such as "Freid Eeg"), you'll know you're getting rock-bottom prices.

You may want to avoid the lakeside eateries, which are generally overpriced and serve average food. Backpackers mostly hang out at the Long Hoa and the Hoang Lang Restaurants. Some of the other places to eat:

Shanghai Restaurant   ★

8 Khu Hoa Binh Square • Vietnamese, Asian, and European fare including "delicacies" such as goat testicles and beef penis. Interesting.

Than Thuy Restaurant

4 Nguyen Thai Hoc Street. ☎ *22262* • On the lake beneath the Triaxco Hotel. Vietnamese, Asian, European cuisine. Average but very popular.

Dang A

82 Phon Dinh Phung Street • Vietnamese and exotic Asian fare.

Cam Do

81 Phon Dinh Phung Street • This is typical of the cheap, good food that can be found outside of the hotels, but close by.

Xuan Huong

Ho Xuan Huong Street. On the west side of the lake overlooking the water • Vietnamese, Western dishes.

Pho Tung

Near the Shanghai Restaurant • Excellent bakery, average food.

My Canh

41 Nguyen Thi Minh Khai Street • Excellent Chinese fare.

Thuy Ta ★

Just below the Palace Hotel • If not for the food, which is decent, come here for the views of the lake. Breakfast is the best time.

Long Hoa

6-3 Thang 2 Street • Western style breakfast, but open all day. Although the morning is the best time to hang out here.

La Tulipe Rouge

1 Nguyen Thi Minh, between the market and the Hai Son Hotel • Vietnamese, Chinese and Western dishes.

Nhu Hai

In front of the Central Market • Known for great vegetable dishes.

Cafe Tung

6 Khu Hoa Binh Street • Not really a restaurant, but a cafe with a rich history. Artists used to hang out here before 1975.

DIRECTORY

TRANSPORTATION

Dalat is about a 110 km from Phan Rang, 210 km Nha Trang, 1510 km from Hanoi, 300 km from Saigon, and 110 km from Bao Loc.

INSIDER TIP

Vietnam's Civil Aviation Department is preparing Da Lat's Camli airport for more commercial air services. Included in the plan is an upgrade of the airport as well as the railway stations, as well as the number of air routes into Da Lat. The airport lies about 4 km from downtown Da Lat. Before 1975, it served as an air base.

By air: There are three flights weekly from Saigon to Dalat (Monday, Wednesday and Saturday) and they cost about US$60 round trip. The Monday flight departs at 7 a.m. The other two flights leave at 10 a.m. From Dalat, there are also flights on Wednesday and Saturday (at 3 p.m.) and another one departs for HCMC on Mondays at 8:10 in the morning. You can also fly to Hue on VN on Wednesdays and Saturdays at 10:40 a.m. Flights to Dalat from Hue leave Wednesdays and Saturdays at 1:20 p.m. Flight time is about 40 minutes to Saigon and 2 hours to Hue (aboard what? A DC-3?).

By bus: Dalat has two bus stations (Dalat Bus Station—the long distance station at the end of Nguyen Thi Minh Street—and the local bus station which is a block north of Rap 3/4 Cinema). From the long distance station, express buses leave for Saigon at about 5 a.m. (11,000 dong, 310 km) and take about 8–9 hours, Nha Trang (8400 dong and 5–6 hours, 205 km), Phan Rang (4,600 dong and 2–3 hours, 100 km), Hue (30,000 dong and a damn long time), Danang (27,000 dong, 745 km), Quang Ngai (22,500 dong), Quy Nhon (16,400 dong), and Buon Ma Thuot (17,000 dong, 395 km). Intra-Provincial buses connect Dalat with Bao Loc, Cau Dat, Da Thien, Di Linh, Ta Nun, Ta In and Lac Duong. The fastest way of getting away is by minibus from the local station, however.

Minibuses leave for Hanoi (69,000 dong), Hue (40,000 dong), Danang (35,000 dong), Vinh (55,000 dong), Quy Nhon (55,000 dong), and Nha Trang (11,500 dong).There is also hourly minibus service to Saigon for about 18,000 dong. Many hotels offer their own minibus services to Nha Trang, and some offer them even as far as Saigon.

By car: Dalat is about a 6-7 hour trip by a late-model sedan. I did the trip in a little under 5-1/2 hours by large cc motorcycle, although I do not recommend you try to break that record. The road from Saigon to Dalat is usually quite wide and primarily in excellent shape (by Southeast Asia standards) but, nonetheless, there is a significant amount of pedestrian, ox cart, motorbike, and bicycle traffic—so driving (or riding a motorcycle) is very dangerous. Fortunately, after the fork that splits off NH1 to Dalat, the traffic becomes quite light, except in the villages. There is far less traffic on Highway 20 than on NH1. Be especially careful on the road that ascends from Bao Loc to Dalat through the forested mountains. The road narrows significantly and becomes very steep and winding. Minibuses seem to take great pains to give their passengers the feeling they're on a roller coaster and frequently use the wrong side of the road when negotiating corners at extremely high speeds.

By train: There is no train service presently to Dalat from anywhere but a couple of suburbs, rides which are usually taken on these ancient trains by tourists.

Around town, the best way to get around is on the back of a **motorbike**. You shouldn't have any problem finding someone willing to lend you their services for a day or two. Some will not even require payment. I paid one driver US$7 for two full days of journeying around the Dalat area. You can also travel by **horse cart** or ancient Peugot **taxis**. You can also rent a **bicycle** (if you're in good shape—the terrain is hilly). But you won't find a **cyclo**, because the drivers aren't in good shape.

POST OFFICE

14 Tran Phu Street.

BANKS AND MONEYCHANGERS

Industrial and Commercial Bank of Vietnam. Hoa Binh Square, above the market.

TOURIST OFFICE

Lam Dong Provincial Tourist Office. *12A Tran Phu Street.* ☎ *22125.*

IMMIGRATION POLICE

Lam Dong Provincial Public Security Immigration Office. *10 Than Benh Trong Street.* Hours are between 7:30–11:30 a.m. and 1:30–4:30 p.m.

BUON MA THUOT

Much of this area of the remote central highlands used to be off-limits to foreigners—especially Americans. But this is no longer the case.

Deep within the Central Highlands on the Darlac Plateau is the Provincial capital of Buon Ma Thuot (population about 67,000 and considered by many as the capital of the Central Highlands), not far from the Cambodian border. This is one of the least accessible areas in Vietnam, although you can get there by car. The immigration police in Dalat told me that because of the lengthy and ridiculous road routes to get there, very, very few Westerners make it out to Buon Ma Thuot. Although it is only perhaps 130 km or so as the crow flies northwest from Dalat, to get there by road, you must first take the highway east to the coastal city of Phan Rang (about 110 km), then NH1 north about another 160 km or so, well above Nha Trang (about 35 km), before heading on the road west to Buon Ma Thuot, a dilapidated roadway, for perhaps another 200 km or so. It means a trip from Dalat to Buon Ma Thuot equals well over a whopping 400 km! But you can get there by air. The immigration police in Dalat were unclear, but they said that there already exists a road linking Dalat with Buon Ma Thuot (but that it is for military use only), or that one is being constructed—although, again, it was unclear whether tourists would be allowed to use this route, as Buon Ma Thuot has traditionally been a militarily sensitive area.

But tourists can visit this city. This is an area that was designated a New Economic Zone after the fall of South Vietnam in 1975. Peoples of the Red River region near Hanoi and a significant number of Saigonese were displaced to this area, where villages were created and the forests cleared. The cleared land has yielded little in the form of crops, although the government calls Buon Ma Thuot a "major commercial center." Coffee is the principal crop grown here.

Buon Ma Thuot has the distinction of being the site of the last major battle between NVA and South Vietnamese troops during March 1975 (guess who won?). Then South Vietnamese President Nguyen Van Thieu ordered a withdrawal from the area (in fact the entire Central Highlands) and it was only a short month later before NVA tanks rolled into Saigon.

Today, Buon Ma Thuot's population is ethnically divided, and there is tension with the Rhade minority groups, who have been considered second-class citizens for a number of years.

Buon Ma That shares a similar rainy season with Dalat, but is usually warmer because of its lower elevation.

Along the 250 kilometers from Buon Ma Thuot to Con Tum there are a number of ethnic minorities, most noticeably the Austronesian tribes Jarai and Raday. Buon Ma Thuot was also home to an American military base during the Vietnam War.

WHAT TO SEE AND DO IN BUON MA THUOT

Museum
1 Me Mai Street. This is a relatively interesting museum devoted to the ethnography of the Central Highlands. There are displays and artifacts representing Montagnard and Rhade traditions, among the traditions of other ethnic groups. There is earthenware here as well as agricultural tools. There are also displays of traditional Montagnard dress, musical instruments, ancient weapons and other artifacts from more than 30 ethnicities of the Central Highlands. There's also a traditional Rhade house here as well.

Draylon, Draysap, Drayling and Draynor Waterfalls
These are the several waterfalls that can be found outside town. None are terribly impressive but they rarely see tourists, which makes them that much more delightful to visit. Draysap Falls in particular is a nice area as the falls are surrounded by massive hardwood trees.

Dac Lap Lake
Former Emperor Bao Dai used small amounts of money to build a small palace at this lake about 50 km south of Buon Ma Thuat.

Local Villages
Foreigners are permitted to visit the local ethnic villages in the vicinity of Buon Ma Thuot, but, at the time of this writing, you need permission from the police to do so. You can visit the Rhade village Buon Tuo—13 km from Buon Ma Thuot. Here there are long houses where matriarchal Rhade families dwell, although, in many instances, a male will preside over the community. There are also elephants in the Buon Don area that are captured and trained by the M'nong ethnic group, although this was only believable hearsay during my brief visit. But there are elephants trained in Buon Don, a M'nong village about 56

km northwest of Buon Ma That. They are captured through the use of domesticated elephants.The M'nong, like the Rhade, are a people whose surnames are passed down through the female rather than male lineage. The M'nong have a lot of animosity against all other ethnicities of the region, including ethnic Vietnamese, although the few Westerners that come to this remote pocket of Vietnam are greeted with great and not unbegrudging curiosity. There is also a 13th century Cham tower in the area, about 35 km to the north in Ya Liao.

WHERE TO STAY IN BUON MA THUOT

Thang Loi Hotel
1 Phan Chu Trinh Street. ☎ *2322* • About US$5. This is the biggest hotel on Buon Ma Thuot. Dingy but comfortable. Inexpensive.
Reservations: Direct.

Hong Kong Hotel
30 Hai Ba Trung Street. ☎ *2630* • Basic accommodations. Public toilet. Inexpensive. *Reservations: Direct.*

Hoang Gia Hotel
62 Le Hong Phong Street. ☎ *2161* • Ditto. Inexpensive.
Reservations: Direct.

WHERE TO EAT IN BUON MA THUOT

Stick to the hotels. Like a number of areas in the Mekong Delta, the folks here don't boil their water. I'd stay away from the food stalls, unless you want to spend quite a bit of time in a stall of quite a different variety.

DIRECTORY

TRANSPORTATION

Buon Ma Thuot is about 350 km from HCMC, 1430 from Hanoi, over 400 km from Dalat, 225 km from Quy Nhon, 665 km from Danang and 190 km from Nha Trang.

By air: VN flies to Buon Ma Thuot Tuesdays and Thursdays at 7 a.m., Mondays and Fridays at 10:20 a.m., and Wednesdays and Saturdays at 12 noon.

By bus: There is regular bus service to Saigon, Hanoi, Dalat, Nha Trang and most other provincial capitals and major cities.

By train: There is no rail service to or from Buon Ma Thuot.

By car: See the above mileage information.

TOURIST OFFICES

Dac Lak Tourist Office. *3 Phan Chu Trinh Street.* ☎ *2108.*

PLEIKU & CON TUM

Pleiku (with a population of about 40,000 and an elevation of 780 meters) is a market town in the center of a massive and fertile plateau whose red soil is of volcanic origin. Most of the town's inhabitants are from a variety of ethnic origins. Pleiku was also the site of an American base that went through vicious shelling and mortar attacks by the VC during the war in February 1965. The attack was used as justification for the U.S. escalating its military presence in Vietnam (there were about 25,000 U.S. military "advisors" at the time in South Vietnam).

Con Tum, about 50 km north of Pleiku, is also inhabited primarily by ethnic minority groups. Some of these peoples include the Sedeng, Jarai, Bahnar and Rengao. Con Tum was the site of massive bombing by American B-52s during the Vietnam War and was essentially leveled by that and the fighting that took place between NVA and ARVN troops in the area in 1972. Con Tum is extremely remote and should be seen by only the hardiest of travelers. Some government immigration officials told me that permits and fees were required to visit Con Tum, while others said such documentation and fees were not necessary to see the region.

INSIDER TIP

Although virtually all of Vietnam is open to independent travel, always check with the local immigration police if you want to visit remote, inaccessible areas. The big problem here is that, in many instances, officers within the same province will tell you different stories, especially the farther away you are from the central tourist areas. And, believe me, Pleiku and Con Tum are off the beaten track.

WHAT TO SEE AND DO IN PLEIKU

There is not much to do here but do see the magnificent **Gia Lai Forest** and **Yali Waterfall**. Also don't miss the elephant village of **Nhon Hoa**, where you may be able to ride an elephant (and that probably depends whether or not you're part of one of Saigon tourist's organized excursions). There are also ethnic dance shows and cultural and folk shows in town.

INSIDER TIP

Unfortunately, one of the few ways to visit Pleiku is through one of Saigon tourist's expensive tours of the area. If you take the tour to Pleiku, you'll have to surrender at least nine days of independent travel time, as the tour will also bring you to sights in Nha Trang, Buon Ma Thuot, Quy Nhon and Dalat, places you can easily reach on your own—and should. The following is the tourist agency's itinerary while stopping in Pleiku: After visiting the hilltribe museum and Tua Village near Buon Ma Thuot, you'll travel overland and spend the night in Pleiku. Here you'll get an elephant ride in the village of Nhon Hoa and spend the evening seeing cultural and folk shows put on by ethnic minorities. That's it, folks. Even if you're on a tight budget, you might want to consider flying to Pleiku, as the cost is relatively cheap at US$65 one way from Saigon. From Hanoi, it's about twice as much. The best bet is to fly to Pleiku from Danang for a day or two. The cost is US$60 round trip.

DIRECTORY

TRANSPORTATION

Pleiku is about 550 km from Saigon, 425 from Nha Trang, 200 km from Buon Ma Thuot and 185 km from Quy Nhon.

By air: VN flies to Pleiku from HCMC on Sundays, Tuesdays and Fridays at 10:10 a.m.; from Hanoi on Fridays at 9:30 a.m., and from Danang on Sundays, Tuesdays and Fridays at 1:35 p.m. From Pleiku, flights depart for HCMC on Sundays, Tuesdays and Fridays at 2:15 p.m.; for Hanoi on the same days at 11:25 a.m., and for Danang on the same days at 11:25 a.m.

By bus: There are non-express buses that leave from Pleiku to the coastal cities between Nha Trang and Danang. From Saigon, there is express bus service to Pleiku (about 22 hours).

WHAT TO SEE AND DO IN CON TUM

The spectacular 40-meter high **Jrai Li Waterfalls** are perhaps the best reason to visit the region. They can be found about 20 km southwest of Con Tum.

DIRECTORY

TRANSPORTATION

Con Tum is about 900 km from HCMC, 50 km from Pleiku, 248 from Buon Ma Thuot, 200 km from Quy Nhon, and 435 km from Nha Trang.

By air: You'll have to fly into Pleiku (see the above VN air schedule) and I suggest combining a trip to Con Tum and Pleiku by flying into Pleiku from Danang.

By bus: Buses leave Con Tum for Danang, Pleiku and Buon Ma Thuot.

By car: You can rent a car (and driver) to get to Con Tum. It's worth only a day trip, as Con Tum has few if any accommodations for foreign travelers.

Phan Thiet

PHAN THIET

Colorful fishing boats flank the Phan Thiet River.

PHAN THIET IN A CAPSULE

Largest city in Binh Thuan province...About 120 miles northeast of Saigon...Population of 75,000...Clean, pine-lined, breezy beaches... Famous in Vietnam for its fish sauce (nuoc mam)...A Cham controlled area until the late 17th Century.

Phan Thiet is usually the first stop travelers stay overnight when heading north from Saigon, and the last when heading south from Hue, Danang, or Nha Trang to Saigon. There's not a lot to note here, but the beaches—both Phan Thiet and Mui Ne, 25 km to the east—are clean and expansive and offer a refreshing way to kick back after a hot ride from Saigon. Crossing over the Phan Thiet River on National Highway 1 near the river's mouth at the South China Sea, you'll see row after row of brightly-colored fishing boats tied along both banks. The roads are wide and tree-lined in and outside of Phan Thiet and are usually uncrowded, making sidewalk dining at food stalls comfortable. The enormous width of National Highway 1 leading to Phan Thiet from Saigon was the work of the U.S. Army Corps of Engineers during the Vietnam War. In the effort to widen this central artery between Saigon and Phan Thiet, engineers razed countless buildings, but only partially. It's a bizarre sight to see houses and other structures that appear as if they had gone through a jigsaw. Their owners simply slapped on corregated metal siding and continued their lives—in half a house. For miles these half-houses flank the highway south of the city.

The north bank of the Phan Thiet River was home to European settlers in the 18th and 19th centuries when Phan Thiet was a relatively bustling port. Prior to European colonization, the city was under Cham control. And this part of Vietnam is still heavily populated with Cham descendents. In fact, even today, the plains and mountains around Phan Thiet possess a population with only about 30% ethnic Vietnamese.

In Phan Thiet, swimmers don't bother donning bathing suits.

Phan Thiet is the southernmost city of the former principality of the Cham. Once known as Panduranga, it was once, until the 18th century, entirely left to itelf by the Vietnamese because of its inhospitable climate. Slanting from the northeast to the southwest, the region remains relatively free of the monsoons, which, like Ca Na to the north, creates an environment not unlike Mexico's Baja peninsula. What was originally the coast of Panduranga extended nearly 250 kilometers. Panduranga once reached 100 kilometers west into the valley of the Ndau Nai, which is now referred to as the valley of the Dong Nai River which flowed down to Saigon (then called Raigauv). The Mnong Plateau to the east once served as a natural[*] barrier between Panduranga and Cambodia. The region possessed a number of towns that still exist today: Tanh Linh, Di Linh, Dalat, and Bao Loc.

The tourist office is located at 82 Trung Trac Street which is just on the south side of the Phan Thiet River near the bridge.

WHAT TO SEE AND DO IN PHAN THIET AND ENVIRONS

Phan Thiet Beach

This is about it folks. The beach. Phan Thiet Beach is covered with Australian pines and isn't your typical palm lined tropical beach, but it's clean and offers some pretty heavy surf, almost the kind of surf you can surf in. But don't get out the board. There are beach chairs for rent in this parklike atmosphere. You can sit and drink for free but you've got to rent a chair. It's a popular place with the locals and, like with the vast crux of Vietnam's beaches, the Vietnamese remain in the protective shade of the pines and coconut palms above the beach, leaving this wide aisle of buttery sand nearly deserted save for occasional bathers. Only the foreigners are stupid enough to lie in the sand nearly naked under a burning sun, the locals muse to themselves.The best way to reach Phan Thiet Beach is to head east at the pointed Victory Monument. You can't miss it. You'll reach the dunes just a few hundred yards later. It's usually pretty windy here.

Harbor
Phan Thiet's harbor, which is usually packed with bright, multi-colored fishing boats make for great photos. Try photographing from the bridge that spans the Ca Ti (Phan Thiet) River.

Mui Ne Beach

This is also a nice strip of sand at the end of the Mui Ne peninsula about 12 miles east of Phan Thiet with rising sand dunes and gusty winds. You can get here either by car or bus. If you're just looking for a beach to relax on, the trip out probably isn't worth it, as Phan Thiet Beach offers as much in scenery and more in amenities.

Vinh Hoa
Vinh Hoa, off NH1 between Phan Thiet and Phan Rang is most famous for its mineral water, which is bottled and sold all over Vietnam. It's a small town just off the highway.

WHERE TO STAY IN PHAN THIET

Phan Thiet Hotel

40 Trang Hung Dao Street. ☎ *2573* • US$15–25. This is where you should stay if you're on a budget while staying in Phan Thiet. It's in the center of town, but it's only about a 10-minute walk to the beach. All the rooms have air conditioning, attached bath, and they're generally quite clean. There are doubles and triples in this hotel. The staff seemed a little unfriendly, however. Inexpensive–moderate.

Reservations: Direct

Khach San 19-4

1 Van Tu Van Street. ☎ *2460* • About US$15. This big hotel is just across the street from the bus station and formerly didn't permit foreigners to stay. But this has changed. Air conditioning, restaurant. Inexpensive. ***Reservations: Direct***

Vinh Thuy Hotel

This expensive hotel is right on the beach *on Ton Tuc Thang Street.* ☎ *21294* or *22394* • US$45. This is a new structure, built in 1989, although it looks older. And it's expensive. But it's the only choice in town if you want to stay on the beach. Air conditioning, restaurant. Rooms are clean. To get to the hotel follow the directions given above to Phan Thiet Beach. You'll see the multi-storied hotel on the left. Moderate–expensive. ***Reservations: Direct***

WHERE TO EAT IN PHAN THIET

Extremely cheap sidewalk foodstalls offering great Vietnamese fare abound in this port city, but if you must:

Phan Thiet Hotel

3rd Floor, Phan Thiet Hotel; 40 Tran Hung Dao Street • Vietnamese. Relatively expensive.

Vinh Thuy Hotel

Ton Tuc Thang Street, on the beach • Great seafood at moderate-expensive prices.

DIRECTORY

TRANSPORTATION

Phan Thiet is about 200 km from HCMC, 248 km from Dalat, and 250 km from Nha Trang.

By bus: From HCMC, buses depart for Phan Thiet at Mien Dong Bus Station. The bus station in Phan Thiet is on Tu Van Tu Street on the northern edge of town. Non-express buses leave here for HCMC, Bien Hoa, Phan Rang,Long Khan, Phu Cuong, Madagoui, Mui Ne Beach and other destinations.Best to purchase your tickets in advance.

By train: The Reunification Express train runs in both directions up and down the coast from the town of Muong Man, which is about 10 km west from Phan Thiet.

Around town: cyclos are the cheapest and only way to get around Phan Thiet.

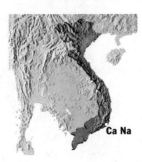

Ca Na

CA NA

Former U.S. military turrets dot the beaches around Ca Na.

CA NA IN A CAPSULE

Isolated and arid...a great overnight stop on National Highway 1...Few people, lots of clean, clear ocean...Take panoramic photos from the tiny mountainside pagoda...Terrain is much like Mexico's lower Baja peninsula...Popular stop for tour buses making their way both north and south.

There's not a helluvalot here, and that's Ca Na's appeal. After a grueling ride over rutted National Highway 1 south from Nha Trang or north from Phan Thiet, Ca Na is what the doctor ordered, as long as you're not expecting a five-star hotel. Or even a one-star hostelry for that matter. The accommodations are a little primitive and you'll think the tiny town is a winter destination for migrating flies. But get it out of your mind, snap the tab off a cold one, and enjoy the lukewarm clear waters of this magnificent bay. The seafood in the town's three restaurants is superb. And the scenery is some of the most unique in Vietnam. If you didn't hear Vietnamese being spoken around you, you'd swear you were in Baja, Mexico. Cacti poke from the rugged, boulder-strewn mountains that lace this semi-circular transparent bay. Australian pines tower from the bluffs overlooking the long, deserted beach. There's even a gun turret and bunker left over from the war facing the ocean defiantly keeping the masses from developing this unique little spike in the South China Sea that will remind you as much of Vietnam as Mazatlan does.

Arid Ca Na offers Baja, California peninsula-like vistas.

WHAT TO SEE AND DO IN CA NA

There's basically nothing to do here but swim in the warm ocean and enjoy the view. Take a hike up into the mountains. (Be careful. Although the locals say the area has been pretty much depleted of its indigenous fauna, there may be snakes). Take a brief visit up the stairs to the Chinese pagoda resting precariously on the hillside opposite the Nah Hang Hai Son Restaurant and take photos of the clear bay. At night, local drunk, new friends that you've made will invite you up into hills to shoot wild animals. Best to decline the offer unless he's got the gun pointed at you.

WHERE TO STAY AND EAT IN CA NA

HOTELS

Ca Na Hotel

National Highway 1. You can't miss it • 10 rooms here, about US$15, a backpacker's type of place, but the accommodations are sufficient for more upscale visitors. Breezy and desertlike. Much of this part of Vietnam reminds me a lot of Mexico, especially the Mazatlan area. The Ca

Na Hotel looks like an American motel, but is right on the beach. The ocean here is very calm and clear, even a little Caribbeanish in its hue. The rooms are large and airy and have ocean views. Private toilet but no hot water. Electricity problems. You'll need the mosquito net more for the flies than for the mosquitos. Moderate to inexpensive if you're traveling with a Vietnamese guide. You may get away with paying as little as US$8 a night.   ***Reservations: Direct***

Hai Son Hotel

Right next to the Hai Son Restaurant • 10 rooms, all facing the sea. A small Chinese pagoda overlooks the town perched on the side of a mountain. You can climb a bunch of steps to get up there. Inexpensive.   ***Reservations: Direct***

RESTAURANTS

Ca Na Quan Restaurant

National Highway 1. Right on the beach, patio over the water. Excellent seafood, from lobster to urchin to squid. Cheap.

Nah Hang Hai Son Restaurant

You can rent cars out of this place; great seafood, right down the street from both hotels.

PHAN RANG

The four brick Po Kiong Gargi Cham Towers date from the 13th century.

Phan Rang (population about 50,000) is sort of a dumpy little nondescript semi-seaside city along the coast a little more than half way between Phan Tiet and Nha Trang. It also serves as the capital of Ninh Thuan Province. Its attractions have nothing to do with the city itself (there are even few hotels for foreigners) but the surrounding Cham towers that rise above the landscape, in particular Po Klaung Garai towers, offer magnificent views of the surrounding mountains. And it is this tower complex which is really the only reason you should veer off NH1 through Phan Rang, unless you need to change money or buy table grapes (which are grown here and sent to Saigon).

The climate of Phan Rang itself is relatively dry and arid, although from the Po Llaung Garai towers, you can view the arid landscape south toward Ca Na and the more lush mountainsides bordering the sea toward Cam Ranh Bay in the north. As well, you can see the concrete remnants of the U.S. airbase called Thanh Son to the north. It was used by Vietnamese Air Force as well as the Soviets until the collapse of that nation. Also you can view from the hill the water tower the Americans built during the war in 1965. Surrounding it are the gun turrets the French built during the First Indochina War. There's a bunch of prickly cacti in the area as well as poinciana trees.

The reason so many towers are in the area is that Phan Rang was once the capital of Champa when it was known as Panduranga. There is still a significant number of Chams that live in the area, and they all seem to be horribly poor, despite the city's trickling trek toward relative economic prosperity.

This is an area where you'll be tempted to try to find a map of the surrounding area identifying sites of Cham towers, but you'll be disappointed. In fact no maps at all (including of Vietnam) are available at any of the newsstand/bookstores in Phan Rang. As we've mentioned earlier, buy all the maps you'll need in Saigon. You'll be hard pressed to find any anywhere else.

WHAT TO SEE AND DO IN PHAN RANG AND ENVIRONS

Po Klong Garai Towers

This is a spectacular set of four brick Cham towers, highly visible at Thap Cham and about 7 km from Phan Rang off the road toward Dalat. To get there take the road to Dalat and turn right onto a dirt road about 2 km past the village Thap Cham. A landmark will be a water tower. When you see it, turn right. The towers are atop a granite, rock-strewn hill called Chak Hala Hill just about 200 meters down the road. The biggest of the four towers (*kalan*)—all of which are in remarkably great shape—built as Hindu temples in the 13th century, was constructed in 1306. There's an image of Siva with six arms appearing to be dancing above the entrance. The image itself is reputedly to have been carved in the 12th century, although recently renovated. The pillars surrounding the entrance have detailed inscriptions. Inside it's dark, and the thick incense constantly burning can be overwhelming and make the visit inside a short one, as you'll soon need fresh air. But inside on a raised dias is a lingam featuring a human face, which is said to be that of King Po Klong Garai. It is believed to have been carved in the 16th century. The face is covered with a white dough mask, which is changed during every ceremony. Inside the narrow vestibule is the carving of a bull which was called Nandin, a symbol of agricultural prosperity. There is a tower opposite the entrance to the kalan that was originally the main entrance to the kalan. Here there are renovated inscriptions carved into the brick. This definitely is worth a visit if you're passing through Phan Rang. And don't be surprised to find a number of young Vietnamese girls dressed in ao dais eager to practice their English with foreign visitors. It was here that I met one such woman who had brought her teacher along to help. The man insisted that the Vietnam War was lost by the Americans because of a mind-control machine a Vietnamese scientist developed in the early 1960s, giving him the power to redirect American opinion of American involvment in the war. He insisted that the device is still in use today, and that it's thought-control waves are delivered through television. Then he said he spent a year in a Saigon mental hospital. Even though he insisted I give him his address, I have yet to receive one of his ears in the mail.

Nha Trang's Po Nagar Cham Towers were built between the 7th and 12th centuries.

Thap Cham Rail Yards

About 300 meters southeast of Po Klong Garai, next to the railroad station. The main purpose of the yards, built by the French around 1915, is to repair the old railroad engines used by Vietnamese Railways. The Vietnamese are ingenious in their repair methods, as spare parts are made by hand or through thoroughly antiquated machinery processes. There was an 85 km long line between Thap Cham and Dalat, but it was closed in 1964 due to repeated VC sabotaging of the tracks. Chains used to pull the trains up the mountainsides. You can see the steepest mountain along the rail line from the road to Dalat from Phan Rang.

Po Re Me Cham Tower

This is more recently constructed than the towers of Po Klong Garai. It can easily be seen from the summit of Chok Hala Hill. It was one of the many towers and sanctuaries that encircled the capital, as these towers do in all Cham capitals. It's on a rocky hill about 10 km southwest of Phan Rang and 5 km toward the mountains south of Phan Rang off NH1. It was named for the last Champa ruler King Po Re Mi (1629–1651). Many archeologists believe the structure was built much earlier than the king's reign, perhaps as early as the beginning of the 16th century. Paintings decorate the interior. There are also two statues of the bull Nandin here. There is an excellent life-size image of Siva carved into a relief on a stele. However, this image of Siva has eight arms rather than the six found at Po Klong Garai. There are five figures that are next to the statue—one is a wife of King Po Re Me (Bai Tan Chun). There's another wife of the king, Princess Po Biah Sucih. A third figure was another wife of the king, the Vietnamese princess Po Bia Ut. There are also chapels in the area which possess Hindu influences, but lack the classic Cham style. They are located in the Huu Duc village of Hau Sanh.

Po Nagar

This pagoda is about 15 kilometers east of Phan Rang. It's a 19th century Vietnamese pagoda that celebrates the Goddess Po Nagar. Here there are statues of women and a stone which represents the Mother Goddess.

Tano Po Riya

This is a small chapel in Malam, 50 kilometers from Phan Rang at the base of the mountains. Ask for directions.

Po Rayak

This means God of the Sea and the Rains and rests on the mountain of Cape Padaran. There is a large festival that takes place, in the southern part of the province in March which draws virtually the entire province's population.

Ninh Chu Beach

This is a relatively nice stretch of unspoiled and deserted beach (for the most part) sand about 4 km south of Phan Rang.

Tuan Tu

South on NH1. Go about 250 meters after you cross a large bridge. Here, you'll come across a smaller bridge, after which crossing you'll turn left onto a dirt path. You'll come to a market which is just after a Buddhist pagoda. Turn right on the road at the market for 2 km. You'll then cross two small foot bridges. This is a small Muslim Cham village 5 km south of Phan Rang. Depending on the mood of the Provincial Immigration office, you may need a permit to visit here, as well as dishing out fees for a guide, even if you already have one. Here there is a Cham Mosque. The elected officials of the village can easily be recognized by their ornate costumes, featuring white robes and a turban with long red tassles. The women wear traditional Cham headdress.

WHERE TO STAY IN PHAN RANG

Huu Nghi Hotel

1 Huong Vong Street (just off the road to Thap Cham). ☎ *22606 • 20 rooms.* About US$12–25. Some rooms with air conditioning here, but the staff is friendly and they welcome foreigners. The lower priced rooms are a little dingy. Inexpensive–moderate. ***Reservations: Direct.***

Phan Rang Hotel

254 Thuot Nhat Street • 20 rooms. US$10–20. Didn't get a chance to visit here, but I'm told it's the most popular hotel in Phan Rang with foreigners. Inexpensive–moderate.

Thong Nhat Hotel

164 Thong Nhat Street. ☎ *2515 • 16 rooms.* US$15–20. This is a relatively new hotel. Restaurant, hot water, air conditioning in the expensive rooms. Moderate. ***Reservations: Direct.***

WHERE TO EAT IN PHAN RANG

Huu Nghi

1 Hung Vuong Street • Great Vietnamese fare.

Nha Hang 426

Across the street from the bus station • Vietnamese, Asian dishes. A good place to hang out while waiting for your bus.

Thu Thuy Restaurant

Thong Nhat Street • Vietnamese, Asian. Delicious and cheap.

Hang 404

404 Thang Nhat Street • Vietnamese.

DIRECTORY

TRANSPORTATION

Phan Rang is about 330 km from Saigon, 105 km from Nha Trang, 110 km from Dalat, and 147 km fro Phan Thiet.

By bus: The Intercity Bus Station is opposite *66 Thong Nhat Street*, about 500 meters north of the center of the city. There are regular connections with Saigon, Danang, Nha Trang, Dalat, Ca Na, Cam Ranh Bay, Don Duong, Long Huong, Phan Thiet, Noi Huyen, Song My, Nhi Ha and Phan Ri, to mention some. Also buses leave for Saigon from Mien Dong Bus Station. The local bus station is at *428 Thong Nhat Street*, south of town.

By train: The station is located at Thap Cham, 5 km west of town and within sight of Po Klong Garai Cham towers. Trains serve all coastal destinations.

By car: From Dalat, the trip takes about 2 hours. From Saigon on NH1, about 7–8 hours.

BANKS AND MONEYCHANGERS

Foreign Exchange Service. *334 Thong Nhat Street.* There are also a couple of jewelry and gold shops along Thong Nhat Street (which is what NH1 is called going through Phan Rang) that will exchange money, but be prepared to accept a sack of small 2000 dong notes.

TOURIST OFFICE

Ninh Thuan Tourist (in Vietnamese: Cong Ty Du Lich Ninh Thuan). Inside the Huu Nghi Hotel.

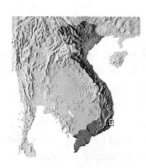

CAM RANH BAY

Scenic Cam Ranh Bay has been used as a naval base by several countries, including the Russians, the Japanese, the Americans and the Soviets since the early 20th century.

CAM RANH BAY IN A CAPSULE

Hawaii of the Orient...Laid back and lush...This was the site of the largest U.S. naval base in Vietnam during the war...Has been utilized as a naval base for five different nations since 1905...The Russians even managed to maintain a presence here after the Soviet Union collapsed...This has outstanding tourist potential, but there seem to be no plans to develop the area into a tourist destination...The Vietnamese government seems to want to keep the area as a restricted site although foreigners can visit the area...The area is a major salt production site....A great place to start your own navy–you wouldn't need to spend money to send your sailors to other areas for R&R.

Traveling up NH1 from Phan Rang toward Nha Trang lies some of the most beautiful coastal topography in southern Vietnam, much of it in the Cam Ranh Bay area. Salt paddies and factories dot the roadside—and on both sides of this beautiful natural harbor are towering, lush mountains interrupted by banana plantations and surrounded by dense coconut palm groves. The water here is a crystal-clear sky blue. Perhaps the most disappointing (or rewarding, depending on your viewpoint) aspect of the area is its distinct lack of tourist facilities. This is simply because the area has traditionally served as a major naval station for nations ranging from the Russians in 1905, the Japanese during WWII, the Americans during the Vietnam War, and the Soviets again after the Americans left. In fact, even after the fall of the Soviet Union, Russia still managed to maintain a small fleet in Cam Ranh Bay (it was once their largest base outside the Soviet Union)—as a symbolic gesture of defiance if nothing else.

In the 1960s, U.S. forces made this area a massive naval institution, and the area has not yet shed it's militarylike milieu. Touring the area today is still difficult—even though the Russians have left. It is still considered militarily sensitive, which is a damn shame, because there's really nowhere to stay, and it's the type of area you could see yourself spending a few days in. The beaches in the area are terrific—unspoiled, empty white sand stretches for kilometers.

Hootches hide behind coconut palms and banana trees south of Cam Ranh.

WHERE TO EAT IN CAM RANH BAY

The number of food stalls along NHI approaching Cam Ranh is staggering. Each proprietor runs out into the middle of the highway with each approaching vehicle to entice them to stop at their eatery. Choose among the dozens that are here. The seafood, including eel, squid, and fresh fish crab is excellent. But be warned. If you're traveling independently without a Vietnamese guide, you will be charged as much as three times higher than a Vietnamese would, or foreigners traveling with a Vietnamese.

INSIDER TIP

When traveling with a Vietnamese, let this person do all the work for you, in both restaurants and in hotels. Never order or ask for anything yourself. Don't even point at what you want. Tell the Vietnamese guide or friend what your wishes are. If the proprietor has even the slightest indication that you are requesting something yourself, you will be charged more, even if your Vietnamese companion is present. You don't believe me? Go ahead and order that 333 beer, and later see on your bill that it cost 10,000 dong, while it would have cost 5 or 6 thousand dong had your Vietnamese companion ordered it for you.

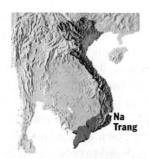

Na
Trang

NHA TRANG

Nha Trang's huge white Buddha was built in 1963.

NHA TRANG IN A CAPSULE

Lazy and beautiful fledgling beach resort city of 200,000 that may one day unfortunately acquire the commercialism and gawdy trappings of Thailand's Pattaya or Bali's Nusa Dua Beach...Possesses some of Vietnam's best year-round weather...The beach here is nearly four miles long...Port was established in 1924 and was a popular recreational spot for American sailors during the Vietnam War...The site of some of Vietnam's most magnificent Cham towers...The Po Nogar Cham towers offer spectacular views of the city and harbor, the ocean and islands, and the surrounding verdant mountains.

Nha Trang (population about 210,000) offers the best combination of clean beaches, clear water and traveler's amenities for the fewest amount of people than any coastal city in Vietnam. Period. And asked what city travelers would return to after doing a coastal tour of Vietnam, most say Nha Trang. Other than its topographical setting, architecturally it's not a particularly beautiful city. It's not a historical and cultural icon like Hue. It lacks the colorful and heart-wrenching Vietnam War sagas of Danang. It is, though, probably Vietnam's closest answer to a developed tropical resort. Its four miles of beaches are clean and uncrowded, especially outside the city center. The water is usually quite clear, making Nha Trang a diving and watersports destination (although parasailing and jet skis have yet to arrive).

INSIDER TIP

Depending upon whom you believe, Nha Trang is developing a reputation as a turkey shoot for pickpockets and other scam artists. Whether this picture being painted by some guides is accurate or not, the jury's still out. But if you're traveling with a guide, he may warn you that the danger is not from the locals, but from foreigners. You may be advised to stay away from foreigners entirely; even casual greetings should be avoided. Why Nha Trang would be selected over other Vietnamese cities by foreign pickpockets, though, is a mystery to me. There is one school of thought that says the guides want to keep you away from other tourists, so you won't realize, through idle conversation, how much you were overcharged by your guide. Nha Trang would be a natural place for your guide to tell you this as it is the first city north of Saigon where you'd have a fair chance of interacting with a significant number of foreign tourists. One thing for sure, though. Only by talking with other tourists will you get any idea of what constitutes a fair price for your tour or the transportation means you've selected. Rather than discriminate against any single group of people, I'd simply not trust anyone.

The clear waters are great for scuba diving and snorkeling, especially off Mieu Island, which can easily be reached by ferry, passenger excursion vessels or small private boats. Unfortunately, this area has the potential of being developed into a major seaside tourist mecca of the likes of Pattaya or Phucket, although this will take some years. The small pockets of tourist areas are packed with foreigners, and rarely do you see any elsewhere in town. The beach-side boulevard of Tran Phu is usually virtually empty of traffic and there are a number of hotels lining the street, although they're across the boulevard from the beach, which is coconut palm-lined and features a number of comfortable cafes.

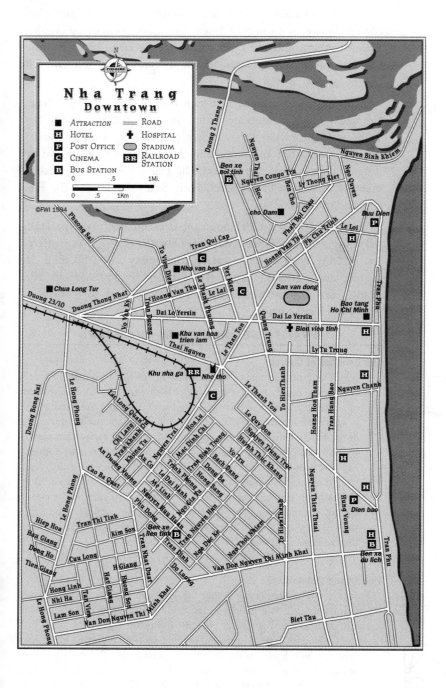

Nha Trang
Downtown

- ■ ATTRACTION
- H HOTEL
- P POST OFFICE
- C CINEMA
- B BUS STATION

- ═══ ROAD
- ✚ HOSPITAL
- ⬭ STADIUM
- RR RAILROAD STATION

0   .5   1Mi.
0   .5   1Km

©FWI 1994

Nha Trang (the name is taken from the Cham word "Yakram," which means bamboo river) also possesses perhaps Vietnam's best coastal climate, as it can cool down significantly here in the evening. Unlike farther south, the rainy season in Nha Trang runs only from October through early December—and even then, rain usually falls only at night.

There are some magnificent Cham towers (the Cham Po Nagar Complex) which sit high atop a hill on the north bank of the Nha Trang River, near its mouth, which offer spectacular views of the city, beaches, the harbor and mountains that reach west far off into the distance. Few tourists visit areas of Nha Trang other than the seaside, except to see the Cham towers, Long Son Pogoda, and the Hon Chong Promontory.

During the Tay Son rebellion in the late 18th century, Nha Trang fell to the rebels after nine bitter days of battle. Now it is a two-tiered city offering both a sleepy seaside community and a bustling city center, which, ironically, offers the best food found in the city. Nha Trang's architecture ranges from French colonial to Chinese to post-1975 Vietnamese.

WHAT TO SEE AND DO IN NHA TRANG

The Beaches of Course

Nha Trang offers some of the best beaches in all of Vietnam. There is Nha Trang Beach, which runs parallel with Tran Phu Blvd. The coconut-palm lined white sands are dotted with cafes and food stalls. This is where most visitors to Nha Trang come to sun themselves and bathe in the warm, clear waters. As you move down the beach south toward the Bao Dai Villas, strollers, sun worshipers, bathers and souvenir hawkers become fewer and farther between. This is a beautiful, clean stretch of sand surrounded by calm waters that is nearly 6 km long. Hon Chong Beach is actually a few beaches which surround the Hon Chong Promontory. The palm-lined sands are amidst a beautiful sky-blue bay and tall, lush, banana and mango tree-covered mountains that surround the bay. Here is where many of the area's fishermen live.

Hon Chong Promontory

Just north of Nha Trang (about 3.5 km from the city center) is a tall granite hillside that overlooks the small crystal-clear bay where Hon Chong Beach is. You can get here by following 2 Thang 4 Street past the Po Nogar Cham Towers and turning right on Nguyen Dinh Chieu Street, which leads up the hill to the promontory. There's a decent restaurant and souvenir kiosks at the promontory and a small run-down hotel nearby (Nha Nghi Hon Chang) that's currently closed. From the bluffs of the promontory, you can view the Fairy

Mountains, three peaks that are supposed to look like a sleeping fairy (I'll tell you, these Vietnamese!) but look like nothing more than three verdant peaks. Toward Nha Trang, down Hon Chong beach, you can see the small island of Hon Do and its Buddhist temple on top. To the northeast is Tortoise Island. You can also see the two islands of Hon Yen in the distance. The giant rocks of the promontory here are reputed in legend to have been carved by the hands of a giant. A large "handprint" is on one boulder on top of the promontory. Local lore has it that the print was made by a drunk male fairy after he was caught peeking at a female fairy swimming in the buff and then fell down. (Unfortunately, today, the only carving in the rocks is being done by drunk vandals with spray paint cans. Grafitti covers some of the stones.) Although the two fairies eventually married, the male was caught by the gods and sent off to "prison" for his previous voyeurism. After the female could wait no longer for her lover to return, she lay down and turned into Fairy Mountain. I think that Disney could use some of these guys as writers, myself. Admission is 6000 dong per car. Not sure what it is for a single individual.

Hon Chong Promontory in Nha Trang offers beautiful vistas of the surrounding mountains.

Gallery

20 Tran Phu. Vietnamese artists and sculptors works on display and for sale. Oil paintings, laquer paintings, wood engravings, silk paper paintings, etc. Universal Sciences of Library of Khanh Hoa Province.

Phong Trung Bay My Thuat Gallery

The various works of a bunch of Vietnamese artists and sculptors. ☎ *22277. 16 Tran Phu.* Works for display and sale.

Pasteur Institute

Phan Thu Street, across from the beach. Andre Yersin, who came to Vietnam from Paris after working for Louis Pasteur and lived for four years in the Central Highlands documenting his experiences, was perhaps the most beloved of all the Frenchmen by the Vietnamese in the late 19th and early 20th centuries. Yersin was the man who "discovered" Dalat and recommended that the French government establish a hill station there. He also was the first to introduce quinine and rubber producing trees to Vietnam. But perhaps he is best known as being the man who discovered the cause of bubonic plague. Yersin founded the Nha Trang institute in 1895 to help research ways of improving Vietnamese hygeine and immune systems. Today, the institute performs the same functions. It develops vaccines and conducts research in microbiology, epidemiology and virology, and develops disease vaccines using primitive equipment. Yersin's library has now been made into a museum. A lot's on display here: antiquated research equipment, personal items, and the doctor's books. Open every day from 7:30–11 except Sunday and holidays.

Po Nogar Cham Towers   ★★★

There were once eight magnificent towers on this granite hilltop *on 2 Thang 4 Street* (just on the north side of the Xom Bong bridge) overlooking the picturesque Nha Trang region, but only four remain today. Po Nagar (locally called Tap Ba) means "Lady of the City," and the towers were built between the 7th and 12th centuries. Well before then, during the 2nd century AD, the area was an important Hindu worshipping hilltop. The largest tower is the 23-meter high Thap Chinh, built in AD 817 by a minister of King Harivarman I named Pangro, which houses the statue of Lady Thien Y-ana (the wife of Prince Bac Hai). Lady Thien Y-ana taught agriculture to the people as well as weaving. The remaining towers were constructed in honor of the gods, the central tower (or Fertility Temple) in honor of Cri Cambhu. The northwest tower was built for Sandhaka (the foster father of Lady Thien Y-ana) and the south tower for Lady Thien Y-ana's daughter, Ganeca.

Some 40 years before the north tower was built, it was raided by Malay corsairs from Sumatra who burned and ransacked the area. A gold mukha-linga was put in the north tower by King Indravarman III in AD 918, although it was later hauled off by raiding Khmer bandits. The mukha-linga was replaced with the stone figure of a shakti of Shiva by King Jaya Indravarman I in AD 965.

The central tower was erected in the 12th century, and is considered the least well-built tower in the complex. Its pyramidal roof possesses no terracing or pilasters.

There's a museum next to the north tower that contains examples of Cham stonework, but relics that hardly rival the magnificent examples of Cham stonework found at the Cham Museum in Danang. The towers are worth a visit if only for the views from the top of the hill. Don't do Nha Trang without seeing them. Although some guidebooks say there is a 500 dong admission to the complex, I paid 5000 dong to get in.

Long Son Pagoda

23 Thang 10 Street. The Buddha in this temple, founded in the late 19th century, is lit by natural light from behind it. The pagoda itself has been rebuilt a number of times and is now dedicated to the monks and nuns that perished through self-immolation protesting the South Vietnamese Diem regime during the Vietnam War. There are ceramic tile and glass images of dragons on the roof and the entrance to the structure. There are also murals telling of jataka legends covering the upper walls of the pagoda. The principal sanctuary is decorated with dragons wrapped around the columns on both sides of the main altar. Stairs on the right side of the complex head up the hill toward an approximately 10 meter high white Buddha seated on a lotus blossom. The big Buddha can be seen from many parts of the city.

Cau Da

This is a tiny, nondescript fishing village about 5 km south of Nha Trang best noted for being a good way to get out to Mieu Island, for the Bao Dai Villas and also for the Aquarium. But there are some superb views of Nha Trang from the promontory which is the site of the villas.There's an abundance of souvenir kiosks in Cau Da for tourists while they haggle over private boat fees to the island. Many of the "souvenirs" are stuffed sealife, but you can purchase some fine, polished seashells and seashell jewelry.

Oceanographic Institute and Aquarium

Built in the early 1920s, this is a disappointing display of ocean creatures and plant life in Cau Da. From Nha Trang, go down (south) Tran Phu Blvd. toward the Bao Dai Villas, which becomes To Do Street south of the airport. The Aquarium's more than 20 tanks contain seahorses, lobsters, turtles and the like. There's a museum of preserved sea creatures behind the aquarium featuring perhaps 60,000 preserved specimens of local sealife. As well, there are stuffed fish and sea birds. I wasn't impressed.

NHA TRANG ENVIRONS

★ *DAI LANH*

National Highway 1 passes through the small hamlet of Dai Lanh about 85 km north of Nha Trang. It's a spectacularly scenic location (the lush green mountains descend virtually to the beach), the bay's beach being surrounded by casuarina trees that were, unfortunately, virtually ripped from their roots by the devastating typhoon that hit the central Vietnamese coast in December 1993. I mean this area really took a battering. The palms and casuarina trees, the few that remain, look as if they had been totally defoliated during the war—and many tourists will ask their guides if this was indeed what happened to what is normally an amazingly lush mountain-to-sea hamlet. The beach is of clean, white sand and virtually void of beachgoers. Despite the massive typhoon damage to the flora in the area, Dai Lanh makes for a perfect beach day trip from Nha Trang. The beach touts are few and far between, but they usually offer what you'd want to buy anyway on a hot day, rich local coconut milk and its soft meat to match. There is a restaurant/cafe at the beach (the Dai Lanh Restaurant) as well as an amazingly drab-appearing, unfinished hotel that seems to have been under construction since the Nguyen Dynasty, which will presumably be called the Dai Lanh Hotel (that's if it's finished before the Bill Clinton Dynasty ends). But no one around the area seems to have any idea when or if ever the structure will be completed. It should be, though. Like Ca Na to the south, Dai Lanh has the potential of being one of the most relaxing, remote and commercially undeveloped and least exploited coastal areas in Vietnam. Stop here.

MIEU ISLAND

The principal village on this island off Nha Trang is Tri Nguyen, a small town that's noted for a fish breeding farm, where dozens of species of sealife are raised in separate compartments. There's one "beach" on the island, Bai Soai, which is really nothing more than where the sea meets a bunch of rocks. If you want to lie out in the sun here, bring a bed. And if you want to go swimming, bring hiking boots. Means of reaching the island are discussed in the Cau Da section of this chapter.

BAMBOO ISLAND

You'll have to hire a private craft to reach this island, about 3 km off the coast of Nha Trang Beach and the largest isle in the vicinity of Nha Trang. A decent beach is here (Tru Beach) on the northern end of the island.

EBONY ISLAND

This is just south of Bamboo Island and is noted for its decent snorkeling. Again, you'll have to hire a boat to get out here.

SALANGANE ISLAND

These are actually two different isles about 17 km offshore (a 3–4 hour boat ride) where salangane nests are gathered for use in bird's nest soup and for their traditional aphrodisiac qualities. The nests themselves are created from the secretions of salangane birds. The red ones are considered the finest and they're harvested about twice a year. It's believed the virile and promiscuous Emperor Minh Mang who ruled Vietnam in the mid 19th century relied on salangane for his legendary sexual longevity.

BA HO FALLS

About 20 km north of Nha Trang and close to the village of Phu Huu is a beautiful set of three waterfalls set amongst a lush forest. You can get there by bus to Ninh Hoa from Nha Trang's local bus station.

DIEN KHANH CITADEL

This 17th century Trinh Dynasty citadel is about 10 km west of Nha Trang and close to the village of Dien Toan. After defeating the Tay Son insurgency, Prince Nguyen Anh, who was later to become Emperor Gia Long rebuilt the structure in 1793. It's worth only a short visit.

WHERE TO STAY IN NHA TRANG

Cau Da Villas (Bao Dai Villas)   ★★★
Tran Phu Street at Cau Da; ☎ *22249 or 21124* • US$30–40-plus. These villas, about 3-1/2 miles south of town off Tran Phu Street, are the classiest accommodations in town and used to be the estate of the former Emperor Bao Dai. The villas were renovated recently and offer incredible views of the sea, the harbour, and Bamboo and Mieu Islands, although it's a little disappointing when freighters are anchored offshore, as they often are down here. But the villas are an outstanding bargain for the price. The rooms are large, open and airy—with bathrooms to match. All the amenities you'd expect at twice the cost. Moderate–Expensive.   ***Reservations: Direct.***

Thuy Duong Hotel & Restaurant
36 Tran Phu • *10 rooms. US$7–15.* Air conditioning in the cheap rooms. Restaurant. Sort of a lazy place frequented by beer-swilling, but polite, locals. Pool tables in front. Not much going on. I saw no tourists here, but they are accepted. Inexpensive.
Reservations: Direct

Hotel Hoa Hong Mini Hotel
26 Nguyen Thien Thuat, ☎ *22778; FAX: 84-5823842* • A bit off the beaten track. Not particularly close to the beach, nor the hustle and bustle of the city center. But clean enough. Few tourists. Inexpensive–Moderate.   ***Reservations: Direct***

Thong Nhat Hotel
18 Tran Phu Street, ☎ *22966 or 22511* • *86 rooms. US$12–27.* On the beach strip. Tall, attractive building—the upper floors offer a great view of the islands if you can get a room facing the water. The cheaper

price gets you a reasonably comfortable room with two beds, a ceiling fan, and hot water. The splurge price gets you the above plus air conditioning, a refrigerator, telephone and TV. Overall, this is a very nice place for the price. Moderate.   ***Reservations: Direct***

Post Hotel

2 Tran Phu Street; ☎ *21181 • 24 rooms (2 suites).* US$20–25. Located on the far north end of the Tran Phu strip across the street from the beach. Brand new building and hotel. Opened only months ago. Friendly, helpful and eager staff—perhaps because they're new. Glamerous white deco building. Clean as a whistle. Get a room on one of the higher floors for a view of the sea. Although it's quiet enough, I'd stay away from the rooms off the lobby if you can. Telephone, refrigerator, TV, air conditioning. Moderate.   ***Reservations: Direct***

Duy Tan Hotel (Khach San 24)

24 Tran Phu Street; ☎ *22671 • 83 rooms.* US$11–30. This building, across Tran Phu from the beach, looks like a toppled ice-cube tray, but it's a popular place. A word of caution. It seems each room has a different price. I counted at least 8 different prices, so know what you're getting into. A number of rooms offer separate meeting areas. Restaurant, car rentals, tours, catering, laundry, barber/beauty salon. Photo developing. Moderate.   ***Reservations: Direct***

Vien Dong Hotel

1 Tran Hung Dao Street; ☎ *21606 or 21608; FAX: 84.58.21912 • 84 rooms (6 suites).* US$7–50. This is the most happenin' place in town. Just up Tran Hung Dao from the beach, this place is truly a bargain if you take one of the cheaper rooms on the top floor. Namely because you'll be able to take advantage of the hotel's amenities which, on a Vietnam scale, make the Vien Dong a full-blown resort. There's a large swimming pool, pool tables, a tennis court, badminton court, and a huge outdoor cafe where traditional Vietnamese dance shows are performed a few times a week. There's a top-shelf gift shop, restaurant, and bicycle rentals. The service is friendly, albeit a little slow. The cheap rooms offer fan, hot water, public WC. The pricier digs come with air conditioning, color TV, telephone (IDD), and refrigerator. This is my choice when in Nha Trang, although it's somewhat sterile, packed with foreigners, and you have to pay to use the pool. Inexpensive–Expensive.   ***Reservations: Direct.***

Hai Au 1 Hotel

3 Nguyen Chanh; ☎ *22862 • 21 rooms.* US$15–20. Tucked away off the beachside drag of Tran Phu, this is a small, unassuming, quiet, and basic hotel that might be just a little overpriced. But the service is friendly and laid-back. It seemed to me to be more popular with overseas Vietnamese than Westerners. Air conditioning, hot water. Moderate.   ***Reservations: Direct.***

Hau Au 2 Hotel

4 Nguyen Chanh; ☎ *23644 • 15 rooms.* US$15–25. This is a more attractive and newer building than its sister up the street. Hot water, air conditioning, restaurant, rest area. Moderate.

Reservations: Direct.

Nha Trang's Khatoco Hotel leaves no guessing what it's owned by—a giant tobacco monopoly.

Khatoco Hotel

9 Biet Thu Street; ☎ *23724, 23725, or 23723; FAX: 84.58.21925 • 26 rooms.* US$30–60. This is the classic example of the invasion of capitalism in Vietnam. In the middle of relative squalor with no particular strategic or marketing reason to be there, rises this modern, elegant, dazzling white monolith founded in marble, smoked glass and chrome that looks right off the set of *Miami Vice.* Atop the roof are suspended giant packs of cigarettes produced by the hotel's owners (the Khanh Hoa Tobacco Company). This is truly a bizarre sight, and worth the short walk from the beach just for the chuckle and a snapshot. Opened in April 1993, it has most of the conveniences: guide services, tours, restaurant, air conditioning, refrigerator, international TV, telephone. Very friendly staff. But for the price, make sure you get a view of the water. Moderate–Expensive.   ***Reservations: Direct.***

Nah Trang Hotel

129 Thong Nhat Street; ☎ *22347 or 22224 • 74 rooms.* US$8–20. This towering (by Vietnamese standards) seven or eight story hotel is clean and priced right but out of the way unless you have business in the vicinity. Air conditioning. Inexpensive–Moderate.

Reservations: Direct.

Hai Yen Hotel

40 Tran Phu Street; ☎ *22828 or 22974; FAX: 84.58.21902 • 107 rooms.* US$7–80. This is a popular place across Tran Phu from the beach, and despite its amenities of conference rooms, car rentals, a dancing hall, restaurant, currency exchange, gift shop, and traditional Vietnamese dance performances, the reception—when I visted—ranged from aloof to rude. I don't see what all the fuss is about. Inexpensive–Expensive.   ***Reservations: Direct.***

Hotel La Fregate (Khach San Thang Loi)

4 Pasteur Street; ☎ *22241 or 22523; Fax: 21905 • 55 rooms.* US$20–38. This hotel has undergone a recent renovation and the staff seem as cheerful as the new masonry. Conference hall, large restaurant, cafe, two bars, two banquet rooms, beauty salon/barber, massage and sauna, and gift shop. Also car and bike rentals, boat tours. The upper-end rooms come with refrigerator, hot water, air conditioning, and bathtub. Luxurious for the price. Moderate.

Reservations: Direct.

The Grand Hotel (Nha Khach 44)

44 Tran Phu Street; ☎ *22445 •* US$10–40. This yellow French colonial mansion sits right across Tran Phu from the beach and has some breezy, large and elegant rooms. But the cheaper prices put you in a barracks-like annex next to the main building with a fan and a hard, thin mattress. The grounds look more like a boarding school campus than a hotel, but the price—at all levels—includes a full breakfast on the patio. It's relaxing in the early morning sunlight. Beauty salon/barber services. Inexpensive–Moderate. ***Reservations: Direct.***

Lehoang

86 Tran Phu; ☎ *24070, 24076* • *9 rooms.* US$8–16. On the road just south of town. The $8 rooms are a bargain that would run as high as $12 or more closer to town. Across the road from the beach. Air conditioning, big beds, hot water, individual baths. Nhat Thong is the manager; a real friendly guy. Tell him Fielding sent you and you may get a Vietnamese's rate. Restaurant right next door. Inexpensive.

Reservations: Direct.

Hung Dao Hotel

3 Tran Hung Dao Street; ☎ *22246* • US$8–10. This is where everyone heads when the cheaper rooms at next door's Vien Hong are full. Consequently, this place is full a lot of the time, too. Call in advance. Or better yet, call the Vien Hong in advance. I've heard a rumor about "nasty" elements frequenting this place. Hookers perhaps? Nonetheless, it's an attractive place with a decent location (although not on the beach) and a good restaurant. Bike rentals, too. Inexpensive.

Reservations: Direct.

Hai Duong Bungelows

Tran Phu Street, about 2 miles south of town on the beach • This place appears to be nothing more than a beachside whore village, for Vietnamese only. As a foreigner, I wasn't allowed to take a "hut." And my inspection of the grounds turned up nothing more accommodating than some drunken Army officers fondling hookers in the bar next to reception. I only mention this place so you'll avoid the temptation to inquire here, because Hai Duong is on the beach and the setting's not bad amid the casuarina trees. And also because the bungalows are listed in the other guidebooks as being accessible to foreigners. If you can get in, I'd like to hear from you. But why bother trying?

WHERE TO EAT IN NHA TRANG

Nam Phi Restaurant

12 Tran Phu Street • Local fare.

Coco Bar

Tran Phu Street, across from the Pasteur museum on the beach. Cafe.

Dich Vu Du Litch

Thui Trang, 9a Le Loi • Vietnamese, Asian.

Ninh Hoa

So9 Le Loi • Specialty is hash.

Hoang Yen Guide and Tourist Services Center

26-28 Tran Phu; ☎ *22961* • Yes, this is a restaurant. Great seafood.

Quan An

11 Le Loi • Seafood.

Ninh Hoa

13 Le Loi • Vietnamese, Asian.

Vi Huong
19 Le Loi; ☎ *22872* • Cuisine of Vietnam.

Quan Nem
1 Hoang Van Thu • Vietnamese.

Com Phan Dia
33 Le Loi • Vietnamese, Asian.

Phong Ngu
33 Le Loi, ☎ *22096* • Vietnamese, Asian.

Dong Anh
17b Yersin • Vietnamese, Asian.

Khanh Phong
6b Yersin • Vietnamese, Asian.

Cafe Tho
1 Quang Trung • Vietnamese, Asian.

The Second Best Ice Creamery in Vietnam   ★
58 Quang Trung • Yogurt, fruit salad, fruit juice, banana splits galore, soft drinks, sour soft drinks, fruit shakes, coffees, teas, a hodgepodge of stuff. Frequented by Westerners. Very friendly. The woman owner says the name is a takeoff on an ice cream parlor in Saigon called The Best Ice Creamery in Vietnam. But her scheming neighbor, hoping to cash in on some of the success she was seeing next door, suspiciously and less than fluently renamed her own food stall as the "First Best Offering" store and posted an identical menu alongside the one hanging in The Second Best Ice Creamery. If you're not careful, you'll think the two shops are one and the same and end up getting served by the imposter. But on my visit, First Best Offering was empty and SBICV nearly packed, mostly with dollar-toting foreigners. The owner says she's changing the name to Banana Splits. That'll screw up her neighbor, who'll proably reciprocate with a name change of her own—perhaps to Banana Divides. We'll keep you posted on this, the first corner gas station war in Vietnam since 1975.

Cafe Vy
2 Ly Tu Trong, just right off the main drag by the beach.

Cafe Giai Khat
Tran Phu • Peaceful, bamboo laden setting. Small tables are very private. Nice for couples. Romantic in sort of a grungy way.

Hai Au Restaurant
3 Nguyen Chanh; ☎ *22862* • Vietnamese specialties.

The Lizard Club and Restaurant
Le thanh ton; ☎ *21206.*

46 Cafe
By the Grand Hotel, Tran Phu • Standard local fare.

Seamen's Club Restaurant
  72-74 Tran Phu, ☎ *22251•* I'm not sure about this place, whether it's for seamen only or not.

Dac San Seafood Restaurant
  Tran Phhu, right on the beach south of town • This is a breezy open air cafe and restaurant under a tent on the beach.

96 Restaurant
  96 Tran Phu.

Kem Cafe
  Tran Phu.

Hanh Green Hat
  Tran Phu.

DIRECTORY

TRANSPORTATION

Nha Trang is 1300 km from Hanoi, 445 km from Saigon, 240 km from Quy Nhon, 215 km from Dalat, 200 km from Buon Ma Thuot, 410 km to Quang Ngai, 105 km from PhanRang.

By air: There are four VN flights a week to Saigon (Wednesday, Thursday, Saturday and Sunday) costing about US$50 one way. Connections to Hanoi are twice a week (Thursday and Sunday) and are extremely expensive (about US$130) one way. Flight schedules are subject to change and the prices will go up soon as mentioned earlier in this edition).

By bus: The bus station for long-distance travel is located at the intersection of Ngo Gia Tu and Nguyen Huu Huan Streets in the southwest area of town. Express tickets can be purchased at *6A Hoang Hoa Tham Street,* and it's best you buy your tickets in advance. Non-express buses to Saigon cost about 16,000 dong, to Danang 19,000 dong, to Vinh 40,000 dong, Hue 25,000 dong, Quy Nhon 9,000 dong, Dalat 8,500 dong, and Phan Rang 4,000 dong. Express buses to Saigon are about 19,000 dong, Hanoi 55,500 dong, Danang 22,000 dong, Vinh 39,000 dong, Quang Hgai 16,000 dong, Dalat 9,400 dong, Vinh 40,000 dong, and Hue 25,000 dong. The local bus station is located across from *115 2 Thang 4 Street,* although there is little reason to travel by local bus.

Bicycles can be rented from most hotels for about 8000 dong a day (they'll try to get 10,000 from you, but just walk away. They'll call you back). A car and driver can be rented for the day from some of the better hotels, such as the Khatoco Hotel, and popular excursions include an afternoon trip to Bai Lanh Beach up the cost about an hour. Cars and microbuses can also be rented at Tourist Car Enterprise, *1 Nguyen Thi Minh Khai Street.* Prices are different everywhere, either for local excursions or long-distance one-way travel.

Lambrettas run to Cau Da from the Central Market.

By train: The train station is located across the street from *26 Thai Nguyen Street*, although you should book in advance at the office at *17 Thai Nguyen Street;* ☎ *22113.*

Cyclos are available all over town. If you want to hire a boat, go to the dock at Cau Da, which is 5–6 km south of Nha Trang. From here, you can visit Mieu Island for about US$8–10. (The prices keep going up as stupid tourists don't negotiate properly—so the locals can expect more.) Some boats can be hired for the day, which include stops for snorkeling for as little as US$10 per day. Again, see if you bargain it down a bit. Ferries also run out to Mieu Island for a pittance.

NHA TRANG TELECOMMUNICATIONS CENTER

2 Le Loi. Tel : 8458, 21510.; FAX: 84-58-210-56. Fax, phone and telex services are here. There's a post office here, too.

CENTRAL POST OFFICE

2 Phan Tru Street.

TNT INTERNATIONAL EXPRESS

☎ *21043.*

HOSPITAL

19 Yersin Street. ☎ *22168.*

BANKS AND MONEYCHANGERS

Vietcom Bank. *17 Quang Trung Street.* Will exchange most major currencies and cash travelers' checks. Also will provide cash advances on major U.S. credit cards.

TOURIST OFFICES

Khanh Hoa Tourism. *1 Trang Hung Dao Street.* ☎ *22753.*

AIRLINE OFFICES

Vietnam Airlines. *86 Tran Phu Street.* ☎ *21147.* You can also book at *94 Tran Phu Street.*

Tuy
Hoa

TUY HOA

TUY HOA IN A CAPSULE

The capital of Phu Yen Province, but a small town of only a few thousand inhabitants...This is a good place to break the journey north or south along NH1 only if you're tired...There are no real attractions here other than sleeping.

Tuy Hoa is a barely noticeable, small town about 100 km south of Quy Nhon. There's little if anything to do here but stop and eat at a food stall or take a cheap hotel room for the night. You virtually could pass through Tuy Hoa without noticing it. It rests on the coast between Quy Nhon and Dai Lanh Beach. Here NH1 passes over a large river. But the beaches in the area aren't worth noting.

Trang Bridge—the longest bridge in south Vietnam, built in 1954 by the French—1100 meters long is close by.

WHERE TO STAY IN TUY HOA

Huong Sen Hotel
> *NH1, center of town* • About US$10. This is a peaceful hotel with a surprisingly good restaurant. Inexpensive.

DIRECTORY

TOURIST OFFICE

Phu Yen Tourist
> *137 Le Thanh Ton Street.* ☎ *23353.*

Quy
Nhon

QUY NHON

Enchanting islands flank the coast of Nha Trang and Danang.

QUY NHON IN A CAPSULE

The capital of Binh Dinh Province...A dingy city that experienced a good deal of fighting between the Viet Cong and American and South Korean troops during the Vietnam War...Beaches are some of the worst along the central Vietnam coast...It makes for a decent overnight stop between Nha Trang and Danang.

Quy Nhon, the capital of Binh Dinh Province, is a major seaport supporting a population of about 250,000 people. There's not a lot to see and do here, but it does make for a decent night night stop on the road between Nha Trang and Danang. In fact, you've got to leave Highway 1 for about 11 km to get here. There are only two hotels of any note, and they both rest on the palm-shaded Quy Nhon Beach, which I found disappointingly grungy and littered (even near the hotels), and the ocean murky and gray (even on a sunny day). Quy Nhon is definitely not a destination, and you really won't find it worth spending even a full day here. The only "attractions" near town are a couple of small Cham towers on the road off NH1 toward town, about 2-3 km from the central area, or the municipal beach, where the breezes can be quite brisk and even chilly toward the evening hours.

The port here used to be internationally recognized during the 17th–19th centuries. The two Hung Thanh towers near here are worth a visit. The larger of the two towers stands at 23 meters tall and they date back to the 13th century. They were once part of a vast Cham complex here that has been largely destroyed. M. Pigneau de Behaine, French missionary and Bishop of Adran, gave protection to defeated Nguyen survivors while his forces were surrounding the city—which was under the control of the Tay Son—in October 1799. Just two years later, the Tay Son fleet was destroyed from offshore by Nguyen Anh.

Quy Nhon itself is an unremarkable and relatively dirty city and was the site of a great deal of fierce fighting during the war between the Viet Cong and a significant number of South Korean troops, as well as ARVN and American forces.

Spend the night in Quy Nhon and go away, although there are some important sites in the area.

WHAT TO SEE AND DO IN QUY NHON AND ENVIRONS

Thap Doi Cham Towers

Because Quy Nhon was a central Cham area during the Cham Empire, there are a significant amount of the towers scattered about the Quy Nhon area. The two Thap Doi towers, near the edge of town, are perhaps the best examples.

Quy Nhon's Beaches

As I explained above, the beach areas of Quy Nhon are unimpressive stretches of dirty, dark sand and seriously dim the temptation of swimming in the ocean, which is surprisingly cold. The pictures you send back home won't inspire your friends and family to hop on a jetliner to Vietnam. Probably the "best" corridor of beach is by the Quy Nhon Tourist Hotel (which is most likely so due to the hotel being run by Saigon Railway Tourism). Along the west side of the beach, you'll find a number of boats and seaside shacks belonging to local fishermen.

Another beach is further west and has fewer people. Its drawback is that part of the beach is flanked by factories and processing plants. Ugh.

Lon Market

Phan Boi Street. This is the town's central market. It's a relatively new, covered structure where the usual Vietnamese goods and produce can be had.

Binh Dinh/Xiem Reap/Ratanakiri Zoo

As the name implies, this is a "zoo" with creatures imported from Cambodia, namely from the provinces of Siem Reap and Ratanakiri. Here you can see monkeys, bears and crocodiles on a site near the sea. The conditions here aren't as dismal as in other Vietnamese "zoos."

Cu Mong Pass

Cu Mong pass is a spectacularly scenic and steeply graded pass south of Quy Nhon that's great for photos but hell on trannies. On the nearly vertical downgrades engineers have cut out ramps for vehicles that have lost their brakes. Shrines dot the roadway here, with incense burning, marking where motorists have fallen victim to the steep grades and ill-prepared vehicles. The Vietnamese believe that they will avoid the same misfortune if they stop at the shrines and pay their respects for the dead drivers/passengers. The Cu Mong Pass represents the point where the Tonkinese prevailed after the fall of the Vijaya in 1471. From the pass, the Chams were able to prevent invasions from both north and south for nearly 150 years until the early 1600s.

Song Cau

This stretch of NH1, which hugs the coast, offers spectacular views of the surrounding hillsides. NH1 on the outskirts of the small town, particularly to the north, is flanked by rows of "truck stops," (i.e., brothels) where women lie in waiting for long distance truck drivers. Here the girls will sit out on the porches and invite you inside for some tea and some sin.

WHAT WAS THE TAY SON REBELLION?

The Tay Son Rebellion was a peasant revolt in 1771 that was led by the three Tay Son brothers as the country was leaning toward famine. Sensing unease and kinetic revolt and animosity toward the Nguyen Lords and the Trinh amongst the peasants of this region, the brothers were able to unify the peasantry into a rag-tag army that soon became a powerful fighting force. The army soon included others, such as shopkeepers and even intellectuals, who all formed behind the Tay Son brothers. This fighting force soon ruled much of the countryside and cities from as far south as Saigon to Trinh. This is where the Chinese stepped in. Realizing the country was in turmoil, they sent large forces of troops, as many as 200,000, to annex Vietnam in 1788. Quang Trung, the oldest of the three brothers proclaimed himself emperor and fought both the Vietnamese and the Chinese viciously and with significant amounts of success. They attacked the Chinese at Thang Long during the Tet new year and decimated the Chinese forces. The Tay Son Battle of Dong Da is considered one of the greatest strategically fought battles in the history of Vietnam. The Tay Son brothers then entertained notions of attacking China. Quang Trung initiated a variety of economic reforms, including land reform, education programs, and less demanding tax structures. He attempted to issue to his followers identity cards with the inscription "The Great Trust of the Empire." But Quang Trung died in 1792 and the movement fell apart to such a degree to not be in a position to fend off the newly arriving French forces. Vietnamese Emperor Gia Long then later, in 1802, exhumed the body of the youngest brother and ordered his soldiers to urinate on the corpse while Quang Trung's wife and son watched. Then the corpse was ripped apart by three elephants.

Cha Ban

About 25 km north of Quy Nhon and 5 km from Binh Dinh are the ruins of what was once an ancient Cham capital. Chan Ban was the capital of Champa from 1000 until about 1470 when it was variously attacked by the Vietnamese, the Chinese, and the Khmers. The Vietnamese were defeated by the Chams here in 1377, where the Champa king was killed. The Vietnamese then invaded Cha Ban and captured the Cham king and his royal family. This was considered the last great battle of the Chams. Tens of thousands of Chams were killed and taken prisoner. While Cha Ban was under the control of the Tay Son in 1771, the city was ruled by the three Tay Son brothers. Cha Ban was unsuccessfully attacked again in 1793 by the Vietnamese (Nguyen Anh, who later became Emperor Gia Long). But the city fell to the Vietnamese in 1799. The Tay Son then moved to what is now Quy Nhon where they conducted their own siege of Cha Ban. The siege of the city continued until 1801, when Vietnamese General Vu Tinh ran out of provisions. Rather than be defeated, Vu Tinh erected a wooden tower, filled it with gun powder and committed suicide inside by blowing the tower into the sky. The Canh Tien Tower, or Tower of Brass, stands in the middle of the compound.

Thap Doi

Thap Doi is about 2 km toward NH1 from the Quy Nhon Bus Station. Head out on Tran Hung Dao Street and turn right onto Thap Doi Street. These four towers don't possess typical Cham architecture, but instead feature pyramid-type roofs and granite doorways. Some of the brickwork is still in evidence on the granite statuary on the peak of the roofs. Torsos of Garudas are on the roofs of the structures.

Duong Long Cham Towers

These are referred to as the Towers of Ivory; they are about 10 km from Cha Ban. There are three towers here with ornamentation depicting elephants and snakes. Huge dragons can be found on the corners of the structures.Bas reliefs over the doorways depict dancers, monsters and animals.

Vinh Son Waterfalls

These unspectacular falls are about 19 km off national Highway 19, which runs between Binh Dinh and Pleiku.

Quang Trung Museum

The museum is in Tay Son District, nearly 50 km from Quy Nhon. It's about 5 km from the main route. Ask for directions in Quy Nhon at the Binh Dinh Tourist Company (see directory). But if you don't want to bother (because they'll try to steer you into an expensive tour of the site), take NH19 toward Pleiku. The museum is dedicated to the middle brother of the three brothers that led the Tay Son Rebellion, Nguyen Hue. Later, in 1789, as Emperor Quang Trang, he led a successful defense against an enormous force of about 200,000 Chinese soldiers. The museum features traditional martial art *binh dinh ho* demonstrations performed with bamboo sticks.

WHERE TO STAY IN QUY NHON

Seagull Hotel

48 Nguyen Hue Street. ☎ *21473; FAX: 84.56.21926 • 45 rooms.* US$8–25. This isn't a bad place save for the suspect staff. It's a beachfront hotel and the rooms on the beach side of the structure offer great views of the ocean and surrounding mountains. The higher up, the better—you won't notice how dirty the beach is. Restaurant, air conditioning, attached bath. But be careful of the staff. Lock your stuff up. I faxed a single page to the U.S. from here and the desk clerk charged me US$9. I asked to see the rate chart, which I had checked the day before with another staff member. The actual charge per page was 67,000 dong (about US$6.70). So beware. This activity might be indicative of the staff at large or not, but beware. Inexpensive-moderate. **Reservations: Direct or through Saigon Railway Tourism.**

Saigon Hotel

Corner of Dao Duy Tu and Tran Hung Dao Streets • US$25. This is a fairly new and well appointed hotel that seems designed to entice NH1 travelers to stop by for the night. Restaurant, air conditioning, attached bath. Moderate. ***Reservations: Direct***

Quy Nhon Hotel

12 Nguyen Hue Street. ☎ *22401* • *47 rooms.* About US$30–50. On the beach. Air conditioning, restaurant, attached bath. This place has had a bad reputation for cleanliness, and at these prices, that's the first thing you'd expect in a tourist-class hotel. Moderate–expensive.
Reservations: Direct

Thanh Binh Hotel

17 Ly Thuong Kiet Street. ☎ *22041* • About US$6–20. Overpriced considering the amenities. The cheaper rooms are grimy, while there is air conditioning in the expensive rooms. Private bath. Restaurant. Inexpensive–moderate. ***Reservations: Direct.***

Hotel Minh Ha Hai

Corner of Hai Ba Trung and Tranh Binh Trong Streets. ☎ *21295* • About US$20. Average, average, average. It's a small hotel but relatively clean (it should be at these prices). Air conditioning, attached bath. Moderate. ***Reservations: Direct.***

Dong Phuong Hotel

39-41 Mai Xuan Thuong Street. ☎ *22915* • *20 Rooms.* About US$10–15. Good location near the center of town and the stadium. Recommended by a lot of travelers. Air conditioning, attached bath. Inexpensive. ***Reservations: Direct.***

Viet Cuong Hotel

460 Tran Hung Dao Street. ☎ *22434* • *22 rooms.* About US$5. There was no one in this shabby, run down place that would speak English with me and I was led to believe the hotel doesn't accept foreigners, although I'm convinced they do. Perhaps they just didn't want me to stay. Very inexpensive. ***Reservations: Direct.***

The Peace Hotel

Across from 266 Tran Hung Dao Street. ☎ *22900* • *64 rooms.* About US$15. Clean, comfortable, friendly service. Attached bath. Inexpensive. ***Reservations: Direct.***

Nha Khach Huu Nghi

210 Phan Boi Chau Street. ☎ *22152* • *22 rooms.* About US$7–8. I didn't get a chance to visit this location, but I've heard it's popular with backpackers. Doubles with private bath. Very inexpensive.
Reservations: Direct.

Olympic Hotel
>*167 Le Hong Phong Street.* ☎ *22375* • *23 rooms.* About US$10–20. Next to the stadium and popular. Restaurant, attached bath, air conditioning. Inexpensive–moderate. ***Reservations: Direct***

WHERE TO EAT IN QUY NHON

Dong Phuong Restaurant
>*39-41 Mai Xuan Thuong Street* • Ground floor of the Dong Phuong Hotel. Vietnamese fare.

Tu Hai Restaurant
>*On the 3rd floor of the Lon Market, Phan Boi Chau Street* • Vietnamese, Asian and Western, but bland.

Gang Rang Restaurant
>*Nguyen Hue Street,* about 3.5 km out of town on the beach, southwest of Municipal Beach. This is a great setting, as the restaurant sits on piling above the water. Vietnamese, Asian.

Vu Hung Restaurant
>*On the roof of the Olympic Hotel, 167 Le Hong Phong Street* • This is a real restaurant. The food's good and relatively cheap for hotel restaurants.

Ngoc Lien Restaurant
>*288 Le Hong Phong Street* • Vietnamese, Asian. Good and cheap.

DIRECTORY

TRANSPORTATION

Quy Nhon is about 680 km from HCMC, 410 km from Hue, 305 km from Danang, 240 km from Nha Trang, 225 km from Buon Ma Thuot, 175 km from Quang Ngai.

By air: VN has flights to Quy Nhon 4 times a week: Tuesdays and Fridays at 6:20 a.m., and Wednesdays and Saturdays at the same time. Flights to HCMC leave Quy Nhon Mondays and Fridays at 8 a.m., and Wednesdays and Saturdays at 9:50 a.m. Flights to Hanoi leave Wednesdays and Saturdays at 7:30, with a connection in Danang. Flights to Danang leave at the same time. Into Quy Nhon flights leave Danang Wednesdays and Saturdays at 9:10 a.m.

By bus: The Quy Nhon Bus station is 1 km northwest of the town center on Tran Hung Dao Street. Express buses leave at 5 a.m. for Hanoi, Hue, Dalat, Danang, Nha Trang and Saigon, as well as other locations. Tickets should be purchased the day before departure. Non-express buses also leave early in the morning for Bong Son, Nha Trang, Am Lao, An Khe, Dalat, Cam Ranh, Danang, Saigon, Hanoi, Phu My, Hoi An, Pleiku, Vinh Than, Tuy Hoa, Van Canh, and Kontum, as well as other destinations.

By train: The train station in Quy Nhon is off the beaten track (express trains do not stop here). The station is 1 km northwest of town on Hoang Hoa Tham Street which is off Tran Hung Dao Street. To catch an express train, you'll have to go to Dieu Tri, which is about 10 km away.

POST OFFICE

127 Hai Ba Trung Street. International calls and faxes can be made from here.

TNT INTERNATIONAL EXPRESS

☎ *22193* or *22600.*

BANKS AND MONEYCHANGERS

Vietcom Bank, *148 Tran Hung Dao Street*, on the corner of Le Loi Street.

HOSPITAL

102 Nguyen Hue Street.

TOURIST OFFICE

Binh Dinh Tourism Company, *4 Nguyen Hue Street.*

Quang
Ngai

QUANG NGAI

QUANG NGAI IN A CAPSULE

Nothing of note in the town itself...gateway to Son My, the site of the My Lai massacre...Great beaches 17 km west of town, although they, also, were the sites of the slaughter of Vietnamese civilians by American troops during the war...Most travelers stop here briefly on their way to Danang.

Most travelers don't spend a lot of time in Quang Ngai, as it's only about 130 km south of Danang, and it's not even on the coast—the beach is nearly 15 km away. It is a small provincial capital of Quang Ngai Province that lies on the banks of the Tra Khuc River (notice the waterwheels as you pass over the bridge). There's a huge market here and a nice cathedral, but the reason why most travelers stop here is to visit Son My (site of infamous My Lai massacre), which lies about 13 km from Quang Ngai.

Quang Ngai was formerly a center of French resistance during the First Indochina War, inhabited by a number of Viet Minh. During the Vietnam War, the area was part of the South Vietnamese government's Strategic Hamlet Program, which relocated a number of villagers from here into fortified hamlets. This caused a considerable amount of dissent among the townsfolk, and many became Viet Cong sympathizers. The area was considered by the Americans as a VC stronghold, which precipitated the murderous massacre at My Lai in the Son My Subdistrict. Fighting in the district was intense, and you can still see the rusted, ruined bridges that were destroyed by both the Viet Minh and the Viet Cong. The third bridge that NH1 crosses today looks as if had been erected in a day, which it probably was.

The beaches are great—deserted and immaculate—when you get out to them.

WHAT TO SEE AND DO IN QUANG NGAI AND ENVIRONS

Son My Subdistrict (My Lai)

Thirteen km from Quang Ngai. Turn right just after crossing the bridge at the monument commemorating the My Lai massacre. This is the site of perhaps the greatest atrocity during the Vietnam War, and perhaps the most heinous military action ever staged by the U.S. American forces believed the hamlet to be a strategic VC stronghold and believed the villagers were not only VC sympathizers, but fighters and sabateurs as well. On March 16, 1968, units of the 23rd Infantry Division (Task Force Barker) were dropped into the village of Son My. Soldiers were dropped into other hamlets as well, including Tu Cong hamlet and Xom Lang sub-hamlet. Two weeks before the massacre, six U.S. soldiers had been killed after coming upon a mine field. The decision was made to search and destroy Son My Subdistrict. Lt. William Calley was responsible for investigating the hamlet of My Lai. Nearly 350 civilians died here under his orders. All were unarmed, and most were women and children. The soldiers of Lt. Calley's 1st Platoon shot and bayonetted fleeing villagers and threw grenades into the hootches and family bomb shelters. As the villagers tried to flee their shelters they were shot. Women were raped and sodomized. At no time during the massacre did American troops encounter any resistance. As many as 150 villagers were ordered to line up and were mowed down with machine gun fire. The 2nd and 3rd platoons of Charlie Company (under the commands of Lt. Stephen Brooks and Jeffrey La Cross respectively) were dropped into the zones and "attacked" Tu Cung. Unspeakable crimes were committed here by U.S. troops. Young women were gang raped—one was reportedly then shot in the vagina. Neil Sheehan reported in his marvelous book, *A Bright Shining Lie*, that, "One soldier missed a baby lying on the ground twice with a .45 pistol as his comrades laughed at his marksmanship. He stood over the child and fired a third time. The soldiers beat women with rifle butts and raped some and sodomized others before shooting them." In all, more than 500 civilians were massacred in Son My, most of them in My Lai. To their credit, some of the soldiers refused to take part in the massacre—one shot himself in the foot. But the vast majority of Capt. Ernest Medina's Charlie Company participated in the worst atrocity committed by any American soldiers during any war involving Americans in U.S. history. In all, more than 500 civilians were killed in the turkey shoot, most in My Lai. The story didn't come out for another eight months as action was taken at every level of the American command to cover up the incident. Finally, soldiers returning home told of the incidents at Son My, and an outraged American public demanded action. This was the "action": A number of American soldiers were disciplined, but only one, Lt. Calley, faced a court martial—he was found guilty of the murders of 22 (eventually 109) civilians and sentenced to life imprisonment. He was paroled by President Nixon in 1974. Some action. Some president. There is a memorial to the slaughter in Son My in a park where Xom Lang sub-hamlet once existed. There is a museum and graves of the victims. Permits are no longer required to visit the sites, but expect busloads of tourists.

This monument in Quang Ngai directs travelers the way to Son My, the site of the My Lai Massacre.

Bien Khe Ky Beach

This a fine, long beach about 17 km from Quang Ngai, and only about 3 km from Son My. This beach was also the site of another massacre by American troops. Bravo Company this time. Near the bridge across Song Kinh Giang, GIs burned down hootches and blasted automatic weapons fire at the fleeing civilians as they ran on the sand toward the sea. Family bomb shelters were annihilated and torched. Women and children were indiscriminately shot. Others were tortured before being killed. As many as 100 civilians were killed in this mass slaughter. Charges against Lt. Thomas Willingham, Bravo Company's leader, were dismissed. These incidents, although there is little left to remind you of the area's recent history, will sober your visit to this otherwise beautiful length of beach.

WHERE TO STAY IN QUANG NGAI

There aren't many places in Quang Ngai where foreigners can stay but this is changing as tourism to My Lai is booming.

Nha Khach Uy Ban Thi

Pan Boi Chau Street. ☎ *2109* • About US$20–40. Absolutely ridiculous price for this place. Restaurant. Used to be a government guesthouse but foreigners can stay here now. Personally, I'd continue on to Danang or Hoi An. Moderate. ***Reservations: Direct.***

Song Tra Hotel

Next to the Tra Truk River bridge • About US$30. Everyone seems to want to cash in on the tourism boon in My Lai. This place is no exception. The service is lacking, especially for the prices. This used to be the only place foreigners could stay in Quang Ngai. Modertate.

Reservations: Direct.

Khach Son So 2

41 Phan Boi Chau Street • I don't know anything about this place, except that foreigners are permitted to stay. Sorry, guys.

WHERE TO EAT IN QUANG NGAI

Food stalls are your best bet in Quang Ngai, but there's a decent restaurant at the Nha Khach Uy Ban Thi hotel, with decent seafood. There are a number of cafes near Khach San So 2, but don't expect much on the menus. Others include:

Nha Hang 155

155 Quang Trung Street • Average Vietnamese fare. Cheap, but not as cheap as the surrounding food stalls.

Tiem An 72 Restaurant

72 Nguyen Nghiem Street • Vietnamese, Asian. Cheap.

DIRECTORY

TRANSPORTATION

Quang Ngai is about halfway between HCMC and Saigon (840 km from HCMC and 890 km from Hanoi). Other distances are 410 kilometers from Nha Trang, 240 km from Hue, 130 km from Danang, 175 km from Quy Nhon.

By bus: Quang Ngai's bus station is across from *32 Nguyen Nghiem Street*, not far from NH1, which is called Quang Trung Street through Quang Ngai. There is service to Danang, Dalat, Hoi An, Nha Trang, Quy Nhon, Kontum, and HCMC.

By train: The railway station is about 3 km west of town. Take Phan Boi Chau Street west from Quang Trung Street. The street name changes to Nguyen Chanh Street, but just keep going. Here you can catch Reunification Express trains either north or south, as the train makes regular stops here.

POST OFFICE

Located at the intersection of Phan Ding Phun and Phan Boi Chau Streets.

TOURIST OFFICE

Quang Ngai Tourism, in the Song Tra Hotel. ☎ *2665* or *3870.*

Hoi An

HOI AN

The Japanese Covered Bridge in Hoi An was built in 1593.

HOI AN IN A CAPSULE

Perhaps the most unique town in Vietnam...Worth a two-day visit...Ancient seaport that did commerce with dozens of nations, from Europe and even America...Unscathed by the Vietnam War, although there was much damage to the city during the Tay Son Rebellion...Ancient buildings here represent influences from both Asia and the West...Narrow streets flanked by buildings that have remained virtually unchanged for 200 years...Similar in flavor and style to Malaysia's famed port of Malacca...A must-see if you're traveling the coast.

AUTHOR'S NOTES

South of Nuon Nuoc is the wonderfully preserved town of Hoi An, a virtually virgin throwback to the European influences which dominated the area up until the 19th century...The city was remarkably left unscathed by the fighting of the Vietnam War...Hoi An was at one time the center of the kingdom of Champa...As a side trip, check out Cua Dai Beach, which is essentially deserted and arguably one of the most pristine beaches in Central Vietnam...Tourism in Hoi An, regrettably, is changing fast and by the time you read this, the town may have become the next Malacca...Hoi An was once the dominant commerce center in the area but eventually played second fiddle to Danang in terms of commerce and shipping...So far, this has worked to the benefit of the tourists that visit this beautiful port, and hopefully it will remain that way, although it is certain that Hanoi will eventually exploit the quaintness and uniqueness of this river/seaport village that has been through the years a major center for Japanese, Portuguese, Dutch, Chinese, and French merchants...More than 840 structures of vast historical significance have been listed in Hoi An, and virtually each one of them is worth visiting...Most of the structures, though, are open for public viewing at no charge, although you will feel a pinch of guilt not offering a small donation...Usually 5000 to 10,000 dong is sufficient...You may also be offered a steaming bowl of cao lau, which is a local delicacy...Once you've had your fill of the local hospitality, take a stroll down the Thu Bon River for excellent views of the river boats and the village itself.

Hoi An is a beautiful, ancient Vietnamese town, a little more than 30 km to the south of Danang, that will seem to you like a time machine. It sits on the banks of the Thu Bon River near the South China Sea. It was virtually untouched by the fighting during the Vietnam War (although it was heavily damaged during the Tay Son Rebellion), and it retains its centuries-old Vietnamese, Chinese, Japanese and European architecture. It distinctly reminds me of Malaysia's port at Malacca, with its narrow streets and low, tiled roof houses. The influences are from the Japanese, the Portuguese, the Dutch and the Vietnamese. In the 17th–19th centuries, Hoi An was one of the most important ports in Southeast Asia, and wasn't eclipsed by Danang until the end of the 19th century, when Thu Bon River had silted up to such a degree, that major commerce by navigation became problematic as the waters became too shallow.

Hoi An was probably inhabited as early as 2000 years or more ago, and also has the distinction of being, by most accounts, the first place in Vietnam where Christianity was introduced. The French priest Alexandre de Rhodes arrived in the 17th century who later transcribed the Vietnamese language into the Latin-based quoc ngu script. Hoi An was also the site of the first Chinese settlers in southern Vietnam. More than 1500 ethnic Chinese live in Hoi An today. Many Chinese come from all over the southern part of Vietnam to celebrate various Chinese congregational gatherings. Unlike in other parts of Vietnam, there is little friction between ethnic Vietnamese and the Chinese, who have adopted Vietnamese as their first language.

From the 2nd–10th centuries, Hoi An was one of the principal cities in the Champa Kingdom. Archeologists have discovered the bases of numerous Cham towers in the region. Its port was visited by sailors from the Middle East for provisioning. During its heyday, Indian, Dutch, Portuguese, French, Thai, Indonesian, Spanish, American, Japanese, Chinese and Filipino ships came to Hoi An to procure its quality silk, sugar, fabrics, tea, ceramics, pepper, elephant tusks and a slew of other goods.

The Chinese and the Japanese usually stayed in Hoi An for the longest periods of time due to the prevailing winds. In fact, there were "seasons" in which Hoi An experienced the presence of such merchants. Many of the nationalities calling on Hoi An left agents of their respective companies, and this is the reason Hoi An developed it's multinational architectural appearance.

Today, parts of Hoi An look precisely as they did two centuries ago. And although Hoi An today remains largely uncommercialized, don't expect this to continue. Foreign tourists were everywhere during my visit and the city is gearing up for more. Within a year or two, walking the streets of this quaint town won't be dissimilar to strolling through an American theme park. But get there now, before Disney does.

WHAT TO SEE AND DO IN HOI AN AND ENVIRONS

There are more than a whopping 840 structures in Hoi An that have been deemed as historical structures. They include houses, shops, pagodas, tombs, etc. We can't possibly describe them all but here are a few worth visiting, especially if you've only got a day to spend in Hoi An. (It's actually worth two or more).

Japanese Covered Bridge   ★ ★

This is Hoi An's most famous landmark, although there are other structures in town equally if not more compelling. It's located at the west end of Tran Phu Street and connects Tran Phu Street with Nguyen Thi Minh Khai Street. The bridge was reportedly built in the 16th century although there are some experts who think it is much older. It's not a long structure. At the western end of the bridge there are statues of two dogs, and on the east end, two monkeys. Legend

has it that the bridge was started in the year of the monkey and finished during the year of the dog. Another tale says that the dogs and
monkeys reflect the years that many of Japan's Emperors had been
born in. It was built by the Japanese (although this isn't for certain)
in the same rigid style they built their own bridges—to avoid damage
during earthquakes, though there are few in southern Vietnam. And it
was constructed to link the Japanese quarter of town with the Chinese
section. In the 17th century it was the hangout for beggars and the
homeless, taking advantage of the hundreds of people who crossed it
everyday. During the 20th century the French flattened the bridge's
roadway to make it easier to cross by car, but it was restored to its
original curvature in 1986. The bridge was once known as the "Faraway People's Bridge," but the name didn't stick. Built on the far side
of the bridge is a small pagoda called Chua Cau, where the old Faraway People's Bridge sign hangs.

Phuoc Kien (or Fukien) Pagoda

46 Tran Phu Street. This Chinese pagoda was built around 1690 and
then restored and enlarged in 1900. It is typical of the Chinese "dialect associations," or "clans" that were established in the Hoi An area.
A hall of worship was also added in 1900. This pagoda is a reflection
of the Chinese communities to establish within their dialect associations their own schools, hospitals, places of worship, and cemeteries.
In Hoi An, there were four different associations. There was the Fukien, Teochiu, Hainan, and Kwangthung associations. This temple,
dedicated Thien Hau Thanh Mau (Goddess of the Sea and Protector
Sailors and Fishermen), is a large complex in a compound. Thien Hau
is the principal figure at the main altar, dressed in an ornate robe. On
the right side after entering the pagoda, you'll see a mural of Thien
Hau rescuing a sinking ship. Outside there is a model of an old Chinese war junk.

Assemby Hall for Maritime Commerce   ★ ★

176 Tran Phu Street. Despite the name, this is also a pagoda that was
constructed in the early 18th century and was a refuge for Chinese
merchants and sailors of all ethnicities. Tien Hau is the diety worshipped here (who else?). The compound is quite beautiful. For a
small donation, the monk will write your name and address on a large
piece of red paper and glue it to the inside wall of the pagoda. I
noticed that there had been quite a few American visitors in recent
months.

Hainan Assembly Hall

Near the corner of Tran Phu and Hoang Dieu Streets. This was built for
the Hainan Chinese congregation in 1833. It is dedicated to the 108
merchants from Hainan island in southern China who were killed after
they were mistaken for pirates by forces of Emperor Tu Duc. There
are many plaques commemorating the killings inside the Hall.

Ong Hoi Pagoda

24 Tran Phu Street, near the intersection of of Nguyen Hue Street. These are actually two temples—Chua Quan Cong and Chua Quan Am behind it. They were probably built sometime early in the 16th century. The pagodas are dedicated to Quan Cong and Quan Am, obviously.

Hoi An Market.

Right next to the Ong Hoi Pagoda. This is a huge market that extends along the river and Bach Dang Street. At the market area at Tran Phu street, the products are mostly consumer goods, while further down, there is a variety of produce and animal meat.

Assembly Hall of the Fujian Chinese Congregation

Opposite 35 Tran Phu Street. Dedicated to Tien Hau, this assembly hall eventually became a temple. There's a mural near the entrance that shows Tien Hau crossing the sea with a lantern to rescue a faltering ship. A mural depicting the heads of the six Fujian families that escaped China for Hoi An in the 17th century after the overthrow of the Ming Dynasty is on the opposite wall. One chamber contains a statue of Tien Hau. Near the goddess are two figures, one red and the other green, One could see for a thousand miles; the other could hear things from long distances and it was their responsibility to inform Tien Hau of ships in trouble. There is a central altar in the last chamber that depicts the six families that fled to Hoi An, Behind the altar is depicted the God of Prosperity. There's also a tall glass dome that contains the figure of Le Huu Trac, a great Vietnamese physician. It is said that married couples without children come here to pray for childbirth.

Chaozhou Assembly Hall

Acrosss from 157 Nguyen Duy Hieu Street. Woodcarvings on the altar and beams are the attractions at this temple, constructed in 1776 as an assembly hall. There are also carvings of Chinese girls on the doors in front of the altar.

Chinese All-Community Assembly Hall

31 Phan Chu Trinh Street. This hall is frequented by all members of the Chinese community in Hoi An. Bamboo blinds and hand-woven carpets are also made here. The hall was built in the early 1770s.

Japanese Tombs

Sugar cane, crushed sea shells, and boi loi leaves were used to build the tomb of Yajirobei, a Japanese Christian merchant who fled his native land and died here in 1647. The Japanese characters inscribed on the tomb are clearly visible to this day. The tomb faces northeast toward Japan. Getting there is a little difficult: Follow Nguyen Truong Street north to its end and then the sand path which curves left until you reach a junction in the path. Here, turn to the right. At the next junction after about 1 km, take a left, and then another left at the next fork. In the open field, you'll cross over an irrigation channel. Take a right on the other side of it and go up the hill. After about 150 meters, turn left for about 100 meters. The tomb is in the middle of rice fields. In the area is also the tomb of Masai, a Japanese who perished in Hoi An in 1629. There are other Japanese tombs in the area. The best bet is to get a guide if you don't already have one.

Cao Dai Pagoda

64-70 Huynh Thuc Kang Street. This is a small Cao Dai pagoda near the bus station. It was built in the early 1950s.

Chuc Thang Pagoda

At the end of Nguyen Trong Street, turn left on the dirt path for about 500 meters. This pagoda, built around 1454 by a Buddhist monk from China named Minh Hai is by far the oldest pagoda in Hoi An. In the main sanctuary, on the roof, Chinese characters depict the pagoda's construction. There are a few big bells here, one made from stone that's at least 200 years old. On the dais is A Di Da Buddha. On each side of the Buddha are Sakyamuni Buddhas. In front of the shrine is the figurine of Thich Ca as a young boy.

Phuoc Lam Pagoda

On the path past Chuc Thanh Pagoda about 350 meters. This pagoda was built around the 1750s. Toward the end of the century, the eventual head monk here, An Thiem, who at 18-years-old left monkhood, joined the army in lieu of his brothers and eventually rose to the rank of general. He felt so bad about the number of people he killed, he asked to clean the market in Hoi An for 20 years. He was then asked to come Phuoc Lam Pagoda as head monk.

Hoi An Church

Corner of Nguyen Truong To and Le Hong Phong Streets. This is a new structure where Hoi An's European population was buried.

Tan Ky House

101 Nguyen Thai Hoc Street. This is one of the three central "monuments" of Hoi An. It is a private house built more than 200 years ago for the worship of ancestors. It's one of the oldest and largest private houses in Hoi An. It was recognized by the government's Ministry of Culture as "an ancient building of high value" in 1985. It's basically unchanged in two centuries and reveals evidence of the period when trade with foreigners in this city was booming. During this time, residents used pulleys to raise goods above the floor. There is a combination of priceless ancient Chinese, Japanese and Vietnamese artwork in the house. The builders of the house had also been involved with constructing royal sites and palaces in Hue. The carpentry in the house represents both Chinese and Japanese influences. The upper reaches of the house reveal 18th century Japanese architecture. The timber in the house is joined with wooden pegs. The floor is made mostly of brick and flagstone imported from abroad. Many of the decorative works of art and carvings reveal Vietnamese, Chinese and Western influences. Chinese poems are inscribed in mother-of-pearl. The carved wooden balcony is adorned with grape leaves, another European import. Seven generations of the family have lived here. Members of the family, as well as a couple of young hired guides, give one-hour presentations and they charge you 2000 dong.

77 Tran Phu Street   ★★

This private house is nearly 300 years old, and it claims to be the oldest private house in Hoi An. Who to believe? There are magnificent carvings in the house on the walls. Around the courtyard balcony, there are ceramic tiles built into the railings. A small fee is charged to visit this home.

Diep Dong Nguyen House

80 Nguyen Thai Hoc Street. Built in the late 1800s, this house was constructed for a Chinese merchant, whose family still live here. The owner has a priceless collection of antiques, including porcelain and furniture, but none are for sale. Some of the items were once on loan to Bao Dai himself. Although there are hours when the house is closed to the public, I just simply knocked on the door and, although I may have spoiled the family's lunch, the owner was more than happy to show me around—without asking for a fee!

Cua Dai Beach

Cua Dai Beach is 5 km from Hoi An, east out on Cua Dai Street, which is what Tran Hung Dao and Phan Dinh Phung Streets become out of town. Although this beautiful stretch of beach has been traditionally deserted, more and more tourists are discovering it. Fortunately Hoi An has so many attractions of its own, only a handful of tourists make it out to the beach and, once there, don't stay very long. There are souvenir and refreshment kiosks here, but the atmosphere is easy and laid back, and you won't find the hordes of young children hawking chewing gum as you'll find at the nearby Marble Mountains.

Cham Island

About 20 km off Hoi An in the South China Sea. The island is best known for swift's nests, which are exported and eventually find their way into bird's nest soup in other Asian countries. Boats leave Hoi An for Cham Island from the Hoang Van Thu Street dock.

Cam Kim Island

This is a nearby island reachable by boat from the Hoang Van Thu Street dock.

WHERE TO STAY IN HOI AN

Hotel Hoi An

6 Tran Hung Dao Street. ☎ *373* • *16 rooms.* About US$10–20. Beautiful old colonial building. Fans, air conditioning, restaurant, attached bath. Clean. Friendly staff. Air conditioning isn't so important during the winter, and the rooms are essentially the same, so that's what you're paying for with the top-end rooms. Very popular. Most tourists stay here. Inexpensive–moderate.   ***Reservations: Direct***

Guesthouse

92 Phan Tru Street • About US$8. This place is a dump. Only for those who like cement, cockroaches and the like. Shared bath. Very inexpensive.

WHERE TO EAT IN HOI AN

Two specialties in Hoi An are cao lau—noodles and croutons with bean sprouts and greens topped with slices of pork. It's mixed with dried rice paper—and Hoi An loanh thanh—a delicious wanton soup. There are a number of restaurants offering the same fare up and down Tran Phu Street. Try:

Cao Lau Restaurant

42 Tran Phu Street • Delicious cao lau.

Floating Restaurant

Bach Dang and Nguyen Thai Hoc Streets • This is a brand new flashy, festive place that sits on the riverfront near the Japanese Covered Bridge. Delicious seafood at reasonable prices. But it's geared for tourists.You can eat more cheaply along Tran Phu Street.

DIRECTORY

TRANSPORTATION

Hoi An is about 30 km south of Danang.

By bus: The bus station is about 1 km west of the city center at 74 Huynh Thuc Kang Street. Connections to Danang are constant. If you're on only a day trip, the last bus leaves for Danang at 5 p.m. The ride takes an hour. Van buses leave for Danang, Que Son, Dai Loc, Tra My and Tam Ky.

By train: You'll have to get off the Reunification Express at Danang and find your way south. See the Danang chapter for transport to Hoi An.

By car: If you're traveling north on NH1, the best way is to get off the highway (a sign is posted) about 27 km from Danang. You'll then travel about 10 km to Nguyen Thi Minh Khai street which forks as you get into town. Nguyen Thi Minh Khai Street turns into Tran Phu Street on the other side of the Japanese Covered Bridge. From Danang, there are two routes. You can drive south on Trung Nu Street to the Marble Mountains and then continue south along the Korean Highway for about 20 km. Or you can take NH1 south, the sign posted for Hoi An, but this is a longer trip.

By boat: You can't actually arrive in Hoi An by boat from other destinations, but the docks at Hoang Van Thu Street provide a great way of getting out to see Cam Kim and Cham Islands.

Danang

DANANG

Linh Ong Pagoda sits high atop the Marble Mountains, a Viet Cong refuge during the war.

DANANG IN A CAPSULE

Third largest city in Vietnam...and the principal port in the central part of the country...a repository of traditional art objects and architecture from the Cham dynasty, which dates from the 2nd century A.D.... it was here that the French originally landed to begin their "excursion" into Vietnam...a century later, the first U.S. combat troops arrived to begin their Vietnam "excursion"...Danang fell to the Viet Cong in March 1975...it signified South Vietnam's defeat in the war...this is an ancient city with a rich cultural history...situated on a peninsula where the Han River flows into the South China Sea...today it's a thriving beach town and worth a couple of days' visit.

The Hai Van Pass, a few kilometers to the north of Danang (or the Pass of the Ocean Clouds), is the thin, snaky stretch of roadway that connects Danang and Lang Co Beach. The weather changes dramatically, truly separating the south from the north. Some of the grades are so steep that the road builders had to construct uphill grades on the downslopes for buses and trucks that lose their brakes, which happens with alarming and deadly frequency. All along the side of the pass, shrines mark where vehicles crashed and their occupants met their demise. It is considered good luck for passing motorists to stop and pay their respects to the dead as it is believed that the life source of the deceased will be absorbed into the spirit of living motorists and thus prevent them from communing with the same fate. Laboriously the pass ascends and then drops to the sugary sands of Lang Co Beach. On top, the pass (also once known as the Mandarin Road because it was reserved only for the use of important ancient mandarin VIPs), snakes through 20 km of spectacular jungle mountains and reaches a height of 500 meters. Here are perhaps the most majestic views in Vietnam. Going by train will not give you these views, as the track cuts through the terrain at the base of the mountains along the sea.

Danang (population about 500,000, and originally known as Cua Han—Market of the Han—and later renamed Tourane by the French in 1787) has meant a lot of things for a lot of people, in particular, some of the history wrought by the war, some spectacular scenery, and the friendliness of the locals. But Danang is on the threshold of becoming a major destination of "resort" tourists from Europe, Australia and the U.S. who are accustomed to the amenities found in Bali, Phuket, Pattaya, and Tahiti. Just check out the old tourists sporting cellulite-ridden thighs with the illusion they're wading in the waters off the US$50 a night hotel beside "China Beach," which actually isn't China Beach at all, but a moniker given to a renamed beach by the the goverment tourism authorities because it's more accessible to tourists than the real China Beach. The locals will tell you; most of the informed ones place the actual China Beach (the popular R&R GI resort of the Vietnam War immortalized by a short-lived, shoddy U.S. television show) about three miles up the coast. But, regardless, the bogus China Beach of lore made popular by the American TV series of the same name a few years ago has become the natural destination of those who want to impress their friends at home with those stupid T-Shirts. "China Beach" today is Hanoi's exploitation of the adventure tourist trade. And it's paying off.

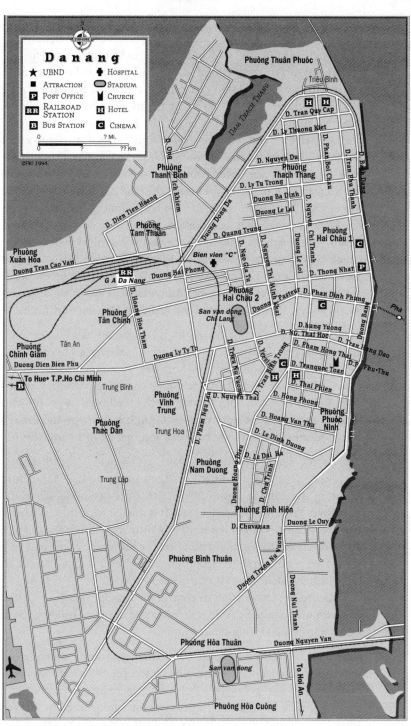

Last October more than 30 international professional surfers, much to the mixed delight/disdain of the local authorities, descended upon "China Beach" in decadent day-glo wetsuits for the first international surfing competition to ever have been held inVietnam. It was a four-day US$ 60,000 competition called the Saigon Floating Hotel Hotel Surf Pro '93, brought to stunning Non Nuoc Beach (the real name for the bogus beach) by Bruce Aitken, director of Sortas Asia.The entrepreneur had already staged two successful events in Vietnam as a way of promoting surfing and tourism in Vietnam. Surfing has now taken root with the locals, and Vietnam now fields a team of four surfers, although the crux of them might be able to more easily accommodate the swells of running bath water than the six-foot peaks that occasionally ascend the waters of "China Beach." Although it's unlikely the perfect wave will ever be found at China Beach, or anywhere else in Vietnam for that matter. So far, Vietnam has some 12 "professional" surfers, who took up the sport about seven years ago after some Americans kindly left some boards for the locals; they're all part of the fledgling Danang Surf Club.

Of course, if you're not into surfing, Danang offers a host of other attractions. It serves as an excellent base to make quests to other area sites. There's May Son, about 60 km away, which is considered Vietnam's most impressive Cham site. Some say it's on par with Cambodia's Angkor Wat but, quite frankly, that's usually said by people who haven't had the opportunity to visit Angkor. Perhaps Indonesia's Borobodur might be a little bit more appropriate of a comparison.

When the French took over Danang (Vietnam's fourth largest city), they renamed it Tourane. It then became Thai Pien before adopting the current name. It's located on a peninsula where the Han River flows into the China Sea. It is the last location in Vietnam that really can be considered southern Vietnam, as both the weather and the people change dramatically on the other side of the pass (the word cold is not entirely unappropriate, however it applies more to the weather). Danang is also the site where some of the first American Marines landed in 1965 to control the airfield. It later, by 1966, had become a strategic American naval and air base, handling both heavy warships and long-range bombers.

After the fall of the south, the communist authorities attempted to reduce the population of Danang by creating agricultural zones outside the city. The policy had little effect in reducing this bustling port's population. Whereas the port was once frequented by ships of Vietnam's socialist allies, today one sees off its shores ships from Taiwan, Singapore and Hong Kong—and soon, no doubt—ships from the U.S.

Danang is perhaps the most progressive city in Vietnam in terms of exploiting Vietnam's new free market principles. It is aggressive in attacting foreign investment, and its cultural and geographical isolation from both Hanoi and Saigon virtually make the region autonomous—not unlike Ha Tien in the Mekong Delta during the 17th and 18th centuries. Danang is the true leader in Vietnam in economic reforms (attacting foreign investment at a pace faster than both in Hanoi and HCMC), and tourism has certainly helped boost the local economy, as 100,000 people visited the city last year alone.

This might not be an example of Vietnam's sandy white beaches, but rocks make for a nice change of pace between Nha Trang and Danang.

Danang has the stature of perhaps being the most chaotic city in South Vietnam during the war. With both Hue, to the north, and Quang Ngai, some 100 km to the south, having fallen to the communists, Danang found itself cut off from the rest of South Vietnam. South Vietnamese troops defected, and on March 29, 1975, truckloads of armed men and women in trucks entered the city and declared it under communist control—without a shot being fired. The only real fighting was between Danang locals and ARVN soldiers battling for space on fleeing aircraft and sea vessels. Two jetliners flew from Saigon to Danang to pick up civilians and soldiers. The scene was utter chaos as soldiers and locals battled one another for space on the planes. Some even attached themselves to the wheel-wells of one of the aircraft as the planes took off. They met their deaths as they fell hundreds of feet into the South China Sea, all captured by TV cameras on the the second Boeing 727. The only civilians that managed to board the flights were a couple of women and a child.

Danang also contains a beautiful assortment of pagodas, as well as an impressive Coa Dai Temple (which is actually only really impressive if you haven't seen the Cao Dai site at Vin Minh). The Ho Chi Minh Museum includes a replica of Ho's House. Along Bach Dang Street on the banks of the Han River is the flower market beside the ferry pier.

WHAT TO SEE AND DO IN DANANG AND ENVIRONS

Cham Museum   ★★

Located where Tran Phu and Le Dinh Duong Streets meet. This houses probably the best collection of Cham art to be found anywhere in the world. There are more than 300 artifacts in the museum, many dating to the 4th century. There are beautiful sculptures reflecting the 1000-year Cham period. The museum was founded the École Française d'Extrême Orient in 1915 and expanded in 1935. Check out the magnificent sandstone carvings. Indonesian and Malay influences are seen in the work before the 10th century, while Khmer influences become more apparent in the work after that date. The museum also features the famous 7th-century altar Tra Kieu, which depicts the wedding of Prince Rama. The museum was founded by a group of French scholars in 1915. The building itself is worth the visit. The large rooms are airy and each is devoted to a different period of Cham art. There are displays that range from the 4th through the 14th centuries. Cham art can be basically broken down into two periods: before the 10th century, when the art reflected Cham relations with Indonesia and Mahayana Buddhism, and between the 10th and 14th centuries, when continued conflict with both the Cambodians and the Vietnamese created art with significant Khmer influences. The "Mother of the Country" (Uroja, which, in Cham, means the breast of a woman) is the pervasive image in the museum. You'll see a lot of nipples here. There is also the phallic symbol of Shiva. There are dozens of sandstone sculptures and altars, many of which have required surprisingly little renovation, that span a period of more than a thousand years. You'll definitely need a guide here, as the lingas, reliefs, and garudas are only marginally explained (really only the name and date of construction are marked) and only in Vietnamese.Worth a few visits. Open 8–11 and 1–5 p.m. every day. There is an admission fee.

Cao Dai Temple

This is an interesting church located at *35 Hai Phong Street*. It's the second largest Cao Dai temple in Vietnam, second only to the sect's base in Tay Ninh. There are more than 20,000 Cao Dais in Danang and this is their centerpiece. Women enter on the left, marked "Nu Phai," and men enter the temple on the right, marked "Nam Phai." As in all Cao Dai temples, above the main altar is the image of the Giant Eye, which is the symbol of Cao Daism. What I found most interesting about the temple was the sign hanging in front of the altar on the ceiling which says "Van Giao Nhat Ly." It means that all religions have the same purpose. I then asked a priest if I could convert to Cao Daism. He told me to get a haircut first and then take off my shoes. I'm thinking of it. There are also portraits of Jesus Christ, Mohammed, Buddha and Confucious. I didn't see any pictures of Marilyn Monroe or William Shakespeare, though. The temple was erected in 1956. Prayers are held four times a day.

Danang Cathedral

Located on Tran Phu Street, this church serves Danang's Catholic community. Built in 1923 by the French, it's worth a peek for its single-spire, pink sandstone architecture.

Ho Chi Minh Museum

Also called Bao Tang Ho Chi Minh. Located on *Nguyen Van Troi Street.* Here you can see various weaponry of the Vietnam War from the U.S., China and the former Soviet Union. There's also a replica of Ho's Hanoi house on display. Open 7–11 a.m. and 1–4:30 p.m. Tues.–Sun.

Pho Da Pagoda

Across from 293 Phan Chu Trinh Street. Not much to see here. Typical Buddhist pagoda. Built in 1923.

Phap Lam Pagoda

123 Ong Ich Khiem Street. The main feature here is the tarnished (at least during my visit) brass statue of Dia Tang, the Chief of Hell. It would make for an interesting business card, I think.

Cho Han Market

At the corner of Tran Phu and Huong Vuong Streets. This is a new market—clean and worth a visit for essentials.

Cho Con Market

At the corner of Ong Ich Khiem Streets. A good place for handicrafts and souvenirs.

Beaches

One of the best parts of any Danang visit is the beaches, and there are some good ones in the Danang area. The best time to visit Danang's beaches is from April through July, when the surf isn't as dangerous and there are fewer undertows. **China Beach** was an R&R area during the war and was made popular by the U.S. TV series of the same name, although the real China Beach (**My Khe Beach**) is some three miles north. There's a hotel and a number of restaurants in the fake China Beach area. There's also **Nam O Beach**, about 15 km northwest of the city. It's a good place to see the locals' fishing boats. **My Khe Beach** is a little more than 5 km from Danang and one of the better beaches in the area. But watch out for the undertow. **Thanh Binh Beach** in the center of Danang is often packed with locals and can be dirty.

Marble Mountains

These are the beautiful limestone peaks that rise above Danang. About 10 km from the city of Hoi An and only a stone's throw from Bai Non Nuoc are the five craggy peaks of the Marble Mountains (each represents one of the five elements of the universe), the site of numerous guerilla attacks on American troops down below from the nearly inaccessible cliff-like edifices overlooking the China Beach area. Because of their relative ruggedness and strategic location overlooking Danang, they were a favorite spot of the VC during the war. The VC could snipe at American troops below virtually uncontested. A trail of steep stairs cuts into the limestone of the most oft-visited peak (Thuy Son), about 900 if I remember correctly. There are a number of natural caves that were once used as Hindu shrines and then of course later by the Viet Cong in their largely successful attempts to harass American troops below who were picked off like flies on many occasions. The caves were also used as a hospital during the war for wounded Viet Cong soldiers. Getting up the stairs is a pain in the ass, and many older people would be foolish making the attempt. (Hell, fit 18-year-old American soldiers didn't, albeit for different reasons.) And be prepared for hordes of children touts hawking everything from candy to guided tours. I mean there are hundreds of these little bastards; all are flawless in their English, as well as fluent in French, German, Italian and a number of other tongues. Each and every single one of them! As many as a dozen at a time won't leave your side from your ascent of the mountain back to the base. If you're lucky you'll only get away with paying one of them for a guided tour. A few thousand dong should do the trick. It's worth it for two reasons. You get a decent tour, and when the other kids see that you already have someone accompanying you as a guide (although he or she may only be three or four years old) they'll tend to leave you alone in terms of trying to pawn off the fake Buddhas and other "relics."

At the top of the main staircase is the Ong Chon gate, which still reveals bullet holes from the war. Behind that is Linh Ong Pagoda. Then there are the caverns (Tang Chon Dong) which contain a variety of concrete buddhas. The passage through the rocks and the caves on the mountain can be very narrow and dark, and it's best to carry a flashlight (the childrens' candles do little to help, especially if you're at the back of a group of visitors. But if you can get up to the top, the scenery is spectacular: miles of crystal clear, unspoiled views of the beaches, Cham Island and the surrounding mountains. You can even see the Hai Van Pass through the Truong Son Mountains to the north. Thuy Son is a village in the mountains that sells local handicrafts. The Tam Thai Pagoda has also been carved into the mountains. The name was given to the limestone mountains by the Nguyen

Emperor Minh Mang, who obviously wasn't a geologist. The numerous caves and grottoes on the main Marble mountain were formed by
chemical treatments. The main temple up here is the Tam Thai
Pagoda, which was built in 1825 by Minh Mang. There's a huge
statue of the Buddha Sakyamuni (historic Buddha) which is next to
Bodhisattva Quan Am (the Goddess of Mercy). There's also another
grotto called Huyen Khong Cave. The roof of the cave has five holes
poked into the ceiling to allow dim sunlight to filter through. At
about 12–2 p.m., the light shines upon the central statue of Sakyamuni. There's also Linh Nham, a vertical cave with an altar inside.
Another cave nearby (Hoa Nghiem) contains a Buddha. There's also
the spectacular Huyen Khong Cave, which possesses an opening to
the sky and contains numerous shrines and inscriptions on the walls.
This was the cave the VC used as a field hospital during the war. When
finished with your visit, you can descend the mountain through the
back staircase, which is a lot easier on the heart and lungs. Cost is
4000 dong and you should spend at least an hour on Thuy Son.

Bai Non Nuoc

The hamlet of Non Nuoc is near China Beach. Accommodations are
limited at Bai Non Nuoc to the Non Nuoc Beach Hotel. The 60-room
Indochina Beach Hotel will reopen in 1995 after renovations. Managed by Majestic International, based in Hong Kong, the hotel's second phase will include about 300 new villas.

My Son and Dong Duong

This is the former site of the Cham's most important cultural, religious and intellectual metropolis back when Tra Kieu was Champa's
capital. Although reaching these areas is difficult, they are actually the
principal reasons many visitors come to Danang. My Son (which
means the Good Mountain) is about 60 km southwest of Danang and
it's not an easy journey. To get there, you have to take the road south
from Danang about 34 km and cross the Thu Bon River Bridge.
About 2 km past the bridge, turn right and follow the tributary of the
Thu Bon toward the valley. You'll come across the small village of Tra
Kieu after about 7–8 km. Continue to travel upstream for another 28
km to Kim Lam. Turn left for another 6 km. The road here is at times
virtually impassable (see INSIDER TIP) at certain times of the year. If
you're going by car, you'll have to leave it at the end of the "road"
and then travel by foot for 8 km on a path that winds through lush
hillsides and a lot of brush to reach My Son.

AUTHOR'S NOTE

*You should definitely have a guide when traveling to My Son. The area
was extensively mined during the war, and many of the mines, still
quite lethal, remain beside the roads and paths leading around My Son.*

There are more than 70 remarkable Cham monuments in the area, constructed between the the 7th and 13th centuries, and it's why many people compare the region with Cambodia's Angkor. (The monuments at My Son are significantly smaller than those found at Angkor in the Cham belief that no grandiose structures should be built.) The small, elegant monuments are surrounded by mountains in a valley with the impressive Cat's Tooth Mountain towering over the basin. There are coffee plantations and clear streams for cooling off.

INSIDER TIP

If you do much traveling into the interior from Danang, remember that roads are often washed out between May and October, which is the wet monsoon season in Vietnam. Medical facilities are next to nonexistent; and doctors will, in many instances, demand cash on the spot or they may not take care of you.

Most of the monuments consist of the classic Cham Tower, which is built high (by Cham standards) to reflect the divinity of the king (Shiva, the founder of the dynasties of Champa). Many of the structures are in incredibly good shape (the bricks were glued together by a vegetable-based cement, according to a number of scientists. And many structures were domed in gold). And it's a shame that the balance are not, the result of incessant B-52 bombing during the war (the area was considered a free fire zone at the time), especially during 1969. Among those buildings demolished by American sappers was perhaps the most important temple at the site, which was a magnificent tower designated as A1 by French archeologists near the end of the 19th century.

My Son became a major religious area in the 4th century and was bustling until the 13th century. The nearly 1000 years of Cham culture far surpasses religious realms in other Southeast Asia locations. During the early centuries of the dynasties, there was much contact with the Indonesians, as the two empires traded both in commerce and in education. Cham pottery has even been found in Indonesia (Java).

The monuments at My Son were separated into 10 groups (A-K, although, curiously, there are two "A's" and no "I"). The neighboring groups that remain are B, C and D. B and C are two temple enclosures which are about 25 by 25 meters, and lie side by side, although you'll have to use your imagination to distinguish the structures as two separate sanctuaries. Group B is the massive main sanctuary of the southern enclosure. There is a sandstone base and the main building once had eight monolithic columns supporting it.

Temple C is similar to Temple B, more modest in size, measuring 5 by 10 meters but it is a well preserved sanctuary. A small building (C3) is at the southeast corner of the Group C enclosure. Restoration is currently being performed on its interior walls. C7 is in bad shape. C5 and C6 are also being restored.

Cham clergymen rarely see foreigners, and are even less likely to give you permission to photograph them.

Temple D is between the Group B and C enclosures and contains six structures. This area is known as the Court of Steles. It's noted for its altars and rows of statues. At the end of the court are two badly demolished buildings. D3 is on the western end where it stands between the gateways to the B and C enclosures.

Dong Duong is about 20 km east of My Son and 60 km south of Danang. In the 9th century the area emerged as the new center of Cham art after King Indravarman II constructed a big Buddhist monastery here. The towers and reliefs at Don Duong are more intricate and flamboyant than those at My Son. But only a century later, the Cham art and cultural capital returned to My Son. The new towers built at My Son during the 10th century more reflected those at Don Duong than those that had been previously built at My Son.

Lang Co Beach

Lang Co Beach is a kilometers' long stretch of sandy white palm-lined beach that has the only (but significant) misfortune of being located on the north side of the Hai Van Pass, where the climate (most of the year) changes dramatically, from hot and sunny to cold and gray. There are incredible views of Lang Co descending Hai Van Pass from Danang when the mountainous region isn't shrouded in fog, which it usually is. You can walk for kilometers on the beach at Lang Co and not see a sole individual for hours. Train travelers like to stop here for the night simply for its pristine peace and quiet. In fact, there's only one place to stay in Lang Co—the Khach San Lang Co—situated up a dirt path off Highway 1. You'll have no problem finding it, just ask someone. It's the only digs in town. The small hotel sits on top of a short path right on the beach and is rather run down. Electricity is only available from about 6 p.m. to 10 p.m. Rooms will have as many as four beds and will cost as little as US$3 if you let a Vietnamese do the negotiating for you, perhaps US$10 if you don't. There's a small restaurant here, but it's a lot easier to simply walk down the hill to NH1 and take advantage of one of the many food stalls lining the highway, where the food is cheaper and company cheerier. The area is a popular rest stop for long distance buses heading both north and south, and passengers in hordes pack the roadside food stalls. It's amazing the small restaurant at the hotel is able to remain in business at all. And another important thing to remember about Lang Co: You can show up at the hotel anytime during the winter and expect to get a room. But the small hotel is generally packed with foreigners during the summer months when the weather is better.

WHERE TO STAY IN DANANG

Danang Hotel

3 Dong Da Street ☎ *21179 • 100 rooms.* US$7–20. This is one of three hotels bunched together on the northern tip of the peninsula and one of the obligatory checkpoints on the backpacker route. The lower end rooms are dreary, but you get air conditioning for $7 so they're a bargain. Shared bath, but check the toilet and shower before accepting the room. Water pressure seems to vary greatly from room to room. For some reason, this hotel seems to be popular with foreign businessmen. One reason may be the hookers. At any given time, you'll run into Cubans, Indians and, of course, the omnipresent French. Downstairs restaurant is okay. Inexpensive–Moderate.

Reservations: Direct.

Marble Mountains Hotel (Ngu Hanh Son Hotel)

5 Dong Da Street ☎ *23258 or 23122* • *60 rooms.* US$8–25. This is a new hotel next to the Danang Hotel and is far more attractive both inside and out than its neighbor.There are also "flats" available here with a living room, kitchen and two double bed rooms. The hotel offers car rentals and says it can handle visa matters. Inexpensive–Moderate.   *Reservations: Direct.*

Dong Da Hotel

7 Dong Da Street ☎ *42216* • *68 rooms.* US$8–15. Next door still is this alternative to the Danang Hotel and the Marble Mountains Hotel. This is, as well, less run down than the Danang Hotel, but a little more expensive for budget travelers. The lower end rooms have a fan, while the others get air conditioning. There is a restaurant. Inexpensive–Moderate.   *Reservations: Direct.*

Ngan Hang Hotel

59 Dong Da ☎ *21909.* I know nothing of this place other than it exists.

Orient Hotel (Phuong Dong Hotel)

93 Phan Chu Trinh Street ☎ *21266; FAX: 84.51.22854* • US$25–50. The lobby is exquisite in this old structure, and many think the Orient is the best lodging in Danang. TV; refrigerators; good restaurant upstairs. Moderate–Expensive.   *Reservations: Direct.*

Dau Khi Ami Motel

7 Quang Trung ☎ *22582 or 24494; FAX: 84.51.25532.* Inexpensive.

Reservations: Direct.

Pacific Hotel

92 Phan Chu Trinh Street. ☎ *22137* • *48 rooms.* US$10–40. Old building. Basic accommodations; TV; refrigerators; restaurant. Inexpensive–Moderate.   *Reservations: Direct.*

Bach Dang Hotel

50 Bach Dang Street ☎ *23649 or 23034* • US$25–50. Situated across Bach Dang Street from the Han River, this may be the nicest place to stay in Danang. There is a restaurant and a nightclub. Moderate–Expensive.   *Reservations: Direct.*

The Fishery Guest House (Nha Khach Thuy San)

12 Bach Dang Street ☎ *22612; FAX: 84.51.21659* • *15 rooms.* US$15–20. This seemed a little overpriced, but there's both a restaurant and a nightclub here and that may be why. Air conditioning, single and double rooms, hot water. Moderate. ***Reservations: Direct.***

Binh Tha Hotel & Restaurant

80 Tran Phu ☎ *2276.* Inexpensive.   ***Reservations: Direct.***

Phuong Dong Hotel

93 Phan Chau Trinh Street. ☎ *21266. FAX: 84.51.22854* • Air conditioning; TV; refrigerators; hot water. Inexpensive.

Reservations: Direct.

Hai Au Hotel

215Tran Phu Street. ☎ *22722. FAX: 84.51.22854* • *40 rooms.* US$20–30. Situated across the street from the Danang Cathedral. Although the location's good, it's overpriced. Air conditioning; telephones; hot water; restaurant; bar; sauna; massage. Moderate.

Reservations: Direct.

Huu Nghi

7 Dong Da Street. ☎ *22563* • Air conditioning. Inexpensive.

Reservations: Direct.

INSIDER TIP

The American Company DeMatteis Development Corp. plans to construct a 20 hectare seaside resort in Danang. The US$150 million project will include a hotel, offices, shops, an aquarium, corporate villas and an aquarium.

WHERE TO EAT IN DANANG

Ngoc Anh

30 Tran Phu ☎ *22778* • Vietnamese, Asian.

Trieu Chau Tuugs

62 Tran Phu ☎ *24002* • Vietnamese.

Nha Akng Restaurant

72 Tran Phu • Vietnamese.

Giai Khat

187 Tran Pu • Vietnamese.

Tudo Restaurant   ★★

172 Tran Phu, ☎ *21869* • Chinese, European and Vietnamese food served in a large courtyard. The food is good and many claim this to be Danang's best eatery.

Chin Do
> *174 Tran Phu* ☎ *21846* • European and Asian specialties as well as Chinese seafood.

Phuong Nam
> *205 Tran Phu* ☎ *22806* • Vietnamese.

Be Thui
> *207 Tran Phu* • Vietnamese.

Tien Hung Restaurant
> *190 Tran Phu* • Vietnamese.

Christies Harbourside Bar/Grill Restaurant
> *9 Bach Bang* • Hamburgers, pasta, Vietnamese, fish and chips. Located right on the Han River. There's also a duty free shop here.

Kim Dinh Restaurant
> *7 Bach Dang Street;* ☎ *21541* • Across the street from the Bach Dang Hotel. Vietnamese and Asian. This sits right out over the Han River.

Thanh Lich Restaurant   ★
> *48 Bach Dang Street* • Vietnamese, Chinese, and European. Excellent seafood. Right next door to the Bach Dang Hotel.

Oue Huong Restaurant
> *1 Bach Dang Street* • Vietnamese food, karaoke, cafe.

Mien Trung Restaurant
> *1 Bach Dang Street* • Vietnamese, Chinese, and European. Expensive.

Kim Dinh Restaurant
> *7 Bach Dang Street* • This stretches out over the Han River. Good food, good views.

Restaurant 72
> *72 Tran Phu Street* • Good shrimp spring rolls.

Tranh Lieh Restaurant
> *42 Bach Dang Street* • Vietnamese, Asian. Extensive menu.

DIRECTORY

TRANSPORTATION

Danang is 965 km from Saigon, 759 km from Hanoi, 108 km from Hue, 541 km from Nha Trang, 303 km from Qui Nhon, 350 km from the Lao border and 130 km Quang Ngai. Danang has an "international" airport (it has been designated as such to create a better reputation as both a tourist and business destination) located about 3 km from the city. There are regular connections to Saigon and Hanoi (both about US$80) as well as Nha Trang (US$60) and Pleiku (US$30).

There are many signs here of the cement hangars that were built by the Americans during the war, when this was one of the busiest airports in the world. See the VN Timetable earlier in this edition for precise domestic flight information. "International" flights (to locations such as Hong Kong, Manila, Paris, Kuala Lumpur, etc.) are always via connections in HCMC or Hanoi; the only difference in the airport being an "international" one is that you can buy a ticket to Bangkok in Danang and not in Nha Trang.

By bus: The long distance bus station in Danang is at *8 Dien Bien Phu Street*, about 2 km west of the city. The ticket office is across the street. Here you can get buses to Vinh, Hue, Haiphong, Hanoi and Quanh Nhai. Next to the Thanh Thanh Hotel is a station (*52 Phan Chu Trinh*) where you can get an express bus to Hanoi (about 32,000 dong), Saigon (about 40,000 dong), Nha Trang (about 22,000 dong), Vinh (about 20,000 dong), Dalat (about 32,000 dong), Haiphong (about 34,000 dong), and Buon Ma Thuot (about 27,000 dong). Buses to local destinations such as Hoi An and Marble Mountain leave from opposite *350 Hung Vuong Street.* There is non-express bus service to Trung Phuoc, Hue, Hoi An, Trao Hiep Duc, Tien Phuoc, Ha Tan, Quy Nhon, Thanh My, Que Son, Dong Ha, Giang Ai Nghia, An Hoa, Giao Thuy, Tam Ky, and Kham Duc, among other destinations.

By train: *120 Haiphong Street*, at the intersection with Hoang Hoa Tham Street. Optimistically, it takes about 20 hours to get to Saigon and a little less to Hanoi. The views along the coast are spectacular. Local transportation is by cyclo or rented bicycle. Motorbike riders hang out in front of the Marble Mountains and Danang Hotels and are always available for hire, for either around town or day trips. I paid one to take the 20 km Hai Van Pass over to Lang Co Beach about 40,000 dong. It was too much, as I subsequently learned you can hire a driver for as little as US$5 per day. But you've got to look hard to find one. The Vietnamese know tourist dollars when they see them.

POST OFFICE

46 Bach Dang Street at the corner of Le Duan Street; ☎ *21327.* International telephone and fax services. Faxes can also be transmitted from the Phuong Dong Hotel.

TOURIST OFFICES

Danang Tourist Office. *48 Bach Dang Street.* ☎ *22226; FAX: 84.51.22854.*

Vietnamtourism. *91/1 Nguyen Chi Thanh Street.* ☎ *22990 or 22999; FAX: 84.51.22854.*

TNT INTERNATIONAL EXPRESS

☎ *21685 or 22582.*

BANKS AND MONEYCHANGERS

Vietcom Bank, *46 Le Loi Street.* Will exchange money and give cash advances on major U.S. credit cards.

HOSPITAL

Hospital C, *35 Hai Phong Street.* ☎ *22480.*

AIRLINE OFFICES

Vietnam Airlines Dometic Booking Office, *35 Phan Tru Street.* ☎ *21130.*

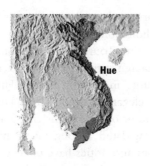

Hue

HUE

Hue was the capital of Vietnam during the Nguyen Dynasty 1802–1945.

HUE IN A CAPSULE

Hue served as the capital of Vietnam for more than 140 years...it houses ancient temples...Imperial buildings...and French-style edifices...was established in the 17th century...invaded by the French in 1833 and by the Japanese in 1945...was hammered by U.S. forces during the Tet offensive...many historical monuments were destroyed during this military action...but a great many remain.

The Ancient Capital of Hue (population about 350,000) began to swell with tourism in 1993. Tourism is now the leading generator of hard currency in this historic city that was battered during the Vietnam War. Today, thousands of residents make their salaries from tourism. The five principal provincial tourism businesses reaped in more than 32 million dong in 1993. Simply, the city is going through a tourist boom. Tourism in Hue doubled in a single year (from 1992–93). Foreign currency earnings increased threefold. Responding to the surge in tourism, Thua Thien Hue authorities quickly opened the elegant riverside Hotel Hue, which is the first joint-venture hotel to be opened in the city. Since 1975, when there existed only the dilapidated Huong Giang hotel with 47 gutted guest rooms, tourism authorities have opened at least six "luxury" hotels of international standards with 335 rooms (620 beds). And over the last several years, dozens of new hotels have opened up and down the south side of the Perfume River—including the Kinh Do, Dong Ha, and Morin Hotels. The Hoa Hong Hotel on Le Loi Street was the first private hotel to open in the city.

Western visitors in Hue can now find a slew of garden houses and villas as accommodations. Most of the accommodations in the Hue area are enjoying occupancy rates greater than 80 percent, and that's why it's a good bet to book with a particular hotel first rather than simply showing up (although you should always be able to find a room in the city).

By the year 2000 it is predicted that tourism levels will climb to five times higher than their current levels. With the pace of infrastructure developments in the region, these forecasts seem reasonable. Officials in the city told me that their predictions will be predicated primarily on the initiation of package tours rather than travel by independent tourists. Hue's Royal Park is being restored and the Tinh Tam Lake recreated. Additionally, under construction is the Bach Ma-Lang Co casino. Visits to the "Nine Underground Bunkers," which show the atrocities of the South Vietnamese Ngo Dinh Diem regime, are in the works. And there are reenactments of ancient and royal ceremonies being devised at various locations. Horse-drawn carriages will soon take tourists to the royal tombs, the mountains and the beaches. As well, recreations of costumes worn by kings, queens, princes, and princesses are being developed. In short, and regrettably I might add, this city is gearing up to become a "tour" tourist's destination.

Frankly, I find Hue cold, rainy and gray (yearly rainfall can total 152 cm or 60 in.). And, although the Citadel and the Forbidden Purple City are well worth visiting, the devastation caused by war to these ancient sites makes them essentially unrecognizable, with patches of weeds and occasional deformed rock formations that were once grand splendors of the Nguyen Dynasty now springing from the earth like outcroppings on a moonscape. I found the city disappointing, and the guidebooks depicting the city's earlier grandeur more awe-inspiring. To make matters worse, it's difficult getting around to the different sites without getting wet. The best way, of course, is by bicycle. This doesn't afford great photo opportunities for those other than professionals, who may have to wait around for a month or two to get a few rays of sun.

Hue (originally called Phu Xuan and built in 1687), during the Nguyen Dynasty, was the cultural, religious and economic capital of Vietnam. Nguyen emperors built the Mandarin Road (Quan Lo) which allowed travelers to remarkably reach Saigon in only two weeks, and Hanoi in under a week. Messengers that were more than two days late were flogged for their tardiness.

Pedestrian crossings don't need to be marked along national highways, because most of the pedestrian users wouldn't recognize one if they saw it.

In addition to the Vietnam War, Hue has had an extensive history of conflict. There were no fewer than 100 peasant uprisings in the area between 1802 and 1820. Royalty bickered and fought constantly. The French attacked Hue in 1833 and decimated the population to such an extent that the Emperor Hiep Hoa permitted the city to become a protectorate of France. The French divided the population by their spreading of Christianity. Although the French, and later the Japanese, felt it in their best interests to allow the Nguyen Dynasty to continue, there remained perpetual feuding and power scheming among the Nguyen royalty—and its influence on the population dropped to such a degree that the last Nguyen Emperor, Bao Dai, ceded the throne in August 1945.

Even after World War II ended, peace would not come to Hue. The Viet Cong took over the Citadel for 25 days during the Tet Offensive in 1968 and their communist flag defiantly flew from the Citadel's flag pole for more than three weeks. U.S. troops ruthlessly counterattacked, and it was this action which caused much of the damage to the ancient royal sites. The Thai Hoa Palace was decimated. More than 10,000 people died in the bitter fighting in Hue during the Tet Offensive. But with the Americans back in control of the area, peace would still not last long. NVA troops, after taking over the city in 1975, massacred thousands of civilians, beheading many, making the massacre at My Lai look like a mugging.

For shopping, the most unique item in Hue is a hat called *non bai tho*, which is made from palm and bamboo leaves. Inside the hats are proverbs, poems, and the lyrics to love songs which can only be seen when facing the hat toward the light. Makes for a great gift.

WHAT TO SEE AND DO IN HUE

Citadel

This is a large, moated and walled area that has a perimeter of some 10 km. It was begun in 1804 by Emperor Gia Long. The Citadel used to enclose the entire city. Its 7 m high walls were originally built of earth but it was decided in the 1820s to cover them with bricks. This laborious process took thousands of workers and years to complete. Even today, it is used as a military fortress. The most famous gate is the **Ngo Mon Gate**.

Imperial City

This is in the Citadel and was built in the early 19th century and modeled after the Forbidden City in Peking. There are numerous palaces and temples within these walls, as well as towers, a library and a museum. There are also areas for religious ceremonies. The South Gate is the main entrance. The Emperor Gia Long began construction of the city in 1804, and the site eventually encompassed eight different villages and covered six square kms. There are 10 gates that surround the four walls of the citadel. It took more than 20,000 laborers to construct the walls alone. Inside two of the gates are sets of large cannons, four through the **Nhon Gate** and five through the **Quang Duc Gate**. These cannons, made of bronze seized from Tay Son rebels, were cast in 1803. They represent the five natural elements and the four seasons. None of the cannons have ever been fired. Each contains a description of how it was constructed as well as firing instructions which, of course, were never followed. The main gate to the Imperial enclosure, the **Ngo Mon Gate** (built during the reign of Emperor Minh Mang in 1834), could only be used by the emperor. On the top of the gate is the Belvedere of the five Phoenixes. The emperor would appear here during important ceremonial occasions. The last Nguyen

Dynasty Emperor Bao Dai formally ended his reign here. A Japanese company is currently in the process of renovating the gate, albeit a slow one.

Forbidden Purple City

The imperial family and its entourage were the only individuals permitted to use this royal palace. There were 60 buildings situated in 20 courtyards. "Feminine" affairs happened in the west area of the complex, while the men did their manly things in the east area. Fighting during the Tet offensive ruined the complex. The entire area is a depressing pile of rubble and small vegetableless vegetable gardens. Sadly, the only structures that can still be identified here are the two **Mandarin palaces**, the **Dien Canh Can** and the **Reading Book Palace**, but even these are in dismal shape. Work was started in 1983 to renovate the structures, but not much has been done. There are two large urns at the far side of the **Thai Hoa Palace**, cast in bronze and decorated with animals, birds and plants. On each side of the urns is a pavilion, the **Huu** and **Ta Pavilions**. One is a souvenir shop. The only really surviving buildings are on the west side of the palace, between the walls of the Forbidden Purple City and the outer walls—and many independent visitors miss them altogether. There is the relatively-well preserved **Hien Lam Cac**, where nine large urns made from copper cast in the mid 1830s stand in front of the pavilion. The **Temple of Generations** is next to the urns. This was built in 1821 and features altars of 10 Nguyen Dynasty Emperors. The **Hung Temple** is north of the Temple of Generations. It was built in 1804 in honor of Nguyen Phuc Luan, considered the "Father of the Nguyen Dynasty," and the father of Gia Long. Most blame the American shelling of Hue for the destruction of the Forbidden Purple City, but the complex had been deteriorating over the course of the previous 50 years due to shelling by the French, vandals, natural disasters and termites. The only shelling being done here now is the whopping US$4 admission price to get into the Imperial City and Forbidden Purple City.

The Flag Tower

This is the tall, 37-meter high flagpole between the Nhon and Quang Duc Gates. It was built originally in 1809 and lengthened in 1831. A typhoon knocked it down in 1904; it was rebuilt in 1915 only to be wrecked again in 1947. It was rebuilt in 1949 and that is how it stands today. The VC hung the National Liberation Front flag here for 24 days during the Tet Offensive. A picture of the flag on the pole can be seen in the Ho Chi Minh Museum in Hue.

Bao Quoc Pagoda

Bien Phu Street, near the the railway line. This pagoda was built by the Buddhist monk Giac Phong in the early 18th century. There is a nice stupa behind the the pagoda to the left. There are beautiful doors here with Chinese and Sanskrit inscriptions.

Tu Dam Pagoda

At the intersection of Dien Bien Phu and Tu Dam Streets. This was built in the late 1930s and has the distinction of being the temple where South Vietnamese President Diem sent troops in to silence the residing monks who were reputedly spreading discontent amongst the populace with the South Vietnamese regime.

Imperial Museum (Museum of Ancient Objects)

3 Le Truc Street. Built in 1845 and restored in 1923, this is a beautiful museum which houses inscribed poems on the walls. Most of the precious artifacts were pillaged during the Vietnam War, but there are many beautiful items here, including lacquerware, ceramics, royal costumes and furniture. In the front courtyard are giant bells and gongs. Admission: 8000 dong. Behind the museum is the **Royal College**, which was moved to this site in 1908 after being built in 1803. This was a school for the sons of princes and high-ranking Mandarins. Nearby, at *23 Thang 8 Street* is the **Military Museum**, which features a collection of tanks, missiles and armed personnel carriers.

AUTHOR'S NOTE

The Vietnamese government has invested 1 billion dong (US$1 million) into the primary restoration of the Hue Ancient Museum. The Center for Hue Historical Heritage Restoration has copied the design of the museum in order to restore the whole wooden structure of the museum and retile the roof of Hoang Luu Ly and Than Luy Ly tiles. The fence surrounding the museum has been rebuilt to coincide with the museum's unique architecture. The restoration is a rapid one and should be completed by the time you read this.

Thien Mu Pagoda

This is a bizarre sight. Yes, it's a pagoda. But your curiosity is more peaked by something else. It's an old Austin. Yeah, a British car. It was the same car that brought the Buddhist monk Thich Quang Duc to Saigon. There he became the subject of Malcolm Browne's famous photo. It shows the monk immolating himself in 1963. A copy of the photo is pasted on the windshield. Weird.

Phu Can Cathedral

The cathedral, at *20 Doan Huu Thrinh Street*, was built in 1963, but wasn't finished until 1975 (although it isn't entirely finished). There are plans to continue the building, which essentially only requires adding a spire to the cathedral. According to reports, this is the eighth church to be built on this site since 1682.

Tang Tau Lake

A royal library was formerly on an island in Tan Tau Lake. There is now a small Hinayana pagoda on the island called Ngoc Huong Pagoda.

Tinh Tam Lake

This lake is about 500 meters north of the Imperial enclosure and close by to Tang Tau Lake. In the middle of the lake are two islands connected by a bridge. Emperors used to spend lazy afternoons on the lake.

Gia Long Tomb

Built between 1814 and 1820, this is a magnificent structure that is unfortunately difficult to visit. There are huge mango trees that surround the tomb. It follows the formula of other royal tombs with a lotus pond surrounding the enclosed compound. Here there is a courtyard with five headless Mandarins. Also there are figurines of horses and elephants. There are steps that lead up to another courtyard where the emperor and his wife are buried. Inscriptions describing the emperor's reign can be found behind the burial area. Gia Long was the first of the Nguyen Dynasty emperors and ruled from 1802–1820, the year he died. He ordered the construction of his tomb in 1814. When the king died, his corpse was washed and clothed in ornate garments. Precious stones and pearls were placed in his mouth. He was then placed in a coffin made of catalpa wood, a kind of wood that wards off insects to prevent decomposition. When a messenger reached the Empress a few days later, he found that she, too, was dead—although she could not have known of her husband's death by all accounts. Although Gia Long died on February 3, 1820, he was not actually buried until around May 20. Next to his tomb is a second grave which contains items placed that would be useful to the emperor in his next life. A small donation will be expected at his tomb.

Khai Dinh Tomb

This was the last monument of the Nguyen dynasty and was constructed between 1920 and 1931. It sits magnificently on the slopes of Chau E Mountain, about 10 km from Hue in Chau Chu village. It has a long staircase flanked by dragons. There are ceiling murals and ceramic frescoes. The emperor reigned over Vietnam from 1916–1925. The tomb looks entirely unlike the other emperors' tombs around Hue. The tomb, combining a gaudy combination of European and Vietnamese influences has become dilapidated over the years. You have to climb 36 steps to get up to the tomb, where you'll reach the first courtyard, surrounded by two pavilions. The Honor Courtyard is 26 steps farther up the hillside and features depictions of elephants and horses, as well as Mandarin soldiers. Then climb another three sets of stairs to reach the tomb, which is called Thien Dinh. It's divided into three halls and decorated with various murals. The emperor lies beneath the statue of Khai Dinh.

Minh Mang Tomb

This complex was built in 1840 by King Minh Mang and is known for its magnificent architecture, military statuaries and elaborate decorations. It is perhaps the most beautiful of Hue's pagodas and tombs. You can get to this location, about 12 km south of Hue by tour boat or car.

Tu Duc Tomb

Seven km from the city, this was once the Royal Palace of Tu Duc, who ruled Hue more than 100 years ago. There are pavilions in a tranquil setting of forested hills and lakes. The tomb was constructed between 1864 and 1867. Tu Duc, who was the longest reigning Emperor (1848–1883), lived a luxurious life. Fifty chefs and 50 stewards presided over the emperor's meals, enough to feed and serve his 104 wives and numerous mistresses (although he never fathered any sons). The tomb is surrounded by a wall; there's a lake inside with a small island where the king constructed replicas of various temples. He used to come here to the surrounding pavilions to relax, hunt animals and recite poetry he composed to his many female companions and listen to music. To the left of the water is the Xung Khiem Pavilion; this was one of the emperor's favorite hangouts. Built on pilings over the lake, it was restored in 1986. The tomb of his Empress Le Thien Anh and adopted son Kien Phuc is to the left of Tu Duc's tomb. Many of the surrounding pavilions are in dire need of restoration, although you can still feel the serenity Tu Duc must have found here. Hell, with 104 women, I would have. It is rumored that Tu Duc was sterile, and therefore forced to write his own eulogy. The eulogy itself recounts a surprisingly sad life (perhaps because of his sterility). Also, the French took control of Vietnam during his reign, which further saddened the emperor.

Dong Khanh Tomb

Seven km from Hue. Built in 1889, this is the tomb of Emperor Dong Khan, the adopted son of Tu Duc. He assumed the throne as a puppet emperor after the French captured Emperor Ham Nhgi, who had fled Hue after the French stormed the palace in 1885. Ham was exiled to Algeria. Dong ruled the dynasty from 1886–1888. The tomb is the smallest of the royal tombs of Hue.

Trieu Tri Tomb

About 7 km from Hue. There are conflicting reports as to when this tomb was built. Some say it was constructed in 1848 and other sources say it was constructed between 1864 and 1867. Trieu Tri ruled Vietnam from 1841 to 1847. The tomb is the only emperor's tomb not to be surrounded by a wall.

WHERE TO STAY IN HUE

Ben Nghe Guest House

4 Ben Nghe Street. ☎ *3687* • Attached bath; hot water. Rave reviews from backpackers. Inexpensive.   ***Reservations: Direct.***

Le Loi Hue Hotel (Hue Guest House)

2-5 Le Loi Street ☎ *24668, 22155, 22153 or 22323; FAX: 84.54.24527*
• US$7–20. This is an interesting-looking compound of several build-
ings that looks a little bit like a college campus. The cheap rooms are
a real bargain. The rooms are small but impeccably clean and comfortable. The more expensive doubles are large and airy. Attached bath in
all private rooms and "mini-dorm" rooms, accommodating 4 or more
people. There are a number of outdoor cafes downstairs, as well as
souvenir stalls.Bicycle rentals.Very comfortable. Inexpensive–Moderate.   ***Reservations: Direct.***

Hue City Tourism Villas

11, 16, 18 Ly Thuong Kiet Street, and 5 Le Loi Street. ☎ *(11) 3753; (16)
3679; (18) 3964; (5) 3945* • These four properties get mixed reviews
from travelers. Basic accommodations; fans; hot water. Inexpensive.
                                                        Reservations: Direct.

Hue Hotel

49 Le Loi Street. ☎ *3390. FAX: 84-54-3399* • *150 rooms.* Largest and
the newest hotel in Hue. Air conditioning; tennis courts; two restaurants; disco; karaoke; swimming pool; post office; gift shop; TV; telephones; refrigerators; barbers; hairdressers; massage; hot water; all the
amenities. Moderate—but for what it buys, it's cheap!
                                                        Reservations: Direct.

Huong Giang Hotel

51 Le Loi Street. ☎ *3958. FAX: 84-54-3424* • *42 rooms.* US$35–100.
Built in 1962, but enlarged in 1983. Right on the river. Most rooms
offer great views (you better get a great view for a hundred bucks).
This is one of the most expensive hotels in town. Whether it's vastly
overpriced will depend on your wallet. Friendly staff. Two great restaurants; cafe; large gardens; reception rooms; gift shop; sauna; massage; car and bike rentals; air conditioning; refrigerators; attached
bathrooms; hot water with good pressure. The works, if you've got
the cash. Great deal if you can afford a lower-priced room. Often full
with the well heeled. If you're on a budget, you can laugh at the
"modern" architecture as you pass by on the way to your US$6 guest-
house. Moderate–very expensive.   ***Resrvations: Direct.***

Kinh Do Hotel

Vo Thi Sau Street. ☎ *3036* • Rooms in three price ranges. Restaurant;
bar; sauna; massage; dancing. Inexpensive to moderate.
                                                        Reservations: Direct.

Thuan Hoa Hotel

7b Nguyen Tri Phuong Street. ☎ *2553 or 2576* • About US$ 20–40.
Basic accommodations if a bit overpriced. Air conditioning, restaurant, attached bath. Moderate.   ***Reservations: Direct.***

Morin Hotel

2a Hung Vuong Street. ☎ *3866* • About US$5–15. This is an excellent value and I highly recommend this hotel, especially to backpackers. The service is friendly, the rooms clean and comfortable. Hot water, good pressure, private bath. Big rooms. Bicycles for rent for 8000 dong. Inexpensive.   ***Reservations: Direct.***

Nha Khach Chin Phu

5 Le Loi Street • About US$20–40. This is another recommendation, although it's a bit pricey. Beautiful building on the Perfume River. Large rooms, private bath, air conditioning. Restaurant. Friendly staff and efficient service. Moderate.   ***Reservations: Direct.***

WHERE TO EAT IN HUE

The food in Hue is generally very good, and there are a number of specialties unique to Hue. One is a dish of shrimp, pork and bean sprouts filled in a deep-fried egg batter (*banh khoai*). It is served usually with a delicious sesame sauce called nuoc tuong. There is also a rice pancake filled with shrimp and herbs called *banh beo*, and a rice pancake with pork called *ram*. The local beer, Huda, is decent but could use some more hops.

Huong Giang Restaurant

51 Le Loi Street • Vietnamese and European cuisine. Excellent.

Ngu Binh Restaurant

7 Ly Thuong Kiet Street • Food is average. Great place to meet new friends.

Song Huong Floating Restaurant

North of the Trang Tien Bridge on the bank of the Perfume River • Great Vietnamese fare at low prices.

Ong Tau Resturant

134 Ngo Duc Ke, on the grounds of the Imperial Palace • Vietnamese, Asian, Western. A little pricey but this is a good restaurant.

Loc Thien

6 Dinh Tien Hoang Street • Service is friendly, the Vietnamese and Asian fare good, Cheap.

Pho Restaurant

6 Na Hoi Street • Vietnamese fare at great prices. The noodle soup is excellent.

DIRECTORY

TRANSPORTATION

Hue is 1070 km from Saigon, 654 km from Hanoi, 370 km from Vinh, 108 km from Danang, 165 km from Dong Hoi, 94 km from the Ben Hai River, 56 km from Quang Tri, 72 km from Dong Ha, 152 km from the Laos border, 400 km from the Thai border, and 60 km from Aloui, which can only be reached by 4-wheel-drive.

By air: VN flies to Hue from Ho Chi Minh City Sunday–Tuesday and Thrursdays and Fridays at 9:40 a.m. Also on Wednesdays and Saturdays at 10 a.m. From Hanoi, flights leave for Hue Sunday–Tuesday and Thursdays and Fridays at 2:30 p.m. Flights from Hue connect to HCMC on Wednesdays and Saturdays at 1:20 p.m., and Sunday–Tuesday and Thursdays and Fridays at 4:10 p.m. To Hanoi Sunday-Tuesday and Thursdays and Fridays at 11:30 a.m.

By bus: The An Cuu bus station is at *43 Hung Vuong Street.* This station serves destinations to the south. Buses connect with Lang Co, Quy Nhon, Danang, Buon Ma Thuot, Nha Trang, Dalat and Saigon. They usually leave very early in the morning, about 5 a.m. The bus station serving the north (An Hoa Station) at the northwest corner of the walled city has connections to Dong Ha, Vinh, Hanoi, Dong Hoi and Khe Sanh. Again buses usually leave around 5 a.m. Tickets for all destinations can be bought at either station. The local bus station is called Dong Ba (downstream from the Trang Tien Bridge on the river side of Tran Hung Dao Street), and from here non-express buses depart for Ban Thanh, Dong Ha, Phu Loung, Cho No, Nong, An Lo, Bao Vinh, Lang Co, Danang, Thuan An, and Cau Hai.

By train: The train station is at the west end of Le Loi Street and serves all points up and down the coast. It takes about 16 hours to get to Hanoi and 24 hours to Saigon. Book well in advance, especially for sleepers.

Transport around town: Cars with drivers can be hired at Thus Thien Tourism, Hue Tourist Office and Hue City Tourism.

By motorbike: I didn't find a place to rent a motorbike, but there are plenty of citizens who will bring you around on the back of their's for a negotiable fee.

By bicycle: Bicycles are easily rented at most hotels for about 8000-10,000 dong. It's the best way of getting around town. Unfortunately, it rains so much in Hue, expect to get wet. Bring a rainsuit.

By boat: There are many ways to rent boats to go up and down the Perfume River. Restaurants can help arrange a boat tour, but they're expensive. Many of the sights in Hue can be reached by boat, including many of the royal tombs, Thuan An Beach, and Thien Mu Pagoda. Also try hiring a boat behind the Dong Ba Market, by the Dap Da Bridge and also the Perfume River Hotel.

POST OFFICE

8 Hoang Hoa Tham Street. You can make international calls and faxes from here.

HOSPITAL

Hue General Hospital. *16 Le Loi Street.* ☎ *2325.*

BANKS AND MONEYCHANGERS

Industrial and Commercial Bank. *2A Le Quy Don Street.* Open from 7 to 11:30 a.m. and from 1:30 to 4:30 p.m. Monday-Saturday.

TOURIST OFFICES

Hue City Tourism. *18 Le Loi Street.* Can arrange for car rentals, guides and traditional Vietnamese musical performances.

Hue Tourist Office. *51 Le Loi Street.* ☎ *2369.* Can arrange for car rentals and guides.

AIRLINES OFFICES

The booking office for Vietnam Airlines is located at *12 Ha Noi Street.* ☎ *2249.* There's not much they can do for you here at this primitive, non-computerized office but get you out of Hue. It's staffed by a sole woman, so expect to wait a while.

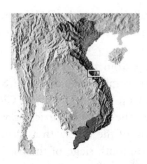

THE DMZ

THE DEMILITARIZED ZONE IN A CAPSULE

The DMZ was the site of the fiercest fighting of the Vietnam War...Tens of thousands of soldiers died here...The siege of Khe Sanh and battles at Hamburger Hill are considered the bloodiest battles of the war...The former DMZ stretched for 5 km in either direction of the Ben Hai River...Thousands of scavengers have been killed since 1975 unearthing old war materiel to sell as scrap metal and souvenirs...The DMZ was officially created in 1954...It extends along National Highway 9 from the South China Sea to the Laos border.

The Demilitarized Zone was the area that extended 5 km both north and south of the Ben Hai river and was the site of some of the bloodiest fighting of the Vietnam War. This was the demarcation line that separated South Vietnam from North Vietnam. The origins of the DMZ were the result of the Potsdam Conference held in Berlin in 1945 (which included representatives of Great Britain, the U.S. and the USSR) that partitioned Vietnam into two separate countries. However, the actual DMZ wasn't established until 1954. What was concluded at the Potsdam conference was that Japanese forces south of the 16th parallel would surrender to the British, while occupying Japanese forces in the north would surrender to the Nationalist Chinese Army led by Chiang Kai Shek.

Eventually, in 1954, the governments of France and of Ho Chi Minh agreed in Geneva to an armistice of sorts that would split the south and north—however, not politically. The demarcation line was to be temporary until general elections could be held in 1956. But when these did not occur, the nation was split in half at the Ben Hai River, also referred to as the 17th parallel.

The DMZ extended from the the sea to the Laos border. Today National Highway 9 runs along this former border to Laos. As well, the Ho Chi Minh Trail cut across the DMZ, forcing American forces to establish a number of bases and fire bases along the southern side of the demarcation line to prevent the transport of troops and war materiel from moving from the north to the South. Some of the bases along the 17th parallel included Khe Sanh, Camp Carroll, Lang Vay, Cua Viet, Con Thien, Dong Ha, Gio Linh, Cam Lo, Ca Lu, and the Rockpile. Khe Sonh, in particular, was the scene of some of the fiercest fighting of the war, with as many as 10,500 soldiers dying during the two-month siege of the base in the beginning of 1968 by North Vietnamese forces—which was only a decoy for the Tet Offensive in February.

Other areas along the DMZ that experienced bitter fighting were Dong Ha, the infamous Hamburger Hill, the Rockpile, Camp Carroll, Quang Tri, the Ashau Valley (where Hamburger Hill is located), Con Thien and Lang Vay.

Although the war has been over for many years, the DMZ remains an extremely dangerous area. Thousands of people have been killed by land mines, unexploded bombs, agonizing and deforming white phosperous shells and other ordnance that is still spread all across the DMZ. Peasants and farmers still comb the area for scrap metal—aluminum, steel and brass—and other items they hope to sell. They earn only a pittance for these efforts and many are killed each year. It is not wise to touch anything on the ground along Highway 9. In fact it would be deadly, because if the Vietnamese have not already scavenged the materiel it is because they are too frightened to move it.

A NOTE ABOUT LAND MINES AND UNEXPLODED ORDNANCE

The Americans recarpeted Vietnam with underground explosives. Even today, scores of Vietnamese and cattle are blown up by land mines and other unexploded ordnance. It seems now that it is the Australians who are trying to remove what's still left, especially in port areas. EXAT is an Australian ordnance disposal firm working with the Vietnamese Army implementing ordnance surveys and clearance services. One contract is with a new cement company on a site near Haiphong heavily bombed by the Americans during the war. Another contract is with a mining company in the Central Highlands. Although thousands of bombs near the ground's surface have already been defused by the Vietnamese, more sophisticated clearance operations are required for port expansion, sites of new factories, bridge and road building, and open-cast mining operations. EXAT believes they will achieve a 95% success rate in Vietnam, a figure based on their operations in Kuwait, Afghanistan, Cambodia and Pakistan. Much of EXAT's efforts will be training local demining technicians to utilize the sophisticated equipment required for intense, large-scale demining operations.

Travel permits to the DMZ area, once required and extremely costly, have largely been removed. But you should only visit the area with a trained, professional guide. The old bases can be visited by either day trips or through Saigontourist's War Veteran Tours (see the War Veterans Tours section earlier in this edition).

A WORD ABOUT AGENT ORANGE

The debate continues even today regarding the effects of Agent Orange on both the Vietnamese and American war veterans exposed to the chemical. Many "experts," particularly in the U.S., insist that the chemical is essentially harmless and that the higher birth defect rates experienced in the south and central parts of Vietnam are due more to malnutrition than anything else. But consider the following: 72 million liters of chemicals, containing 15 types of poisons, were dropped on 1.7 million hectares of forest during the war. That's nearly 20 percent of the total forest area in southern Vietnam. Of these 72 million liters dropped, 47 million of them were Agent Orange, which contained a blend of 170 kg of dioxin. And this estimate of the total amount of Agent Orange (called Operation Ranch Hand, which lasted from 1961–1971) dropped on Vietnam is considered conservative at best. It is believed that 4600 flying sorties sprayed the herbicide mainly in the following areas: Phuoc Long, Binh Dinh, Thua Thien, Tay Ninh, Long Khan, Binh Duong, Bien Hoa, Quan Nam, Quang Tri and Kontum. There were between

300–700 drops in each of these areas. Nearly 50% of the Agent Orange dropped fell in these areas. Despite protests from around the world and the U.S. government's assurance that the chemical would have no long term effects on the Vietnamese people, American soldiers and foliage in the environment, it became undisputedly evident that the chemical would have long-term harmful effects as early as 1970 at an international conference in France of Scientists at Orsay University. Regardless, the American military continued to drop the chemical on Vietnam until 1973.

Surveys by scientists have revealed that dioxin is still evident in the blood of the people of Vietnam and in the environment, particularly in the DMZ area and southern Vietnam. For instance, in northern Vietnam, blood tests have shown an average of 2.2 picograms (pg) of dioxin in the blood of the people. (In the U.S., the figure is 5.2 pg per person and in Japan 3.2 pg.). However the levels of dioxin in the blood of southern Vietnamese is staggering. The general figure is between 11.7–14.6 pg per person. Particularly whopping are the amounts of dioxin found in the people of Song Be Province (32 per person!), Bien Hoa (28 pg per person) and Danang (18 pg per person).

An analysis of fat tissue taken from 73 people between 1987 and 1992 revealed that of the 25 people living in areas where the chemical was dropped by U.S. warplanes, 84 % of them contained large traces of dioxin in their blood. Of the 48 people not living in affected areas, 81% also showed high levels of dioxin in their blood. This is essentially conclusive evidence that the dioxins of Agent Orange were and still are spread through the consumption of affected food. In fact, people directly exposed to the dioxin absorb about 25% of the pesticide, while those exposed to the chemical indirectly through the consumption of food grown in affected areas absorb 98% percent of the dioxin content!

It is conclusive now, most scientists believe, that exposure to Agent Orange causes fetus damage. Newborn babies today usually have about 0.02 pg of the dioxin in their blood. Death rates of children born in sprayed areas is about 30% higher than those born in non-sprayed areas. Most believe that the mother's milk containing the dioxin is the principle cause of the higher death rates. Deformities and abnormalities, such as mental retardation are also higher in these areas. Instances of stillbirth, cancer and congenital deformity are also higher in these areas.

Only recently has the U.S. government admitted that Agent Orange and dioxin may cause cancer and skin diseases, as well as nervous, lymphatic and respiratory disorders and diseases such as Hodgkin's Disease. There have also been similar long-term effects on the American soldiers who fought in the affected areas. Of the nearly 40,000 lawsuits filed by American soldiers against the government based on their exposure to Agent Orange, to date only about 470 of them have been settled by most recent accounts. It is believed that as many as 200,000 U.S. soldiers were affected by the chemical.

Today, the Vietnamese are still poisoned by Agent Orange through the food they eat and the soil they till. Scientists hope that the spread and effects of Agent Orange will last only another 5–10 years.

WHAT TO SEE AND DO AROUND THE DMZ

Ben Hai River

This river, about 20 km north of Dong Ha marks the former border between South Vietnam and North Vietnam. NH1 passes over the river via a dilapidated bridge. During the war the southern half of the bridge was painted yellow, the northern half red. It was destroyed during a U.S. bombing raid in 1967. After the ceasefire agreements in 1973, the rebuilt bridge had two flag towers built. There are nice stretches of beaches on both the south and north sides of where the river empties into the sea.

Dong Ha

Along National Highway 1 at the intersection of the American-built Highway 9 south of the Ben Hai River. This was the site of a former U.S. Marine command center and later a South Vietnamese Army base. It was fiercely attacked during the spring of 1968 by NVA regulars. Dong Ha is now the capital of Quang Tri Province. Here you can see the **French-built blockhouse** on Tran Phu Street (about 400 meters of NH1), the perimeter of which can be seen captured war equipment, including tanks. The blockhouse was once used by American and South Vietnamese forces. Near the blockhouse you can stay at the **Dong Ha Hotel** (☎ *361, 24 rooms*). Other hotels in town include the **Buu Dien Tinh Buu Quang Tri Hotel** (on the south side of town, about US$20), **the Ngoai Thuong Hotel** (also near the French blockhouse and very inexpensive), and the **Dong Truong Son Hotel** (about 3 km out from the blockhouse and rather expensive) on Tran Phu Street. There are a slew of roadside restaurants along NH1 in Dong Ha to choose from. There's a decent restaurant next to the Buu Dien Tinh Buu Quang Tri hotel. There is also a restaurant at the Dong Truong Son Hotel.

Quang Tri

Quang Tri is about 60 km north of Hue and was the site of the Eastertide Offensive in 1972, in which several NVA divisions crossed the

DMZ and, using tanks, mortars and heavy artillery, captured both the city and the province. The Americans then carpet bombed the area with B-52 sorties. South Vietnamese artillery was also employed in the total destruction of the city. In short, the city was leveled in order to retake what was left of it. As a result, there's nothing to see here save for the Quang Tri Memorial and perhaps the ruined citadel, which was formerly an ARVN HQ. There's also another ruined building here, that was formerly a Buddhist secondary school, between NH1 and the bus station. If you want, you can visit the bombed out church where American and VC soldiers fought. It is pockmarked with bullet holes. There are two beaches in the vicinity: Gia Dang Beach and Cua Viet Beach.

Vinh Moc Tunnels   ★

Unlike the tunnels at Cu Chi, these elaborate tunnels used by the VC and NVA troops have not been enlarged to accommodate Western tourists (they average 1.2 meters wide and are only 1.7 meters high) and look exactly as they did in the mid-1960s. There are nearly three kilometers of tunnels here, with at least 12 entrances. Seven of them are at the beach. The entrances have been embraced by shrubs and trees. The tunnels themselves were built on three different levels. Inside the tunnels, there are small chambers where families and soldiers lived. There is even a conference hall that could fit as many as 150 people who would gather for military meetings and social events. They can easily be visited by tourists, but only with a guide, because it's easy as hell to get lost in these dark, narrow caverns. If you're on the lam and under five feet tall, this would be where the bill collectors definitely wouldn't find you. As well, the government uses poisons to keep away snakes tempted to make the tunnels their home. During the war, the tunnels were bombed, but little damage was inflicted. What the inhabitants feared most were the drilling bombs, which burned their way deep into the earth before exploding. Although electric lighting was added to the tunnels in 1972, bring a flashlight.

Doc Mieu Base

Eight km south of the Ben Hai River along NH1. This was the site of "McNamara's Wall," which housed an intricate electronic surveillance site used by the Americans to detect VC and NVA troop movements, as the soldiers would cross electrical wires informing the surveillance station. All around you can see remnants from the war: military uniforms and boots, huge craters leftover from the bombing and shelling, artillery shrapnel and live ammunition rounds. These have largely been scavenged by the locals.

Cua Tung Beach

Bao Dai used to vacation here, which is on the north side of where the Ben Hai River spills into the South China Sea. Off the coast of Cua

Tung Beach is Con Co Island, which can be reached via a three-hour boat ride. Bomb craters of all sizes can be found in the area around the beach. It's a grizzly sight.

Dakrong Bridge

About 12.5 km to the east past the Khe Sanh bus station. This bridge, which spans over the Dakrong River was built after the "official" withdrawal of American troops. It was constructed by the North Vietnamese with Cuban assistance. The route that heads south from the bridge to Aluoi was once part of the Ho Chi Minh Trail. Although the villagers in the area today are peaceful, they still sling on their backs automatic weapons and assault rifles leftover from the war. It's a little unnerving, but there's little danger for tourists.

Camp Carroll

This former U.S. base is 3 km off Highway 9, 24 km east past the Dakrong Bridge and about 36 km east of the Khe Sanh bus station. There's not much today worth visiting here but jackfruit trees, shrubs, and small weapons shells that litter the ground, but this is a historical military site that was established in 1966 and named after a U.S.Marine who was killed during a battle on a nearby ridge. There were giant artillery pieces at the camp, 175mm cannons that could fire volleys as far away as Hue. Today the area is used to grow pepper. This was also the site where the South Vietnamese commander of the base, Lt. Col. Ton That Dinh, deserted the base and joined the North Vietnamese Army.

Con Thien Firebase

This was the scene of intense fighting between U.S. and North Vietnamese troops. When the North Vietnamese attacked the firebase in September 1967 as a diversion leading to the upcoming Tet Offensive, the Americans responded by dropping more than 40,000 tons of bombs on the area via fighter bombers and B-52s. In total, there were more than 4000 sorties flown by American war planes. The normally lush and verdant hills surrounding were entirely blown apart, making the area look like a desert of craters and rotting wood. The Americans eventually fought off the siege, but at great expense. Even today, the former firebase is too dangerous to visit due to vast amounts of unexploded ordnance in the area.

The Rockpile

26 km from Dong Ha toward Khe Sanh. This was exactly as the name implies, a giant pile of rocks, which U.S. Marines used as a lookout and long-range artillery camp. Today, local villagers live in stilt houses and subsist on slash-and-burn agriculture.

Truong Son National Cemetery

This is a cemetery filled with white tombstones of the thousands of North Vietnamese and VC fighters who lost their lives carrying equipment and weaponry down the Ho Chi Minh Trail in the Truong Son

Mountains. They were exhumed from where they were originally buried and brought here after the reunification of Vietnam. However, a number of the graves are empty, representing the untold hundreds of thousands of VC and North Vietnamese soldiers missing in action. Above each stone is the inscription *Liet Si*, which translates into "martyr." Disabled veterans maintain this Arlington-type cemetery. The cemetery is divided into 5 zones, each representing the regions where the soldiers had lived. There is a separate area for decorated heros and officers.

THE HO CHI MINH TRAIL

The famous and vast networks of roads and paths that connected North Vietnam and South Vietnam were used by VC and North Vietnamese Army troops to transport war supplies, primarily to VC strongholds in the south. Many tributaries of the trail were constructed to avoid any one point from being cut off via the constant U.S. bombing of the intricate path. As many as 10 secret roadways were constructed, entirely camouflaged in many places. Defoliants and other chemicals the Americans used to reveal the trail were largely ineffective. More than 300,000 full-time workers and another 200,000 part-time North Vietnamese laborers maintained the trail. NVA loss rates along the trail are estimated to be only 10 percent, and perhaps only a third of the machinery and vehicles being transported down the trail were ruined by the Americans. At first, supplies were carried on the backs of men and women on bicycles, but trucks from China and Russia later traversed the route(s). By the end of the Vietnam War, the Ho Chi Minh Trail totaled more than 13,350 km of all-weather roadways. One "trailsman" was reputed to have carried more than 55 tons of supplies down the trail, a distance totalling about 41,000 km—roughly equalling the circumference of the world. Although American bombing did relatively little to ruin the trail and its travelers, the mission of ferrying equipment down the Ho Chi Minh Trail was a damned dangerous one.

Aluoi

60 km west of Hue and about 65 km southeast of the Dakrong Bridge. Here, in 1966, U.S. Army Special Forces units were besieged by the communists and the base here was abandoned. Consequently, it became an important link in the Ho Chi Minh Trail. LZs (landing zones) where bitter fighting took place are located nearby. Included are Hill 1175, Hill 521, Erskine and Razor, and Cunningham LZs. Farther south is Hamburger Hill. This was the site of an incredibly fierce battle in May 1969 and no one seemed to have any reason why it should have taken place, as there was absolutely no strategic advantage of controlling the hill other than "saving face." More than 240 U.S. soldiers died in a week of fighting here that saw possession of the hill change repeatedly. The Americans eventually ceded the area to the North Vietnamese and withdrew.

Lao Bao

On top of a Co Roc Mountain, overlooking the Vietnamese town of Lao Bao from the Lao side of the border was a North Vietnamese artillery position near the Tchepone River.

Lang Vay

This was an American Army Special Forces camp established in 1962 but overrun by north Vietnamese troops in 1968. The base primarily was composed of South Vietnamese, Bru, and U.S.-trained Montagnard soldiers—as well as a handful of U.S. Green Berets. During the attack more than 300 of the ARVN troops died. Ten of the Americans were killed.

Khe Sanh ★

The 77-day siege of Khe Sanh, which started on January 21, 1968, was seen by the American forces as an attempt by the North Vietnamese to create another Dien Bien Phu, when, in actuality, the siege was nothing more than a diversion in preparation for the Tet Offensive. However, as many as 15,000 NVA soldiers lost their lives here, compared to 248 American fatalities (43 of them in a C-123 transport crash). General William Westmoreland, convinced that Khe Sanh was the prime target of NVA forces (reconnaissance revealed that between 20-40 thousand NVA troops had surrounded the area), had the region carpet-bombed by B-52s and entirely defoliated. More than 100,000 tons of bombs and explosive were dropped by aircraft. The U.S. Marines at Khe Sanh fired 159,000 shells, including the dreaded white phosphorous type, at NVA positions. Westmoreland would not permit another military humiliation, such as that which happened to the French at Dien Bien Phu in 1954, to happen to American troops. He even considered the use of tactical nuclear weapons! The area surrounding Khe Sanh was thoroughly leveled. It was a resounding military victory for the Americans (who were able to reopen Highway 9 on April 7, linking the Army with the Marines), but an even greater psychological one for the North Vietnamese—despite their massive losses—as it paved the way to another psychological victory that changed the course of the war: the Tet Offensive, which started a week after the siege of Khe Sanh began. (Westmoreland amazingly continued to believe that Khe Sanh was the primary target, and thought the Tet Offensive was merely a diversion!) After the general's tour of duty was up and he was replaced as Vietnam's military commander-in-chief, American military experts reassessed the significance of Khe Sanh, and forces in the area were silently redeployed after destroying or burying anything of significance. Today villagers inhabit this lush area, many searching for scrap metal and military ordnance, and it's very difficult to believe this was the site of the deadliest battle of the Vietnam War. But all around are shells and remnants of the siege. The area is littered with shell casings. The town of Khe Sanh is set amongst serene hillsides and green fields. Most of the inhabitants here are Bru tribespeople. The thought that comes to mind when visiting here is that the whole affair was an ugly, bloody human travesty. A small (five-room) guesthouse is at Khe Sanh just south of the Khe Sanh Bus Station.

DMZ DIRECTORY

DONG HA

TRANSPORTATION

Dong Ha is about 1170 km from Saigon, 617 km from Hanoi, 190 km from Danang, 73 km from Hue, 295 km from Vinh, 40 km from Vinh Moc, 65 km from Khe Son, 95 km from Dong Hoi, 22 km from the Ben Hai River, 80 km from the Laos border, and 30 km from the Trong Son National Cemetery, The Dong Ha Bus station is located at the intersection of National Highways 1 and 9. There are connections to surrounding towns, including Quang Tri, Ho Xa, Khe Sanh, Dong Koi, Lao Bao, Hue and other coastal and interior cities. There is service to Hanoi at least twice a week. It leaves at 5 in the morning, stops in Vinh 12 hours later and Hanoi after another 12 hours. Buses south leave for Danang, Con Thien and Ha Tri. The Reunification Express also stops here, with regular connections to the north and south along the Vietnamese coast. The Da Hong Railway station is south of the bus station on NH1 by about a kilometer. Then cross a field to the right of the highway.

TOURIST OFFICE

Quang Tri Tourism. Dong Truong So Hotel. ☎ *261.* There are cars and guides available here, but a better situation is making tour arrangements in Hue through Thua Thien-Hue Tourism.

QUANG TRI

TRANSPORTATION

Buses and Citroën Tractions from the Quang Tri Bus Station (Le Duan Street) connect Quang Tri with Hue, Khe Son, and Ho Xa.

VINH MOC TUNNELS

TRANSPORTATION

The best way to get to the tunnels if you're not on a tour is by taking a private car north of the Ben Hai River about 6.5 km to Ho Xa. The tunnels are about 12–13 km from the village.

DOC MIEU BASE

TRANSPORTATION

This is right off NH1 on the right side about 8 km south of the Ben Hai River.

CUA TUNG BEACH

TRANSPORTATION

The beach is 8 km on a dirt road to the south of Vinh Moc. If you're headed north, turn right off NH1 exactly 1.2 km north of the Ben Hai River.

DAKRONG BRIDGE

TRANSPORTATION

Dakrong Bridge is along NH9 13 km east of the Khe Sanh Bus Station.

CAMP CARROLL

TRANSPORTATION

To get to Camp Carroll, go about 11–12 km past Cam Lo west on Highway 9 and turn left off NH9 for about 3 km. It's about 25 km east of the Dakrong Bridge and almost 40 km east of the Khe Sanh Bus Station.

CON THIEN FIREBASE

TRANSPORTATION

Jusr south of the Ben Hai River, the firebase can be reached from either Cam Lo on Highway 9 or from a turnoff on Highway 1.From Highway 9, Con Thien is about 12 km to the north and 5–6 km from the Truong Son National Cemetery. Con Thien is 7 km east of the Truong Son National Cemetery and 10 km west of NH1. You can reach it by continuing on the road past the cemetery. From the road that connects Cam Lo with the cemetery, you can see the firebase to the east of the road.

THE ROCKPILE

TRANSPORTATION

To get to The Rockpile, take Highway 9 from Dong Ha for 26 km. The site is off to the right.

TRONG SON NATIONAL CEMETERY

TRANSPORTATION

Thirteen km to the north of Dong Ha, the cemetery is 17 km off of NH1 and 9 km south of the Ben Hai River. A dirt path (only accessible by 4-wheel-drive) connects Cam Lo on Highway 9 with the cemetery. This an 18 km bumpy trip.

ALUOI

TRANSPORTATION

Aluoi is about 60 km west of Hue and about 65 km southeast of the Dakrong Bridge. If you're already in the DMZ, take Highway 9 go south at the the Dakrong Bridge toward the Ashau Valley and Hamburger Hill.

LAO BAO

TRANSPORTATION

Lao Bao is about 80 km from Dong Ha, 150 km from Hue, 18 km west of Khe Sanh and 45 km east of the Lao town of Tchepone along Highway 9 near the Tchepone River marking the Lao border.

LANG VAY SPECIAL FORCES CAMP

TRANSPORTATION

Only 9 km west from the Khe Son Bus Station, just off Highway 9 on the southwest side on top of a hill was the Lang Vay Camp. You can also reach it by traveling 7 km toward Khe Sanh from the Lao Bao Market.

KHE SANH

TRANSPORTATION

The Khe Sanh Bus Station is along Highway 9 less than 1 km from the junction where the northward road veers off toward the former base of Khe Sanh. There is bus service to Hue, Dong Ha, and Lao Bao. Now that the border with Laos is open, the station has become particularly busy and has added new routes in the last six months.

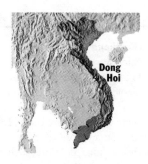

Dong Hoi

DONG HOI

DONG HOI IN A CAPSULE

The capital of the Quang Binh Province...Inhabitants regularly struggle with the elements, from constant flooding to typhoons...During the Vietnam War, the area was obliterated by the bombing of U.S. war planes...Millions of unexploded devices are still scattered across the area...Some estimates say that a million unexploded bombs have been unearthed since the war...Dong Hoi makes for a good rest stop along NH1.

Dong Hoi is the capital of the central province of Quang Binh, an area that was obliterated during the Vietnam War due to its proximity to the 17th parallel—the border between South and North Vietnam. Just south of town is the Hien Luong Bridge spanning the Ben Hai River, which split Vietnam in half.

After the war, millions of unexploded bombs and live ordnance have been dug up in the area and, even today inhabitants of the region are inadvertently killed or dismembered by unexploded materiel. The area was also heavily defoliated during the war, and the effects of Agent Orange are probably more in evidence in this region than in any other area of Vietnam. Dong Hoi, of anywhere in Vietnam, is the best testimony to the alleged effects of the chemical.

Today, Dong Hoi is a fishing port where numerous significant archeological finds have been made. In the vicinity of Dong Hoi is the Ke Bang Desert, which is the site of perhaps the most extensive and beautiful cave network in the world.

WHAT TO SEE AND DO IN DONG HOI AND ENVIRONS

The Ke Bang Desert & The Phong Nha Cave

Ke Bang Desert, which covers more then 10,000 square kilometers from Quang Binh Province in Vietnam to Laos, is the world's largest limestone desert. Geologically evolving over the course of almost three million years, the area has been thinly populated due to harsh living conditions. There are also more than 41,000 hectares of primeval forests where biologists and forestry engineers have discovered rare and threatened species of fauna and flora, such as stiped leopards, gayals and 1000-year-old perennial trees.

The people of the region can only reside in the limestone valleys, which are linked with the outside world by tracks clinging on mountains averaging more than 1000 meters in height. Water from rivers and rainstorms is absorbed completely by the limestone, which has created spectacular underground rivers.

The Ke Bang desert really possesses one community, the remote mountainous village of Son Trach, with a population of about 7000. Although only about 50 km from the city of Dong Hoi, the capital Quang Binh Province, and 35 km from the smaller community of Hoan Lao, getting to Son Trach is like getting from Belize to Panama—but around Cape Horn on the tip of South America.

Son Trach's population, an ethnic enclave of Kinh and Arem people, is spread out through the Son Trach Valleys and in the limestone grottos of the Ke Bang Desert. There is so little water during the dry season there is none available for the rice crops, as canals cannot be dug into limestone.

The weather in the Ke Bang Desert is the most unpredictable in Vietnam. It can be hot and sunny one day and cold and rainy the next, regardless of the season.

But the most spectacular elements of the Ke Bang desert are its caves and grottos, a network called Phong Nha. The Phong Nha cave itself is 7729 meters in length. Discoveries of other caves have also been made, such as the 5258-meter-long Toi Cave, Ruc Mon Cave at 2863 meters, Vom Cave at 13,969 meters, Cha Ang Cave at 667 meters, and Ruc Ca Ron Cave at 2800 meters in length. Eventually, scientists expect to find that this circumference of cave networks is the largest and most beautiful in the world. The natural light in Phong Nha gives the cave a cosmic appearance, with its 10-meter high vault ceilings. There are various compartments, some lacking the beautiful natural light found in Phong Nha's first compartment, where water softly drops from the ceilings like from tree leaves after a spring rain. The fourth compartment contains an array of different stalactites, which look like tree trunks made of diamonds. As you move further into the cave it becomes narrower. Conversation should be avoided. Just the resonance of a human voice can cause the frail columns of stalactite to fall from the ceiling.

This is a spectacular place that is essentially unknown to the outside world. After the discovery of a 2 km long cave in Malaysia, the Malaysian government poured huge sums of money into making the cave a tourist attraction. They built roads, and soon 11,000 visitors and scientists visited the site annually, pumping millions of dollars into the local economy. But today, the people of Son Trach remain poor, despite their proximity to one of the world's most magnificent geological sites. To date, there have been but a mere 400 visitors to Ke Bang Desert's caves, the majority being geologists. The road to Ke Bang is in dismal condition and there are no plans to improve it.

Khe Sanh and The Ho Chi Minh Trail

This is a bit of a trip from Dong Hoi, where you'll really want to stop only to see the caves. Travel about 95 km south to Highway 9 toward Laos. Here, you'll be among the most active areas of the Vietnam War. The Ho Chi Minh Trail crosses Route 9. See the Khe Sanh section and the Ho Chi Minh Trail sidebar in the DMZ chapter for more details.

Beaches

There are a number of sand dunes that line the beaches around Dong Hoi. Kilometers of beach stretch both south and north from the town. The best swimming beach in the vicinity is **Ly Hoa Beach**. **Nhat Le Beach** lines the mouth of the Nhat Le River.

Deo Ngang Pass ★

Representing the border between Quang Binh and Ha Tinh Provinces, this is a beautiful pass through the Hoanh Son Mountains which reach from the South China Sea all the way to the Lao border, close to the 18th parallel. The range used to form the border between the Kingdom of Champa and Vietnam up until the 11th century.

Cam Xuyen and Ha Tinh

Although these small towns are not really at all in the vicinity of Dong Hoi (Cam Xuyen is about 150 km north of Dong Hoi and Ha Tinh a little farther up the coast), they really aren't worthy of chapters of their own, as they're both essentially attractionless—although a surprising amount of foreigners stay at Cam Xuyen's cheap and only guesthouse. There is absolutely nothing to see or do in Ha Tinh, save stop for a beer and be surrounded by the locals.

WHERE TO STAY IN DONG HOI

The **Hoa Binh Hotel** used to be the only hotel in town allowed to accept foreigners. But also check out **Chuyen Gia**, the **Dong Hoi Hotel** and **Nhat Le Hotel**.

DIRECTORY

TRANSPORTATION

Dong Hoi is about 500 km from Hanoi, 200 km from Vinh, 65 km from Hue, 165 km from Hue, and 94 km from Dong Ha. The highway north of Dong Hoi, because it's north of the DMZ, is improving but is not in nearly as good shape as NH1 to the south. There's a ferry crossing 34 km to the north at Cua Gianh. Sometimes it's a long wait.

By bus: Buses from Dong Hoi serve most major coastal provincial capitals, as most buses traveling along NH1 from Saigon to Hanoi or vice versa stop in Dong Hoi.

By train: There are regular connections with Hanoi and Saigon.

TOURIST OFFICES

The Dong Hoi Tourist Office is located near the Hoa Binh Hotel in the central part of town.

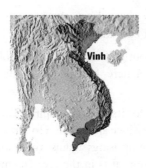

VINH

VINH IN A CAPSULE

Vinh is about halfway between Hue and Hanoi...Perhaps the ugliest city in Vietnam...It is located in one of the poorest provinces in Vietnam...Beggars outnumber the geckos...It was pounded by American shelling during the war and completely destroyed...Rebuilt by the East Germans...Ho Chi Minh was born near here...This would be a good place to exile someone you don't particularly care for.

Annihilated during the Vietnam War by American and South Vietnamese war planes, Vinh is the capital of Nghe Tinh (or Nghe An, depending on who you talk to) Province (one of Vietnam's most populous and poorest provinces)and a major north central Vietnamese industrial and commerce center. Despite its economic importance, because of the climate, its people are the poorest in Vietnam. And if you think you've had your fill of beggars in other Vietnamese cities, Vinh will infuriate you. The town had the unfortunate geographical position of being located on a narrow coastal plain, where roads and railways were required to pass through. The city was rebuilt by the East Germans after the war and, consequently, Vinh, along with Haiphong farther north, has the distinction of being perhaps the ugliest city in Vietnam. There's little, if anything, of note in the city to see and do. Its only real attractions are the hotel beds to break up the road journey between Hue and Hanoi.

Its weather is essentially horrible—hot and and dry in the summer and cold and rainy in the winter. But it's essentially under gray skies the year round. The area is under the constant threat of flooding and typhoons.

But west of Vinh lie thickly forested mountains inhabited by tribespeople and wild creatures alike. The Muong people live here, as well as the Tai, Meo, Khmer, and Tho ethnic groups. The jungles are roamed by elephants, tigers, leopards, deer, rhinoceros, gibbons and other monkeys, fiant bats and flying squirrels.

Because Vinh is about halfway between Hanoi and Hue, hotel and eatery owners prosper here, but they're about the only ones in the province who do.

The area is known for its insurgent spirit. The Ho Chi Minh Trail was started in this province and Uncle Ho himself was a native of the province. There were uprisings against the French led by the population here, and communists in the area (members of the Indochinese Communist Party) in the early 1930s staged uprisings and workers' strikes. These uprisings were generally successfully resisted by the French, utilizing fighter planes to disperse unruly demonstrators.

U.S. bombers and warships off the coast obliterated the area between 1964–1972. It is said that fewer than five buildings remained standing here after the Americans left Vietnam in 1973 (some say only two structures were left intact). But this was also the area where the greatest amount of American warplanes were downed in North Vietnam, and naval pilots killed or captured.

Vinh (population about 200,000) is located about 15 km from the coast.

WHAT TO SEE AND DO IN VINH AND ENVIRONS

Chua and Sen Villages

The small village of Chua, about 14 km northwest of Vinh, was where Ho Chi Minh was born in 1890. The house is now a sacred shrine, but visitors are welcome. There's a small and unimpressive museum, given the historical significance of this place, close by. Sen Village, which is close to Chua, is where Uncle Ho lived starting at the age of six with his highly-educated father. Ho was actually born to relatively wealthy parents, his neighbors were dismally poor. Although Ho's house itself is nothing more than a crude, thatched shack, it was considered upscale for the area.

Cau Lo Beach

This beach, located about 20 km from Vinh, isn't bad. It's clean and rarely visited, perhaps because the weather here is cold and windy most of the time. There's a modest hotel located here.

Vinh Central Market

At the end of Gao Thang Street. Despite the amount of people who live here, there is surprisingly little offered, although, like most city markets in Vietnam, it is a bustling, colorful place. But there are hordes of beggars.

Restoration Project Clinic

Nguyen Phong Sac Street near the Children's Hospital. (I couldn't find any street numbers here, or anywhere in Vinh for that matter.) A group of California-based war veterans and humanitarians built this structure as a hospital and physical therapy center in 1989. They worked in conjunction with Vietnamese war vets as well. Nothing of any real interest here. The Nghe Tinh Children's Hospital is also on these grounds.

Anti-Aircraft Guns

Le Hong Phong Street. These giant guns are still active and pointed to the sky to fend off an air attack, by whom, I couldn't imagine. Perhaps the Belize Air Force.

Worker's Cultural Complex

Le Mao and Dinh Cong Trang Streets. This is Vinh's "community center," a big structure that features a movie and performance theater as well as a dance hall.

WHERE TO STAY IN VINH

Vinh Railway Station Hotel

Le Ninh Street. ☎ *24* • US$6. This is right next to the railway station as you might guess it would be. It's a little run down but it's cheap and popular with backpackers. Inexpensive. ***Reservations: Direct.***

Hotel Kim Liem

Quang Trung Street in the middle of town • US$25–35. This is the biggest hotel in Vinh and the only one you might cautiously refer to as being up to "international standards." There's hot water, fairly large rooms, air conditioning, restaurant, massage, moneychanging, private bath and a travel agency downstairs. This is the best place in town to rest on the road between Hue and Hanoi. Moderate.

Reservations: Direct.

Xi Nghiep Dich Vu Hotel

Le Loi Street near the corner of Nguyen Si Sach Street, east of the railway station • US$6. The cheapest accommodations in Vinh and usually quite filled with backpackers. Don't expect much here but a hard mattress to put your head on. Very inexpensive. ***Reservations: Direct.***

Hotel Huu Nghi

Le Loi Street • US$20–25. This, like the Kim Lien Hotel, is a decent place for Vinh. The price tag will get you air conditioning, attached bath, restaurant and hot water. Also recommended if you're staying in Vinh. Moderate. ***Reservations: Direct.***

Chuyen Gia Giao Te Hotel

Thanh Ho Street. ☎ *4175* • About US$15–45. Vastly overpriced, rather ugly hotel. Air conditioning, attached bath, hot water, restaurant. I'd stay somewhere else in this price range. Inexpensive–moderate.

Reservations: Direct.

Ben Thuy Hotel

Nguyen Du Street, just a kilometer from the Lam River toward the middle of Vinh. ☎ *4892* • US$8. This is another popular place with backpackers, although it's a hike from the train station. No air conditioning, but it does have a small, decent restaurant. Inexpensive.

Reservations: Direct.

WHERE TO EAT IN VINH

The best place to eat in town is at the restaurant at the **Hotel Kim Lien**, or perhaps the restaurant at the **Hotel Huu Nghi**. But it's less expensive and equally as filling to eat at one of the many restaurants and food stalls at the Vinh Central Market or near the Railway Station, which has a slew of eateries with decent prices.

DIRECTORY

TRANSPORTATION

Vinh is about 291 km from Hanoi, 365 km from Hue, 197 km from Dong Hoi, 470 km from Danang, 98 km from the Laos border, and 140 km from Thanh Hoa.

By air: There are currently no air connections to Vinh from anywhere. Rumor has it that pilots can't stand the layover in Vinh. Plus, there's nowhere to land.

By bus: The bus station is on Le Loi Street north of the Central Market by about 1 km. There are express buses that depart for Hanoi, HCMC, Danang and Buon Ma Thuot early in the morning around 5 a.m. There are also express buses that leave for Hanoi at other times of the day as well. Ask at the ticket office (you'd be wise to purchase your tickets in advance). Non-express buses depart for Hanoi, Pleiku, Ba Hai, Ky Anh, Huong Son, Lat, Cau Giat, Hue, Hoa Binh, Yen Thanh, Que Phong, Nghia Dan, Do Luong, Phuc Son and Dung, as well as other destinations.

By train: The Vinh Railway Station is located about 3 km west of the Central Market about 1 km from the intersection of Le Loi and Phan Boi Chau Streets. The Reunification Express stops here. It's about a 7 hour trip to Hanoi, and 35 hours to HCMC.

POST OFFICE

Nguyen Thi Minh Khai Street, about 280 meters northwest of Dinh Cong Trang Street. Hours are from 6:30 a.m. to 9 p.m. International and domestic calls and faxes can be made from another office across from the Workers' Cultural Complex (Cong Ty Dien Bao DienThoai) on Dinh Cong Trang Street close to the intersection of Nguyen Thi Minh Khai Street.

BANKS AND MONEYCHANGERS

Vietcom Bank, *at the corner of Le Loi and Nguyen Si Sach Streets,* can provide advances on American issued credit cards.

TOURIST OFFICE

Vinh Tourist Office. *Quang Trung Street.* ☎ *4629.* The travel agency in the Hotel Kim Lien can book airline flights.

HOSPITAL

General Hospital. *Le Mao and Tran Phu Streets.*

NORTH OF VINH

The northern central region of Vietnam contains only one highway, National Highway 1 along the coast. From Vinh to Than Hoa, the road runs at many points right along the coast of the South China Sea through tiny, nondescript villages and towns that offer virtually no amenities to travelers save for a sparce number of roadside cafes and restaurants. The northern provinces in this area are the poorest in Vietnam—the soil isn't good for cultivation and the region runs havoc with the ravages of flooding and seasonal typhoons. The villagers exist on only a marginal subsistence.

The people of this region did not share in the prosperity the Americans brought to the southern half of the country during the Vietnam War. There is little for the independent traveler to do and see between the 140 km that separate Vinh and Thanh Hoa. By the time you've reached this point, you'll have little interest in stopping and exploring these small hamlets.

Some will tell you that the people of north-central Vietnam are not as warm to foreigners (especially Americans) as those in the south. While I do not find this to be entirely correct—indeed, smiles were everywhere—there is more reserve on the part of the people of this region, as they rarely see foreigners, and are unaware of the warm feelings most southerners had for Americans during the war, due mainly to their being North Vietnamese. But even the North Vietnamese bear little animosity toward Americans and are generally quite friendly. Keep in mind that very little English is spoken in this area, and that you should carry dong rather than dollars if stopping in small hamlets and towns along NH1. There are few if any places that will change money for you.

THANH HOA

Thanh Hoa is the capital of Thanh Hoa Province (which was the site of the Lam Son Uprising between 1418–1428) and the northernmost point in north-central Vietnam. The 160-meter bridge that spans the Ma River south of Thanh Hoa (Ham Rong Bridge, or "Dragon's Jaw") was an important North Vietnamese military link moving south and was bombed repeatedly by U.S. warplanes during the war. In fact, all around Thanh Hoa are craters left by the bombs of American planes. The North Vietnamese heavily fortified the bridge and the U.S. lost as many as 70 planes during raids on the bridge in the mid-1960s. Finally, in 1972, they were able to take out the bridge using laser-guided bombs, but the NVA quickly erected a

pontoon bridge to replace it. There is a big church on the north side
of town, the Citadel of Ho, which was built in 1397 when this town
was the capital of Vietnam. In Thuan Hoa, you can stay at the Tourist Hotel, at *21A Quang Trung Street* (☎ 298); the 25B and 25A
Hotels along NH1, or the Thanh Hoa Hotel on the west side of
NH1 in the middle of town. Rooms are in the US$6–10 range. Near
the southern edge of town are a slew of cheap restaurants and cafes.
The Reunification Express train does stop here, linking Thanh Hoa
with the rest of the Vietnamese coast. Buses link the provincial capital with a number of coastal towns, including Vinh (140 km), Hue
(500 km), and Hanoi (153 km). There are two decent beaches in the
area called the Sam Son Beaches, about 15 km southeast of Thanh
Hoa. They are mainly frequented by monied Hanoi residents to escape the summer heat. But keep in mind that the weather here is
usually cool and damp, and the northerly winds can make a trip to
the beaches quite cold. There are some cheap hotels and bungelows
here. You can also see the remains of fortifications built here by the
NVA to protect the Ham Rong Bridge.

NINH BINH

This is the capital of Ha Nam Ninh Province on the Day River,
about 60 km north of Thanh Hoa. There is little here for the tourist,
and it serves as not much more than an overnight spot. It is linked to
other coastal communities by both rail and bus service. Perhaps the
best reason to come to this region, other than just passing through,
is to make the short 10-km trip to the ancient capital of Vietnam in
the Truong Son Mountains called **Hoa Lu**. Hoa Lau was built as the
new capital of Vietnam in AD 968 and remained so until AD 1010.
This was the time of the Dinh and early Le Dynasties. It was selected
for its location: in a narrow valley surrounded by limestone mountains with paths that were easily defendable against Chinese invaders.
Some say it is like Ha Long Bay without the bay. There are still the
remnants of ancient temples in Hoa Lu. Elephants and horses were
carved into the stonework.

Although today there is little to see here, this was once an area covering 200 hectares that was dotted with temples and shrines. Hoa Lu
was the birthplace of Dinh Bo Linh, the founder of the Dinh Dynasty. There are ruins of the ancient royal citadel here that once covered
three square kilometers, and the Dinh Tien Huang royal temple of
the Dinh kings. Inscribed on the pillar in the central temple are the
words *Dai Coa Viet*, which the name Vietnam was derived from. Inside this temple are statues of Dinh and his sons.

The Vault of Dinh is at the base of Mount Yen. During the 960s, Bo Linh was able to pacify the area, and even the warring Ngos accepted his dominance of the region. But Bo Linh's kingdom was wracked with insubordination. He placed a tiger in the center courtyard and announced that anyone who violates his rule will be "boiled and knawed." But rather than make his oldest blood son, Din Lien, the heir to the throne (he chose instead his younger son, Hang Lang), the king faced enormous trouble. Legend says that violent climactic events occurred, and, in 979, Lien ordered an assassin to kill Hang Lang. Just a few months later, a court official named Do Thich murdered both Bo Linh and Din Lien as they lay sleeping in a drunken stupor. Do Thich was caught for his crime, and it's said he was executed and his body fed to the people. Hoa Lu is at the southern edge of the Red River Delta in Truong Yen Village. You'll have to take a car from either Hanoi or Ninh Binh to get here.

Near Ninh Binh you can also visit **Bich Dong Pagoda**, a three-hour boat ride on a tributary of the Hoang Long River. Getting there by car is much quicker. The boat ride offers magnificent scenery of limestone caves and surrounding mountains. After getting to the pagoda's landing, there's about a 20 minute walk to reach the pagoda. Also visit **Binh Cach**, 20 km to the north of Ninh Binh. Here are the remains of the citadels of **Bo Co** and **Co Long**. The Chinese army was crushed here by General Tran Gian Dinh in 1408. You can also visit the remains of the **Van Phong Citadel** deep in the nearby Ngo Xa Mountains. The small village of Van Lam possesses the **Bic Dong Grottoes**. They can be reached by boat from Hoa Lu or Binh Dinh. The grottoes have been around since the 10th century, and they were used as hideouts during the First Indochina War by the Viet Minh.

Ke So is 34 km northwest of Binh Dinh on the Song Day River. There is a big cathedral here built between 1879 and 1884 by the French Monseigneur Puginier. **Nam Trang** (35 km north of Ninh Binh) is where Black Flag rebel leader Dinh Kong Trang was born. **Phat Diem** (30 km southeast of Ninh Binh) was a major Catholic center during the French colonial era. The cathedral built here was built of marble, granite and wood. It stands 16 meters high and is 80 meters long. There is also the nearby **Thuan-Dao Church** (built in 1926) which is a strange looking structure. Monseigneur Nguyen Ba Tong in Phat Diem was pronounced the first Vietnamese Bishop by the Vatican in 1930. Places to stay in Ninh Binh include the *Hoa Lu Hotel* (about US$15) on the west side of NH1 and the *Ninh Binh Hotel*, also on the west side of NH1 (about US$10). Ninh Binh is a scheduled stop on the Reunification Express train route. Ninh Binh is about 115 km south of Hanoi, 200 km north of Vinh and 60 km north of Thanh Hoa.

NAM DINH

Nam Dinh (population about 250,000) is a smoky, ugly gray industrial city about 90 km south of Hanoi. The city is primarily known for its textiles (and lack of tourists). The French built the **Nam Dinh Textile Mill** here in 1899 and it's still up and running. Western missionaries arrived here as early as 1627. Nam Dinh is considered to be the third largest industrial area in the north. There was a giant square citadel here, built in 1804, that faces southeast toward the sea, that was eventually destroyed by the French in 1891 (only the watchtower is marginally intact) after they seized the city in 1882.

Nam Dinh, which was continually attacked by the Chams during the Champa Empire, was designed as sort of a mini-Hanoi, where quarters were built to house areas of tradesmen and craftsmen. For instance, there was a section for cobblers, another for blacksmiths, one for embroiderers, another for goldsmiths, one for coffin makers, and so on. Some of the "sights" of Nam Dinh are outside the city itself, much of them areas of historical rather than architectural interest, as many of the ancient structures have been ruined. **My Loc**, about 2 km north of the city, is where the Tran Dynasty began and was the birthplace of Tran Bich San. All inhabitants of the city were forced to adopt the name Tran to their own names. **Tuc Mac** is 3 km north of the city. Tu Mac's **Den Thien-truong** (Royal Temple) was built here. Of the many buildings it consisted of, one, the **Tran Mieu**, was built in 1239. **Den Co Trach** was constructed in 1895, and was a temple dedicated to Tran Hung Dao. **Pho Minh Thu** was the stupa for King Tran Nhan Ton, who ruled the area in the 13th century. It's a 14-story tower built in the early 14th century that was demolished by the Mings and rebuilt in the 15th century. Subsequent restorations took place in the 17th and 18th centuries.

Fifteen km northwest of Nam Dinh is **Yen Do**, where Nguyen Khuyen was born. **Ky Lan Son (The Mountain of the Unicorn)** was home to Le Hoan, who founded the Early Le Dynasty and was its ruler from 980-1005. He was crowned "The King Who Pacified the South" in 981 after driving back an attacking Chinese force. There were also numerous battles with the Chams during his reign. **Chua Dien Linh**, **Doi Son**, and **Doi Dep Pagodas** were built in the 12th century on the hills 46 km northwest of Nam Dinh in Hung Yen Valley close to where the Red River spills into the Gulf of Tonkin. **Phy Giay** is a temple dedicated to the immortal Leiu Hanh about 17 km south of Nam Dinh. Leiu Hanh was the daughter of the Heavenly Emperor, who returned to Earth after he died to make amends for a goblet he broke during festival. A pilgrimage still arrives here each year on the third day of the third lunar month to celebrate the Pure Light Festival (or the Festival of the Dead, *Thanh Minh*). You might also want to visit the nearby villages of **Dong Dai** (10 km from Nam Dinh), where stands the Phoc Lam Pagoda and stupas of Hung Thien and Hoang Hai; **Van Diem** (20 km north of Nam Dinh) where there is an ancient citadel, and **Doc Bo** (27 km southeast of Nam Dinh), that has a pagoda dedicated to Trieu Viet Vuong, a general who declared himself king of Vietnam in AD 549. In Nam Dinh, you can stay at **Vi Hoang Hotel** (*115 Nguyen Du Street.* ☎ *439262*). The post office is on Ha Huy Tap Street. Ninh Binh Tourist is at the Vi Hoang Hotel.

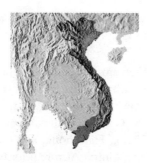

HANOI AND THE NORTH

As the border between Vietnam in the north and China becomes increasingly open, a burgeoning amount of travel between the two countries has begun. It has also opened the routes for smugglers. In Lon Son province, which was opened up only last January, one can see swarms of Asian travelers carrying on their backs sometimes many times the weight of their bodies. **Duong Dang** has become something of a boom town, and one can see the prosperity in this once shanty town as imported tires, fruit, beer and other consumer items are now offered for sale, lining the streets like a gauntlet of entrepreneurialism. As you head south, you'll notice the rapid construction of multistoried brick and tile buildings as this newly-found prosperity heads southward. However, a large degree of this southward-bound caravan of consumer goods has been smuggled into the country or been allowed in through bribery. Be cautious in this region. If you're asked by any traveler to help carry goods that appear too burdensome to the carrier, don't be overcome by your sympathies. Carry only your own belongings on both sides of the border.

The beautiful northern Vietnam region of **Son La** province is getting the gears in motion for tourism. To bolster the local economy, the province has been divided into three separate regions. The first, along Highway 6, will be allocated to developing mulberry silk production, coffee and fruit trees. Son La has installed 4000 mini hydro-electric plants to provide power for lighting and agriculture. And the telecommunications network is now in synch with the national grid. Tourism is on the rise in the province, mainly because of the magnificent beauty of the surrounding mountains. To date, though, the roads reaching the province from all areas in the north are in dismal shape, though the views from the rutted path are spectacular.

Road travelers in Vietnam may soon have an easier selection of routes to take to both urban and rural destinations in the north—a four-lane highway linking Bac Ninh (30 kn to the north of Hanoi) and Mong Cai, near the Chinese border. As part of the economic triangle that includes Hanoi, Hai Phong, and Quang Ninh, the 314 km route is a government infrastructure priority. Additionally, there will also be bridges constructed at Pha Lai (260 meters) and Bai Chay (800 meters), which will replace the present ferries. As well, a new highway is being built from Bac Ninh town to Hanoi's Noi Bai International Airport. The road projects are important as they will connect the Cai Lan port, which is currently under construction in Hai Phon with Hanoi and with the Chinese border crossing at Mong Cai.

INSIDER TIP

A new national Route 5 is currently under construction through Hai Duong Town. The road will have only a distance of 15 km, but it's still 15 km of less dilapidated roadways that are the main infrastructure blight of Vietnam.. There will be six traffic lanes, and the road will run over three bridges, in Dong Nieu, Phu Luong and Lai Vu.

INSIDER TIP

If you're traveling through Hai Duong, you have to make a point of trying the town's special cuisine, in particular the green bean cake and Tan Cuong Tea. There is an array of green bean cake dealers (you'll see a sign saying Rong Vuong (Golden Dragon) along the street in the town. Bao Hien Restaurant is where the specialty was originally created, using green beans, white sugar, pig fat, shaddock scent and vanilla. There's a lot of protein in the concoction. These cakes can now be found in other areas of Vietnam, but the real thing comes from Hai Duong. The townsfolk consider the preparation of green bean cake an art form. Green bean cakes are often part of wedding meals and engagement ceremonies, and are offered on the altars of ancestors during the Tet holiday in Hanoi and other northern rural areas. Green bean cakes are also offered to visiting foreign businessmen by government representatives at official functions. The authentic green bean cake comes with the trademark Bao Long. The best restaurants for green bean cake in Hai Duong are the Bao Hien Restaurant (now called the Ngoc Bich) and Nguyen Huong Restaurant. Bao Long green bean cakes are now reaching customers at Hanoi's Noi Bai International airport, upscale eateries in Hanoi, the railway station, Quang Ninh Province and Haiphong, just to mention a few of the areas where the delicacy is available. Green bean cake is now just beginning to be exported to foreign countries. The cakes are perhaps northern Vietnam's best representation of the use of its agricultural products. Try some. Absolutely delicious.

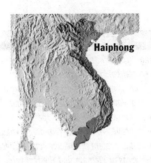

HAIPHONG

HAIPHONG IN A CAPSULE

A basically ugly city that was heavily bombed by the Americans during the Vietnam War...This is Vietnam's major port...The city itself offers few attractions...But there remains some nice colonial architecture...The First Indochina War started here with the French bombing of the port in 1946...Thousands of civilians died...During the American War, the U.S. lost more than 300 warplanes here...The nicest areas of the region are Cat Ba Island and Do Son Beach.

Haiphong, with a population of more than 1.2 million people, is the second largest city in the north and Vietnam's major port. For the most part, much of the area surrounding the city is actually an eyesore—a gray urban sprawl pockmarked with factories and bombed-out buildings, despite massive rebuilding in the city.

Now Greater Haiphong, which sits on the mouth of the Cua Cam River, covers an area more than 1520 square meters now. In 1872–1874, when the French took possession of the city, it was nothing more than a small port and market town. With the French in control, Haiphong grew at rocket speed. It soon became a major port, in part, because of its proximity to coal supplies. The French didn't leave until 1955, after their defeat at Dien Bien Phu. In fact, the biggest instigation of the First Indochina War was the 1946 French bombardment of Haiphong's civilian residential areas, an action that killed at least hundreds of civilians; perhaps, by some estimates, as many as 5000 people were killed in the raids. All this happened because a French Navy ship had seized a Vietnamese junk. Vietnamese troops fired on the French ship, which so incensed the French commanders, they decided to bomb the hell out of the city. A month later, the war started.

The Americans pounded Haiphong during the Vietnam War and, in 1972, President Nixon ordered the mining of the city's harbor to prevent the shipment of Soviet-made war equipment that was being moved south. As part of the Paris Peace Agreement the same year, the Americans agreed to help dispose of the mines.

The Vietnamese purportedly downed more than 300 U.S. aircraft from the city's antiaircraft batteries during the war. But the Americans achieved many of their objectives in Haiphong. More than 80 percent of the city's above-ground petrol facilities were destroyed in 1966 in the U.S. effort to prevent these precious supplies from reaching the south—although American intelligence was unable to glean that the North Vietnamese suspected such action would be taken and had moved much of their supplies to underground locations.

Today, there's a resort and even Vietnam's first casino. The hotels, though, are generally overpriced. Surprisingly, much of the old French colonial architecture survived the bombardment, mostly in the downtown area around the **theater square**. A couple of kilometers south of the city center is the **Du Hang Pagoda**, said to have been built in the 1600s. Also check out the numerous street markets near Cau Dat Street.

Despite the "resurgence" of the city, it remains an ugly, dirty metropolis. Tourists don't particularly care for it and, apparently, neither do the Vietnamese. Since 1980, massive amounts of Vietnamese have left the city—and not merely as boat people in search of a new land and economic opportunities, but to other areas in Vietnam itself.

WHAT TO SEE AND DO IN HAIPHONG

The Colonial-Style Architecture

If you're going to spend any time in the city at all, at least check out the old French buildings that remained largely undamaged through both Indochina wars. The best area for seeing the old structures is in the center of the city, particularly where Tran Hung Dao and Quang Trung Streets intersect, which is where an old theater can be found.

Du Hang Pagoda

121 Du Hang Street. This mildly interesting pagoda was built in the 17th century and has been remodeled many times since. Today, it is being renovated again as you read this. The small pagoda was dedicated to Le Chan, who battled the Chinese alongside the Trung Sisters. There's a courtyard and some impressive Vietnamese-style traditional wood carvings.

Nghe Pagoda

51 Ngo Nghe Street. This pagoda was also built to honor Le Chan, and was constructed during the early part of the 20th century.

Dang Hai Flower Village

About 5 km from the city center. All types of tropical and perennial flowers are grown here and sold to countries all over the world. Worth only a brief stop.

Hang Kenh Tapestry Factory

Wool tapestries are produced at this factory, founded some 66 years ago, and are exported to other nations. Again, worth just a brief stop.

Hang Kenh Communal House

Hang Kenh Street. This is where you can find an impressive display of about 500 wooden relief sculptures. The area here once belonged to the village of Kenh.

Other Temples

If you're forced to spend the the time in Haiphong, you might also want to check out the **Thien Phuc Pagoda**, built in 1551, where there is a statue of Queen Mother Tra Huong; the **Le Chan Temple**, which was built in honor of a military commander of the 1st century and **Linh Quang Pagoda**, which was built in 1709 and possesses many fine wood carvings.

HAIPHONG ENVIRONS

BACH DANG RIVER

Bach Dang River (also called the Cua Cam River, Cam River or the Haiphong Channel) is about 10 km east of Haiphong. This is where the river flows into the sea. It is actually a maze or network of waterways between Ha Long Bay and Haiphong that has an impressive history. Vietnamese forces prevented the Chinese from landing here to do battle three different times: in AD 938, AD 981 and in 1288 by Tran Hung Dao. Anticipating the Mongol invasion, Tran Hung Dao stopped the Mongols from taking over the region by pounding three stone spikes in the harbor during high tide. The Mongol ships ran into them when they tried to sail away at low tide and sank. The buried remains of the stakes were discovered in 1985 in the nearby district of Yen Hung.

DO SON BEACH

This beach resort, established in 1888 on what is actually an islet (or a series of islets), is 20 km southeast of Haiphong and is popular with the locals. It's not a bad beach but a little dirty due to the hotels that have gone up along the beachfront in recent years. The peninsula is best known for the nine hills called "The Mountain of Nine

Dragons," or *Cuu Long*. There's a small temple on Doc Mountain called **Den Ba De Temple**, which is dedicated to a young woman who leapt to her death after spending the night with a man she didn't want to be with.

CAT BA NATIONAL PARK

30 km to the east of Haiphong and 135 km from Hanoi. Daily ferries leave for Cat Ba from Haiphong's Ben Bach Dang Street Ferry Terminal, usually early in the morning (however, the schedules are subject to change). Cat Ba Island is the largest island in the Ha Long Bay region. The park represents a small section of the island of Cat Ba that covers a forested area of 120 square km. The total area of Cat Ba is close to 355 square km. The area was declared a national park in 1986 to preserve the island's diverse flora and fauna. The mainly forested park is covered with tropical evergreens, coastal mangrove forests, freshwater swamps and lakes (the biggest being Ech Lake), and surrounded by fine beaches with coral reefs offshore. The principal beaches in the park include Hong Xoai Be, Cai Vieng and Hong Xoai Long beaches. There are reportedly three hotels on the island, although I could only locate one, the Cat Ba Hotel. It's said the other two go by the same name. Don't make plans to meet anyone at the Cat Ba Hotel.

Cat Ba Island also features small waterfalls and grottoes in limestone rock formations (as many as 350 limestone outcroppings). There are high winds at the top of the grottoes and, frankly, sitting on the beach can be a little nippy at any time of the year. In fact, there's no real "season" to visit the island, as the winters are cold, drizzly and gray and the summers rattled by typhoons. Of particular interest have been the discoveries of stone tools and human bones on the island which indicate Cat Ba was inhabited as long ago as 7000 years ago. Nearly 20 such sites have been found. Today, the island possesses at least a dozen species of mammals, including the rare Francois monkey. There are also deer and wild boar in addition to birds such as hornbills, hawks and cuckoo birds. Other species stop here on their migration paths to other areas. Most of the island's population of 10,000–12,000 people is located in Cat Ba Town. They eke out a living mainly through fishing and rice farming and by growing apples, oranges and cassava. Electricity on the island is limited to only a brief few hours in the evening. Some of the best beaches in Vietnam can be found here, or that's what Hanoi officials would have you believe. And it may be accurate. Cat Ba Island has largely been declared a protected region and, as mentioned, features tropical forests, mangrove swamps, towering dolomite hills, water-falls, lakes, caves and, of course, gorgeous beaches. There's also a thriving animal population, including, of course, the Francois monkey.

WHERE TO STAY IN HAIPHONG & DO SON

Hotel De Commerce

62 Dien Bien Phu Street. ☎ *47206 or 47290 • 40 rooms.* US$10–40. This Rench-era hotel has been renovated and is a very comfortable place to stay in a very uncomfortable place. All the rooms have air conditioning, attached bath. Restaurant. Hot water, refrigerators. The lower priced rooms are especially a bargain. Inexpensive-moderate.

Reservations: Direct.

Duyen Hai Hotel

5 Nguyen Tri Phuong Street. ☎ *47657 or 42157 •* About US$ 15–30. This is also an attractive French colonial style hotel not unlike the Hotel of Commerce, in price, ambiance and service. Air conditioning, hot water, attached bath. Recently renovated. Moderate.

Reservations: Direct.

Cat Bi Hotel

30 Tran Phu Street. ☎ *46306 •* About US$20. The best thing about this hotel is its proximity to the railroad station. Air conditioning, attached bath. Nothing special. Moderate.   *Reservations: Direct.*

Hang Hai Hotel

282 Danang Street. ☎ *48576 • 38 rooms.* About US$30. This may be the nicest hotel in Haiphong, and if you're spending more than a day or two, this would probably be the best place, even though it's located in a grimy area 3 km from the city center. Large, quiet rooms with air conditioning, refrigerators, telephone, attached bath, hot water. Two restaurants and a disco on the top floor. Moderate.

Reservations: Direct.

Bach Dang Hotel

40-42 Dien Bien Phu Street. ☎ *47244 •* About US$ 12–40. All different classes of rooms in this hotel. But it's a little seedy, especially if you're considering the higher priced rooms. Air conditioning, restaurant, attached bath, hot water. Moderate.   *Reservations: Direct.*

Hong Bang Hotel

64 Dien Bien Phu Street. ☎ *42229 • 30 rooms.* About US$40. Recently renovated. Rooms have attached bath, color TV, air conditioning, refrigerators. Restaurant, massage and sauna. Nice amenities for the price. Moderate.   *Reservations: Direct.*

Thang Nam Hotel

55 Dien Bien Phu Street. ☎ *42820* • About US$15–20. Average. Rooms have air conditioning, attached bath. There's a restaurant and beauty shop. Inexpensive-moderate. ***Reservations: Direct.***

Ben Binh Gesthouse

6 Ben Binh Street, across from the ferry dock. ☎ *57260* • About US$30. These are large, attractive and spacious villas. Air conditioning, attached bath, hot water. Friendly service. Moderate.

Reservations: Direct.

Hoa Binh Hotel

104 Luong Khanh Thien Street, opposite the railway station. ☎ *46909* • About US$10–15. The lower priced rooms come with fan; air conditioning in the higher-priced rooms. A convenient and relatively cheap place for backpackers. Inexpensive. ***Reservations: Direct.***

Hai Au Hotel

Do Son Beach • *45 rooms.* About US$20–30. This hotel is run by Haiphong Tourism and is a reasonably good value. Air conditioning, attached bath, hot water, restaurant. There are a slew of hotels strung out along the beach, but this may be the best. Moderate.

Reservations: Direct.

Hoa Phuong Hotel

Right near the Hai Au Hotel on Do Son Beach • Also run by Haiphong Tourism. These are villas that were once used by members of the Politburo. Moderate. ***Reservations: Direct.***

Ministry of Energy Guest House

Do Son Beach • *100 rooms.* About US$20–35. This is one of the newest hotels at the beach but it doesn't overlook the beach itself. Air conditioning, hot water, balconies with the higher-priced rooms, telephone. A decent deal for foreigners, but the Vietnamese pay half these prices. Moderate. ***Reservations: Direct.***

Van Hoa Hotel

Do Son Beach, at the tip of the peninsula • About US$8. A favorite among backpackers. Long walk to the beach, however. Bizarre architecture. Rooms have a fan. Very Inexpensive. ***Reservations: Direct.***

WHERE TO EAT IN HAIPHONG & DO SON

Haiphong has a great many small and cheap restaurants. The most expensive food can be found at the hotel restaurants, the cheapest on the streets. But the seafood in Haiphong is excellent. At Do Son Beach, try the **Van Hoa Restaurant** at the end of the peninsula in a small park.

DIRECTORY

TRANSPORTATION

Haiphong is 103 km southeast of Hanoi on National Highway 5.

By air: VN flights leave HCMC for Haiphong Sunday–Tuesday and Thursdays and Fridays at 7:30 a.m. From Haiphong, flights depart for HCMC Sundays, Tuesdays and Thursdays at 5:15 p.m. At presstime, these were the only available air routes in and out of Haiphong, although VN told me this will change at some point in 1994, perhaps the addition of flights to Hanoi and Danang.

By bus: There are regular connections to Hanoi via the minibuses that cruise around the theater area. The trip takes about 2-1/2 hours and costs about 10,000 dong. Buses also depart from Haiphong's bus station in the Thuy Nguyen District, which is on the north bank of the Cua Cam River, for Bai Chay and Ha Long Bay's Hong Gai (about 3 hours). To reach the station, you have to take a ferry to the north bank of the river. Buses leave Hanoi for Haiphong from the Long Bien Bus Station on the east side of the Red River.

By train: This is a more popular means of reaching your destination even though the Reunification Express doesn't stop in Haiphong. There is one train that links Hanoi with Haiphong every day early in the morning. From Haiphong, there are two daily trains to Hanoi.

By car: This is actually a relatively difficult trip considering the short distance between the two cities. There are a number of bridges that both cars and the train share. If a train is coming, you've got to stop and wait, sometimes for quite a while. This short distance along Highway 5 can take as long as three hours to cover.

By boat: You can also reach Haiphong from Hanoi by boat. The schedule changes often. If you want, you can even go to Saigon by boat from Haiphong. The trip takes 2-1/2 days. Ferries also leave from the dock on Ben Binh Street for Hon Gai in Ha Long Bay. The trip takes about four hours and costs about US$1. Ferries from Ha Long Bay usually have the same schedules. As I mentioned, boat schedules in the area change frequently, so find out first. You may end up in Haiphong a day or two longer than you anticipated.

POST OFFICE

3 Nguyen Tri Phuong Street. International calls and faxes can be made from here.

BANKS AND MONEYCHANGERS

Vietcom Bank is located at *11 Hoang Dieu Street,* not far from the Post Office. Will give advances on American-issued credit cards.

TOURIST OFFICES

Haiphong Tourist. *15 Le Dai Hanh Street.* ☎ *42957.* This is one of the more useful tourist offices in Vietnam for independent travelers. It offers car rentals and boat charters to Ha Long Bay and Cat Ba National Park.

HOSPITALS

Vietnam-Czech Friendship Hospital on Nguyen Duc Canh Street or the Traditional Medicine Hospital on Ben Vien Dong Y Street. The best bet, though, is to get your ass back to Hanoi ASAP if you've gotten sick or badly hurt.

TNT INTERNATIONAL EXPRESS

☎ *47180.*

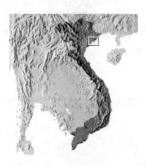

HA LONG BAY

HA LONG BAY IN A CAPSULE

165 km from Hanoi to the Bai Chai bus station...Perhaps the most beautiful area of Vietnam...Possesses more than 3000 islands in the bay...Spectacular limestone outcroppings and caves...Stalagmite and stalactite formations perhaps the most beautiful in the world...Huge limestone rock formations appear out of the bay like giant deformed monoliths...Bay Chai and Hong Gai are the major "towns" in the region...Reachable by bus or boat.

Ha Long Bay, 20 km past Haiphong, is targeted for tourism, but it's anyone's guess what form it will take and when it will take form. Nonetheless, the area has some rather breathtaking scenery, including beautiful limestone formations, sheer edifice cliffs, huge rock arches, peaceful coves and seemingly thousands of limestone islets that rise from the sea like plaster monsters. If Ha Long Bay was perhaps 1000 km to the south, this would be paradise on Earth.

INSIDER TIP

It seems like Ha Long Bay is pretty close to the capital—after all, how long could it take to go a hundred miles? A long darn time.It's a trip that can easily take six hours or more—one way. The trip includes both a river and harbor crossing by ferry. So be warned; it's no day trip. If you're traveling alone you might be required to travel with a guide. As an American, you may be refused access to some areas, such as Pleiku, the former U.S. air base down south.

Ha Long Bay (the name means "Where the Dragon Descends Into the Sea") is perhaps the most beautiful area in Vietnam. It's only drawback, and it's a major one at that, is that the area is perpetually shrouded in a cold, drizzly fog, particularly during the winter months when, frankly, a stay in the area can be a damn uncomfortable one.

Myth says that an enormous beast created the bay and outcroppings as it thrashed its way toward the sea to prevent the forward progress of enemy fleets, even though two major battles were fought here in the 10th and 13th centuries. Legend maybe, but there are sailors who even today report sightings of a giant sea beast called the Tarasque. Locals, in their effort to make a few bucks, offer foreigners a chance to to sail out in search of the creature.

Ha Long Bay was also the site where, in 1882, French Captain Henri Rivière was beheaded after sending troops into the area to seize the region's coal deposits. His head was put on a stick and paraded from village to village. The incident prompted the French government to launch a full-scale effort to make the country of Vietnam a colony of France. The two ports of Hong Gay (called the Pointed Peak, about 120 km from Hanoi in Quang Ninh Province) and Cam Pha (150 km east of Hanoi) are areas of vast coal deposits and are mined by the Cai Bao, Mon Duong and Cham peoples. The area, in Quang Ninh Province, is Vietnam's largest coal-producing region. And archeological evidence suggests an ancient culture in the area dating back to the Neolithic Era (2000) BC following the Bac Son people.

Ha Long Bay is the north's major tourist center; any trip to Vietnam should include a visit to the area on the itinerary. There are magnificent, fragmented limestone outcroppings in this bay which possesses, by the best estimate, more than 3000 islands. Beautiful Chinese-type sailing junks dot the waters between the outcroppings, many of which ascend to heights of 300 meters or more. Many more reach a height of 100 meters. The area looks like a mountain range in the sea. The mountains, consisting of mainly dolomite and limestone, reach for a distance of more than 100 km and cover 1500 square km. The outcropping formations, caves, grottoes, fjiords and tunnels possess perhaps the most exotic appearance of any natural wonders in the world. They've been given names founded in wonderment. There is the Isle of Surprise (which is not a surprising name), the Isle of Wonders, and so forth. There are isles named after monkeys, marionettes, toads and buzzards.

Most foreigners travel to the two principal areas where there is food and accommodations: Bay Chai and Hong Gai on the northern side of the bay. Although some of the more hardy travel to Tra Co next to the Chinese frontier.

WHAT TO SEE AND DO IN HA LONG BAY

Limestone Outcroppings and Grottoes

From Hong Gai, junks can be rented to see the spectacular caves and grottoes in the bay, some of which possess names such as Fighting Cocks and Customs House Cave. Get your guide to bring you to Hang Manh Cave, a giant cave that reaches more than 2 km and offers incredible stalagmite, stalactite and other fantastic rock formations. There is also the Hang Dao Go Grotto, a massive cave of three chambers that can be reached after climbing nearly 100 steps. In the first hall are scores of stalactites that look like a congregation of small creatures out of a George Lucas film. The cave (translated to the "Cave of Wooden Stakes") derived its name from the famous 13th-century warrior named Tran Hung Dao who used the third chamber of the cave to store pointed stakes which he later pounded into the bed of the Bach Dang River to sink an invading Mongol fleet. Other boats will stop at Deu Island, where visitors can view a rare species of monkey characterized by its red buttocks. You should also see Drum Grotto, which is so called because the wind that blows through the stalagmites and stalactites sounds like the faraway beating of drums. Other visitors to Ha Long Bay can also stop at the Grotto of Bo Nau.

WHERE TO STAY IN HA LONG BAY

HON GAI

Hon Gai Floating Hotel

Near the ferry dock • About US$8. Very inexpensive. No amenities. A place to lay your head. Very inexpensive.

Reservations: Just show up.

Hai Au Hotel

About halfway between the Hon Gai and Bai Chay docks • About US$10. Hot water, when it works. Basic accommodations. Inexpensive.

Reservations: Just show up.

BAI CHAY

Bach Dang Hotel

Near the ferry dock. ☎ *6630* • About US$25. Comfortable accommodations. One of the best in town. Hot water, private bath. Moderate.

Reservations: Direct.

Hoang Long Hotel

☎ *6318* • About US$30. Expensive, but the air conditioning is worth it during the summer. Hot water, private bath. Moderate.

Reservations: Direct.

Bach Long Hotel

☎ *6445* • *40 rooms.* About US$25. This is a good deal, as the rooms are bright, relatively large and clean. Hot water, clean attached bathrooms. Friendly staff. Restaurant. Moderate. ***Reservations: Direct.***

Navy Guest House

☎ *4603* • *6 rooms*. About US$30. These are two colonial mansions overlooking the bay, 3 rooms in each house. Attached bath, hot water. Moderate. **Reservations: Direct.**

Trade Union Guest House

Overlooking the beach • About US$25 The biggest building in town and relatively new. Make sure the air conditioning is working during the summer before you choose a room. Moderate.

Reservations: Direct.

Post Office Hotel

2 km on the road back to Hanoi • New and comfortable. Attached bath, air conditioning, hot water. Moderate.Next door are three relatively new hotels managed by Quang Ninh Tourism: the Bach Long, Ha Long, and Hoang Long Hotels. Each are comfortable and in the US$25–40 price range. For those bucks, you get air conditioning, hot water, attached bath and so on. Restaurant. Each of these 4 hotels are in the moderate price range. **Reservations: Direct.**

Worker's Guest House (Nha Khach Cong Doan)

I didn't find this place, but it's supoosed to be the cheapest place in town at about US$5. **Reservations: Direct.**

Van Hai Hotel

In the middle of town. ☎ *6403* • About US$10. Shared bath. Rooms overlook the sea. Inexpensive. **Reservations: Direct.**

DIRECTORY

TRANSPORTATION

Ha Long Bay is about 165 km from Hanoi, 55 km from Haiphong, and 45 km from Cam Pha.

By air: Hanoi is the closest airport unless you find a way of hiring a sea-plane.

By bus: Buses depart Haiphong for Bai Chay from the bus station on the north bank of of the Cua Cam River. The trip takes about 2 hours. The bus station in Bai Chay is on the waterfront road near the Van Hai Hotel. There are also regular connections with Hanoi until the afternoon. The trip takes 5–6 hours and there are two ferry crossings (where most of the time is spent).You can also make connections to points south.

By train: For budget travelers in Hanoi, the best way to get to Ha Long Bay is by train, first to Haiphong in the morning, and then the afternoon ferry to Bai Chay. From Bai Chay you can either return to Haiphong by boat or Hanoi by bus.

By car: This is the best way to get to Ha Long Bay. Go to Bai Chay, spend the night, take a boat tour the next day, and return to Hanoi on the third day. To hire a car and driver from Hanoi will set you back at least

US$100 (usually more) for the round trip. The Japanese cars are more expensive to rent than the Russian ones, namely because they're more comfortable. Also expect to pay for the driver's meals and accommodations.

By boat: Getting around the area isn't much fun unless you've got a boat to tour the islands. You won't need to rent a boat yourself as there will be a slew of foreigners as well as Vietnamese also seeking the same trips. Large boats, carrying up to 100 passengers cost between US$12–20 an hour. But smaller boats holding up to a dozen people can be had for around US$8 an hour. And the smaller boats are privately-owned, so you can negotiate.

By ferry: Ferries depart for Hong Gai about three times a day—in the early morning, mid-morning and late afternoon. But these schedules seem to continually change. The one-way trip takes about 3–4 hours and will set you back at least 10,000 dong, and sometimes much more if you're stupid and don't let your independent (i.e., non-Vietnamtourism) guide buy your ticket for you. Ferries for Haiphong leave from the dock at Hon Gai at 6 a.m., 11 a.m. and 4 p.m. (Again, these schedules are subject to change). You can also take a ferry from Hon Gai to Bai Chay that leaves constantly during the day and early evening.

By helicopter: Yes, this is possible, either through Vietnamtourism or Vietnam Airlines.

TOURIST OFFICE

Quang Ninh Tourism. *Bai Chay Street in Bai Chay.* ☎ *6321.*

Quang Ninh Tourism & Ship Chandler. *Bai Chay Street in Bai Chay.* ☎ *46405; FAX: 84.33.46226.*

POST OFFICE

Bai Chay opposite the ferry dock. Also at the Post Office Hotel.

BANKS AND MONEYCHANGERS

Ha Long Hotel in Bai Chay.

HANOI

HANOI IN A CAPSULE

Hanoi is the capital of the Socialist Republic of Vietnam...it's a city of lakes and parks...about 70 km inland from the Gulf of Tonkin...it sits on the banks of the Red River...the streets are tree-lined...trees are uplifting the pavement...it's been a major settlement since A.D. 1010....it became capital of North Vietnam after the Geneva Agreement of 1954...it's not nearly as kinetic and energetic as Saigon...it is inferior in both tourism and infrastructure...because it's more dreary than its sister to the south, it's probably the best place to launch your tour of Vietnam...was heavily bombed during the Vietnam War...Like Ho Chi Minh City, Hanoi has had more than a half-dozen names over the years.

Although not as popular with tourists as Ho Chi Minh City, and certainly lacking the hustle and bustle of its sister to the south, there's still plenty to see and do in the capital. Some of the sights include the Fine Arts Museum, which houses traditional Vietnamese art as well as European-influenced works; the Water Puppet Theater, Vietnam's humorous version of Punch and Judy; Ho Chi Minh's mausoleum (the Vietnamese hero's body reposes in a glass coffin); the Ho Chi Minh Museum, which opened in 1990 in honor of the 100th anniversary of Ho's birth; and the Hanoi Hilton, the prison where U.S. soldiers were kept (and which may soon be torn down to make way for an actual hotel).

Hanoi was founded in A.D. 1010 at the beginning of the Lu Dynasty; it is the oldest capital city in Southeast Asia. The city was racked by constant bombing from U.S. Air Force B-52 bombers from 1966 to 1972. The center of Hanoi itself doesn't reveal a lot of scars, but the outlying areas do. The French colonial buildings of the capital are in desperate need of renovation—at the very least a coat of paint. But like the big city in the south, Hanoi's people are extremely friendly and seem to bear few ill feelings toward Westerners,

Americans in particular. In fact, you can almost call this city of more than 3 million charming.

Whereas movement of Westerners in the city was once strictly controlled, tourists today move about Hanoi freely. Bicycles can be hired, and even sights off the beaten track are within easy reach of the traveler.

Perhaps what is most interesting about the city is the enormous changes the war ultimately has brought to the architecture of the capital. Many Hanoi dwelling owners are tearing down their properties and rebuilding in such a way that seriously threatens the character of the capital. These building owners are evidently preparing for what they believe will be a deluge of American customers descending on the capital after the embargo is lifted. Residents are tearing down centuries' old structures as well as ramshackle wooden dwellings and replacing them with multistoried mini-motels complete with expensive TV satellite dishes. There seems to be little regard for style in these new structures, and they neither conform to any traditional or modern Asian or Western style—nor do they conform to each other. They look odd and out of place.

And these new building trends haven't gone unnoticed by Hanoi authorities, who are caught in the dilemma of preserving tradition while faced with the demands of a changing and growing economy so thoroughly dependent on foreign investment—and, yes, buildings that look like six-story inverted railroad cars.

Up to now, Hanoi has been one of the few cities in Asia left entirely void of the western-style boxy business architecture that has completely redefined urban areas like Bangkok, Manila, and Kuala Lumpur. There are two very unique historical areas: the ancient city of Hanoi near Hoan Kiem Lake that was settled in the 11th century, and the large French Quarter that was built by the French during their reign in the region from 1880-1930. The French Quarter is really quite attractive, with its tree-lined streets and small French-style houses. Old Hanoi, or the ancient city, is an old network of narrow alleys with dilapidated, crumbling houses set on nearly 40 streets named after the original craftsmen and artisans who settled the area: Gold Street, Baker Street, etc.

Urban planners in Hanoi, not eager to see either area become infected by modernization, are seeking to zone areas specifically for the development of business and residential centers that will become necessary as the Vietnamese economy expands. But the problem is which areas to earmark.

Although independent travel has become extraordinarily easy throughout Vietnam, the government is still somewhat wary of travelers straying from the traditional, government approved sights (many of which are drab and, quite frankly, boring). This is evident by the fact that Hanoi is one of 10 localities in the country where tourist offices administer entire tourist establishments and other tourist activities in the area. But it is still very possible to move about the city and its environs quite easily on your own, usually with little or no hassle from the authorities.

Hanoi has a lot of interesting things to see besides the formaldehyde immersed corpse of Ho Chi Minh. The capital has a history of more than 1000 years. Ho Guam (Restored Sword Lake) features water that has been dyed with green ink! There are the golden buffalo in the West Lake (Ho Tay). There's the bronze-casting village of Ngu Xa, the snake village Le Mat, and the flower villages of Ngoc Ha and Nhat Tan.

Besides the hundreds of pagodas and temples in the city (if you're not already entirely "pagodaed"-out) there are more than 35 ancient streets blooming with the same lotus flowers that have existed here for centuries.

But remember that tourism infrastructure in Hanoi is still substandard, well below amenities offered in HCMC. There are only a total of about 2000 hotel rooms in the city, and only about a quarter of these are considered worthy of "international standards." Roads are in dilapidated condition, except in central Hanoi. Electricity and the water supply continue to be unpredictable. (Foreign-invested joint projects with Vietnamese firms, however, are changing these conditions, but at a tortoiselike rate.)

Hanoi is looking for ways to improve its tourist industry. It's predicted, since the inception of the new laws pertaining to foreign investment, that by the year 2000, Hanoi will be attracting US$10 billion in foreign investment capital. Hanoi predicts that in order for the region to become an area of mass tourism that per capita income will need to increase to US$1000 by the year 2000. By then the capital expects to have nearly 10 hotel rooms of international standards. And just as important, infrastructure projects largely consisting of good accessible roadways to the provinces will have to be implemented.

WHAT TO SEE AND DO IN HANOI AND ENVIRONS

Army Museum

If you want to see tanks and planes and grenades and shells, this is the place. Better to see this museum before checking out the War Crimes Museum in Saigon. It's not as shocking and sobering. However, here you'll find the wreckage of B-52s and American fighter jets, such as F-111s—if this kind of stuff fascinates you.

Ho Chi Minh Mausoleum and Museum ★

Somehow you're not surprised when your guide tells you that this mausoleum was modeled after the Lenin tomb in Moscow. The structure itself is a huge imposing building polygonal in shape. It's no doubt the best-maintained building in all of Hanoi. The inner chamber is where the embalmed body of Ho rests; guards surround it. The old man's an eery-looking sight, and his impact on all of our lives this half of the century is felt through the glass. From the mausoleum, you can tour **Ho's house** near the Communist Party guesthouse— which was the former **presidential palace** and residence of the former French governors of Indochina. When the North's quest for independence finally came to fruition in 1954, Ho refused to live in the palace, opting instead for the meager electrician's house on the palace grounds; he claimed the palace belonged to the people. Open 7:30–11:30 a.m. Tues.–Thurs. and Sat.–Sun.

Hanoi Hilton ★

This is the morbidly humorous name given to the grisly, forboding Hanoi prison structure that housed U.S. POWs, namely American flyers, during the Vietnam War. Prisoners were tortured here up until at least 1969. Some were held seven years or longer. This is a dark, eery sight. Off of Hai Ba Trung Street.

National Arts Museum

Vietnamese sculpture is exhibited in this small museum located next to the Van Mieu, Vietnam's first university. The museum also features bronze drums and modern Vietnamese painting. Open 8–12 and 1–4 p.m. Tues.–Sun.

National History Museum ★

This is actually a great place to visit, especially after seeing all the other sights and coming to the conclusion that the Vietnamese must love to yawn. This is Vietnam's leading museum and the center for cultural and historical research. Granted it's tough to know exactly what you're looking at if you don't read Vietnamese or don't have a guide, but the exhibits here are impressive. It's all designed so you can walk though the different periods of Vietnamese history. There are some beautiful bronze Dongson drums and funeral urns, Nguyen Dynasty pieces, models of ancient cities, weapons from the Tay Son revolt, and much more. If you're lucky, you may even get a private tour from one of the museum's curators. Open 8–12 and 1–4 p.m. Tues.–Sun. There is an admission fee.

Old Hanoi (The French Quarter)   ★ ★

Check out the old quarter of Hanoi, a maze of narrow back alleys with shops selling antiques, flowers and handicrafts. This area is located in Central Hanoi, and was once located in the southeast part of the city as part of the royal plan for placing foreigners. But the quarter's location was far from the city center (down the Red River, susceptible to pollutants spilled into the river, near cemeteries and a leper colony). When the French took the city in 1882, they moved into the area south of Hoan Kien, between the former area and the Ambassador Pagoda. This is where they built their new city. In 1884, the first permanent houses were built, replacing the huts that existed in the area at the time. But in order to do so, they had to ruin numerous monuments that stood in the area at the time. The Museum of Mines, which is now called the Museum of the Revolution, is on Tong Dan Street, behind the Opera. So is the History Museum. The style of the two buildings contrast with their surroundings. The Museum of History, especially, is built in a neo-Vietnamese style. St. Joseph's Cathedral is between the French and Vietnamese Quarters. It was built in the mid-1880s at the site formerly occupied by Bao Thien Pagoda by Monseigneur Puginier. There are two large towers on the cathedral which was built in the neo-gothic style. According to the local Catholic population, this is the highest seat of Vietnam's Catholics. When the communists took control of the city, the size of the congregation dwindled, but has now again grown with the relaxing of religious restrictions. Vietnam is second only to the Philippines in Asia in its number of Catholics. The Ambassador Pagoda is at *73 Quan Su Street.* This was formerly a reception house for visiting Buddhist ambassadors. The main temple is in front, while the rear is dedicated to the monk who cured Emperor Ly Than Tong of a disease.

Botanical Garden

In the 15th century, King Le Thanh Tong ordered a ring built on an earthen mount so he could better view martial arts demonstrations. After Le died, a temple was built in his honor. For centuries the area was a peaceful sanctuary from the densely populated city. In 1890, the French moved the local residents away and created the Botanical and Zoological Park, which was later named simply the Botanical Garden. The native bamboo and banana trees, as well the rattan trees were replaced with perennial plants and trees. They created ponds and small hills and, after a short time, the garden became luxuriantly green. Today, many of the trees and plants are imported from Africa, as well as vegetables and flowers from temperate zones. During the first part of the 20th century, the French began bringing in cages for lions, tigers and bears—as well as for leopards, goats, deer, elephants, peacocks and pheasants. Now it's a popular attraction for both tourists and locals alike. It's a great place to spend a hot summer afternoon.

Quan Su Pagoda

Built in the late 1930s this pagoda is on a site that once served as the quarters for visiting Buddhist VIPs. Some of the Buddha sculptures inside the temple are exquisite. This place is usually packed with wayfarers.

Temple of Literature (Van Mieu Pagoda)

This is the biggest temple attraction in Hanoi. It was founded in 1070 during the reign of Ly Thanh Tong. It is dedicated to Confucious and purportedly modeled after a temple in Shantung, China. There are courtyards, a big bronze bell, and multistoried roofs in the complex. The courtyards feature beautifully carved stelae.

HANOI ENVIRONS NEARBY

★ TAY PHOUNG PAGODA

Three km from the first left turn at the 34th km marker of Highway 11A from Hanoi. Its initial name was Sung Phuc Pagoda and then it became Hoanh Son Thien Lam Tu before acquiring its current name. It's located in the Thach Xa commune in the Thach That district of Ha Tay Province. On the horizontal board at the pagoda's gate are written four hieroglyphs, *Tay Phoung Co To* (meaning the West Ancient Pagoda). It was built on a 50-meter tall mountain that locals say looks like a hook. They say that viewing it from a distance, the mountain and the surrounding hills remind them of a buffalo herd. Cau Lau is the herd's leader turning his head back for a drink of water from a lotus pond. After climbing 239 laterite paved steps, you reach the pagoda's gate. There is a main temple and a temple behind it which represent three treasures: Buddha, his law, and the bonze (the Buddhist Trinity). Each building features two roof layers. The upper layer is formed by tile with fig leaf reliefs. The bottom layer is paved with square tiles, painted in the five colors of a monk's robe. The surrounding wall of the pagoda is constructed of Bat Trang bricks. The wooden supporting pillars are on bases of blue limestone and decorated with lotus petal ornaments. The roof edges are carved in the form of rolled leaves. On top of the roofs are small figurines. The curved corners of the roofs also feature carved flower, dragon and phoenix reliefs. Its architecture is outstanding, true sculptural art. All over the pagoda are carved mulberry and fig tree leaves, lotus, chrysanthemums, dragons and tiger heads. There's a collection of 76 statues at the pagoda, red lacquered, carved out of jact-tree wood and trimmed with gold. The statues bear only Vietnamese inscriptions, and each has its own facial expression. These sculptures are perhaps unparalleled in Vietnam. Perhaps the most famous is the statue of Tuyet Son. Intricate lines are cut deeply into his face. His thin body and solitary appearance are designed to elicit remorse and loneliness. According to ancient inscriptions on the pagoda, it was restored in 1632. A three-sector upper temple and a back temple with a 20-sector corridor were also added. Four years later a giant bell was cast and the statues carved. The pagoda was again rebuilt during the Tay Son period in 1794. Definitely worth the visit.

THAY PAGODA

This pagoda is in Ha Tay Province about 40 km southwest of Hanoi. This is also known as the Master's Pagoda and is dedicated to the historical Thich Ca Buddha (Sakyamuni) as well as to the 18 monks that achieved Nirvana.The monks are on the central altar. There is also a statue of the 12th century monk the pagoda was named after, Tu Dao Hanh. As well, there is a statue of King Ly Nhan Tong, who was reincarnated from Tu Dao Hanh. There's also a stage here where puppet shows are performed during festivals. There are some magnificent caves in the area. The annual festival here is held for three days during the third lunar month.

DEN HAI BA TRUNG TEMPLE

This temple, well south of Hanoi, was dedicated to the heroines of an aborted revolt against the Chinese in AD 40-43. It was built in 1142 and restored in both the 19th and 20th centuries. Once a year, legend has it, the two sisters return to the temple and walk around it. There's a stone relief depicting the battle, probably carved in the late 15th century.

CHUA LIEN PHAI PAGODA

Bach Mai Street, 2 km south of Petic Lac. Built by the Ly in the early 1730s, it was restored in 1884. There are many interesting stupas here and a nine-story octagonal tower. There weren't many pagodas built of this style for the tombs of the laity. Interestingly enough, the temple was built over the remains of the wife of an actor from Saigon.

HANOI ENVIRONS TO THE SOUTH

HUNG YEN (FORMERLY PHO HIEN)

Next to the Red River 60 km southeast of Hanoi, this historic town with its rich multicultural influences makes for an excellent day or half-day trip. During the 17th century, a number of different cities in Vietnam prospered through trade with other Asian nations as well as with the Europeans. Hung Yen was such a place, and brings to mind cities such as Hoi An, south of Danang. Because of its superb geographic location, Pho Hien was developed and thriving as early as the 15th century, and was once considered Vietnam's second largest commercial center. In the late 16th and early 17th centuries it became a major foreign trade center. The Japanese had quite an amount of influence on the area during the early 17th century. Shortly after, ships from the Philippines, Malaysia, Portugal, England, Holland and France came in to call at Pho Hien. But the Chinese, who had arrived centuries earlier, still played the strongest economic role in the region, especially in the handicraft area. The first Europeans to arrive were the Portuguese in the first part of the 16th century. Long term business relationships lasted between the Portuguese and businessmen from Pho Hien through the rest of the century. British influence began to be felt in the area around the 1670s. However, by the end of the 17th century, European traders were forced to abandon Pho Hien through a magistrate's order, and commerce was performed only with the Japanese and Chinese. Many of the goods traded were for royalty and include gold, bronze, weapons and gunpowder, silver, herbal medicine, textiles, jewelry, and ceramic products. Exported material from the area included silk and painted wood handicrafts. Today, there are still many signs of the past on Pho Hien. Its architecture reflects the Tonkin Delta, China's Fukien Province, and there are other buildings with strong Western influences. The city is packed with ancient antiques and architectural relics. Many of these items can be found in the city's pagodas and the Pho Hien Museum. There are Chinese and Vietnamese ceramic goods, brass bells and laquerware items. Even today, ancient relics are still being discovered in Pho Hien.

CUC PHUONG NATIONAL PARK

This is quite a trip, as it's about 150 km south of Hanoi and west of Nam Dinh. Set amidst deeply cut limestone mountains, this national park covers more than 25,000 hectares. It is an important archeological site discovered in 1974 in the Hang Dang (Bat) and Con Mong (Animal) grottoes. There have been numerous discoveries here of prehistoric tools and artifacts. This park is home to thousands of different species of endangered and exotic tropical wildlife. A nature preserve was established here in 1962.

KIEP BAC PAGODA

This is 60 km from Hanoi and about 30 km from Bac Ninh. This recently restored pagoda (founded in the early 1300s) was built to honor the Tran Quoc Tuan, the famous general who aided Tran Hung Dao in defeating more than a quarter of a million Mongol soldiers in the mid 1280s.

HOA BINH

Hoa Binh is 74 km southwest of Hanoi and the capital of Hoa Binh Province. The city, famous for its hill tribes and a large dam on the Song Da River (which created the Song Da Reservoir) can be visited from Hanoi in a day trip. There is a major hydro-electric operation at the dam that generates electricity for much of the north of the country, in fact enough to keep Hanoi from experiencing the constant power failures that put HCMC in the dark. This is also home to members of Muong hill people as well as the Thai. Although there have been problems with foreigners visiting the dam in the past, these obstructions have been largely removed. The tourist office (Hoa Binh Tourism. ☎ *37*) is located only about 10 km from Hanoi in Ha Dong, at *24 Tran Hung Dao Street.*

★ PERFUME PAGODA

Located about 60 km southwest of Hanoi in Hoa Binh Province, this is a complex of pagodas constructed into the sides of the limestone cliffs of Huong Tich Mountain. Here is found Huong Tich Chu Pagoda (Pagoda of the Perfumed Vestige), Giai Oan Chu Pagoda (Pagoda of Purgatory), and Thien Chu (Pagoda Leading to Heaven). This region experiences a great number of pilgrims who come here to fish, hike, explore caves and go boating. There is a festival that begins during the second lunar month and concludes the last week of the third lunar month.

KEO PAGODA

Keo Pagoda is 10 km from the town of Thai Binh in Thai Binh Province, close to Thai Bac. There's a beautiful wood-carved bell at this pagoda, which was built to honor Buddha and the monk Khong Minh Khong who cured Emperor Ly Than Ton of leprosy. It was constructed in the 12th century. There's a dike nearby that makes for good photo opportunities of the pagoda grounds.

HANOI ENVIRONS TO THE NORTH & EAST

BUC THAP PAGODA

In Ha Bac Province and nearby Van Phuc Pagoda, about 28 km northeast of Hanoi. This pagoda is perhaps best known for its stone four-story stupa dedicated to the monk Chuyet Cong. The exact date of its construction isn't known, however it was built either before or during the 17th century.

VAN PHUC PAGODA

About 28 km northeast from Hanoi. This pagoda was built in 1037 and is surrounded by lush hills.

HANOI ENVIRONS TO THE NORTH & WEST

TAM DAO HILL STATION

About 85 km northwest of Hanoi. In 1907 this hill station (some call it Dalat of the north) was founded by the French so that monied colonists could make summer retreats to this elevation of 935 meters to escape the heat of the Red River Delta. This is a beautiful, lush mountainous area featuring giant fern trees about two hours by car from Hanoi. Few foreign tourists reach this hill station, unlike Dalat, so that Tam Dao has yet to suffer from those damned duck boats and Vietnamese cowboys dressed like Roy Rogers astride defecating ponies that plague Dalat. Tam Dao Mountain features three summits. Each is about 1200 meters in height. The highest is 1265 meters. They're easily seen from Tam Dao. The hills are teeming with rare animals and plants. The area is also home to a number of hill tribe people. Although the buildings in Tam Dao are somewhat dilapidated, this makes for a beautiful excursion. The summertime is the best time of the year to come here. It gets quite cold up here in the winter. You can stay at the Tam Dao Hotel (virtually all foreigners do). The tourist office is located in the hotel. ☎ *306* for both.

VINH YEN

Vinh Yen is about 60 km northwest of Hanoi. It's a tiny village cut off from most everything (even though it's on the main road!) that sees few, if any, foreigners. It lies between the Song River and the Tam Dao Mountains. It was the site of battles during the First Indochina War. It has the distinction of being the first place in Vietnam where napalm was used (not by the Americans, but by the French). The attacks killed and wounded thousands of Viet Minh soldiers. The French General who engineered the strategy, Gen. de Lattre, was called the Fire General by the locals.

SON TAY

About 40 km northwest of Hanoi. Son Tay is located at the end of the delta region around Hanoi. There's a small citadel in the middle of the complex which was fortified in 1822, but captured in 1883 by French Admiral Courbet.

A HUNG HOA

A Hung Hoa is 66 km from Hanoi upriver. There's a famous citadel here (at least for the architecture of its watchtower) that used to stand watch over the Song River. Here the topography descends into the valley where the Lo and Black rivers flow. The local population depends on the river for its livelihood, and the inhabitants here tend to be less friendly to foreigners. Legend has it that this was the area where the Hong Bang Dynasty started in 2880 BC and ended in 258 BC. It was part of the Van Long Kingdom. Its capital was Bach Hach (then called Phong Chau), about 80 km from Hanoi to the northwest in Vinh Phu Province. The site of the Hong Bang kings' temple, Den Hung, is close to here in the Nung Hills (80 km west of Hanoi). The temple, the ruins of which are still precariously standing, dates back to the Ly Dynasty. There is the tomb of the mythical leader Hung Huy Vuong in front of the temple.

TUYEN QUANG

Tuyen Quang is located 165 km northwest of Hanoi in Ha Tuyen Province. Tuyen Quang faces Yen Bay from the banks of the Lo River. It was a strategic hamlet for the Nguyen on the path to Yunnan. From 1884-1885, the town was occupied by the French and then was occupied by the Chinese. The Second National Congress of the Vietnamese Communist Party was held here in 1951 in honor of the start-up of the Worker's Party.

BINH SON

Binh Son is 85 km west of Hanoi on the Lo River. There's an 11-story tower here dating from at least the 11th century. When archeologists were working to restore the tower in 1979, they discovered a "blueprint" (inscribed on a brick) of the temple that dates back to the 8th century. Between Vinh Yen and Tuyen Quang is the village of Thien Khe, which is the site of numerous Buddhist rock paintings. Fifteen km before reaching Tuyen Quang is the former Binh Ca Fortress. It was built in the early 16th century by Vu Cong Mat, a famous general. The walls around the fortress are still visible.

TAN TRAO

Tan Trao is situated 150 km from Hanoi, northwest in Ha Tuyen Province. This town has the distinction of once being the capital of revolutionary Vietnam. Ho Chi Minh organized a mass upheaval here in May 1945. Most of the mandates of the Communist Party were drawn up here. Also in Tan Trao, the Central Committee of the National Liberation was elected. Uncle Ho was elected president.

HANOI ENVIRONS TO THE EAST

The Dong Trieu Ridge and the surrounding area are historically extremely significant in Vietnamese history, particularly to scholars of the country. The ridge averages 500–1000 meters high and borders northern Vietnam with China. During the Cham and Mongol invasions of the 14th century, Tran Dynasty rulers used the area as a hideout and sanctuary. The following areas are extremely remote and rarely, if ever see Western tourists. If you want to visit these areas, as well as the remote areas described earlier in the west, it's extremely important you find a good (a very good) private guide in Hanoi. Do not, I repeat, do not rely on Vietnamtourism to provide any help in reaching many of these destinations. These communities and sites are well off the beaten track and many are inaccessible by vehicle. Only the hardiest of travelers should attempt visiting these sites. And don't expect any accommodations or decent food and water. Bring your own from Hanoi.

DONG TRIEU

Dong Trieu in Quang Ninh Province is 85 km east of Hanoi. This is an important coal mining area. There are vast deposits in the vicinity. The Trans virtually worshipped the surrounding area at the base of Nui Yen Tu. About 4 km away is the village of Ha Loi where there is the Quynh Lam Pagoda, which dates from the Tran Dynasty. There's a giant bell here. Almost 4 km to the north lies the village of Yen Sinh and a temple and tombs of Tran rulers of the 14th century.

KIEP BAC

Kiep Bac is located 60 km northeast of Hanoi. This "quaint" village is north of Hai Duong by about 15 km on the eastern border of the Dong Trieu Ridge, above the Hom Hills. Refuge was taken in the hills here by Prince General Hung Dao, better known as Than Quoc Tuan, in 1285 after being defeated by the Mongolians from Loang Son. The prince then regrouped his forces here and later attacked and beat the Mongols in 1289. After his death in 1300 he was buried in a pagoda that was built here earlier in his honor. Hung Doa is considered a national hero in Vietnam. After his death soldiers used to come to the pagoda when war was pending for luck and signs of the battle's outcome. If a soldier's sword was heard to be removed from its sheath, it meant that the battle would be lost. Pregnant women also came to the temple to pray to the spirits for a safe delivery of the child.

HAI DUONG

Hai Duong is in Hai Duong Province, 60 km east of Hanoi. This was a strategic location on the road from Hanoi to Ha Long Bay, as it is located near the summit of the delta in Thai Binh. Today, you can view the remains of a fort that was built here in 1804 by the Nhuyen Dynasty.

NUI YEN TU

Nui Yen Tu is 45 km east of Hanoi. Here there are many pagodas in the surrounding hills that were constructed by Tan rulers, who used Nui Yen Tu as a retreat. It's damned difficult to get here, but once you reach the area, the views of Ha Long Bay are magnificent.

MAO KHE

About 8 km east of Dong Trieu. This is the most eastern point of the Co Bang Hills. The Dong Trieu Ridge begins here.

CON SON

Con Son is 80 km northeast of Hanoi, and 30 km north of Hai Duong. The village offers gorgeous views of the surrounding hillsides. Nguyen Trai, the trusted advisor and aide to Le Loi used this location as a retreat.

WHERE TO STAY IN HANOI

It wasn't that long ago that one could stroll down the tree-shaded streets of Hanoi and run into nothing more than a few cyclo drivers clamoring for a fare in this sleepy, slow-paced capital. Although it has a long way to go to catch up with the hustle and bustle of Saigon, some pretty damn good hotels have been springing out of the concrete recently. Sidewalk cafes, nightclubs, and restaurants seem to be opening like barbers at a heavy metal concert. It is said that each week a new hotel opens its doors in Hanoi, most to cater to the hordes of businesspeople converging on the capital in recent years. Even so, the current hotel glut is still hard pressed to meet the demand, and it can be damned difficult to find a hotel room in Hanoi, at any time of the year. Building more hotels in the capital has been problematic at best due to the government's increasing involvement in the integrity of the structures being razed to make room for the new hotels (see section on architecture). At present, it seems that most new structures are being being born from exisiting ones, although I've seen a good many exceptions to this "rule."

Construction of the US$30 million Ever Fortune Plaza in Hanoi opposite the United Nations compound and the Australian and Egyptian embassies will begin construction during the third quarter of 1994 and be completed by the end of 1996. The hotel and office plaza will feature a five-story base structure and a 16-floor, 242-room hotel tower. The base area will include offices, restaurants, a bar, meeting rooms and a ballroom. Roof-top swimmimg facilities will be available as well as a health and beauty center. The new structure will tower high over the opposite seven-story Saigon Hotel on the opposite corner.

Also, an American company (New York-based DeMatteis Development Corp.) will build a 14-story tower on the southern bank of Hanoi's West

Lake, an area that will cover 4000 square meters. The building will include office and retail space as well as a restaurant, health club, conference facilities and a movie theatre. DeMatteis hopes to build a number of movie theatres throughout Vietnam. The following establishments are already in operation.

Army Guest House, Army Hotel

These two hostelries are run by the defense ministry and are surprisingly clean and well run considering the ominous sounding monikers. *Just 2 blocks from the municipal theatre, and just down the street from the museum of history on Pham Ngu Lao Street,* these two establishments offer 84 rooms with modern facilities, including satellite TV and IDD at moderate prices. Both are popular with ExPats. Moderate.

Reservations: Direct.

The Dong Loi

Ly Thuong Street and Le Duan Street, close to the Hanoi Railway Station. This hotel is operated by the Hanoi Tourist Services Company (Torseco). It offers old world charm at moderate prices. Built in the 1930s, this 30-room stucci structure features a spiral staircase and wrought iron bannisters as well as molded ceilings and art nouveau light fixtures. Moderate.   *Reservations: Direct.*

Hoa Binh Hotel

Ngo Quyen Street and the corner of Ly Thuong Kiet. This place has been around since 1923 and it has an excellent location which ensures a steady stream of both tourists and business people alike. The top floor bars offer an excellent view of the city and the tree-lined boulevards below of central Hanoi. Hanoi Tourism runs the place and is in the process of renovating a number of the rooms; at the last count, there were 112. Moderate–Expensive.   *Reservations: Direct.*

Thang Loi Hotel

Hanoi Tourism runs seven hotels in the Hanoi area in addition to the Metropole. It is the biggest hotel operator in the region. Many consider the Thang Loi to be the flagship hotel which was built as a gift from Cuba in 1975. There are a number of new lakeside bungalows built from bamboo bringing the existing amount of rooms to 175. They're all on beautifully landscaped grounds on a small peninsula jutting out into the West Lake. There is a swimming pool and a tennis court. Although the hotel is several kilometers from the city center, you won't mind unless your business brings you into central Hanoi frequently. Tourists will relish the rest and relaxation the Thang Loi affords. Expensive.   *Reservations: Direct*

Tay Ho Palace

This hotel also borders the lake, and it takes quite a drive to get there. It's a modern building flanked by lotus paddies, but the service leaves a bit to be desired for an international standard hotel. I'd avoid it. Expensive.   *Reservations: Direct.*

Boss Hotel

60 Nguyen Du Street. ☎ *252-690. FAX: 84-4-257-634* • *15 rooms.* This is a lot closer to the center of Hanoi and faces Thien Quang Lake. It's a small and modern hotel, and its VIP lounge is probably the closest thing to a disco in Hanoi (at least at the time of this writing, but expect this to change soon.) Air conditioning; TV; telephone; refrigerators; hot water. Expensive.   ***Reservations: Direct.***

Hanoi Hotel

Giang Vo Street, Ba Binh District • *76 rooms.* Hong Kong built and owned, it is managed by the foreign partner Ever Universal Company, and is distinctively Hong Kong in taste and styling, and perhaps even in snotty attitude according to a number of visitors. It's a bit cramped but the 10-year-old structure was recently renovated at a cost of about US$6 million. The structure is 11 stories high and features a huge Chinese restaurant, a business center, nightclub and karaoke. Soon there will be a tennis court overlooking the Giang Vo Lake. Its luxury suites are in the neighborhood of US$300 per night, making this an anomaly in a communist state. Very Expensive. ***Reservations: Direct.***

Heritage Hotel   ★

This is on the same street as the Hanoi Hotel and is under Singaporean management. This is a favorite among foreign businesspeople, and I'm told this is Hanoi's only completely new hotel, although I find this hard to believe. The 41-room structure is run by Singapore's Orient Vacation and a Vietnamese local partner Coal Company No. 3 (another typically creative Vietnamese company name). There is a nightclub with Karaoke booths, and a restaurant offering a full range of Southeast Asian cuisine. Expensive.   ***Reservations: Direct.***

The Dong Do

Close to Giang Vo Lake • On the top floor is the Sunset Bar, which is run by a Finn and his Vietnamese wife. It's popular with Expats. They claim to have the longest bar in Hanoi. When you've imbibed too much, proprietors can usually get away with such claims. The drink list here includes more than 100 concoctions. Try half of them and you'll be convinced the Finn's claim to the longest bar in Hanoi is absolutely correct, especially when you're trying to find the toilet. Expensive.   ***Reservations: Direct***

Bin Minh Hotel

27 Ly Thai To Street. ☎ *266-441. Fax: 84-4-257-725* • *43 rooms.* Air conditioning; telephones; hot water. Good location. Moderate.   ***Reservations: Direct.***

Bong Sen Hotel

34 Hang Bun Street. ☎ *254-017* • *26 rooms.* New hotel (1991) with air conditioning rooms; TV; refrigerator; attached bathrooms. Moderate.   ***Reservations: Direct.***

Dan Chu Hotel

29 Trang Tien Street. ☎ *253-323* • A 100-year-old building and it shows. Friendly service. Air conditioning; telephone; TV; dining room; lounge bar. Moderate. ***Reservations: Direct.***

Dong Loi

94 Ly Thuong Kiet Street. ☎ *255-721* • *35 rooms.* Recently renovated. Basic accommodations. Restaurant. Inexpensive.

Reservations: Direct.

Friendship Hotel

23 Quan Thanh Street. ☎ *253-182* • Singles and doubles. Bar; gift-shop. Moderate. ***Reservations: Direct.***

Hong Ha Hotel

78 Yen Phu Street. ☎ *253-688* • *30 rooms.* North of the railway bridge. Air conditioning; telephones; TV; hot water; refrigerators. Not a bad deal. Inexpensive. ***Reservations: Direct.***

Pullman Metropole ★★★★

15 Ngo Quyen Street. ☎ *266-919. FAX: 84-4-266-920* • *109 rooms (16 suites).* Totally renovated. This is the grande dame of Hanoi's hotels. It was first opened in 1910 and was beginning to show signs of aging before US$9 million was pumped into renovations back in 1989. The original hardwood floors remain as do the original shuttered windows. Expats and tourists alike congregate here to share news, read the news and take all this luxury in. All the rooms have air conditioning; attached bathrooms; IDD telephones; satellite TV; private safe deposit boxes; bar; restaurant with French and Asian cuisine with chefs from China and France; live music—traditional Vietnamese, classical, American jazz; airport shuttle. A new renovation and expansion, costing some US$34 million, will add 135 rooms and 6000 square meters of office space and should be finished by mid-1995. Book a month in advance. Undeniably the classiest and the most expensive hotel in Hanoi.There have been some serious renovations here. As mentioned, it was first opened as a hotel in 1910, and was showing its age in 1989 when a group of French investors along with local financiers in Hanoi with Hanoi Tourism and Unimex pumped US$9 million into the complex. Architects were careful to preserve the integrity of the structure, including retaining the hardwood floors in the bedrooms and the shuttered French windows. Sooner or later, most visitors to the capital end up here, not necessarily to stay, but at least to sample the fine food created by both French and Vietnamese chefs. This is the only five-star experience in Hanoi.The hotel also features live music, including jazz, traditional Vietnamese music, as well as classical and contemporary. The French and Chinese chefs make their own pastries, pates, and ice cream. The hotel's wine selection is the most extensive in Vietnam.Typically, the hotel runs at 95 occupancy and you should book at least a month in advance. Another $34 million expansion is due to be completed in mid-1995 that will add 135 rooms as well as 6000 square meters of office space.Very Expensive. ***Reservations:*** ☎ *(800) 221-4542 in the U.S.*

Rose Hotel

20 Phan Boi Chau Street. ☎ *254-438. FAX: 84-4-254-437* • Near the railway station. Singles and doubles. Moderate. ***Reservations: Direct.***

Tay Ho International Hotel

Quang An, Tu Liem. ☎ *232-379. FAX: 84-4-232-390* • *118 rooms.* Nice digs but a bad location. Out in the boonies. Restaurant; bar; swimming pool; air conditioning; telephones; car rental; massage; TV; refrigerators. Moderate. ***Reservations: Direct.***

Thang Long Hotel

Giang Vo. ☎ *252-270* • Drab 10-story structure near Giang Vo, with service to match. Air conditioning; TV; two restaurants; shop; bar. Inexpensive. ***Reservations: Direct.***

Trang Tien Hotel

35 Trang Tien Street • Basic guesthouse fare, but popular with the backpacker set. Restaurant downstairs. A good place to trade trail stories. Inexpensive. ***Reservations: Direct.***

There are also a ton of mini-hotels in Hanoi (the numbers change daily), the type that the government has discouraged due to the decimating of historic architecture. But not ones to turn down hard currency, the government has allowed these establishments to proliferate as if it were rebuilding the city after a war, which in many ways it still is. According to Vietnamtourism's 1992 figures, there are more than 80 such guesthouses, although I suspect the number has gone up substantially in the last two years. Among the better mini-hotels are the **Bac Nam Hotel**, just a few blocks from the Metropole on Ngo Nguyen Street. There's also the **Phu Gia Hotel** on Hang Trong Street which overlooks Hoan Kiem Lake in the center of the city. The **Trang An Hotel** has been getting good reviews, on Hang Gai Street. The narrow, wedding-cake-like building is squeezed between shops in the 36 historic streets section of the city.

WHERE TO EAT IN HANOI

Where in Hanoi can you order a plate of bangers and mash and a pint of Bass? Amidst the faded pastel architecture of the capital's Old Quarter, try the Emerald (53 Hang Luoc Street, ☎ 259258). This is one of the newest eateries and drinking establishments in Hanoi, an authentic Irish pub. There's also Guiness and a variety of Scottish malts. The proprietors–Steven, Patrick, and David–go by the acronym SPUD and decided to create their home away from home about a year ago. The interior is graced with gaellic motifs and glasses hang in brass rail holders over a dark wood counter. The pub offers hamburgers,chili con carne, soups, fries, fish pie, shepherds's pie, and a chicken and mushroom-stuffed pie that some folks complain is too stuffed. The big disappointment is the price of the Bass, which runs US$6 a pint. The owners say it's because the stuff has to go through hell and back, and worse–the Malacca Strait–before it reaches Hanoi.

A Restaurant

Thang Long Hotel • One of two of perhaps the most creatively named eateries in Tomorrowland. Basic Vietnamese fare. The place seats hundreds. **B Restaurant** is a lot smaller and has a menu in English. Hooray.

Bodega Cafe

57 Trang Tien Street • For good pastries.

Dan Chu Hotel Restaurant

Where else? • Cheery atmosphere, average food. Menus in three languages.

Darling Cafe

33 Hang Quat Street • Decent Western food, cheap. Popular with backpackers.

Hoa Binh Hotel Restaurant

Hoa Binh Hotel • This is good, cheap, food.

Piano Restaurant

Hang Vai Street • Features some imported wines and beers; good shrimp and crab; live music.

Restaurant 202

202 Nha Hang Street • This may be the best restaurant in Hanoi. Both Vietnamese and Western food, but specializes in the latter.

Rose Restaurant

15 Tran Quoc Tian Street. ☎ *254-400* • This place is usually quite crowded. Both Asian and Western cuisine.

Sophia Restaurant

6 Hang Bai Street. ☎ *255-069* • There's a cafe downstairs and restaurant upstairs. Average.

The Green Bamboo ★

42 Nha Trung Street ☎ *2.64949.* Just opened in Jan. '94 and still undiscovered, this place could become a hit with expats and tourists alike. Music, outdoor dining, cheap prices in the heart of Hanoi.

DIRECTORY

AUTHOR'S NOTE

Hanoi will invest close to US$500 million to upgrade Hanoi International Airport's facilities, as nearly 10 million travelers are expected to pass through the airport in the near future. Additionally, 10 tube lines for incoming aircraft are expected to be built. The total airport area will increase to 50,000 square meters, including a three-story terminal building. Take-off areas, runways, and technical stations are also anticipated to be improved.

TRANSPORTATION

Hanoi is 1710 km from Saigon, 765 km from Danang, 660 km from Hue, 420 km from Dien Bien Phu, 165 km from Ha Long Bay, 153 km from Thanh Hoa, 103 km from Haiphong, and 90 km from Ninh Binh.

By air: Hanoi's airport, Noi Bai Airport is about 50 km from the center of Hanoi and is about an hour's drive by microbus, the cheapest and fastest way of reaching the city center, although there are local buses that pick up passengers at the airport's domestic terminal. Expect to pay about US$.60 for the bus ride and at least US$2 for a microbus ride that brings passengers to their destinations in Hanoi and then ends up at the Vietnam Airlines offices at *60 Nguyen Du Street* or *1 Quang Trung Street.* Be duly warned that coming into Hanoi by air is an absolute pain in the ass. The airport itself resembles a warehouse, and the wait for your baggage can take some time indeed. Incoming planes park well away from the terminal, and there is only one baggage conveyor belt in the domestic terminal, sometimes handling luggage from three or four different aircraft. Microbuses also depart for the airport many times during the day, but contact the VN office for the exact schedules, as they change and are infrequently adhered to. Microbuses tend to leave when full no matter what time they are scheduled to depart. International passengers can arrange to depart for the airport at the VN office located at *1 Quang Trung Street.* Again, buses leave when they are full. But remember to buy a ticket for the microbus a day in advance. By taxi, the hour trip will set you back at least US$10 and I've talked with people who have paid as much as US$20 for the ride. You can arrange for a taxi to meet you at your hotel or you can hire one at the VN office for the airport. If you're negotiating with a taxi driver, it's better to do it in dong, and be sure the rate agreed upon is for either the car itself or your own personal fare if you're being joined by other passengers.

Note: Much less English is spoken in the north, and this is particularly frustrating at the airport, where few, if any transportation directors have the ability to say many more than just a few words. They certainly know the meaning of $ signs, however. Conditions are a little more modern at the international terminal, but certainly not up to international standards

See "Author's Note" above on the proposed expansion of the airport's facilities. Also see the VN timetable found earlier in this edition for selected international and domestic routes and schedules on Vietnam Airlines.

By train: Trains leave daily for Saigon from Hanoi's Ga Hanoi train station, about a 15 minute cyclo ride from the city center. Expect a 50-hour train ride to Saigon from Hanoi.(See the railway timetable earlier in this edition.)

By bus: Hanoi has 4 "bus stations." One station *5 Le Thong Street* has two buses a day which depart for Ha Long Bay. The trip takes about 5 hours. They leave early in the morning, around 7–9 a.m. The Kim Ma station on Nguyen Thai Hoc street services the northwest of Vietnam., including Son Tay, Hat Lot, Phu To, Trung Ha, Moc Chau, Bat Bat, Da Chong, Son La, Yen Bai, and Hoa Binh. Kim Lien station is on the southwest edge of Thien Quang Lake and serves destinations in the south, including Vinh, Hue, Danang, Qui Nhon, Ninh Binh, Nam Dinh, Cam Ranh, Nha Trang, and Saigon to mention a few. Again, buses leave early in the morning. The fountain at the northern tip of Hoan Kiem Lake has microbuses that leave regularly for Haiphong.

Transportation around town is usually done by conventional **cyclo**. But their charges to foreigners are usually outrageous. Agree upon a price and put it in writing is the suggestion of many travelers, as the scam in Saigon whereby cyclo drivers claim to be cheated at the end of the ride is an even worse problem in Hanoi. Hiring a bicycle (for about US$1 per day) is the best way of seeing the sights of Hanoi. They can be rented from a number of hotels and bike rental shops across Hanoi.

GENERAL POST OFFICE

85 Dinh Tien Hoang Street. The International Post Office is next door at *87 Dinh Tien Hoang Street.*

INTERNATIONAL TELEPHONE, FAX SERVICES

The necessary international communications services can be had at the International Post Office or at *66-68 Trang Tien Street* and *66 Luong Van Can Street.*

TNT INTERNATIONAL EXPRESS OFFICE

3 Hang Kay Street. ☎ *257615; FAX: 255829.*

IMMIGRATION POLICE STATION

89 Tran Hung Dao Street.

HOSPITALS

Bach Mai Hospital. *Giai Phong Rd.* ☎ *253731.* K Hospital is at *43 Quan Su Street.* ☎ *252143.*

TOURIST OFFICES

Vietnamtourism
54 Nguyen Du Street. ☎ *255963; FAX: 252707.*

Hanoi Tourism Service Co. (TOSERCO)
1 Trang Tien Street. ☎ *250876; FAX: 259209.* Also at *25 Tran Dung Dao Street.* ☎ *254347.*

Oscan Enterprises
60 Ngyuen Du Street. ☎ *52690; FAX: 57634.*

Vung Tau International Tourist Services
136 Hang Trong Street. ☎ *252739.*

BANKS AND MONEYCHANGERS

Bank of Foreign Trade. *49-49 Ly Thai To Street.* This bank, like others in Vietnam, will not change dong back into dollars. On the black market you can change dong back into US dollars. Locations are usually found on Trang Tien Street.

AIRLINE OFFICES

Vietnam Airlines
International address: *1 Quang Trung Street.* ☎ *253842.* Domestic address: *60 Nguyen Du Street.* ☎ *255194.*

Singapore Airlines
15 Ngo Quyen Street at the Hotel Sofitel Metropole.

Air France
1 Ba Trieu Street. ☎ *253484; FAX: 266694.*

Thai Airways
1c Quang Trung Street. ☎ *266893; FAX: 267394.* Note: This is also the offices for **Cathay Pacific** and **Malaysian Airlines**.

USEFUL TAXI NUMBERS

Hanoi Taxi
☎ *265252.*

Thang Long Taxi
☎ *265241.*

EMBASSIES IN HANOI

Afganistan
> D1 Van Phuc Quarter. ☎ 253249.

Algeria
> 15 Phan Chu Trinh Street. ☎ 253865.

Australia
> 66 Ly Thuong Kiet Street. ☎ 252763.

Belgium
> D1 Vann Phuc Quarter, Rooms-105-108. ☎ 252263.

Bulgaria
> 358 Street, Van Phuc Quarter. ☎ 257923.

Cambodia
> 71A Tran Hung Dao Street. ☎ 253789.

Canada
> 39 Nguyen Dinh Chieu Street. ☎ 265840.

China
> 46 Hoang Dieu Street. ☎ 253737.

Cuba
> 65 Ly Thuong Kiet Street. ☎ 254775.

Czech and Slovakia
> 6 Le Hong Phong Street. ☎ 254335.

Egypt
> 85 Ly Thuong Kiet Street. ☎ 252944.

Finland
> b3b Giang Vo Quarter. ☎ 256754.

France
> 49 Ba Trieu Street. ☎ 252719.

Germany
> 29 Tran Phu Street. ☎ 252836.

Hungary
> 47 Dien Bien Phu Street. ☎ 253353.

India
> 58-60 Tran Hung Doa Street. ☎ 253409.

Indonesia
> 50 Ngo Quyen Street. ☎ 253353.

Iran
> 54 Tran Phu Street. ☎ 232068.

Iraq
> 66 Tran Hung Dao Street. ☎ 254141.

Italy
> *9 Le Phing Hieu Street.* ☎ *256246.*

Japan
> *E3\Trung Tu Quarter.* ☎ *L 257902.*

Democratic Peoples' Republic of Korea
> *25 Cao Ba Quat Street.* ☎ *253008.*

Korea (Republic of)
> *60 Nguyen Du Street.* ☎ *L 269161.*

Laos
> *22 Tran Binh Trong Street.* ☎ *254576.*

Libya
> *A3 Van Phuc Quarter.* ☎ *253371.*

Malaysia
> *A3 Van Phuc Quarter.* ☎ *253371.*

Mongolia
> *39 Tran Phu Street.* ☎ *253009.*

Myanmar
> *A3 Van Phuc Quarter.* ☎ *253369.*

Palestine
> *E4b Trung tu Quarter.* ☎ *254013.*

Philippines
> *E1 Trung Tu Center, Rm. 305-308.* ☎ *257-948.*

Poland
> *3 Chua Mot Cot Street.* ☎ *252027.*

Romania
> *5 Le Hong P`hong Street.* ☎ *252014.*

The Russia Federation
> *58 Tran Phu Street.* ☎ *254632.*

Singapore
> *BVan Phuc Quarter, Rms. 301-302.* ☎ *233966.*

Sweden
> *2-358 Street, Van Phuc Center.* ☎ *254824.*

Switzerland
> *77b Kim Ma Street.* ☎ *232019.*

Thailand
> *63-65 Hoang Dieu Street.* ☎ *253092.*

United Kingdom
> *16 Ly Thuong Kiet Street.* ☎ *252510.*

Yugoslavia

47 Tran Phu Street. ☎ 252343.

DIEN BIEN PHU

DIEN BIEN PHU IN A CAPSULE

Famous site of the French defeat to Viet Minh forces in May 1954...The battle marked the end to French colonial rule of northern Vietnam...Extremely remote near the Laos border...Transportation by ground is long, tedious, and treacherous...Can now be reached by twice-weekly flights from Hanoi...Spectacular scenery in the Muong Thang Valley...15 km from the Lao border.

Dien Bien Phu, the site in Northern Vietnam which marked the astounding and tactically brilliant defeat of French forces by Vietnamese patriots in May 1954, has become another hot tourist destination—it has become particularly popular with French tourists.

Dien Bien Phu, about 15 km form the Lao border, is a highly inaccessible area 300 km west of Hanoi and has, up to now, been only reached after an exhausting 15–17 hour road trip by 4-wheel-drive. If you choose to go by 4-wheel-drive, the trip is perilous, especially along the 40-km pass known as "Where Heaven and Earth Meet," a path that reaches 1000 meters into the sky. It is the only "thoroughfare" that links Lai Chau Province in northern Vietnam with the rest of the country.

It was here, across Pha Din, that the Vietnamese cut a path and painfully moved their supplies toward Dien Bien Phu in 1954.

Myth has it that that a Meo king once lived in the mountain with a bevy of beautiful women, both Meo and Thai girls. His son fell in love with one of the Thai girls and the woman was mercilessly beaten and punished by the king. After fleeing into the forest to study mag-

ic, the prince was finally able to liberate the Thai girl from the clutch-
es of his cruel father. But because there was no path in the mountains
to flee, the couple decided to "fly" to heaven. The young prince carried the woman on his back up to Pha Din, where they confronted
cold weather and were able to continue no further. As the story
goes, they couldn't find the gate to heaven so they embraced each
other and turned to stone.

But it was the battle between French and Viet Minh forces that put
the location on the map. The day before the Geneva Conference on
Indochina was to begin on May 7, 1954, 55,000 Viet Minh forces
decisively overran the French unit stationed at Dien Bien Phu. It was
a remarkable battle. In the early stages of 1954, the commander of
the French forces in Indochina, Gen. Henri Navarre, deployed 12
battalions to control the Muong Thanh Valley with the purpose of
preventing the Viet Minh from crossing into Laos to take over the
Lao capital of Luang Phubang. The high command thought the area
to be impregnable. The French forces were then besieged for 57
days by the Viet Minh, who overcame incredible obstacles to ferry
soldiers and supplies to the area (nearly 200,000 porters were employed to carry the equipment)over impossibly steep mountainsides,
and attacked on May 6, 1954. The French soldiers, nearly a third of
whom were ethnic Vietnamese, were routed by 33 Viet Minh infantry battalions, six artillery regiments equipped with 105-mm guns
and anti-aircraft weapons, and a corps of engineers under the leadership of Gen. Vo Nguyen Giap. The weaponry was carried by hand
through jungles and over mountains and then camouflaged in state-
gically-located sites overlooking the valley.

The first assault on the compound failed. But the Viet Minh then
shelled the French encampment continuously for nearly two months
and dug a network of trenches and tunnels that were undetected by
the French and allowed the Viet Minh to harass the French units
without coming under fire themselves. As the situation became more
perilous for the French, the French high command parachuted a
half-dozen batalions into Dien Bien Phu to fortify the compound.
But a combination of bad weather and the constant bombardment
by Viet Minh artillery pieces made reinforcing Dien Bien Phu to any
great deal of effectiveness largely ineffective.

The situation worsened for the French to such a degree that they
considered, along with the Americans, the use of tactical nuclear
weapons to dislodge the Viet Minh positions. However, on May 6,
the Viet Minh attacked the garrison in force and killed or captured
all 13,000 Frenchmen and Vietnamese defending the valley, despite

the loss of nearly 25,000 soldiers of their own units. But the battle was decisive and catastrophic, and it signified the beginning of the entire French withdrawl of Vietnam. Interestingly enough, the night before the attack, the Viet Minh played a recording of the song "Song of the Partisans,"which was the theme of the French Resistance during WWII, the night before they attacked. There was a unit of French paratroopers that continued to defend the valley for another 24 hours but, they, too, were overran.

On July 20, 1954, the French asked for peace and Vietnam was divided into the communist north and the capitalist south at the 17th parallel. Terms set up at the conference included the honorable burial of all forces from both sides killed in the battle. But when South Vietnamese President Ngo Dinh Diem urinated over dead Viet Minh soldiers in the south as a symbolic gesture, Ho Chi Minh decided to let the French lay where they died. During the course of the nine-year war between the French and the Vietnamese, as many as one million civilians died, about a quarter million Viet Minh perished, and nearly 95,000 French troops died.

Today, at the site, French artillery guns and tanks litter the valley. There is a museum dedicated to the battle as well as a hotel to accommodate the increasing number of tourists wishing to visit the area. Additionally, the headquarters of French Col. Christian de Castries has been recreated. There is a monument to the Viet Minh killed at the former French position called "Elaine."

Today, Route 6 from Hanoi to Pha Din, which passes through the villages of Hoa Binh, Moc Chau and Son La, is crowded with vehicles. Highway 6 ends at Tuan Giao. You then have to head southwest for 90 or so kilometers to reach the battlefield at Dien Bien Phu.

Of course, there are easier ways. Vietnam Airlines has inaugurated flight service to the historic battle site, spurred mostly by French tourist demand to visit the area. Japanese and Thai tourists have also expressed an overwhelming desire to visit the battlefield that marked the end of French colonial rule more than 40 years ago. The one-hour flights from Hanoi leave twice weekly on ATR-72 aircraft, each Tuesday and Friday. In Hanoi, contact ☎ *250888*; in Danang *21130*, or in Saigon ☎ *292118, 230697*, or *299910*.

DIEN BIEN PHU ENVIRONS

SON LA

Son La is the capital of Son La Province on the Laos border. Hmong, Black Thai, Muong and White Thai hillpeople live in this heavily mountainous and forested region. Only early in the 20th century was the area annexed by Vietnam; it had been an independent "state" prior to this time, ruled primarily by the Black Thais. This area is within an extremely mountainous area and is highly inaccessible. The road from Hanoi is in treacherous condition, and it worsens even still after Ha Dong and Hoa Binh as it turns north. There is a prison here built at the turn of the century, which is the town's only attraction. Other than that, it serves as not much more than a stopping off point for travelers on their way to Dien Bien Phu. Son La is about two thirds of the way between Hanoi and Dien Bien Phu. It was the site of a surprisingly successful uprising against the French by the Thai people, who took control over the town for a brief period. When the French regrouped and recaptured Son La, their revenge on the ethnic minorities of the town was savage. There is a small guesthouse here where most travelers between Hanoi and Dien Phu stay, going in both directions. Bring your own food and water. Buses leave for Son La from Hanoi's Kim Ma Station, near the intersection of Giang Vo and Nguyen Thai Hoc Streets.

LAO CAI

Lao Cai is on the Chinese border at the end of the rail line, 346 km northwest of Hanoi and 40 km northeast of Sa Pa. This was a former Black Flag capital after the Black Flags drove out the Yellow Flags. The Black Flag leader, known in Vietnam as Luu Vinh Phuoc, was the former Taipang army general who battled the Manchus. Lao Cai was the last station in Vietnam on the French-built train line to Yunnan in the early 20th century. It cost the French perhaps hundreds of lives to build the train line in this rugged area. In 1979, the Chinese took control of Lao Cai.

The border into China is now open, and that's the main reason you'll need to come to Lao Cai. Most travelers will want to head for China's city of **Kunming**, the beautiful capital of Yunnan Province. The scenery around the area is magnificent. Most of the townsfolk have never seen Westerners, although this is changing rapidly. But you will be followed by hordes of villagers wherever you go. If you decide to stay in Lao Cai, there is reportedly a hotel being built for visiting foreigners, but more than likely, you'll be spending the night in the house of a villager. A gift to the host would be appropriate.

There is a hotel in Pho Lo near the railway station (see Hanoi's "Directory"), but it's run down and dilapidated. You can get to Pho Lo by train from Hanoi and, although it continues on to Lao Cai, it is usually reserved for freight. But with the border being open, there have been reports of Westerners reaching Lao Cai by train. Even so, you can change trains at Pho Lo and reach a small village about 10 km from Lao Cai. You can get to Lao Cai by motorbike. Lao Cai is also the gateway to Sa Pa, a magnificent, scenic small town about 30 km from Lao Cai. (See the chapter SA PA.)

DIRECTORY

TRANSPORTATION

Dien Bien Phu is 420 km west of Hanoi, 345 km from Hoa Binh and 110 km from San La.

By air: VN flies to Dien Bien Phu from Hanoi on Tuesdays and Fridays.

By bus: This is an extremely arduous and lengthy trip although the scenery is spectacular. The road is in horrendous condition. When it rains, buses and other vehicles can get stuck in the mud for hours. Buses do leave for Dien Bien Phu from Hanoi but terminate in Son La. I don't recommend getting to Dien Bien Phu by bus.

By 4-wheel-drive: This also is an arduous drive (but far more comfortable than by bus) that takes two full days, but it is a beautiful drive, especially as it nears Dien Bien Phu through hilltribe villages in the mountains. The best way to do it is by renting a Russian jeep and sharing the costs with three or four other people. Count on at least 5–6 days for the round-trip journey. The trip will set you back US$500-plus.

THE CHAY AND HONG RIVERS

These are areas where there was a strong colonial presence, and the French influence in the region is evident everywhere. The French called Hoang Lien Mountains the Tonkin (or Tonkinese) Alps. There are two valleys that parallel the Chay and Hong Rivers which form a topographical pass to China's Yunnan and the provincial capitals of Kunming and Dali.

The area was a strategic trade route, although access was difficult, between Burma and Sichuan. It became a stronghold of Pon Yi refugees who fled Guizhou and now populate the upper valleys. Vietnam's Hoang Lien Son Province is considered to possess the highest mountains in Vietnam. Tourists in the region are few, and only recently have foreigners been allowed basically unrestricted access to the region. Visits to the area will elicit intense curiosity amongst the ethnic hill people, and now that the border to China is open, the inhabitants of this area will be seeing more foreigners, although I dare say that there won't be many, as the following villages are highly inaccessible from Hanoi. But where there's a will, there's a way. And if you haven't drawn up your own will, you might consider doing so before visiting the far north of Vietnam.

SA PA

SA PA IN A CAPSULE

Not easily reached; in fact, it can be treacherous...Sees few tourists but the numbers are growing...Unbelievable mountain scenery...Still retains many French cultural and architectural influences...Has been under the control of at least four different countries over the centuries...Unlike other Vietnamese hill towns, different ethnicities cohabitate peacefully here.

Sa Pa is nearly 1600 meters above sea level in the northern province of Lao Cai, 30 km from the border city and provincial capital of Lao Cai. It is known for spectacular scenery (the craggy hills around the area are called the Tonkinese Alps—at least by tourists—and Vietnam's highest mountain, Fan Si Pan, stretching to more than 3100 meters, is in the area) and the amazing hillpeople called the Hmong. Other ethnic minorities in the region are the White Thai people.

The town has changed hands so many times over the generations, it's difficult to count. It has been under Japanese, French, Chinese, and Vietnamese control at various times in its history. It was most recently rebuilt by the Vietnamese, although the French legacy survives in the form of spacious villas. The place was devastated and pillaged by the Chinese in 1979, and all that remains of the Catholic church are crumbling walls and a statue of Notre Dame De France, which has been haphazardly restored by improvization. The remaining chunks of the statue are held together by pieces of brick.

More ruins of the Chinese aggression include the remains of a fort that stands on an isolated hill overlooking the Sa Pa valley. The countryside is broken up by rice terraces surrounded by the clay and thatch houses of ethnic Hmong. These people wear intricately embroidered collars and dark blue oufits fitted with sashes. They also don bizarre-looking black Chinese umbrellas. Many can be seen carrying wicker baskets on their backs carrying produce, firewood and clothing for trade at the marketplace, which is becoming a main tourist attraction.

The French influence is still evident among the Hmong, many of whom still wear Christian crosses around their necks. The Hmong people welcome the presence of Western tourists who have increasingly become the villagers best customers of items ranging from hats, handbags, bracelets, and sashes to locally-produced medicines, produce, and liquor—a potent locally-produced libation that'll knock you on your ass.

Unlike a number of other ethnic minorities in Vietnam, the Hmong speak Vietnamese (it's a little more bothersome trying to communicate with the White Thais).

Sa Pa is not easily reached. It's better to do it from Lao Cai by horse than any mechanized means. Some of the roadway is under construction, but the ride is a fitful one—the road is hideously rutted and cratered. Lao Cai itself is accessible by train from Hanoi, and cars can be hired for the final leg to Sa Pa, which even at less than 30 km, can take a couple of hours.

INSIDER TIP

The Hmong are a friendly and warm people, but most will not tolerate having their pictures taken. Instead, use your camera for photos of the verdant countryside. In Sa Pa, if you find yourself surrounded by hordes of curious townsfolk and want to be alone, simply take out your camera. They'll react the way most people react to a skunk—they'll flee. You'll find yourself quite alone rather instantly.

WHAT TO SEE AND DO IN SA PA

Sa Pa Market

The market at Sa Pa is the principal tourist attraction. Here, all kinds of locally-made handicrafts, clothes, jewelry, and ornaments can be purchased at prices you'll have to bargain for. Despite the Hmong people's friendliness, they are shrewd negotiators. Chances are they'll make out better than you did. But who else on your block back in Indiana will have a genuine Hmong beaded collar?

WHERE TO STAY AND EAT IN SA PA

Currently there are five guest houses in Sa Pa, none of which exceed minimum accommodation standards—two of them close in the winter time, when temperatures can dip below freezing. But this is expected to change as the number of tourists to the region increases.

Eating is at your own risk. There are no "restaurants" (if you've found one, let me know!) in the town. There are food stalls, but be careful of the cutlery and make sure that any water you consume is either purified or has been boiled for at least 20 minutes. Put simply, Sa Pa is off the beaten track—way off it.

SA PA ENVIRONS

Of course, there's Fan Si Pan, Vietnam's highest peak. It is part of the Hoang Lien Mountains (the Tonkinese Alps), and is accessible by foot from Sa Pa. At present, few foreigners attempt to climb the peak, but the number is growing, as are the number of "guides" in both Sa Pa and Lao Cai who will offer you their services by either car or motorbike (a 4-wheel-drive is the best alternative). Also within walking or driving distance of Sa Pa are the Thac Bac (Silver Falls) and Cau May (Cloud Bridge) which spans the Muong Hoa River.

YEN BAI

Yen Bai is located about 155 km from northwest of Hanoi. This is at the base of the delta. In February 1930, a Vietnamese "army" started an uprising here against the French colonial authorities based on the initiative of the Vietnamese Nationalist Party of Vietnam (Quoc Dan Dang).

PHAN SI PAN

Phan Si Pan is 395 km northwest of Hanoi. This area is the site of Vietnam's tallest mountain, at 3145 meters high. The mountain is climbable, but best done in December. There are tremendously steep slopes, and the wind and rain here make the ascent a treacherous affair.

PACKAGE TOURS

FIELDING WORLDWIDE VIETNAM TOUR PROGRAMS

As a special service to our readers, Fielding Worldwide has by contract associated itself with a select number of Vietnamese tour operators, those we feel our discerning readers will get the most from. If a tour package is the route you decide to embark on for either a brief or extended stay, the following programs come heavily recommended by travelers to Vietnam.

To book a Fielding tour of Vietnam is the easiest possible way of getting the most out of your Vietnam adventure without the hassles associated with trying to book tours once you're inside Vietnam. And remember, group bookings usually include significant discounts.

To book a Fielding Vietnam tour is a snap. Simply call toll free ☎ *(800) FW2-GUIDE.*

We'll take care of the rest. It's that easy.

Or you can book directly through the tour agency by using the addresses and phone numbers provided. But always use the Fielding code "F" when booking a tour directly.

Remember, all tour prices and itineraries listed are subject to change without notice. Call us if you have any questions.

TRAVELER'S INSURANCE

It is strongly recommended that you purchase your own traveler's insurance in your own country, as insurance provided by the Vietnamese Bao Viet Co. (the state insurance company that most Vietnamese tour companies are covered through) provides a minimum amount of coverage, usually not exceeding US$10,000. Fielding Worldwide, Inc. assumes absolutely no legal liability nor financial responsibility in the event of death, accident, illness or injury while participants are enroute to or from and during any of the Vietnamese tour packages mentioned below.

Additionally, you can, for a cost of US$12 for your entire stay in Vietnam, purchase International SOS Assistance. SOS is an organization that provides prompt assistance in the event of an emergency situation while in Vietnam. SOS must be purchased prior to the start of your tour through either Fielding or our associate tour company in Vietnam. SOS members receive the SOS Tourist Program Card which identifies you as eligible for the organization's benefits. The card lists 24-hour contact numbers in Vietnam and Singapore. The card should be carried by you at all times.

In Vietnam, SOS has been approved by the National Administration of Tourism to carry out the evacuation and repatriation of foreign tourists. SOS can provide assistance and send medical teams to the most remote parts of Vietnam. Services available include 24-hour medical consultation and evaluation, referral to doctors and hospitals, emergency medical evacuation, post evacuation medical expenses (hospitalization and medical fees incurred by the member after evacuation will be borne by SOS up to US$10,000), medically supervised repatriation, hospital admittance deposits (any required hospital admittance fee deposit up to US$2,500 will be guaranteed if you are without immediate means of payment), return of dependent children, dispatch of doctors and medicine, companion visit assistance, repatriation of mortal remains, interpreter access and referral, 24-hour emergency message transmission, and legal assistance.

But, again, remember, SOS is not an insurance policy in the traditional sense. Any serious medical problem abroad should be covered by insurance you've purchased in your country. It's wise to purchase SOS if your stay in Vietnam will last more than a few days and/or you plan to travel to areas other than major urban centers. Fielding still strongly recommends you acquire your own personal travel insurance.

Cancellation penalties differ with the tour companies. While some tour companies offer complete or nearly complete refunds in the event of a cancellation, others levy large cancellation fees. It would be wise to check with Fielding or the Vietnamese tour company regarding refunds in the event of cancellation.

When booking a tour offered through Fielding's *Vietnam*, always refer to the full tour number, each of which begins with the letter "F." This signifies to the tour operator that you are a Fielding customer. Even if you book a tour through the following mentioned Fielding-associated tour operators once in Vietnam, still use the full tour number preceded with the letter "F." This lets the tour operator know that you were referred to the tour(s) through its U.S. associate Fielding Worldwide.

Our representative in Vietnam, *Vietnam*'s author Wink Dulles, will also usually be available in Ho Chi Minh City for assistance in making your stay in Vietnam as adventurous and/or as relaxing as possible. The choices in Vietnam are yours, thanks to Fielding.

FIELDING/VOILES VIETNAM TOUR PROGRAMS

Voiles Vietnam
No. 17 Pham Ngoc Thach, District 3
Ho Chi Minh City, Vietnam
☎ *: 84.8.296750, 231589, 231590, 221841, 222844*
FAX: 84.8.231591

"Song Saigon" Cruises off Nha Trang

Off the idyllic and easily accessible coastal city of Nha Trang, countless tropical islands dot the emerald blue South China Sea with precipitous rocks; coconut palm-lined bright sandy beaches, sand dunes, and an undersea world teeming with brightly-colored coral reefs and an array of electric-hued sea life–plus an incredibly diverse environment of flora and fauna. Giant angelfish, white-tip sharks, batfish sweetlips, damselfish, moorish idols, rays, pastel gorgonias, sea fans, sponges, morays, grouper, fighting shrimp and lobsters inhabit these crystal-clear waters. Steep walls of underwater canyons are carpeted with colorful nudibranches, Christmas tree worms and hard and soft corals. Not to mention the number of historical wreck sites.In short, a diver's paradise.

If you're not a diver, you can stroll on untouched, isolated islands of Hon Ho and Hon Cha La, home to thousands of sea swallows. Discover Bamboo Island and the beautiful natural harbor of Vung Coco as well as the primitive villages of Hon Lon Island.

All this and much more is yours through voyages aboard the "Song Saigon," a remarkable and luxurious 30-meter long traditional junk that has been appointed to give 10 passengers the adventure and pampering of a lifetime.

"Song Saigon" has been regally fitted with five air-conditioned, two-person cabins, three bathrooms, a sitting and dining room equipped with video and audio cassette equipment and tapes. On the wide back deck, under the braided palm roof, there are deck mattresses, hammocks and large hardwood tables for meals, including American-style breakfasts and the best Vietnamese food off the coast of Vietnam.

From May through September 1995, Voiles Vietnam offers two cruise packages–one for divers and one for nondivers–with weekly departures from Nha Trang.

FSSGNT1   Departure from Nha Trang aboard the junk "Song Saigon." (4 days - 3 nights)

Day 1   *Transfer from hotel or airport in Nha Trang to Cauda Pier for embarkation at 8 a.m. Sailing between the rocky islands to the south of Nha Trang, including Hon Mun and Hon Mot, where local fishermen can be observed netting their catches. Anchorage at Bich Dam. Bathing, snorkeling. Visit to local fishing village. Discover the pristine beaches on the north side of Hon Tre Island. Dinner and night aboard.*

Day 2   *Navigation to the northern islands of Hon Don and Hon Cha La, where thousands of sea swallows nest. Then on to Hon Lon and the pass of Lach Cua Be to enter the crystalline waters of the natural port of Vung Coco. Anchorage, with dinner and night aboard.*

Day 3   *Sunning and bathing. Meet the inhabitants of Vung Coco. Then set sail for the Hon My Giang peninsula and the magnificent bay of Cay Ban, which teems with rich varieties of coral and tropical sealife. The colorful fishing boats you'll see leave for Nha Trang once a week for food supply. You'll see Ghe Thung, round canoes made from braided bamboo, traditional island families in their huts in the palm-lined shade. Bathing at the beach, snorkeling, village visiting. Dinner and night aboard.*

Day 4   *After breakfast, the junk anchors beneath the green heights of Hon Thi, the monkey island. These mysterious monkeys welcome visitors by leaping from hidden places in the trees into the clear water of a small creek. Then a sail by Tortoise Island and entry into the Song Cai River by canoe past the fishing boats to the Po Nagar Cham Towers of Nha Trang. Lunch aboard and sailing in Nha Trang Bay near the Bao Dai Villas. Leave the "Song Saigon" for transfer back to hotel*

Dates of Departure

All Mondays from May 15–September 15, 1995. Programs leaving on May 22, June 26, July 24 and August 28 are reserved for certified divers. Contact us regarding nondiver programs.

FSSGNT1 — Departure from Nha Trang aboard the junk "Song Saigon." (4 days - 3 nights)

Price Schedule:

US$665
Supplement Cabin Single: US$479
Note: Price includes full-boarding cruise, double cabin accommodation, services, excursions, air-conditioned transportation from hotel or airport to junk, French- and English-speaking guides. The price does not include personal expenses, insurance and extra beverages.

FSSGNTPL1 — Diving Cruise on "Song Saigon" from Nha Trang (4 days - 3 nights)

This itinerary is similar to the one above but is reserved for certified divers only. The land excursions are in the function of the dive program. There will be two or three dives a day led by NAUI instructor Christian.

Price Schedule:

US$865
Supplemental Cabin Single: US$479
Note: Price includes full-boarding cruise, double cabin accommodation, services, excursions, air-conditioned transportation from airport or hotel to the junk, 2-3 dives per day, all heavy equipment (tank and weight system), air and the assistance of a NAUI instructor. The price does not include personal expenses, insurance and extra drinks. Supplemental diving equipment can be rented.

FSSGNT2 — Departure from Nha Trang aboard the junk "Song Saigon" (2 days - 1 night)

Day 1   *Transfer from hotel or airport in Nha Trang to Cauda Pier for embarkation at 8 a.m. Sailing between the rocky islands to the south of Nha Trang, including Hon Mun and Hon Mot, where local fishermen can be observed netting their catches. Anchorage at Bich Dam. Bathing, snorkeling. Visit to local fishing village. Discover the pristine beaches on the north side of Hon Tre Island. Dinner and night aboard.*

Day 2   *After breakfast, the junk anchors beneath the green heights of Hon Thi, the monkey island. These mysterious monkeys welcome visitors by leaping from hidden places in the trees into the clear water of a small creek. Then a sail by Tortoise Island and entry into the Song Cai River by canoe past the fishing boats to the Po Nagar Cham Towers of Nha Trang. Lunch aboard and sailing in Nha Trang Bay under the Cap Mui Chut near the Bao Dai Villas. Leave the "Song Saigon" at Cau Da village for transfer back to hotel.*

Dates of Departure:

All Saturdays from May 15-September 15. The programs leaving May 27, June 24, July 22 and August 26 are reserved for certified divers only.

FSSGNT2   **Departure from Nha Trang aboard the
                      junk "Song Saigon" (2 days - 1 night)**

Price Schedule:

US$280
Supplement Cabin Single: US$200
*Note: Price includes full-boarding cruise, double cabin accommodation, services, excursions,
air-conditioned transportation from hotel or airport to junk, French- and English-speaking
guides. The price does not include personal expenses, insurance and extra beverages.*

FSSGNTPL2   **Diving Cruise on "Song Saigon" from
                  Nha Trang (2 days - 1 night)**

*This itinerary is similar to the one above but is reserved for certified divers only. The land
excursions are in the function of the dive program. There will be two or three dives a day led
by NAUI instructor Christian near Khanh Hoa.*

Price Schedule:

US$380
Supplement Cabin Single: US$200
*Note: Price includes full-boarding cruise, double cabin accommodation, services, excursions,
air-conditioned transportation from airport or hotel to the junk, 2-3 dives per day, all heavy
equipment (tank and weight system), air and the assistance of a NAUI instructor. The price does
not include personal expenses, insurance and extra drinks. Supplemental diving equipment can
be rented.*

"Song Saigon" Cruises of the Mekong Delta and Cambodia

From November 1994–April 1995 Voiles Vietnam offers three
cruise programs, one to and from Cambodia via the Mekong Delta
in Vietnam, one from Phnom Penh, Cambodia to Ho Chi Minh
City and the other exploring Vietnam's Mekong Delta by junk.

Visa Applications and Passing Port Formalities

To get the Vietnam exit visa and the Cambodia entry visa via the
Mekong River, Voiles Vietnam must receive three (3) passport photos and three (3) copies of your passport at least 15 days before the
beginning of the cruise. Passengers must arrive in HCMC at least
two working days prior to the cruise. The Vietnam entry visa can be
obtained at the same time.

Coming from Cambodia into Vietnam via the Mekong River, Vietnamese entry visas are obtained at the Embassy of Vietnam in
Phnom Penh. Two (2) passport photos and one (1) copy of your
passport must arrive at Voiles Vietnam at least 15 days before the beginning of the cruise. Passengers must arrive in Phnom Penh at least
two working days prior to the departure of the cruise.

FSSG MEK1   HCMC/My Tho/Phnom Penh (7 days - 6 nights)

Day 1   *Leave HCMC by air-conditioned van for My Tho. Embark on the junk "Song Saigon." Sail to My Luan, a small village at the junction of a number of canals. Junk anchors. By small boat a visit to a Chinese brick factory with dome-shaped stoves. Tour of the village. Return to junk for dinner.*

Day 2   *Sail through narrow arroyos and bamboo farms. Anchorage off Sa Dec. Visits to a Chinese pagoda adorned with Chinese paintings amid old sampans and the bustling central market. Then by boat to a Cao Dai temple and towers offering fantastic vistas of the delta. Return to junk. Dinner and night aboard.*

Day 3   *Sail up the Mekong. Anchorage in Cao Lanh Province. Disembark and stroll through village. Visits to a Buddhist monastery and a small sugar processing workshop. Dinner and night aboard the junk.*

Day 4   *Leave for Hong Ngu, the last village of any significance before the border with Cambodia. Received by family for meal of local delicacies. Boat trip in the floating markets. Dinner and night aboard the junk.*

Day 5   *Visit a small shipyard on the way to Vinh Xuong port. Dinner and night aboard junk.*

Day 6   *After border formalities, the junk is in Cambodia. The population becomes less dense, cultivating fertile riverside land. Pass pagoda beneath a canopy of sugar palms. At sunset, we reach Phnom Penh's Royal Palace. Anchor in Phnom Penh for the night.*

Day 7   *During breakfast, junk sails up the Tonle Sap River at Phnom Penh. Disembark at 10 a.m.*

Dates of Departure From HCMC:

December 29, 1994
January 9, 1995
March 9, 1995
April 6, 1995

Price Schedule:

US$1300
Supplement cabin single: US$845
Note: Price includes full-boarding cruise, services, excursions, air-conditioned transportation, guide, visa application and port formalities. Not included are personal expenses, insurance and extra drinks.

FSSG MEK21 — Phnom Penh/My Tho/HCMC (6 days - 5 nights)

Day 1 *Meet at port in Phnom Penh and embark on the "Song Saigon." Set sail down the delta passing the Royal Palace, locals cultivating the Mekong region and a pagoda beneath sugar palms. Anchor at Koom San Nar border area at sunset. Dinner and night aboard junk.*

Day 2 *After border formalities, junk moves into the Mekong Delta. Observe small shipyard on the river's bank. Sail on to Hong Ngu. Small boat trip to the floating markets. Family receives passengers for meal of local delicacies. Dinner and night aboard junk.*

Day 3 *After breakfast, junk sets sail for Sa Dec. Visit to the central market and Cao Dai temple and towers for a magnificent panorama of the delta. Dinner and overnight aboard junk near Sa Dec.*

Day 4 *Sail on to Vinh Long in the heart of the delta. Observe markets and sampans loaded with produce. Visit Chinese Pagoda with remarkable ink inscriptions. Return to junk. Anchor at the village of My Luan at the junction of numerous canals. Through narrow arroyos, gardens and bamboo farms are visited under a vault of palms. Dinner and overnight aboard junk at My Luan.*

Day 5 *After breakfast, a visit to a Chinese brick factory with dome-shaped stoves. Tour the village and return to the junk. Junk anchors at sugar processing workshop. Dinner and overnight aboard junk.*

Day 6 *Breakfast. Arrive at My Tho. Junk anchors among brightly colored fishing boats. Disembark junk for air-conditioned car ride to HCMC.*

Dates of Departure From Phnom Penh:

January 7, 1995
February 18, 1995
March 18, 1995
April 15, 1995

Price Schedule:

US$ 1100
Supplement Cabin Single: US$740
Note: Price includes full-boarding cruise, services, excursions, air-conditioned transportation, guide, visa application and port formalities. Not included are personal expenses, insurance and extra drinks.

FSSG MEK3   HCMC/My Tho/Vinh Long/Sa Dec/HCMC (3 days- 2 nights)

Day 1   *Morning departure from HCMC by air-conditioned van to My Tho. Embark on the junk "Song Saigon." Sail the Mekong to My Luan, a small fishing village at the junction of a number of canals. The junk anchors and guests travel by small boat to visit a Chinese brick factory with dome-shaped stoves. Tour of the village. Dinner and overnight aboard the junk.*

Day 2   *Traveling through narrow arroyos under palm vaults, guests will visit bountiful gardens and bamboo farms. Sailing on the junk with anchorage at Vinh Long. Lunch aboard. By small boat, visits to the floating market and a Chinese pagoda with elaborate ink inscriptions. Sail on to Sa Dec. Dinner and overnight.*

Day 3   *Market tour of Sa Dec. Visit to a Cao Dai temple through a flotilla of old ferries and sampans. The towers of the temple offer magnificent vistas of the Mekong Delta. Lunch aboard the junk. Disembark and return to HCMC via the My Thuan ferry and local buses.*

Dates of Departure:

December 20, 1994
January 17, 1995
January 24, 1995
January 31, 1995
February 28, 1995
March 28, 1995

Price Schedule:

US$470
Supplement Cabin Single: US$350
Note: Price includes full-boarding cruise, services, excursions, air-conditioned transportation, guide, visa application and port formalities. Not included are personal expenses, insurance and extra drinks.

FSSG MEK4   HCMC/Sa Dec/Vinh Long/My Tho/HCMC (3 days - 2 nights)

Day 1   *Leave HCMC by air-conditioned van along the banks of the Mekong to the ferry at My Thuan. Cross to Sa Dec. Embarkation on the junk "Song Saigon." Lunch aboard. Visit to a Cao Dai temple through a flotilla of old ferries and sampans. The towers of the temple offer magnificent vistas of the Mekong Delta. Sail to Vinh Long. Dinner and overnight aboard.*

Day 2   *Anchorage at Vinh Long. Breakfast aboard. Tour bustling Vinh Long. By small boat, visits to the floating market and a Chinese pagoda with elaborate ink inscriptions. Lunch aboard. Sail to My Luan, a small fishing village at the junction of a number of canals. The junk anchors and guests travel by small boat to visit a Chinese brick factory with dome-shaped stoves. Tour of the village. Dinner and overnight aboard the junk.*

FSSG MEK4   HCMC/Sa Dec/Vinh Long/My Tho/HCMC
(3 days - 2 nights)

Day 3   *Traveling through narrow arroyos under thick palm vaults, guests will visit boun-tiful gardens and bamboo farms. Return to junk and have lunch while sailing on to My Tho, where the junk anchors amongst colorful fishing boats and sampans. Dis-embark and take van back to HCMC.*

Dates of Departure:

December 23, 1994
January 20, 1995
January 27, 1995
February 3, 1995
March 3, 1995
March 31, 1995

Price Schedule:

US$470
Supplement Cabin Single: US$350
Note: Price includes full-boarding cruise, services, excursions, air-conditioned transportation, guide, visa application and port formalities. Not included are personal expenses, insurance and extra drinks.

FIELDING/DALAT TOUR PROGRAMS

Dalat Tourist

Head Office: No. 4 Tran Quoc Toan Street
Dalat City, Lam Dong Province, Vietnam
☎: 84.63.22725, 22304
FAX: 84.63.22667

Representative Office

Ho Chi Minh City: No. 21 Nguyen An Ninh Street
District 1, Ho Chi Minh City, Vietnam
☎: 84.8.230227, 230485
FAX: 84.8.222347

General Information

1. Tour charges comprise:

- Accommodation based on double occupancy
- Entrance fees (for sightseeing)
- Tour guide
- Domestic Air fares
- Service Charge
- Food (breakfast, lunch and dinner)
- Visa application fee

- Transportation

2. Tour charges do not include:
   - Beverages
   - Airport tax

3. All prices are subject to change without notice.

FDLT1   HCMC/Dalat/HCMC (4 days - 3 nights)

Day 1   *Airport transfer and/or meeting guests at the hotel. Leave for Dalat. Lunch at Bao Loc restaurant. Then a visit to Prenn Waterfalls. Continue to Dalat. Check in at the hotel. Dinner. Free evening.*

Day 2   *Breakfast. Then visits to the Flower Garden, Valley of Love and LiSon Pagoda. Lunch. Then visits to Cam Ly Waterfall, Bao Dai's Palace, and the Dalat Market. Dinner. Free evening.*

Day 3   *Breakfast. Hiking tour to Lang Bian mountains. Lunch. Visit to a Chinese pagoda and a stroll around beautiful Xuan Huong Lake. Dinner. Free evening.*

Day 4   *Breakfast. Leave for HCMC. Lunch at a Bao Loc restaurant. Then on to HCMC. Check in at the hotel. Tour concludes.*

1 Person: US$590 ea.	*5 Person: US$277 ea.*	*9 Person: US$242 ea.*
2 Person: US$386 ea.	*6 Person: US$261 ea.*	*10 Person: US$236 ea.*
3 Person: US$318 ea.	*7 Person: US$259 ea.*	*11 Person: US$231 ea.*
4 Person: US$284 ea.	*8 Person: US$249 ea.*	*12 Person: US$227 ea.*

FDLT2   HCMC/Vung Tau/HCMC (3 days - 2 nights)

Day 1   *Meeting of guests at Ho Chi Minh City's TSN Airport. Transfer to the luxurious Saigon Floating Hotel.*

Day 2   *Breakfast. Leave for Vung Tau, the Saigon area's premier beach resort. Check-in at the Rex Hotel. Sunbathing, swimming. Lunch. Visits to Gautama Buddha Statue and the White Palace. Then leisure and swimming at Bai Dua Beach.*

Day 3   *Breakfast. Swimming and sunbathing. Return to HCMC for dinner and overnight.*

Day 4   *Breakfast. Transfer to TSN Airport and the seeing off of guests.*

1 Person: US$745 ea.	*5 Person: US$504 ea.*	*9 Person: US$477 ea.*
2 Person: US$590 ea.	*6 Person: US$492 ea.*	*10 Person: US$473 ea.*
3 Person: US$538 ea.	*7 Person: US$490 ea.*	*11 Person: US$470 ea.*
4 Person: US$512 ea.	*8 Person: US$483 ea.*	*12 Person: US$467 ea.*

FDLT3 — HCMC/Cu Chi/Tay Ninh/MyTho/HCMC (5 days - 4 nights)

Day 1 *Guests are met at the airport. Transfer to hotel. Free to explore HCMC.*

Day 2 *Breakfast. Leave for My Tho in the Mekong Delta. Boating excursion along the Mekong River. Lunch. A visit to Vinh Trang Pagoda. Back to HCMC.*

Day 3 *Breakfast. Visit to the famed Cu Chi tunnels. Then on to the Cao Dai capital of Tay Ninh. Visit Cao Dai Pagoda. Lunch at "Cay Mai" restaurant. Back to HCMC.*

Day 4 *Day tour of HCMC, visiting the Museum of History, Vinh Nghiem Pagoda, Thong Nhat Conference Hall, the War Crimes Museum and Ben Thanh Market.*

Day 5 *Breakfast. Transfer to TSN Airport. End of the tour.*

1 Person: US$541 ea.	5 Person: US$317 ea.	9 Person: US$292 ea.
2 Person: US$396 ea.	6 Person: US$306 ea.	10 Person: US$288 ea.
3 Person: US$348 ea.	7 Person: US$304 ea.	11 Person: US$285 ea.
4 Person: US$324 ea.	8 Person: US$297 ea.	12 Person: US$282 ea.

FDLT4 — Hanoi/Ha Long/Haiphong/Hue/Danang/HCMC (8 days - 7 nights)

Day 1 *Meeting of guests at Noi Bai Airport, with transfer to Saigon Hotel.*

Day 2 *A half-day city tour of Hanoi before leaving for Ha Long Bay, where you'll check in at the Ha Long I Hotel.*

Day 3 *Cruising tour of Ha Long Bay. Check in at the Peace Hotel. Evening free.*

Day 4 *Return to Hanoi. Check-in at Saigon Hotel. Evening free.*

Day 5 *Transfer to airport and flight to Hue. Visits to Tu Duc Mausoleum and the Museum of Hue. Check-in at Century Hotel.*

Day 6 *Leave for Danang. Visit to the Marble Mountains. Check-in at Hai Au Hotel.*

Day 7 *Fly to HCMC. Half-day city tour. Check-in at the Majestic Hotel.*

Day 8 *Transfer to Saigon's TSN Airport. End of tour.*

1 Person: US$1165 ea.	5 Person: US$786 ea.	9 Person: US$744 ea.
2 Person: US$920 ea.	6 Person: US$768 ea.	10 Person: US$737 ea.
3 Person: US$838 ea.	7 Person: US$764 ea.	11 Person: US$731 ea.
4 Person: US$797 ea.	8 Person: US$753 ea.	12 Person: US$727 ea.

FDLT5 — HCMC/Vung Tau/Dalat/HCMC (8 days - 7 nights)

Day 1 *Meeting of guests at TSN Airport. Transfer to the Floating Hotel.*

Day 2 *Breakfast. Departure for Vung Tau. Check-in at the Rex Hotel. Swimming and sunbathing. Lunch. Visits to Gautama Buddha Statue and White Palace. Swimming and sunbathing at Bai Dua Beach. Dinner.*

FDLT5 — HCMC/Vung Tau/Dalat/HCMC (8 days - 7 nights)

Day 3   *Breakfast. Leave for Dalat. Lunch at Bao Loc restaurant. Visit to Dam Ri Waterfall. Continue to Dalat. Check-in at Anh Dao Hotel.*

Day 4   *Breakfast and visits to the Valley of Love and Linh Son Pagoda. Lunch. Visit Cam Ly Waterfalls and Bao Dai's Summer Palace.*

Day 5   *Breakfast. Visits to the Dalat Market and ethnic villages.*

Day 6   *Breakfast. Leave for HCMC.*

Day 7   *Half-day city tour of HCMC. Rest of the day free.*

Day 8   *Breakfast and transfer to TSN Airport. Guests will be seen off. End of tour.*

1 Person: US$1348 ea.	5 Person: US$874 ea.	9 Person: US$822 ea.
2 Person: US$1042 ea.	6 Person: US$851 ea.	10 Person: US$813 ea.
3 Person: US$940 ea.	7 Person: US$846 ea.	11 Person: US$806 ea.
4 Person: US$889 ea.	8 Person: US$832 ea.	12 Person: US$800 ea.

FDLT6 — Hanoi/Ha Long Bay/Haiphong/Danang/Quy Nhon/Nha Trang/Dalat/HCMC (13 days - 12 nights)

Day 1   *Meeting of guests at Noi Bai Airport. Transfer to Saigon Hotel. Visits to Ngoc Son Temple and the Fine Arts Museum.*

Day 2   *Visits to Ho Chi Minh's Mausoleum and Quan Thanh Temple. Leave for Ha Long Bay. Check-in at the Ha Long 1 Hotel.*

Day 3   *Cruising tour of Ha Long Bay. Overnight on Peace Island.*

Day 4   *Depart for Haiphong with a visit to Cat Ba Island. Check-in at Huu Nghi Hotel.*

Day 5   *Breakfast and departure for Hanoi. Check-in at the Saigon Hotel. Evening free.*

Day 6   *Transfer to airport for flight to Danang. Then transfer to Hue. Visits to Thien Mu Pagoda and Tu Duc Mausoleum. Check-in at the Century Hotel.*

Day 7   *Leave for Danang. Half-day city tour and then check-in at Hai Au Hotel.*

Day 8   *Leave for Quy Nhon. Check-in at Quy Nhon Hotel.*

Day 9   *Leave for Nha Trang. Check-in at Hai Yen Hotel. Visits to the Oceanographic Institute and Hon Chong Beach for swimming and sunbathing.*

Day 10   *Leave for Dalat with a visit to the Prenn Waterfalls on the way. On to Dalat. Check-in at Anh Dao Hotel.*

Day 11   *Visits to Linh Son Pagoda, Bao Dai's Summer Palace, and the Dalat Market for shopping before departure to HCMC. Check-in at the Majestic Hotel.*

Day 12   *Visits to Thong Nhat Conference Hall, Vinh Nghiem Pagoda, Nha Rong Wharf and the Lacquerware Factory. Shopping at Ben Thanh Market. Rest of the day free.*

FDLT6	Hanoi/Ha Long Bay/Haiphong/ Danang/Quy Nhon/Nha Trang/ Dalat/HCMC (13 days - 12 nights)

Day 13　Check-out and transfer to TSN Airport. End of the tour.

1 Person: US$1920 ea.	5 Person: US$1082 ea.	9 Person: US$989 ea.
2 Person: US$1377 ea.	6 Person: US$1041 ea.	10 Person: US$974 ea.
3 Person: US$1196 ea.	7 Person: US$1034 ea.	11 Person: US$961 ea.
4 Person: US$1106 ea.	8 Person: US$1009 ea.	12 Person: US$951 ea.

FDLT7	Hunting Tour in Dalat (6 days - 5 nights)

Day 1　Meeting of guests at Saigon's TSN Airport. Transfer to hotel for check-in before a city tour of HCMC. Rest of the day free.

Day 2　Leave for Dalat. Lunch at Bao Loc restaurant. On to Dalat. Check-in at Ngoc Lan or Duy Tan Hotels. Dinner. At 7 p.m., leave for Tuyen Lam Lake where canoes will take guests to the hunting area. Return to hotel at midnight.

Day 3　Breakfast. Morning free. Half-day city tour of Dalat. Dinner at the hotel. Depart for Da Nhim Lake at 5 p.m., entering the hunting area by canoe. Return to the hotel the next morning.

Day 4　Breakfast. Morning free. Visit Dalat Market. Dancing at 10 p.m.

Day 5　Breakfast. Leave for HCMC. Lunch at Bao Loc restaurant with regional specialties. City tour of HCMC. Evening free.

Day 6　Breakfast and transfer to airport. End of tour.

1 Person: US$1119 ea.	5 Person: US$538 ea.	9 Person: US$476 ea.
2 Person: US$732 ea.	6 Person: US$508 ea.	10 Person: US$463 ea.
3 Person: US$603 ea.	7 Person: US$496 ea.	11 Person: US$452 ea.
4 Person: US$540 ea.	8 Person: US$477 ea.	12 Person: US$443 ea.

FDLT8	The Golfer's Tour. HCMC/Dalat/HCMC (5 days - 4 nights)

Day 1　Meeting of guests at TSN Airport. Transfer to hotel. City tour of HCMC.

Day 2　Breakfast and departure for Dalat. Lunch at Bao Loc restaurant. On to Dalat. Check-in at Anh Dao, Ngoc Lan or Duy Tan Hotels. Dinner. Free evening.

Day 3　Breakfast and transfer to the golf course. Lunch. City tour.

Day 4　Breakfast before checking out for HCMC. Stops at Prenn Waterfalls and Bao Loc for lunch. Visit Dam Ri Waterfalls. On to HCMC. Check-in at the hotel. Free evening.

FDLT8 — The Golfer's Tour. HCMC/Dalat/HCMC (5 days - 4 nights)

Day 5 *Breakfast before check-out. Shopping and then transfer to TSN Airport for send-off. End of tour.*

1 Person: US$1065 ea.	5 Person: US$703 ea.	9 Person: US$663 ea.
2 Person: US$831 ea.	6 Person: US$685 ea.	10 Person: US$656 ea.
3 Person: US$753 ea.	7 Person: US$681 ea.	11 Person: US$651 ea.
4 Person: US$714 ea.	8 Person: US$671 ea.	12 Person: US$646 ea.

FDLT9 — HCMC/Nha Trang/Danang/Hue/Hanoi/Ha Long Bay (12 days - 11 nights)

Day 1 *Meeting of guests at HCMC's TSN Airport. Transfer to hotel. Lunch. Half-day city tour.*

Day 2 *Breakfast. Leave for Nha Trang. Check-in at the hotel. Lunch. Rest of the day free for sight-seeing and entertainment.*

Day 3 *Breakfast before visiting and bathing in the Mineral Stream of Truong Xuan (Long Youth). Lunch at Ninh Hoa. Visits to Hon Chong Beach, Po Nagar Cham Temple and Long Tu Pagoda. Swimming and sunbathing. Shopping. Dinner. Evening free.*

Day 4 *Breakfast. Leave for Danang. Lunch and then a city tour of Danang.*

Day 5 *Swimming and sunbathing at China Beach. Lunch. Leave for Hue. Check-in at the hotel. Rest of the day free.*

Day 6 *Breakfast. Visits to Tu Duc Mausoleum and the Hue Museum. Rest of the day free for sight-seeing and entertainment.*

Day 7 *Breakfast. Transfer to airport for flight to Hanoi. Check-in at the hotel. Rest of the day free.*

Day 8 *Breakfast. Half-day city tour of Hanoi. Lunch. Leave for Ha Long Bay. Check-in at the hotel. Rest of the day free.*

Day 9 *A cruising tour on Ha Long Bay. Overnight stay on Peace Island.*

Day 10 *Leave for Hanoi. Check-in at the hotel.*

Day 11 *Transfer to airport for flight to HCMC. Check-in at the hotel. Rest of the day free.*

Day 12 *Breakfast. Transfer to TSN Airport. Seeing off of guests. End of the tour.*

1 Person: US$1809 ea.	5 Person: US$1114 ea.	9 Person: US$1037 ea.
2 Person: US$1357 ea.	6 Person: US$1079 ea.	10 Person: US$1024 ea.
3 Person: US$1207 ea.	7 Person: US$1074 ea.	11 Person: US$1013 ea.
4 Person: US$1132 ea.	8 Person: US$1053 ea.	12 Person: US$1004 ea.

FDLT10 — HCMC/Vung Tau/Dalat/ Nha Trang/HCMC/Tay Ninh (9 days - 8 nights)

Day 1   *Meeting of guests at TSN Airport. Transfer and check-in at the Saigon Hotel. City tour with visits to Giac Lam Pagoda, the HCMC Zoo and Ben Thanh Market. Dinner. Evening free.*

Day 2   *Breakfast. Leave for Vung Tau. Check-in at the Song Hong Hotel. Sea swimming and sunbathing. Lunch. Visits to the White Palace, Village of Fishers and Niet Ban Tinh Xa Pagoda. Swimming and sunbathing. Dinner. Evening free.*

Day 3   *Breakfast. Leave for Dalat. Photo stops along the way. Visits to Dam Ri Waterfalls in Bao Loc and silkworm reeling factories. Lunch in Bao Loc. On to Dalat with stops at tea and coffee plantations as well as ethnic group villages. Check-in at Anh Doa Hotel. Dinner. Evening free.*

Day 4   *Breakfast. Visits to the Railway Station, the Flower Garden and the Valley of Love. Lunch. Visits to Bao Dai's Palace, Linh Son or Linh Phong Pagoda and the Cathedral.*

Day 5   *Breakfast. Leave for Nha Trang. Stops at Prenn Waterfalls and Ngoan Muc Pass. Visit Cham temple. Check-in at Nha Trang Hotel. Rest of the day free.*

Day 6   *Breakfast. Visits to the Oceanographic Institute and Tri Nguyen Aquarium. Lunch. Visits to Po Nagar Cham Temple, Hon Chong Beach and Long Son Pagoda. Dinner. Evening free.*

Day 7   *Breakfast. Visiting and bathing in the Mineral Stream of Truong Xuan (Long Youth). Lunch at Ninh Hoa. Back to Nha Trang. Sea swimming, sunbathing and additional visits to Po Nagar Temple and Long Tu Pagoda. Shopping. Dinner. Evening free.*

Day 8   *Breakfast and check-out. Leave for HCMC. Check-in at the hotel. Dinner. Evening free.*

Day 9   *Breakfast. Shopping. Lunch. Transfer to the airport. End of tour.*

1 Person: US$1126 ea.	*5 Person: US$577 ea.*	*9 Person: US$516 ea.*
2 Person: US$769 ea.	*6 Person: US$549 ea.*	*10 Person: US$506 ea.*
3 Person: US$650 ea.	*7 Person: US$546 ea.*	*11 Person: US$497 ea.*
4 Person: US$591 ea.	*8 Person: US$529 ea.*	*12 Person: US$490 ea.*

FDLT11 — HCMC/Vung Tau/Dalat/ Nha Trang/HCMC (10 days - 9 nights)

Day 1   *Meeting of guests at TSN Airport. Transfer and check-in at the hotel. Dinner. Evening free.*

Day 2   *Breakfast. Visit to Cu Chi Tunnels. Lunch. Depart for Vung Tau. Check-in at the hotel. Dinner. Evening free.*

Day 3   *Breakfast. Visits to the White Palace, the Reclining Buddha Temple, the Whale Shrine, the New Market and Front Beach. Dinner. Evening free.*

FDLT11	**HCMC/Vung Tau/Dalat/ Nha Trang/HCMC (10 days - 9 nights)**

Day 4   *Breakfast. Leave for Dalat. Sight-seeing stops at Suoi Tien (Fairy Stream) and Suoi Ba Co (Three Spinster Stream). Lunch in Bao Loc. Stop at Prenn Waterfalls. On to Dalat. Check-in at the hotel. Dinner. Evening free.*

Day 5   *Breakfast. Visits to Domaine de Marie, Linh Son Pagoda, the Valley of Love and Bao Dai's Palace. Lunch. Visits to Cam Ly Waterfalls, Chinese Pagoda, the Mayor's Palace and Xuan Huong Lake. Rest of the day free.*

Day 6   *Breakfast. Visits to Tuyen Lam Lake and Datanla Waterfalls. Lunch. Visits to the Lake of Sighs, Twin Tomb Pine Hill and the Garden of Orchids. Dinner. Coffee at Thuyta.*

Day 7   *Breakfast. Check-out. Visit Dalat Market. Leave for Nha Trang. Visits to Da Nhim Hydro-Electric Dam and the Cham Tower in Phan Rang. Lunch. On to Nha Trang. Check-in at the hotel. Evening free.*

Day 8   *Breakfast. Visiting and bathing in the Mineral Stream of Truong Xuan (Long Youth). Lunch in Ninh Hoa. Back to Nha Trang. Visits to Hon Chong Beach, Po Nagar Cham Temple and Long Tu Pagoda. Sea swimming and sunbathing. Shopping. Dinner. Strolling along the beach.*

Day 9   *Breakfast. Leave for HCMC. Check-in at the hotel. Dinner. Evening free.*

Day 10 *Breakfast. Shopping. Lunch. Transfer to TSN Airport for departure and send-off. End of the tour.*

1 Person: US$1201 ea.	*5 Person: US$631 ea.*	*9 Person: US$567 ea.*
2 Person: US$831 ea.	*6 Person: US$602 ea.*	*10 Person: US$557 ea.*
3 Person: US$707 ea.	*7 Person: US$598 ea.*	*11 Person: US$548 ea.*
4 Person: US$645 ea.	*8 Person: US$581 ea.*	*12 Person: US$540 ea.*

FIELDING/SUPERBCO PROGRAMS

Superb Tourist & Trading Co., Ltd.
110A Nguyen Hue Ave., District 1
Ho Chi Minh City, Vietnam
☎: 84.8.225111
FAX: 84.8.242405

Superbco's Conditions & General Information

1) Charges include transportation, hotel accommodations (based on double occupancy), gourmet meals and guide/interpreter assistance.

2) Charges do not include laundry, taxi for personal use, mail, faxes, long-distance calls, airport taxes, medical and personal travel insurance and all other expenses of a purely personal nature.

3) Superbco Tours shall not be responsible for any personal injury, damage, property loss, burglary, accidental delays and other factors beyond the company's control.

4) Tour itineraries, prices and modes of transportation as described are subject to change without prior notice.

5) Superbco reserves the right to substitute hotels and means of transportation regarding the tours if such changes are necessary due to prior unforeseen circumstances.

Vietnam Veterans' Tours

These tour programs are designed to allow Vietnam War veterans to visit sites in Vietnam where their former units were based, areas of military activity and former battlefields. These tours were specially designed specifically for Fielding readers who were veterans of the Vietnam conflict, as well as for family members and relatives of those who returned home and those who didn't. These tours are not advertised to the general public. Many of these areas cannot be visited by means of any other program than through Fielding/Superbco's packages. Clients will have the opportunity to meet with and reminisce with former soldiers of Viet Cong, ARVN and NVA units.

The tours below are exclusive programs for Fielding readers, both American and otherwise, who served in Vietnam and wish to return to these areas for a number of personal reasons. Fielding/Superbco veterans' tours can take you back to the "Ho Bo Secret Zone," the "Iron Triangle," the Cu Chi Tunnels or to the Tay Ninh Forest, where "Operation Junction City" took place. You can revisit the former Dong Tam base at My Tho in the Mekong Delta or Quang Tri in the former DMZ–even more remote former battlefields in the Central Highlands and farther north.

Additionally, at your request, more specialized tours can be arranged–where you can attend seminars and embark on personal fact-finding trips. You can visit with former field commanders and officers of both sides of the conflict, as well as the different Vietnamese ethnic groups that were involved in the war–all in the spirit of friendship and hospitality.

FSC-VET1   HCMC/Lai Khe/An Loc/Cu Chi (7 days - 6 nights)

This tour has been arranged for veterans of the U.S. 1st Infantry Division (The Big Red One), attached elements of the U.S. 101st Airborne Division, 1st Cavalry Division and the 11th Armored Cavalry Brigade to visit locations of former military action and to visit places of interest and historical significance in HCMC.

Price Schedule:

1 person: US$965
2-3:   US$883
4-8:   US$637
9-14:   US$546

FSC-VET2   HCMC/Tay Ninh/Dong Pan/Cu Chi (6 days - 5 nights)

This tour has been arranged for veterans of the U.S. 25th Infantry Division, 3rd Brigade, the 82nd Airborne Division and their coordinated units, and the 1st Philippine Civic Action Group.

Price Schedule:

1 Person: US$998
2-3:   US$937
4-8:   US$660
9-14:   US$568

FSC-VET3   HCMC/Nui Dat/Long Tan/Vung Tau/ Cu Chi (7 days - 6 nights)

This tour has been primarily designed for veterans of the Royal Australian Regiment, the New Zealand "V Force" and the Royal Thai Army Regiment.

Price Schedule:

1 Person: US$782
2-3:   US$731
4-8:   US$527
9-14:   US$452

FSC-VET4   HCMC/Rach Kien/Tan An/Dong Tam (My Tho)/Cu Chi (7 days - 6 nights)

Specifically designed for veterans of the U.S. 9th Infantry Division and those who saw action in the Mekong Delta.

FSC-VET4   HCMC/Rach Kien/Tan An/Dong Tam (My Tho)/Cu Chi (7 days - 6 nights)

Price Schedule:

1 Person: US$998
2-3: US$925
4-8: US$643
9-14: US$550

FSC-VET5   HCMC/Nha Trang/Quang Ngai/Quang Nam/Danang/Hue/Quang Tri/Cu Chi (12 days - 11 nights)

This tour has been designed for former members of the U.S. 1st and 3rd Marine Corps Divisions and the U.S. 101st Airborne Division to revisit the northern provinces of the central part of Vietnam where a significant amount of fighting occurred.

Price Schedule:

1 Person: US$2143
2-3: US$1843
4-8: US$1235
9-14: US$1204

FSC-VET6   HCMC/An Khe/Pleiku/Kontum/Cu Chi (10 days - 9 nights)

This tour has been formatted for veterans of the U.S. 1st Cavalry Division, 4th Infantry Division and the 173rd Airborne Brigade to visit the principle areas of fighting in the Central Highlands area.

Price Schedule:

1 Person: US$1758
2-3: US$1417
4-8: US$935
9-14: US$765

FSC-VET7   HCMC/Nha Trang/Quy Nhon/Quang Ngai (11 days - 10 nights)

This tour has been specifically designed for veterans of the Republic of Korea Capital Division "Tigers," the 9th Infantry Division, Division "White Horse" and the 2nd Marine Corps Brigade "Blue Dragons" to visit central areas of Vietnam where their units were based and saw action.

Price Schedule:

1 Person: US$1282
2-3: US$1176
4-8: US$873
9-14: US$775

ADDITIONAL FIELDING/SUPERBCO VIETNAM TOURS

FSC1	HCMC/Vung Tau/ HCMC (3 days - 2 nights)

Day 1 *Arrive at TSN Airport. Transfer to hotel. Afternoon city tour with visits to Nha Rong Wharf and Thien Hau Temple in Chinatown. Overnight in HCMC.*

Day 2 *Day trip to Vung Tau. Visits to Nirvada Retreat and Buddhist Shrine and the White Palace. Swimming and sunbathing. Return to and overnight in HCMC.*

Day 3 *Leisure in HCMC before check-out. Transfer to TSN airport for departure.*

Price schedule:

1 Person: US$260
2-3: US$215
4-8: US$137
9-14: US$122

FSC2	HCMC/Cu Chi/HCMC (3 days - 2 nights)

Day 1 *Arrival at TSN Airport. Transfer to hotel. Afternoon city tour with stops at Nha Rong Wharf and Thien Hau Temple in Chinatown. Overnight in HCMC.*

Day 2 *Morning excursion to the Cu Chi Tunnels. Afternoon visits to Reunification Hall, lacquerware workshop, Vinh Nghiem Pagoda or Historical Museum and Giac Lam Pagoda. Overnight in HCMC.*

Day 3 *Leisure before check-out. Transfer to TSN airport for departure.*

Price Schedule:

1 person: US$260
2-3: US$215

FSC3	HCMC/Cu Chi/Vung Tau/HCMC (4 days - 3 nights)

Day 1 *Arrive at TSN Airport. Transfer to hotel. Afternoon city tour with a stop at Thien Hau Temple in Chinatown. Overnight in HCMC.*

Day2 *Morning excursion to Cu Chi Tunnels. Afternoon visits to Reunification Hall, lacquerware workshop and Vinh Nghiem Pagoda. Overnight in HCMC.*

Day 3 *Day trip to Vung Tau for swimming and sunbathing with a visit to Nirvada Retreat and Buddhist Shrine. Overnight in Vung Tau.*

Day 4 *Free morning before check-out. Back to HCMC for transfer to airport for departure.*

FSC3 — HCMC/Cu Chi/Vung Tau/HCMC (4 days - 3 nights)

Price Schedule:

1 Person: US$395
2-3: US$313
4-8: US$237
9-15: US$212

FSC4 — HCMC/My Tho/Vung Tau/HCMC (4 days - 3 nights)

Day 1 *Arrival at TSN Airport. Transfer to hotel. Afternoon city tour with stops at Nha Rong Wharf and Thien Hau Temple in Chinatown. Overnight in HCMC.*

Day 2 *Day trip to My Tho with visits to the Orchard Garden and Vinh Trang Pagoda. Overnight in HCMC.*

Day 3 *Day trip to Vung Tau for sunbathing and swimming, as well as a visit to Nirvada Retreat and Buddhist Shrine. Overnight in Vung Tau.*

Day 4 *Free morning before check-out. Back to HCMC for transfer to airport for departure.*

Price Schedule:

1 Person: US$405
2-3: US$313
4-8: US$227
9-15: US$202

FSC5 — HCMC/Tay Ninh/Cu Chi/Vung Tau/HCMC (4 days - 3 nights)

Day 1 *Arrive at TSN Airport. Transfer to hotel. Afternoon city tour with a stop at Thien Hau Temple in Chinatown. Overnight in HCMC.*

Day 2 *Morning excursion to Cu Chi Tunnels. Afternoon visits to Reunification Hall, lacquerware workshop and Vinh Nghiem Pagoda. Overnight in HCMC.*

Day 3 *Day trip to Cu Chi Tunnels and Tay Ninh. Visit to Cao Dai Holy Temple. Overnight in HCMC.*

Day 4 *Day trip to Vung Tau for sunbathing and swimming, as well as a visit to Nirvada Retreat and Buddhist Shrine. Overnight in Vung Tau.*

Day 5 *Free morning before check-out. Back to HCMC for transfer to airport for departure.*

Price Schedule:

1 Person: US$520
2-3: US$445
4-8: US$316
9-15: US$293

FSC6 — HCMC/Vung Tau/Dalat/HCMC (6 days - 5 nights)

Day 1 *Arrival at TSN Airport. Transfer to hotel. Afternoon city tour with stops at Nha Rong Wharf and Thien Hau Temple in Chinatown. Overnight in HCMC.*

Day 2 *Day trip to Vung Tau. Visits to Nirvada Retreat and Buddhist Shrine and the White Palace. Swimming and sunbathing. Return to and overnight in HCMC.*

Day 3 *Morning excursion to Dalat. Lunch enroute with a stop at Suoi Tien (Fairy Stream) and Prenn Waterfalls. Overnight in Dalat.*

Day 4 *Full day of sight-seeing, with stops at the Valley of Love, Lake of Sighs, the Flower Garden and Bao Dai's Palace.*

Day 5 *Return to HCMC. Lunch enroute. Overnight in HCMC.*

Day 6 *Leisure before check-out. Transfer to TSN Airport for departure.*

Price Schedule:

1 Person: US$735
2-3: US$588
4-8: US$410
9-15: US$366

FSC7 — HCMC/My Tho/Dalat/HCMC (6 days - 5 nights)

Day 1 *Arrival at TSN Airport. Transfer to hotel. Afternoon city tour with stops at Nha Rong Wharf and Thien Hau Temple in Chinatown. Overnight in HCMC.*

Day 2 *Day trip to My Tho with visits to the Orchard Garden and Vinh Trang Pagoda. Overnight in HCMC.*

Day 3 *Leave for Dalat. Lunch enroute with stops at Suoi Tien (Fairy Stream) and Prenn Waterfalls. Evening free. Overnight in Dalat.*

Day 4 *Full day of sight-seeing, with stops at the Valley of Love, Lake of Sighs and Bao Dai's Palace. Overnight in Dalat.*

Day 5 *Return to HCMC. Lunch enroute. Overnight in HCMC.*

Day 6 *Leisure before check-out. Transfer to TSN Airport for departure.*

Price Schedule:

1 Person: US$640
2-3: US$572
4-8: US$362
9-15: US$343

FSC8   **HCMC/Cu Chi/Nha Trang/Dalat/HCMC**
                              (7 days - 6 nights)

Day 1   *Arrival at TSN Airport. Transfer to hotel. Afternoon city tour with stops at Nha Rong Wharf and Thien Hau Temple in Chinatown. Overnight in HCMC.*

Day 2   *Morning excursion to Cu Chi Tunnels. Afternoon visits to Reunification Hall, lacquerware workshop and Vinh Nghiem Pagoda. Overnight in HCMC.*

Day 3   *Leave for Dalat. Lunch enroute with stops at Suoi Tien (Fairy Stream) and Prenn Waterfalls. Evening free. Overnight in Dalat.*

Day 4   *Sight-seeing at the Valley of Love, Lake of Sighs and Bao Dai's Palace. Leave for Nha Trang in the afternoon.*

Day 5   *Full day of sight-seeing in Nha Trang, with stops at Po Nagar Cham Towers, Overlapping Rocks and Long Son Pagoda. Sunbathing and sea swimming. Overnight in Nha Trang.*

Day 6   *Return to HCMC. Lunch enroute. Overnight in HCMC.*

Day 7   *Leisure before check-out. Transfer to TSN Airport for departure.*

Price Schedule:

    1 Person: US$820
       2-3:   US$712
       4-8:   US$657
      9-15:   US$627

FSC9   **HCMC/Cu Chi/Danang/Hue/Hanoi/**
                          Ha Long (10 days - 9 nights)

Day 1   *Arrival at TSN Airport. Transfer to hotel. Afternoon city tour with stops at Nha Rong Wharf and Thien Hau Temple in Chinatown. Overnight in HCMC.*

Day 2   *Morning excursion to Cu Chi Tunnels. Afternoon visits to Reunification Hall, lacquerware workshop and Vinh Nghiem Pagoda. Overnight in HCMC.*

Day 3   *Fly to Danang; transfer to hotel. Visits to Cham Museum, Marble Mountains and China Beach. Overnight in Danang.*

Day 4   *Leave for Hue via spectacular Hai Van Pass. Afternoon visits to Tu Duc and Khai Dinh Mausoleums. Overnight in Hue.*

Day 5   *Morning cruise on the Perfume River to Thien Mu Pagoda, with later stops at the Museum of Royal Relics and the Imperial Citadel. Return to Danang for overnight.*

Day 6   *Flight to Hanoi, with transfer to hotel. Afternoon city tour with stops at the Historical Museum, Quan Thanh Temple, Ambassador Pagoda and the Literature Temple. Overnight in Hanoi.*

Day 7   *Visit to Ho Chi Minh's Mausoleum. Leave for Ha Long Bay for overnight stay.*

Day 8   *Boat cruise on Ha Long Bay. Afternoon return to Hanoi. Overnight in Hanoi.*

FSC9   HCMC/Cu Chi/Danang/Hue/Hanoi/ Ha Long (10 days - 9 nights)

Day 9   *Day trip to Hoa Binh with a visit to a Muong ethnic village. Late afternoon return to Hanoi.*

Day 10   *Leisure before check-out. Transfer to airport for departure.*

Price Schedule:

   1 Person: *US$1850*
     2-3: *US$1292*
     4-8: *US$860*
    9-15: *US$703*

FSC10   HCMC/Cu Chi/Nha Trang/Buon Me Thuoc/Quy Nhon/Danang/Hue/HCMC (12 days - 11 nights)

Day 1   *Arrival at TSN Airport. Transfer to hotel. Afternoon city tour with stop at Thien Hau Temple in Chinatown. Overnight in HCMC.*

Day 2   *Morning excursion to Cu Chi Tunnels. Afternoon visits to Reunification Hall, lacquerware workshop and Vinh Nghiem Pagoda. Overnight in HCMC.*

Day 3   *Leave for Nha Trang with lunch enroute. Overnight in Nha Trang.*

Day 4   *Full day of sight-seeing in Nha Trang, with stops at Po Nagar Cham Towers, Overlapping Rocks and Long Son Pagoda. Sunbathing and sea swimming. Overnight in Nha Trang.*

Day 5   *Leave for Buon Me Thuoc. Afternoon visits to the New Economic Zone and Drong Ksack Waterfalls. Overnight in Buon Me Thuoc.*

Day 6   *Leave for Quy Nhon. Picnic or lunch enroute. Overnight in Quy Nhon.*

Day 7   *Leave for Danang. Visits to the Cham Museum and the Marble Mountains. Overnight in Danang.*

Day 8   *Leave for Hue via Hai Van Pass. Afternoon visits to Tu Duc and Khai Dinh Mausoleums. Overnight in Hue.*

Day 9   *Morning excursion to Imperial Citadel and Tinh Tam Lake. Afternoon boat trip on the Perfume River to Thien Mu Pagoda and Minh Mang Tomb. Overnight in Hue.*

Day 10   *Return to Nha Trang. Overnight in Nha Trang. Free evening.*

Day 11   *Leave for HCMC. Overnight in HCMC. Free evening.*

Day 12   *Leisure before hotel check-out. Transfer to TSN Airport for departure.*

Price Schedule:

   1 Person: *US$3175*
     2-3: *US$1680*
     4-8: *US$979*

FSC11   HCMC/Cu Chi/Nha Trang/Hue/HCMC
(10 days - 9 nights)

Day 1   *Arrival at TSN Airport. Transfer to hotel. Afternoon city tour with stop at Thien Hau Temple in Chinatown. Overnight in HCMC.*

Day 2   *Morning excursion to Cu Chi Tunnels. Afternoon visits to Reunification Hall, lacquerware workshop and Vinh Nghiem Pagoda. Overnight in HCMC.*

Day 3   *Leave for Nha Trang with lunch enroute. Overnight in Nha Trang.*

Day 4   *Visits to Long Son Pagoda, Po Nagar Cham Towers and Overlapping Rocks. Overnight in Nha Trang.*

Day 5   *Flight to Danang. City tour with stops including the Cham Museum. Overnight in Danang.*

Day 6   *Visits to the Marble Mountains and China Beach. Afternoon departure for Hue. Overnight in Hue.*

Day 7   *Boat trip on Perfume River to Thien Mu Pagoda. Also visits to the Museum of Royal Relics and the Imperial Citadel. Overnight in Hue.*

Day 8   *Visits to Tu Duc and Khai Dinh Mausoleums. Afternoon return to Danang. Overnight in Danang.*

Day 9   *Flight back to HCMC. Rest of the day free.*

Day 10   *Transfer to airport for departure.*

Price Schedule:

1 Person:	*US$1285*
2-3:	*US$980*
4-8:	*US$674*
9-15:	*US$493'*

FSC1-   HCMC/Tay Ninh/Mekong
CAMBODIA   Delta/HCMC/Cambodia/HCMC
(10 days - 9 nights)

Day 1   *Arrival at TSN Airport. Transfer to hotel. Afternoon city tour with stop at Thien Hau Temple in Chinatown. Overnight in HCMC.*

Day 2   *Morning visit to the War Crimes Museum. Afternoon visits to Reunification Hall, lacquerware workshop and Vinh Nghiem Pagoda. Overnight in HCMC.*

Day 3   *Day trip to Cu Chi Tunnels and Tay Ninh, with a visit to the Cao Dai Holy Temple. Overnight in HCMC.*

Day 4   *Day trip to My Tho. Boat trip to Phung Island or the Island of the Coconut Monk. Then visits to the Orchard Gardens and Vinh Trang Pagoda. Overnight in HCMC.*

Day 5   *Flight to Phnom Penh, Cambodia. Visa delivery at the airport. Transfer to hotel. Full day city tour with stops at the National Museum, Genocidal Toul Sleng Museum, the Killing Fields and Wat Phnom. Overnight in Phnom Penh.*

FSC1- CAMBODIA
HCMC/Tay Ninh/Mekong Delta/HCMC/Cambodia/HCMC (10 days - 9 nights)

Day 6   *Morning flight to Siem Reap. Full-day tour of the Angkor temple complex. Overnight in Siem Reap.*

Day 7   *Full day of sight-seeing in the Siem Reap area.*

Day 8   *Further excursions of the Angkor complex or an optional tour to Bateay Srei. P.M. return to Phnom Penh. Transfer to hotel and overnight.*

Day 9   *Flight to HCMC. Transfer to hotel. Free day. Overnight in HCMC.*

Day 10   *Leisure before check-out. Transfer to TSN Airport for departure.*

Price Schedule:

1 Person: US$1569
2-3: US$1253
4-8: US$1144
9-14 US$1059

FSC2- CAMBODIA
HCMC/Cu Chi/Tay Ninh/Cambodia/ Nha Trang/Danang/Hue/Hanoi/ Ha Long/Hanoi (18 days - 17 nights)

Price to be arranged. Call for details

FSC3- CAMBODIA
HCMC/Cu Chi/Tay Ninh/Vung Tau/HCMC/Cambodia/HCMC (9 days - 8 nights)

Day 1   *Arrival at TSN Airport. Transfer to hotel. Afternoon city tour with stop at Thien Hau Temple in Chinatown. Overnight in HCMC.*

Day 2   *Day trip to Cu Chi Tunnels and Tay Ninh, with a visit to the Cao Dai Holy Temple. Overnight in HCMC.*

Day 3   *Day trip to Vung Tau for swimming and sunbathing, with visit to Nirvada Retreat and Buddhist Shrine. Overnight in HCMC.*

Day 4   *Flight to Phnom Penh, Cambodia. Visa delivery at the airport. Transfer to hotel. Full day city tour with stops at the National Museum, Genocidal Toul Sleng Museum, the Killing Fields and Wat Phnom. Overnight in Phnom Penh.*

Day 5   *Morning flight to Siem Reap. Full-day tour of the Angkor temple complex. Overnight in Siem Reap.*

Day 6   *Full day of sight-seeing in the Siem Reap area. Overnight in Siem Reap.*

Day 7   *Further excursions of the Angkor complex or an optional tour to Bateay Srei. P.M. return to Phnom Penh. Transfer to hotel and overnight.*

Day 8   *Flight to HCMC. Transfer to hotel. Free day. Overnight in HCMC.*

Day 9   *Leisure before check-out. Transfer to TSN Airport for departure.*

FSC3- CAMBODIA	HCMC/Cu Chi/Tay Ninh/Vung Tau/HCMC/Cambodia/HCMC (9 days - 8 nights)

Price Schedule:

1 Person: US$1569
2-3: US$1253
4-8: US$1144
9-14: US$1059

FIELDING/SOUTH SEA
TOUR & TRAVEL PROGRAMS

South Sea Tour & Travel
75 Pasteur
Ho Chi Minh City, Vietnam
☎: *84.8.297526*
FAX: 84.8.298155

South Sea Tour & Travel - The Vietnam Experts
210 Post Street, Suite 910
San Francisco, CA 94108, U.S.A.
☎: *415-397-4644/800-546-7890*
FAX: 415-391-3752/415-397-4643

FSS1: Vietnam Highlights	Ho Chi Minh City/Mekong Delta/ Cu Chi/Tay Ninh/Danang/Hue/ Ha Long/Hanoi

Day 1   *Arrival in HCMC (Formerly Saigon). Welcome ceremony before transferring to the hotel. City tour and "get-acquainted" dinner with the guide.*

Day 2   *City tour: Chinatown, the Lam Son lacquerware workshop, the Presidential Palace and the Saigon markets. Traditional Vietnamese dinner in a Vietnamese family's home.*

Day 3   *Transfer to My Tho. Visit to the Vinh Trang Pagoda and farmers' villages. Boat cruise on the Mekong River. Visit to tropical fruit orchards and the Snake Farm. Return to HCMC.*

Day 4   *Transfer to Tay Ninh for a visit to the Cao Dai's Holy See Temple. Excursion of the Tunnels of Cu Chi. Return to HCMC.*

Day 5   *Flight to Danang. Visit to the Marble Mountains and China Beach. Transfer to Hoi An (one of the most important trading ports in Southeast Asia during the 17th Century) for a city tour. Overnight in Danang.*

Day 6   *Transfer to Hue. Visit to the Tu Duc and Khai Dinh Shrines and the Imperial Citadel. "King's Night" and overnight.*

FSS1: Vietnam Highlights — Ho Chi Minh City/Mekong Delta/ Cu Chi/Tay Ninh/Danang/Hue/ Ha Long/Hanoi

Day 7   *Visit to the Royal Relics Museum and the Dong Ba Market. Afternoon sampan cruise on the Perfume River ending at the Thien Mu Pagoda.*

Day 8   *Flight to Hanoi. City tour: One Pilar Pagoda, Ho Chi Minh Mausoleum, Temple of Literature and the Old French Quarter. Water Puppet Show or traditional opera performance in the evening.*

Day 9   *Transfer to Ha Long. Visit to Haiphong. Overnight in Ha Long.*

Day 10   *Boat excursion of Ha Long Bay. Lunch on the boat. Return to Hanoi.*

Day 11   *At leisure before transferring to the airport for departure.*

Price Schedule:

U.S. $ / Person (Double Occupancy)
Class A: $2190, Class B: $1990, Class C: $1650

FSS2: Heaven & Earth — Ho Chi Minh City/Mekong Delta/ Dalat/Nha Trang/Qui Nhon/Danang/Hue/Hoa Binh/Ha Long/Hanoi

PLEASE REFER TO OUR BROCHURE "THE NEW VIETNAM, CAMBODIA & LAOS"

Price Schedule:

U.S. $ / Person (Double Occupancy)
Class A: $4390, Class B: $3790, Class C: $3150

FSS3: Out Of Asia — Ho Chi Minh City/Dalat/ Nha Trang/Buon Me Thuot/Pleiku/ Qui Nhon/Danang/Ho Chi Minh

PLEASE REFER TO OUR BROCHURE "THE NEW VIETNAM, CAMBODIA & LAOS"

Price Schedule:

U.S. $ / Person (Double Occupancy)
Class A: $2600, Class B: $2400, Class C: $1990

FSS4: Trekking Expedition — Hanoi/Hoa Binh/Hanoi

Day 1   *Arrival in Hanoi. Welcome ceremony before transferring to the hotel. City tour and "get-acquainted" dinner with the guide.*

Day 2   *Transfer to Hoa Binh. Overnight.*

Day 3   *Transfer to Pa Co. Trekking to Hang Kia. Overnight in a H'Mong village.*

Day 4   *Trekking to Bao La. Overnight in a Thai village. (15 kms)*

FSS4: Trekking Expedition — Hanoi/Hoa Binh/Hanoi

Day 5 *Trekking to Ban Lac. Overnight in a Thai village. (15 kms)*

Day 6 *Trekking to Bac Son. Overnight in a Thai village. (15 kms)*

Day 7 *Trekking to Lung Van. Overnight in a Muong village. (15 kms)*

Day 8 *Trekking to Cho Lo. Transfer back to Hoa Binh. Overnight in Hoa Binh.*

Day 9 *Transfer to Hanoi. City tour: One Pilar Pagoda, Ho Chi Minh Mausoleum, Temple of Literature. Water Puppet Show or traditional opera performance in the evening.*

Day 10 *At leisure before transferring to the airport for departure.*

Price Schedule:

U.S. $ / Person (Double Occupancy)
Class A: $2050, Class B: $1850, Class C: $1500

FSS5: Excursion To Northern Vietnam — Hanoi/Hoa Binh/Son La/ Dien Bien Phu/Hanoi

Day 1 *Arrival in Hanoi. Welcome ceremony before transferring to the hotel. City tour and "get-acquainted" dinner with the guide.*

Day 2 *Morning city tour: One Pilar Pagoda, Ho Chi Minh Mausoleum, Temple of Literature. Afternoon transfer to Hoa Binh. Meeting with the Muong minority in their village. Overnight in Hoa Binh.*

Day 3 *Transfer to Son La.*

Day 4 *Transfer to Dien Bien Phu.*

Day 5 *Full-day visit to Dien Bien Phu and its historical sites.*

Day 6 *Return to Son La. Encounter with the H'mong tribe.*

Day 7 *Return to Hanoi. Shopping at the 36 Guilds. Water Puppet Show or traditional opera performance in the evening.*

Day 8 *At leisure before transferring to the airport for departure.*

Price Schedule:

U.S. $ / Person (Double Occupancy)
Class A: $1650, Class B: $1450, Class C: $1200

FSS6: Hilltribe Discovery Tour — Ho Chi Minh City/Dac Lac/ Buon Me Thuot/Ho Chi Minh City

Day 1 Arrival in HCMC (formerly Saigon). Welcome ceremony before transferring to the hotel. City tour and "get-acquainted" dinner with the guide.

Day 2 Flight to Buon Me Thuot. City tour. Overnight.

Day 3 Visit to the Krong Bong District, the D'Sap and Virgin Gia Long waterfalls. Hiking expedition to the Chu Kty village. Evening tribal party with the Ede tribe.

Day 4 Excursion of the Lak Lake on piraguas and elephant-back ride to M'nong villages. Evening tribal party with the locals (music, dance, food). Overnight in the tribal village.

Day 5 Boat excursion on Krong Ana River and Eao Don Lake.

Day 6 Visit to the Don Village and the "Elephant Hunters" cemetery.

Day 7 Morning at leisure in Buon Me Thuot before transferring to the airport for departure to HCMC.

Day 8 Visit to the Cu Chi Tunnels. Afternoon city tour: Chinatown, the Lam Son lacquerware workshop and the Presidential Palace. Traditional Vietnamese dinner in a Vietnamese family's home.

Day 9 At leisure before transferring to the airport for departure.

Price Schedule:

U.S. $ / Person (Double Occupancy)
Class A: $1800, Class B: $1600, Class C: $1400

FSS7: Mekong Delta 1 — Ho Chi Minh City/My Tho/ Ho Chi Minh City

Day 1 Arrival in HCMC (formerly Saigon). Welcome ceremony before transferring to the hotel. City tour and "get-acquainted" dinner with the guide.

Day 2 Visit to the Cu Chi Tunnels. Afternoon city tour: Chinatown, the Lam Son lacquerware workshop and the Presidential Palace. Traditional Vietnamese dinner in a Vietnamese family's home.

Day 3 Transfer to My Tho. Visit to the Vinh Trang Pagoda and farmers' villages. Boat cruise on the Mekong River. Visit to tropical fruit orchards and the Snake Farm. Return to HCMC.

Day 4 At leisure before transferring to the airport for departure.

Price Schedule:

U.S. $ / Person (Double Occupancy)
Class A: $800, Class B: $700, Class C: $600

FSS8: Mekong Delta 2 — Ho Chi Minh City/Can Tho/ Long Xuyen/Rach Gia/Ha Tien/ Ho Chi Minh City

Day 1 *Arrival in HCMC (formerly Saigon). Welcome ceremony before transferring to the hotel. City tour and "get-acquainted" dinner with the guide.*

Day 2 *Transfer to Can Tho. City tour: Central Market, Can Tho University.*

Day 3 *Transfer to Long Xuyen. Visit to Chau Doc and the Holy Lady Temple.*

Day 4 *Transfer to Rach Gia. City tour.*

Day 5 *Transfer to Ha Tien. City tour featuring the Tam Bao Pagoda and the Thach Dong "Stone" Cavern.*

Day 6 *Transfer back to Vinh Long. Boat cruise on the Mekong River and visit to the Bonsai Garden.*

Day 7 *Return to HCMC. City tour: Chinatown, the Lam Son lacquerware workshop, the Presidential Palace and the Saigon markets. Traditional Vietnamese dinner in a Vietnamese family's home.*

Day 8 *At leisure before transferring to the airport for departure.*

Price Schedule:

U.S. $ / Person (Double Occupancy)
Class A: $1600, Class B: $1400, Class C: $1200

FSS9: Mekong Delta 3 — Ho Chi Minh City/Soc Trang/ Can Tho/Chau Doc/Dong Thap/ Ho Chi Minh City

Day 1 *Arrival in HCMC (formerly Saigon). Welcome ceremony before transferring to the hotel. City tour and "get-acquainted" dinner with the guide.*

Day 2 *Visit to the Cu Chi Tunnels. Afternoon city tour: Chinatown, the Lam Son lacquerware workshop and the Presidential Palace. Traditional Vietnamese dinner in a Vietnamese family's home.*

Day 3 *Transfer to My Tho. Visit to the Vinh Trang Pagoda, farmers' villages, tropical fruit orchards and the Snake Farm. Transfer to Vinh Long.*

Day 4 *Boat cruise on the Mekong River and visit to the Bonsai Garden.*

Day 5 *Transfer to Soc Trang. Visit to the Kmer "Bat Temple" before transferring to Can Tho. City tour: Central Market, Can Tho University.*

Day 6 *Transfer to Chau Doc. Afternoon on your own.*

Day 7 *Visit to the local fishermen's floating houses, the Ba Chua Xu Temple and the Sam Mountain.*

Day 8 *Leave for Dong Thap. Visit to the central market and to the Bonsai Garden.*

Day 9 *Boat cruise on the Mekong River and visit to Tram Chim.*

FSS9: Mekong Delta 3 — Ho Chi Minh City/Soc Trang/ Can Tho/Chau Doc/Dong Thap/ Ho Chi Minh City

Day 10   *Return to HCMC. Visit to the local markets and shopping.*

Day 11   *At leisure before transferring to the airport for departure.*

Price Schedule:

U.S. $ / Person (Double Occupancy)
Class A: $2190, Class B: $1990, Class C: $1650

FSS10: Ha Long Bay 1 — Ho Chi Minh City/Ha Long/Hanoi

Day 1   *Arrival in HCMC (formerly Saigon). Welcome ceremony before transferring to the hotel. City tour and "get-acquainted" dinner with the guide.*

Day 2   *Visit to the Cu Chi Tunnels. Afternoon city tour: Chinatown, the Lam Son lacquerware workshop and the Presidential Palace. Traditional Vietnamese dinner in a Vietnamese family's home.*

Day 3   *Flight to Hanoi. City tour: One Pilar Pagoda, Ho Chi Minh Mausoleum, Temple of Literature and the Old French Quarter. Water Puppet Show or traditional opera performance in the evening.*

Day 4   *Transfer to Ha Long. Visit to Haiphong. Overnight in Ha Long.*

Day 5   *Boat excursion of Ha Long Bay. Lunch on the boat. Return to Hanoi.*

Day 6   *At leisure before transferring to the airport for departure.*

Price Schedule:

U.S. $ / Person (Double Occupancy)
Class A: $1190, Class B: $1080, Class C: $990

FSS11: Ha Long Bay 2 — Ho Chi Minh City/Hanoi/Nam Dinh/ Hoa Lu/Ha Long/Hanoi

Day 1   *Arrival in HCMC (formerly Saigon). Welcome ceremony before transferring to the hotel. City tour and "get-acquainted" dinner with the guide.*

Day 2   *Visit to the Cu Chi Tunnels. Afternoon city tour: Chinatown, the Lam Son lacquerware workshop and the Presidential Palace. Traditional Vietnamese dinner in a Vietnamese family's home.*

Day 3   *Flight to Hanoi. City tour: One Pilar Pagoda, Ho Chi Minh Mausoleum, Temple of Literature and the Old French Quarter. Water Puppet Show or traditional opera performance in the evening.*

Day 4   *Transfer to Nam Dinh. Visit to Tran King's Temple, Minh and Co Le Temple. Transfer to Hoa Lu.*

FSS11: Ha Long Bay 2 — Ho Chi Minh City/Hanoi/Nam Dinh/ Hoa Lu/Ha Long/Hanoi

Day 5   *Visit to Phat Diem Cathedral in Luu Phuong. Boat excursion of the underground river of Tam Coc and visit to the Bich Dong Temple.*

Day 6   *Transfer to Ha Long. Visit to Haiphong. Overnight in Ha Long.*

Day 7   *Boat excursion of Ha Long Bay. Lunch on the boat. Return to Hanoi.*

Day 8   *At leisure before transferring to the airport for departure.*

Price Schedule:

U.S. $ / Person (Double Occupancy)
Class A: $1580, Class B: $1380, Class C: $1190

FSS12: Former Battlefield Tours — Ho Chi Minh City/Danang/Hue/ Quang Tri/Khe Sanh/Ho Chi Minh City

Day 1   *Arrival in HCMC (formerly Saigon). Welcome ceremony before transferring to the hotel. City tour and "get-acquainted" dinner with the guide.*

Day 2   *Flight to Danang. Transfer to Quang Tri and visit to the Quang Tri Citadel. Transfer to Dong Ha and overnight.*

Day 3   *Visit to the Ben Hai River (the former demarcation line between South and North Vietnam) and the Tunnels of Vinh Moc. Visit to the Doc Mieu Base (Mc Namara's Electronic Fence), Camp Carroll, The Rockpile, Khe Sanh Combat base, Ashau - Aluoi Valleys and Hamburger Hill. Transfer to Hue and overnight.*

Day 4   *Visit to the Tu Duc and Khai Dinh Shrines, the Imperial Citadel and Thien Mu Pagoda. Coach transfer to Danang and overnight.*

Day 5   *Visit to the Marble Mountains and China Beach. Transfer to Hoi An (one of the most important trading ports in Southeast Asia during the 17th Century) for a city tour. Overnight in Danang.*

Day 6   *Flight to HCMC. Sightseeing tour: the former South Vietnam Presidential Palace, the War Museum, the former U.S. Embassy and Chinatown. Visit to the Cu Chi Tunnels. Traditional Vietnamese dinner in a Vietnamese family's home in Saigon.*

Day 7   *At leisure before transferring to the airport for departure.*

Price Schedule:

U.S. $ / Person (Double Occupancy)
Class A: $1550, Class B: $1380, Class C: $1190

FSS13: The "Reunification Train" Across Vietnam — Ho Chi Minh City/Nha Trang/Danang/Hue/Hanoi

Day 1 *Arrival in HCMC (formerly Saigon). Welcome ceremony before transferring to the hotel. City tour and "get-acquainted" dinner with the guide.*

Day 2 *City tour: Chinatown, the Lam Son lacquerware workshop, the Presidential Palace and the Saigon markets. Traditional Vietnamese dinner in a Vietnamese family's home.*

Day 3 *Transfer to Tay Ninh for a visit to the Cao Dai's Holy See Temple. Excursion of the Tunnels of Cu Chi. Return to HCMC and overnight.*

Day 4 *Early morning departure to Nha Trang on the "Reunification Train." Lunch on the train and late afternoon arrival in Nha Trang.*

Day 5 *Morning boat excursions to islands and visit to the Tri Nguyen Aquarium. Afternoon visit to the Po Nagar Cham site and the Linh Son Pagoda. Late afternoon train departure to Danang. Dinner and overnight on the train.*

Day 6 *Early morning arrival in Danang. Visit to the Marble Mountains and China Beach. Transfer to Hoi An (one of the most important trading ports in Southeast Asia during the 17th Century) for a city tour. Overnight in Danang.*

Day 7 *Early morning train departure to Hue. Lunch on the train. Afternoon visit to the Tu Duc and Khai Dinh Shrines and the Imperial Citadel. "King's Night" and overnight.*

Day 8 *Visit to the Royal Relics Museum and the Dong Ba Market. Afternoon sampan cruise on the Perfume River ending at the Thien Mu Pagoda.*

Day 9 *Morning at leisure. Train departure to Hanoi. Dinner and overnight on the train.*

Day 10 *Early morning arrival in Hanoi. City tour: One Pilar Pagoda, Ho Chi Minh Mausoleum, Temple of Literature and the Old French Quarter. Water Puppet Show or traditional opera performance in the evening.*

Day 11 *Excursion to the Chua Huong Pagoda. Boat cruise. Return to Hanoi and overnight.*

Day 12 *At leisure before transferring to the airport for departure.*

Price Schedule:

U.S. $ / Person (Double Occupancy)
Class A: $2390, Class B: $2150, Class C: $1800

FSS14: Ho Chi Minh City/Dalat/Phan Rang/
Vietnam Nha Trang/Tuy Hoa/Qui Nhon/Sa Huynh/
Bicycle Tour Quang Ngai/Danang/Hue/Hanoi

Day 1 *Arrival in HCMC (formerly Saigon). Welcome ceremony before transferring to the hotel. City tour and "get-acquainted" dinner with the guide.*

Day 2 *Visit to the Cu Chi Tunnels. Afternoon city tour: Chinatown, the Lam Son lacquerware workshop and the Presidential Palace. Traditional Vietnamese dinner in a Vietnamese family's home.*

Day 3 *Transfer to Dalat. Visit to the Prenn waterfall. Check in the hotel.*

Day 4 *Cycle to the Lat village and encounter with hilltribes. Afternoon return to Dalat for city tour: Flower Garden, Whisper Lake, Cam Ly Waterfall.*

Day 5 *Cycle to Phan Rang. Picnic en route. Mid-afternoon arrival. Transfer to the hotel.*

Day 6 *Cycle to Nha Trang. Picnic en route. Mid-afternoon arrival. Transfer to the hotel.*

Day 7 *Cycle to Tuy Hoa. Picnic en route. Mid-afternoon arrival. Transfer to the hotel.*

Day 8 *Cycle to Qui Nhon. Picnic en route. Mid-afternoon arrival. Transfer to the hotel.*

Day 9 *Cycle to Sa Huynh. Picnic en route. Mid-afternoon arrival. Transfer to the hotel.*

Day 10 *Cycle to Quang Ngai. Picnic en route. Mid-afternoon arrival. Transfer to the hotel.*

Day 11 *Cycle to Danang. Picnic en route. Mid-afternoon arrival. Transfer to the hotel.*

Day 12 *Early morning arrival in Danang. Visit to the Marble Mountains and China Beach. Transfer to Hoi An (one of the most important trading ports in Southeast Asia during the 17th Century) for a city tour. Overnight in Danang.*

Day 13 *Cycle to Hue. Picnic en route. Mid-afternoon arrival. Transfer to the hotel.*

Day 14 *Visit to the Tu Duc and Khai Dinh Shrines and the Imperial Citadel. Afternoon sampan cruise on the Perfume River ending at the Thien Mu Pagoda. "King's Night" and overnight.*

Day 15 *Morning at leisure. Afternoon train transfer to Hanoi. Dinner and overnight on the train.*

Day 16 *Early morning arrival in Hanoi. City tour: One Pilar Pagoda, Ho Chi Minh Mausoleum, Temple of Literature and the Old French Quarter. Water Puppet Show or traditional opera performance in the evening.*

Day 17 *At leisure before transferring to the airport for departure.*

Price Schedule:

U.S. $ / Person (Double Occupancy)
Class A: $3400, Class B: $3050, Class C: $2550

FSS15: Scuba-Diving Tour — Ho Chi Minh City/Nha Trang/Dalat/Vung Tau/Ho Chi Minh City

Day 1   *Arrival in HCMC (formerly Saigon). Welcome ceremony before transferring to the hotel. City tour and "get-acquainted" dinner with the guide.*

Day 2   *Visit to the Cu Chi Tunnels. Afternoon city tour: Chinatown, the Lam Son lacquerware workshop and the Presidential Palace. Traditional Vietnamese dinner in a Vietnamese family's home.*

Day 3   *Transfer to Nha Trang. Scuba-diving activities in the afternoon.*

Day 4   *Early morning fishing expedition with local fishermen. Afternoon visit to the Tri Nguyen Aquarium and the Oceanography Institute.*

Day 5   *Transfer to Dalat. Visit to the Datanla Waterfall and the Orchid Market.*

Day 6   *City tour: Cam Ly Waterfall, Flower Garden, Prenn Waterfall, Whisper Lake and Love Valley.*

Day 7   *Transfer to HCMC in the morning. Afternoon visit to the local markets.*

Day 8   *Transfer to Vung Tau. Scuba-diving activities. Return to HCMC.*

Day 9   *At leisure before transferring to the airport for departure.*

Price Schedule:

U.S. $ / Person (Double Occupancy)
Class A: $1780, Class B: $1650, Class C: $1350

FSS16: Business Tour — Ho Chi Minh City/Danang/Hue/Hanoi

Day 1   *Arrival in HCMC (formerly Saigon). Welcome ceremony before transferring to the hotel. City tour and "get-acquainted" dinner with the guide.*

Day 2   *Visit to manufacturing factories and meeting with the managing staff: Thanh Cong Textile Factory, Thang Loi Textile Factory and Legamex.*

Day 3   *Morning meeting with the State Committee for Cooperation and Investment (SCCI) and the Department of Foreign Economic Relations. Afternoon visit to the main locations of investment: Linh Trung and Tan Thuan Export Processing Zone.*

Day 4   *Morning flight to Danang. Meeting with The People's Committee of the Quang Nam Danang Province. Afternoon visit to some potential development sites: graphite mining - glass processing - wood processing - China Beach resorts.*

Day 5   *Transfer to Hue. Visit to local businesses and sightseeing tour.*

Day 6   *Flight to Hanoi. Meeting with the State Committee for Cooperation and Investment, the Ministries of Finance, Power, Communication & Transportation.*

Day 7   *Meeting with the Ministries of Construction, Commerce & Tourism, Culture & Information, Foreign Trade and Commerce. Visit to potential investment sites.*

FSS16: Business Tour — Ho Chi Minh City/Danang/Hue/Hanoi

Day 8   *At leisure before transferring to the airport for departure.*

Price Schedule:

U.S. $ / Person (Double Occupancy)
Class A: $1980, Class B: $1700, Class C: $1580

FIELDING/VYTA TOURS

Vyta Tours

> *52 Hai Ba Trung Street, District 1*
> *Ho Chi Minh City, Vietnam*
> ☎: 84.8.230767
> *FAX: 84.8.243524*

FV1: Vietnam by Bicycle — HCMC/Dalat/Nha Trang/Tuy Hoa/Quy Nhon/Quangai/Hue/Hanoi/Ha Long Bay (20 days - 19 nights)

This tour covers virtually the entire country of Vietnam, and will bring you through diverse flora and fauna, climates and cultures. You should be in pretty good shape for this one. However, we provide trucks and vans for the weary. Although bicycles of touring quality can be obtained in Vietnam, they're few and far between. We suggest you pack your own set of wheels. Accommodations are of international standards.

Day 1   *Arrival at TSN Airport. Transfer to hotel. Tour of Chinatown with a stop at Thien Hau Pagoda. Dinner. Evening free.*

Day 2   *Breakfast. City tour with visits to Reunification Hall, Historical Museum and the War Museum. Lunch. Then visits to the Lacquerware and Handicrafts Center and Giac Lam Pagoda. Dinner. Evening free.*

Day 3   *Breakfast. Excursion to Cu Chi Tunnels. Lunch. Back to HCMC to prepare for the next day's departure. Dinner.*

Day 4   *Breakfast. Bicycle to Bao Loc toward the Central Highlands. Lunch on the way. Check-in at Bao Loc hotel. Dinner.*

Day 5   *Breakfast. Bicycle to Dalat. Check-in at the hotel. Lunch. City tour with stops at Xuan Huong Lake, Tuyen Lam Lake and the Valley of Love. Dinner.*

Day 6   *Breakfast. Cycle via magnificent mountain scenery to Phan Rang. Lunch and a stop at the Cham Towers. Arrival in Phan Rang. Hotel check-in. Dinner.*

Day 7   *Breakfast. Cycle up the coast to the beautiful beach resort of Nha Trang. Lunch on the way. Arrival and hotel check-in. Rest of the day free. Dinner.*

Day 8   *Breakfast and city tour of Nha Trang, with stops at the Po Nagar Cham Towers and Tri Nguyen Aquarium. Lunch. Then stops at the Marine Institute and the Hon Chong Promontory. Dinner.*

FV1: Vietnam by Bicycle	HCMC/Dalat/Nha Trang/Tuy Hoa/Quy Nhon/Quangai/Hue/Hanoi/Ha Long Bay (20 days - 19 nights)

Day 9 *Breakfast. Cycle via a spectacular pass to Tuy Hoa. Lunch at Dai Lanh Beach. Arrival and check-in at the hotel. Dinner.*

Day 10 *Breakfast. Cycle to Quy Nhon via the Cu Mong Pass. Lunch on the way. Arrival and hotel check-in. Dinner.*

Day 11 *Breakfast. Cycle to Sahuynh. Lunch on the way. Arrival. Sunbathing and sea swimming. Dinner.*

Day 12 *Breakfast. Cycle to Quan Gai. Arrival and hotel check-in. Visits to a famous war relic in Son My village and My Khe Beach. Dinner.*

Day 13 *Breakfast. Cycle to Danang. Lunch on the way. Stop to visit the historical town of Hoi An. Arrival in Danang and hotel check-in. Dinner.*

Day 14 *Breakfast and a visit to the Cham Museum. Cycle to Hue via the spectacular Hai Van Pass. Lunch on the way. Hotel check-in and dinner.*

Day 15 *Breakfast and city tour of Hue, with stops at the mausoleums of Minh Mang, Tu Duc and Khai Dinh. Lunch. A boat cruise on the Perfume River to Thien Mu Pagoda. Dinner.*

Day 16 *Breakfast. Trip by train to Hanoi. Lunch, dinner and overnight on the train.*

Day 17 *Morning arrival in Hanoi. Transfer to hotel. Breakfast and a city tour with stops at the Temple of Literature, Ho Chi Minh's Mausoleum, the 1-Pillar Pagoda, West Lake and Ho Guam Lake. Dinner.*

Day 18 *Breakfast. Trip by bus to Ha Long Bay. Visit to Haiphong. Lunch. Arrival in Ha Long. Hotel check-in. Leisure. Dinner.*

Day 19 *Breakfast and a boat cruise on Ha Long Bay with a seafood lunch. Afternoon departure to Hanoi. Hotel check-in and dinner.*

Day 20 *Breakfast. Shopping. Transfer to airport for departure.*

Price Schedule:

5-8 Persons US$1400   *16 and up US$1150*

9-15 US$1250

Note: Fielding/Vyta customers can also choose an opposite itinerary from north to south, with departure from HCMC. Prices include international standard hotel accommodations, meals, entrance fees and boat cruises, transportation and transfers, train ticket, foreign language speaking guides, visa assistance and sightseeing tours. Prices do not include international airfares, personal expenses, airport tax and insurance. However, customers may purchase insurance before the start of the trip through Bao Viet at a cost of US$1.50 per day. However, Fielding strongly recommends you purchase your own travelers' insurance before embarking on a tour in Vietnam.

VIETNAM WAR VETERANS' TOURS

These tours are designed for war veterans to revisit their former bases and camps, areas of military activity and locations of historical significance.

FV-VET1
Program 1

HCMC/Cu Chi/Nha Trang/Quy Nhon/Quangai/Quang Nam/Hue (12 days - 11 nights)

Day 1 *Arrival at TSN Airport. Transfer to hotel. Half-day city tour with a visit to the Army Museum and other areas of interest in HCMC. Dinner.*

Day 2 *Breakfast. Visit to the Cu Chi Tunnels. Lunch. Return to HCMC. Water puppet show and a visit to the Historical Museum. Dinner.*

Day 3 *Breakfast. Trip to Nha Trang with a stopover at Ca Na Beach. Lunch. Arrival in Nha Trang and hotel check-in. Dinner.*

Day 4 *Breakfast. Seabathing. City tour with stops at Po Nagar Cham Towers, Tri Nguyen Aquarium. Lunch. Then on to the Institute of Marine Research and Hon Chong Promontory. Dinner.*

Day 5 *Breakfast. Trip to Quy Nhon. Lunch on the way. Of particular interest to Korean veterans will be Phu Cat Airport, Korean camps, Lo Boi Church, and the Korean-Cuong De High School. U.S. vets will get a chance to visit Cho Cat, Trang Pass, De Duc Airport and Hoang Dieu in Hoai Nhon Quy Nhon. Check-in at Quy Nhon hotel. Dinner.*

Day 6 *Breakfast. Trip to Quan Gai. Check-in at the hotel. Lunch. Visit the 1968 massacre site of Son My (My Lai). Dinner.*

Day 7 *Breakfast. Trip to Danang. Visit to U.S. military base Chu Lai. Lunch. Arrival in Danang. Hotel check-in. Visit to Cham Museum. Dinner.*

Day 8 *Breakfast. Visit to Hoi An and continue to Hue via the Hai Van Pass. Arrival and hotel check-in in Hue. Leisure. Dinner.*

Day 9 *Breakfast. City tour with visits to the mausoleums of Khai Dinh, Tu Duc and Minh Mang. Boat cruise on the Huong River. Visit to Thien Mu Pagoda. Dinner.*

Day 10 *Breakfast and transfer to airport for flight back to HCMC. Boat cruising and island hopping along the Mekong River in the Mekong Delta. Dinner.*

Day 11 *Breakfast. Shopping. Free time. Lunch. Dinner.*

Day 12 *Breakfast. Transfer to TSN Airport for departure.*

FV-VET1 **Program 1**	**HCMC/Cu Chi/Nha Trang/Quy Nhon/Quangai/Quang Nam/Hue (12 days - 11 nights)**

Price Schedule:

1 Person US$1600	*7-10 US$870*
2 US$1300	*11-15 US$800*
3-6 US$1000	*16 and up US$730*

Note: Prices include deluxe hotel accommodations (double occupancy), meals, entrance fees and boat cruises, transportation and transfers, tour guide, domestic airfare and visa assistance. Prices do not include international airfares, personal expenses, airport tax, insurance (an optional US$1.50 per day policy can be purchased, but it is recommended you carry your own travelers' insurance) and visa fee.

FV-VET2: **Program 2**	**HCMC/Lai Khe/Binh Long/Cu Chi (7 days - 6 nights)**

This tour has been designed for veterans of the U.S. 101st Airborne Division, 11th Armored Cavalry Brigade and the 173rd Airborne Brigade to revisit former battle sites, camps, bases and areas of historical significance.

Day 1   *Arrival at TSN Airport. Transfer to hotel. City tour of HCMC. Dinner.*

Day 2   *Breakfast and continued city tour with stops in Chinatown, Thien Hau Pagoda and Phu Tho Hoa War Vestige Site. Lunch. Then stops at the Army Museum of South Vietnam East Zone and Independence Palace. Dinner.*

Day 3   *Breakfast. Visits to the Ben Suc area (the Iron Triangle) and Dau Tieng. Lunch. Visit to An Tay village and nearby areas. Dinner. Overnight in Thu Dau.*

Day 4   *Breakfast. Visits to Lai Khe base and the former battlefield at Bau Bang. Lunch in Bau Bang restaurant. Visits to the An Loc and Soc Xiem areas with a stop at a rubber plantation. Dinner and overnight at Soc Xiem Bungalow.*

Day 5   *Breakfast. Visits to Bong Trang and Nha Do battlefields. Lunch in Thu Dau Mot. Visit to a lacquerware and ceramics factory. Return to HCMC. Dinner and overnight in HCMC.*

Day 6   *Breakfast. Visit to Cu Chi Tunnels. Lunch. Return to HCMC. Shopping, dinner and overnight in HCMC.*

Day 7   *Breakfast. Shopping. Transfer to airport for departure.*

FV-VET2: Program 2 — HCMC/Lai Khe/Binh Long/Cu Chi (7 days - 6 nights)

Price Schedule:

1 Person US$940		7-10 US$500	
2 US$750		11-15 US$450	
3-6 US$590		16 and up US$420	

Note: Prices include deluxe hotel accommodations (double occupancy), meals, entrance fees and boat cruises, transportation and transfers, tour guide, domestic airfare and visa assistance. Prices do not include international airfares, personal expenses, airport tax, insurance (an optional US$1.50 per day policy can be purchased, but it is recommended you carry your own travelers' insurance) and visa fee.

EXOTIC TOURS

FV-EX1: Touring the Exotic — HCMC/Nha Trang/ Buon Me Thuot/Pleiku/Kontum (8 days - 7 nights)

Day 1   *Arrival at TSN Airport. Transfer to hotel. Half-day city tour with stops at the Historical Museum and a water puppet show, as well Independence Palace or Chinatown with a stop at Gia Clam Pagoda.*

Day 2   *Breakfast. Then drive to Nha Trang with a stopover at Ca Na Beach for lunch. Arrive in Nha Trang. Hotel check-in. Dinner.*

Day 3   *Breakfast and seabathing in the morning. Then visits to Po Nagar Cham Towers, Tri Nguyen Aquarium by boat, the Institute of Marine Research and Hon Chong Promontory. Dinner and overnight in Nha Trang.*

Day 4   *Breakfast. Drive to Buon Me Thuot with visits to the hot springs Duc My, the Eaphe War Monument, Draystrap Waterfalls and forests in the western highlands. Hotel check-in. Dinner.*

Day 5   *Breakfast. Drive to Nhon Hoa for a visit to an elephant village. Then on to Pleiku and a visit to a Bana ethnic minority village. Local music and dance. Dinner and overnight in Pleiku.*

Day 6   *Breakfast. Drive to Quy Nhon. Visits to an ethnic minority convent and Quang Trung King's Museum. Hotel check-in and dinner.*

Day 7   *Breakfast. Flight back to HCMC. Visit to Cu Chi Tunnels. Return to HCMC for hotel check-in and dinner.*

Day 8   *Breakfast. Shopping. Departure from TSN Airport.*

Price Schedule:

1 Person US$1100		7-10 US$580	
2 US$900		11-15 US$520	
3-6 US$690		16 and up US$490	

FV-EX1:
Touring the   **HCMC/Nha Trang/**
Exotic   **Buon Me Thuot/Pleiku/Kontum**
    (8 days - 7 nights)

Note: Prices include deluxe hotel accommodations (based on double occupancy), meals, transportation and transfers, domestic airfare, tour guide, boat cruising fees and visa assistance. Prices do not include international airfares, personal expenses, airport tax, insurance (an optional US$1.50 per day policy can be purchased, but it is recommended you carry your own travelers' insurance) and visa fee.

FV-EX2:
Bird and   **Hanoi/Tam Dao/Cuc Phuong/HCMC/**
Wildlife Tour   **Cat Tien/Bao Loc/Dalat/Tam Nong**
(Vietnam   **(18 days - 17 nights)**
Photo Safari)

Day 1   *Arrival at Noi Bai Airport. Pick-up and drive to Tam Dao Hill Station. Dinner and overnight at Tam Dao Hotel.*

Day 2   *Breakfast. Full day of bird and wildlife watching in Tam Dao Forest. Dinner. Overnight at Tam Dao Hotel.*

Day 3   *A full repeat of the previous day's activities.*

Day 4   *Breakfast. Drive to Cuc Phuong National Jungle Park. Lunch. Extensive excursion into the jungle. Dinner and overnight in Cuc Phuong or nearest hotel.*

Day 5   *Breakfast. Full day of nature watching in Cuc Phuong National Park. Lunch. Dinner and overnight in the park or at the nearest hotel.*

Day 6   *Breakfast. Bird and wildlife watching in the morning. Back to Hanoi. Lunch on the way. Hotel check-in and city tour. Dinner.*

Day 7   *Transfer and flight to HCMC. Drive to Nam Cat Tien National Jungle Park. Excursions into the jungle. Dinner and overnight at National Park Headquarters.*

Day 8   *Breakfast. Full day of nature watching in Nam Cat Tien National Park. Dinner and overnight at the park's headquarters.*

Day 9   *Breakfast. Nature watching in the morning. Drive to Bao Loc. Visit to Dam Ri Waterfalls. Hotel check-in. Dinner.*

Day 10   *Breakfast. Visit to Deo Nui San in Di Linh. Lunch. Drive to Dalat. Dinner and overnight in Dalat.*

Day 11   *Breakfast. Full day of bird and nature watching on Mt. Liang Biang. Dinner and overnight.*

Day 12   *Breakfast. Boat cruise to Tuyen Lake for a full day of bird and nature watching in the forest near the lake. Dinner and overnight in Dalat hotel.*

Day 13   *Same itinerary as Day 11.*

Day 14   *Breakfast. Drive to HCMC. Hotel check-in. Half-day city tour with stops at the Historical Museum, a water puppet show and Ben Thanh Market. Dinner and overnight.*

FV-EX2:
Bird and
Wildlife Tour   **Hanoi/Tam Dao/Cuc Phuong/HCMC/**
(Vietnam   **Cat Tien/Bao Loc/Dalat/Tam Nong**
Photo Safari)   **(18 days - 17 nights)**

Day 15 *Breakfast. Drive to Tam Nong National Park. Lunch. Then a boat excursion through the jungle. Dinner and overnight in Tam Nong National Park Headquarters.*

Day 16 *Breakfast. Full day of bird and nature watching in Tam Nong National Park. Dinner and overnight at the park's headquarters.*

Day 17 *Breakfast. Bird and nature watching in the morning. Lunch. Return to HCMC. Hotel check-in and dinner.*

Day 18 *Breakfast. Birdwatching in the HCMC area. Transfer to airport for departure.*

Price Schedule:

1 Person US$2500		*7-10 US$1200*
2 US$1900		*11-15 US$1050*
3-6 US$1500		*16 and up US$1000*

Note: Prices include deluxe hotel accommodations (based on double occupancy), meals, transportation and transfers, domestic airfare, tour guide, boat cruising fees and visa assistance. Prices do not include international airfares, personal expenses, airport tax, insurance (an optional US$1.50 per day policy can be purchased, but it is recommended you carry your own travelers' insurance) and visa fee.

SHORT TOURS

Note: Price schedules for the following Fielding/Vyta tours are based on hotel class accommodations. Class A price schedules are for accommodations in the US$90-120 range. Class B schedules are for accommodations in the US$50-70 range. Class C schedules denote accommodations in the US$30-45 range. Tour prices include double-occupancy hotel accommodations, foreign language-speaking guides, domestic airfares, boat cruising fees, attraction and site entrance tickets, meals and air-conditioned transportation via car, van or bus. Prices do not include international airfare, airport taxes and personal expenses. For children under 11, the price is 50% if the child is sharing the parents' accommodations. An extra charge will be levied on any guest requesting a single room.

FV2A   HCMC (2 days - 1 night)

Day 1   *Arrival at TSN Airport. Transfer to hotel. Half-day city tour with stops at Independence Palace, Historical Museum, Thien Hau Pagoda and Chinatown. Also a traditional Vietnamese music show.*

Day 2   *Shopping. Transfer to the airport.*

Price Schedule:

1 Person (A) US$215, (B) US$180, (C) US$155

2 (A) US$160, (B) US$135, (C) US$125

3-6 (A) US$145, (B) US$120, (C) US$110

7-10 (A) US$135, (B) US$120, (C) US$100

11-14 (A) US$130, (B) US$105, (C) US$95

15 and up (A) US$125, (B) US$100, (C) US$90

Single room request (A) US$45, (B) US$30, (C) US$15

FV3A   HCMC/Cu Chi Tunnels
(3 days - 2 nights)

Day 1   *Arrival at TSN Airport. Transfer to hotel. Half-day city tour with stops at Independence Palace, Historical Museum, Thien Hau Pagoda and Chinatown. Also a traditional Vietnamese music show.*

Day 2   *Morning visit to the Cu Chi Tunnels. Afternoon city tour of HCMC with stops in Chinatown and the War Museum.*

Day 3   *Shopping and transfer to the airport.*

Price Schedule:

1 Person (A) US$335, (B) US$275, (C) US$225

2 (A) US$245, (B) US$195, (C) US$175

3-6 (A) US$225, (B) US$175, (C) US$155

7-10 (A) US$210, (B) US$160, (C) US$140

11-14 (A) US$200, (B) US$150, (C) US$130

15 and up (A) US$190, (B) US$140, (C) US$120

Single room request (A) US$90, (B) US$60, (C) US$30

FV3B   HCMC/Vung Tau (3 days - 2 nights)

Day 1   *Arrival at TSN Airport. Transfer to hotel. Half-day city tour with stops at Independence Palace, Historical Museum, Thien Hau Pagoda and Chinatown. Also a traditional Vietnamese music show.*

Day 2   *Travel to Vung Tau Beach. Sun and seabathing as well visits to pagodas and the White Palace. Return to and overnight in HCMC.*

FV3B   HCMC/Vung Tau (3 days - 2 nights)

Day 3   *Shopping and transfer to the airport.*

Price Schedule:

1 Person (A) US$345, (B) US$275, (C) US$235

2 (A) US$255, (B) US$205, (C) US$185

3-6 (A) US$235, (B) US$185, (C) US$165

7-10 (A) US$220, (B) US$170, (C) US$150

11-14 (A) US$210, (B) US$160, (C) US$140

15 and up (A) US$200, (B) US$150, (C) US$130

Single room request (A) US$90, (B) US$60, (C) US$30

FV3C   Hanoi (3 days - 2 nights)

Day 1   *Arrival at Noi Bai Airport and transfer to hotel. City tour with stops at The Literature Temple and Quan Thanh Temple. Dinner and overnight in Hanoi.*

Day 2   *City tour with stops at Ho Chi Minh's Mausoleum, Ho Chi Minh Museum, the
One-Pillar Pagoda, Hoan Kiem Lake, the Fine Arts Museum, West Lake and the Old
Town area of Hanoi. Dinner and overnight in Hanoi.*

Day 3   *Transfer to airport for departure.*

Price Schedule:

1 Person (A) US$410, (B) US$340, (C) US$300

2 (A) US$320, (B) US$270, (C) US$230

3-6 (A) US$290, (B) US$240, (C) US$200

7-10 (A) US$270, (B) US$220, (C) US$180

11-14 (A) US$260, (B) US$210, (C) US$170

15 and up (A) US$250, (B) US$200, (C) US$160

Single room request (A) US$90, (B) US$60, (C) US$30

FV4A   HCMC/Vung Tau/Cu Chi
(4 days - 3 nights)

Day 1   *Arrival at TSN Airport. Transfer to hotel. Half-day city tour with stops at Independence Palace, Historical Museum, Thien Hau Pagoda and Chinatown. Also a traditional Vietnamese music show.*

Day 2   *Morning visit to Cu Chi Tunnels. Afternoon return to HCMC for a city tour with
stops at a lacquerware product center and the War Museum. Dinner and overnight
in HCMC.*

Day 3   *Morning travel to Vung Tau. Sun and seabathing as well visits to pagodas and the
White Palace. Return to and overnight in HCMC.*

FV4A — HCMC/Vung Tau/Cu Chi (4 days - 3 nights)

Day 4   *Transfer to airport for departure.*

Price Schedule:

1 Person (A) US$485, (B) US$380, (C) US$ 320

2 (A) US$355, (B) US$280, (C) US$250

3-6 (A) US$325, (B) US$250, (C) US$220

7-10 (A) US$305, (B) US$230, (C) US$200

11-14 (A) US$295, (B) US$220, (C) US$190

15 and up (A) US$285, (B) US$210, (C) US$180

Single room request (A) US$135, (B) US$90, (C) US$45

FV4B — HCMC/Cu Chi/Mekong Delta (4 days - 3 nights)

Day 1   *Arrival at TSN Airport. Transfer to hotel. Half-day city tour with stops at the Independence Palace and the Historical Museum. Dinner and overnight in HCMC.*

Day 2   *Morning visit to Cu Chi Tunnels. Afternoon return to HCMC with a half-day city tour. Stops at pagodas, Chinatown, the War Museum and a traditional Vietnamese music show. Dinner and overnight in HCMC.*

Day 3   *Travel to My Tho for a boat cruise along the Mekong River. Visits to Vinh Trang Pagoda and the Dong Tam Snake Farm. Return to HCMC for dinner and overnight.*

Day 4   *Shopping and transfer to the airport for departure.*

Price Schedule:

1 Person (A) US$485, (B) US$380, (C) US$320

2 (A) US$355, (B) US$ 280, (C) US$250

3-6 (A) US$325, (B) US$250, (C) US$220

7-10 (A) US$305, (B) US$230, (C) US$200

11-14 (A) US$295, (B) US$220, (C) US$190

15 and up (A) US$285, (B) US$210, (C) US$180

Single room request (A) US$135, (B) US$90, (C) US$45

FV5A	HCMC/Mekong Delta/Floating Market/Cu Chi (5 days - 4 nights)

Day 1   *Arrival at TSN Airport. Transfer to hotel. Half-day city tour with stops at the Independence Palace and the Historical Museum. Vietnamese traditional music show, dinner and overnight in HCMC.*

Day 2   *Morning visit to the Cu Chi Tunnels. Afternoon HCMC tour with stops including the War Museum. Dinner and overnight in HCMC.*

Day 3   *Trip to the Mekong Delta with visits to the Khmer Museum and Bat Pagoda. Overnight in Can Tho with a Cailong (Vietnamese traditional music) show.*

Day 4   *Boat cruise on the Mekong Delta with a visit to Phung Hiep Floating Market on the river. Experience the delicacies of the region's exotic tropical fruit. Return to and overnight in HCMC.*

Day 5   *Shopping and transfer to the airport for departure.*

Price Schedule:

1 Person (A) US$640, (B) US$510, (C) US$420

2 (A) US$510, (B) US$370, (C) US$330

3-6 (A) US$470, (B) 330, (C) US$290

7-10 (A) US$ 440, (B) US$330, (C) US$290

11-14 (A) US$420, (B) US$280, (C) US$240

15 and up (A) US$410, (B) US$270, (C) US$230

Single room request (A) US$180, (B) US$115, (C) US$55

FV5B	HCMC/Dalat/Cu Chi (5 days - 4 nights)

Day 1   *Arrival at TSN Airport. Transfer to hotel. Half-day city tour with stops at the Independence Palace and the Historical Museum. Dinner and overnight in HCMC.*

Day 2   *Morning visit to the Cu Chi Tunnels. Afternoon return to HCMC with visits to a lacquerware center, Chinatown and the War Museum. Dinner and overnight in HCMC.*

Days 3 & 4   *Travel to Dalat by road. Visits to Prenn, Datala, Camly and Dam Ri Waterfalls as well as the Minhy Tam Flower Garden, the Valley of Love, Linh Son Pagoda and Xuan Huong and Tuyen Lam lakes. Return to HCMC during the afternoon of Day 4. Dinner and overnight.*

Day 5   *Shopping and transfer to the airport for departure.*

Price Schedule:

1 Person (A) US$660, (B) US$520, (C) US$440

2 (A) US$520, (B) US$390, (C) US$350

3-6 (A) US$450, (B) US$350, (C) U$310

7-10 (A) US$420, (B) US$320, (C) US$280

FV5B   HCMC/Dalat/Cu Chi (5 days - 4 nights)

11-14 (A) US$400, (B) US$300, (C) US$260

15 and up (A) US$390, (B) US$290, (C) US$250

Single room request (A) US$180, (B) US$115, (C) US$55

FV5C   HCMC/Phan Rang/Nha Trang (5 days - 4 nights)

Day 1   *Arrival at TSN Airport. Transfer to hotel. Half-day city tour with stops at Independence Palace, Historical Museum, and the War Museum. Dinner and overnight in HCMC.*

Days 2 & 3   *Travel via air-conditioned car or van to Nha Trang. Sea and sunbathing and visits to the Husband's Rock, Tri Nguyen Aquarium, Po Nagar Cham Towers and the Marine Biological Research Institute. Dinner and overnight in Nha Trang.*

Day 4   *Visit Cham towers in Phan Rang and the beaches of Ca Na. Return to HCMC.*

Day 5   *Shopping and transfer to airport.*

Price Schedule:

1 Person (A) US$660, (B) US$520, (C) US$440

2 (A) US$520, (B) US$390, (C) US$350

3-6 (A) US$450, (B) US$350, (C) U$310

7-10 (A) US$420, (B) US$320, (C) US$280

11-14 (A) US$400, (B) US$300, (C) US$260

15 and up (A) US$390, (B) US$290, (C) US$250

Single room request (A) US$180, (B) US$115, (C) US$55

FV5D   HCMC/Hanoi (5 days - 4 nights)

Day 1   *Arrival at TSN Airport. Transfer to hotel. Half-day city tour with stops at Independence Palace, Historical Museum, and the War Museum. Dinner and overnight in HCMC.*

Day 2   *Morning visit to the Cu Chi Tunnels. Afternoon visits to HCMC's pagodas, Chinatown and the War Museum. Dinner and overnight in HCMC.*

Day 3   *Fly to Hanoi. Transfer to hotel. City tour of West Lake and Tran Quoc Pagoda. Dinner and overnight in Hanoi.*

Day 4   *Hanoi city tour with stops at Ho Chi Minh's Mausoleum, 1- Pillar Pagoda, Literature Temple, Hoan Kiem Lake, the Fine Arts Museum and the Old Town area of Hanoi.*

Day 5   *Shopping and transfer to airport.*

FV5D   HCMC/Hanoi (5 days - 4 nights)

Price Schedule:

1 Person (A) US$850, (B) US$710, (C) US$630

2 (A) US$660, (B) US$560, (C) US$520

3-6 (A) US$610, (B) US$510, (C) US$470

7-10 (A) US$590, (B) US$490, (C) US$450

11-14 (A) US$570, (B) US$470, (C) US$430

15 and up (A) US$550, (B) US$450, (C) US$410

Single room request (A) US$180, (B) US$115, (C) US$55

FV5E   Hanoi/Ha Long Bay (5 days - 4 nights)

Day 1   *Arrival at Noi Bai Airport. Transfer to hotel. Half-day city tour with stops at the Literature Temple and Quan Thanh Temple. Dinner and overnight.*

Day 2   *City tour with stops at Ho Chi Minh's Mausoleum, 1-Pillar Pagoda, Hoan Kiem Lake, the Fine Arts Museum, West Lake and the Old Town section of Hanoi. Dinner and overnight.*

Day 3   *Morning departure for Ha Long Bay with a general visit of the bay area. Dinner and overnight at Ha Long.*

Day 4   *Boat cruising on Ha Long Bay with an afternoon return to Hanoi. Dinner and overnight.*

Day 5   *Breakfast and transfer to airport for departure.*

Price Schedule:

1 Person (A) US$750, (B) US$610, (C) US$530

2 (A) US$560, (B) US$460, (C) US$420

3-6 (A) US$520, (B) US$420, (C) US$380

7-10 (A) US$500, (B) US$400, (C) US$360

11-14 (A) US$480, (B) US$380, (C) US$340

15 and up (A) US$460, (B) US$360, (C) US$320

Single room request (A) US$180, (B) US$115, (C) US$55

FV6A   HCMC/Nha Trang/Dalat/HCMC
(6 days - 5 nights)

Day 1   *Arrival at TSN Airport. Transfer to hotel. Half-day city tour with stops at Independence Palace, the Historical Museum and the War Museum. Traditional Vietnamese music show. Dinner and overnight.*

Day 2   *Travel to Nha Trang. Dinner and overnight.*

FV6A — HCMC/Nha Trang/Dalat/HCMC (6 days - 5 nights)

Day 3   City tour and visits to Prenn Datala, Camly, Damry Waterfalls. Also Gougah, Linh Son Pagoda, Bao Dai's Palace, Minh Tam Flower Garden, Xuan Huong Lake and the Valley of Love.

Day 4   Travel to Dalat. City tour with stops at Bao Dai's Palace, Minh Tam Flower Garden and Xuan Huong Lake. Dinner and overnight.

Day 5   Dalat city tour with stops at the Prenn, Datala, Camly and Dam Ri Waterfalls. Also Gougah and Linh Son Pagoda. Afternoon return to HCMC. Dinner and overnight.

Day 6   Shopping and transfer to the airport.

Price Schedule:

1 Person (A) US$820, (B) US$645, (C) US$545

2 (A) US$590, (B) US$465, (C) US$425

3-6 (A) US$550, (B) US$425, (C) US$375

7-10 (A) US$515, (B) US$390, (C) US$340

11-14 (A) US$495, (B) US$370, (C) US$320

15 and up (A) US$485, (B) US$360, (C) US$310

Single room request (A) US$200, (B) US$140, (C) US$70

FV7A — HCMC/Danang/Hue/HCMC (7 days - 6 nights)

Day 1   Arrival at TSN Airport. Transfer to hotel. Half-day city tour with stops at Independence Palace, the Historical Museum and the War Museum. Traditional Vietnamese music show. Dinner and overnight.

Day 2   Fly to Danang. City tour and stops at China Beach and the Marble Mountains, including Ngu Hanh. Dinner and overnight.

Day 3   Visit to the ancient town of Hoi An and the Cham Sculpture Museum. Car trip to Hue. Dinner and overnight.

Day 4   Morning city tour with stops at Tu Duc's, Khai Dinh's and Minh Mang's Mausoleums. Also the Hue Citadel. Afternoon boat trip on the Huong River with a stop at Thien Mu Pagoda. Dinner and overnight.

Day 5   Fly back to HCMC. Visit to the Cu Chi Tunnels. Dinner and overnight in HCMC.

Day 6   Visit to the Mekong Delta with a boat cruise on the Mekong River. Visits to Vinh Trang Pagoda and the Dong Tam Snake Farm. Dinner and overnight in HCMC.

Day 7   Shopping and transfer to the airport.

Price Schedule:

1 Person (A) US$1090, (B) US$885, (C) US$765

2 (A) US$830, (B) US$680, (C) US$620

FV7A	HCMC/Danang/Hue/HCMC (7 days - 6 nights)

3-6 (A) US$780, (B) US$630, (C) US$570

7-10 (A) US$750, (B) US$600, (C) US$540

11-14 (A) US$720, (B) US$570, (C) US$510

15 and up (A) US$700, (B) US$550, (C) US$490

Single room request (A) US$230, (B) US$160, (C) US$80

FV7B	HCMC/Hanoi/Ha Long Bay (7 days - 6 nights)

Day 1   *Arrival at TSN Airport. Transfer to hotel. Half-day city tour with stops at Independence Palace, the Historical Museum and the War Museum. Traditional Vietnamese music show. Dinner and overnight.*

Day 2   *Visit to either the Cu Chi Tunnels or the Mekong Delta. Shopping. Dinner and overnight in HCMC.*

Day 3   *Fly to Hanoi. Transfer to hotel. City tour with stops at West Lake and Tran Quoc Pagoda. Dinner and overnight.*

Day 4   *City tour with stops at Ho Chi Minh's Mausoleum, 1-Pillar Pagoda, Hoan Kiem Lake, the Fine Arts Museum, West Lake and the Old Town section of Hanoi. Dinner and overnight.*

Day 5   *Trip to Haiphong and Ha Long Bay. City tour of Haiphong. Dinner and overnight.*

Day 6   *Boat cruise on Ha Long Bay in the morning. Afternoon return to Hanoi. Dinner and overnight.*

Day 7   *Transfer to the airport for departure.*

Price Schedule:

1 Person (A) US$1140, (B) US$930, (C) US$810

2 (A) US$870, (B) US$720, (C) US$660

3-6 (A) US$820, (B) US$670, (C) US$610

7-10 (A) US$790, (B) US$640, (C) US$580

11-14 (A) US$760, (B) US$610, (C) US$550

15 and up (A) US$740, (B) US$590, (C) US$530

Single room request (A) US$230, (B) US$160, (C) US$80

FV7C — HCMC/Nha Trang/Dalat/HCMC (7 days - 6 nights)

Day 1 *Arrival at TSN Airport. Transfer to hotel. Half-day city tour with stops at Independence Palace, the Historical Museum and the War Museum. Traditional Vietnamese music show. Dinner and overnight.*

Day 2 *Morning visit to the Cu Chi Tunnels. Afternoon city tour with stops at a lacquerware product center, the War Museum and Chinatown. Dinner and overnight in HCMC.*

Days 3 & 4 *Travel to Dalat. Hotel check-in. City tour and visits to Prenn Datala, Camly, Damry Waterfalls. Also Gougah, Linh Son Pagoda, Bao Dai's Palace, Minh Tam Flower Garden, Xuan Huong Lake and the Valley of Love. Leave for Nha Trang in the afternoon of Day 4. Dinner and overnight in Nha Trang.*

Day 5 *Sea and sunbathing as well as visits to Husband's Rock, Tri Nguyen Aquarium, Po Nagar Cham Towers and the Marine Biological Research Institute. Dinner and overnight.*

Day 6 *Return to HCMC, visiting Cham towers on the way back. Dinner and overnight in HCMC.*

Day 7 *Shopping and transfer to the airport.*

Price Schedule:

1 Person (A) US$950, (B) US$740, (C) US$620

2 (A) US$710, (B) US$560, (C) US$500

3-6 (A) US$650, (B) US$500, (C) US$440

7-10 (A) US$610, (B) US$460, (C) US$400

11-14 (A) US$580, (B) US$430, (C) US$370

15 and up (A) US$565, (B) US$415, (C) US$355

Single room request (A) US$230, (B) US$160, (C) US$80

FV8A — HCMC/Danang/Hue/Hanoi (8 days - 7 nights)

Day 1 *Arrival at TSN Airport. Transfer to hotel. Half-day city tour with stops at Independence Palace, the Historical Museum and the War Museum. Traditional Vietnamese music show. Dinner and overnight.*

Day 2 *Morning visit to the Cu Chi Tunnels. Afternoon HCMC city tour with stops at a lacquerware product center, the War Museum, Chinatown and various significant pagodas.. Dinner and overnight in HCMC.*

Day 3 *Fly to Danang. City tour and visits to China Beach and the Marble Mountain Ngu Hanh. Dinner and overnight.*

Day 4 *Visits to Hoi An and the Cham Sculpture Museum. Travel to Hue. Hotel check-in. Dinner and overnight in Hue.*

FV8A	**HCMC/Danang/Hue/Hanoi** **(8 days - 7 nights)**

Day 5   *City tour with visits to the Hue Citadel and the mausoleums of Tu Duc, Khai Dinh and Minh Mang. Afternoon boat trip on the Huong river with a stop at Thien Mu Pagoda. Dinner and overnight in Hue.*

Day 6   *Fly to Hanoi and hotel check-in. General city tour with stops at the Temple of Literature and Hoan Kiem Lake. Dinner and overnight.*

Day 7   *City tour with stops at Ho Chi Minh's Mausoleum, West Lake, 1-Pillar Pagoda, Tran Quoc Pagoda, the Fine Arts Museum and the Old Town area. of Hanoi. Dinner and overnight.*

Day 8   *Shopping and transfer to airport.*

Price Schedule:

1 Person (A) US$1250, (B) US$1000, (C) US$870

2 (A) US$970, (B) US$800, (C) US$730

3-6 (A) US$880, (B) US$710, (C) US$640

7-10 (A) US$840, (B) US$670, (C) US$600

11-14 (A) US$810, (B) US$640, (C) US$570

15 and up (A) US$780, (B) US$610, (C) US$540

Single room request (A) US$270, (B) US$180, (C) US$90

FV9A	**HCMC/Dalat/Nha Trang/** **Danang/Hue/HCMC (9 days - 8 nights)**

Day 1   *Arrival at TSN Airport. Transfer to hotel. Half-day city tour with stops at Independence Palace, the Historical Museum and the War Museum. Traditional Vietnamese music show. Dinner and overnight.*

Day 2   *Morning visit to the Cu Chi Tunnels and then travel to Dalat. Check-in at the hotel. Dinner and overnight.*

Day 3   *City tour and visits to Prenn Datala, Camly, Damry Waterfalls. Also Gougah, Linh Son Pagoda, Bao Dai's Palace, Minh Tam Flower Garden, Xuan Huong Lake and the Valley of Love. Dinner and overnight in Dalat.*

Day 4   *Travel to Nha Trang. Hotel check-in. Sea and sunbathing as well as visits to Husband's Rock, Tri Nguyen Aquarium, Po Nagar Cham Towers and the Marine Biological Research Institute. Dinner and overnight.*

Day 5   *Travel to Danang observing the remarkable scenery. Dinner and overnight.*

Day 6   *Visits to the ancient town of Hoi An and the Cham Sculpture Museum. Car travel to Hue. Hotel check-in, dinner and overnight.*

Day 7   *City tour of Hue with visits to the Hue Citadel and the mausoleums of Tu Duc, Khai Dinh and Minh Mang. Afternoon boat trip on the Huong river with a stop at Thien Mu Pagoda. Dinner and overnight in Hue.*

FV9A — HCMC/Dalat/Nha Trang/ Danang/Hue/HCMC (9 days - 8 nights)

Day 8   *Fly back to HCMC. Dinner and overnight.*

Day 9   *Shopping and transfer to airport.*

Price Schedule:

1 Person (A) US$1380, (B) US$1100, (C) US$940

2 (A) US$1080, (B) US$880, (C) US$800

3-6 (A) US$980, (B) US$780, (C) US$700

7-10 (A) US$940, (B) US$740, (C) US$660

11-14 (A) US$910, (B) US$710, (C) US$630

15 and up (A) US$880, (B) US$680, (C) US$600

Single room request (A) US$300, (B) US$195, (C) US$100

FV9B — HCMC/Mekong Delta/ Danang/Hue/Hanoi (9 days - 8 nights)

Day 1   *Arrival at TSN Airport. Transfer to hotel. Half-day city tour with stops at Independence Palace, the Historical Museum and the War Museum. Traditional Vietnamese music show. Dinner and overnight.*

Day 2   *Morning visit to the Cu Chi Tunnels. Afternoon HCMC city tour with stops at a lacquerware product center, the War Museum, Chinatown and various significant pagodas. Dinner and overnight in HCMC.*

Day 3   *Visit to the Mekong Delta. Boat cruise on the Mekong River and visits to Vinh Trang Pagoda and the Dong Tam Snake Farm. Return to HCMC. Dinner and overnight.*

Day 4   *Fly to Danang. City tour and stops at China Beach and the Marble Mountain of Ngu Hanh. Dinner and overnight in Danang.*

Day 5   *Visits to the ancient town of Hoi An and the Cham Sculpture Museum. Car travel to Hue. Hotel check-in, dinner and overnight.*

Day 6   *City tour of Hue with visits to the Hue Citadel and the mausoleums of Tu Duc, Khai Dinh and Minh Mang. Afternoon boat trip on the Huong river with a stop at Thien Mu Pagoda. Dinner and overnight in Hue.*

Day 7   *Fly to Hanoi. Transfer to hotel. Visits to West Lake and Tran Quoc Pagoda. Dinner and overnight.*

Day 8   *City tour with stops at Ho Chi Minh's Mausoleum, West Lake, 1-Pillar Pagoda, Hoan Kiem Lake, the Fine Arts Museum and the Old Town area. of Hanoi. Dinner and overnight.*

Day 9   *Shopping and transfer to the airport.*

FV9B — HCMC/Mekong Delta/ Danang/Hue/Hanoi (9 days - 8 nights)

Price Schedule:

1 Person (A) US$1420, (B) US$1140, (C) US$980

2 (A) US$1120, (B) US$920, (C) US$830

3-6 (A) US$1010, (B) US$810, (C) US$730

7-10 (A) US$960, (B) US$760, (C) US$680

11-14 (A) US$930, (B) US$730, (C) US$650

15 and up (A) US$900, (B) US$700, (C) US$620

Single room request (A) US$300, (B) US$195, (C) US$100

FV11A — HCMC/Danang/Hue/Hanoi/Ha Long Bay (11 days - 10 nights)

Day 1 *Arrival at TSN Airport. Transfer to hotel. Half-day city tour with stops at Independence Palace, the Historical Museum and the War Museum. Traditional Vietnamese music show. Dinner and overnight.*

Day 2 *Morning visit to the Cu Chi Tunnels. Afternoon HCMC city tour with stops at a lacquerware product center, the War Museum, Chinatown and various significant pagodas. Dinner and overnight in HCMC.*

Day 3 *Visit to the Mekong Delta. Boat cruise on the Mekong River and visits to Vinh Trang Pagoda and the Dong Tam Snake Farm. Return to HCMC. Dinner and overnight.*

Day 4 *Fly to Danang. City tour and stops at China Beach and the Marble Mountain of Ngu Hanh. Dinner and overnight in Danang.*

Day 5 *Visits to the ancient town of Hoi An and the Cham Sculpture Museum. Car travel to Hue. Hotel check-in, dinner and overnight.*

Day 6 *City tour of Hue with visits to the Hue Citadel and the mausoleums of Tu Duc, Khai Dinh and Minh Mang. Afternoon boat trip on the Huong river with a stop at Thien Mu Pagoda. Dinner and overnight in Hue.*

Day 7 *Fly to Hanoi. Transfer to hotel. Visits to West Lake and Tran Quoc Pagoda. Dinner and overnight.*

Day 8 *City tour with stops at Ho Chi Minh's Mausoleum, West Lake, 1-Pillar Pagoda, Hoan Kiem Lake, the Fine Arts Museum and the Old Town area. of Hanoi. Dinner and overnight.*

Day 9 *Trip to Ha Long Bay. Visits to Yen Lap Lake and Hon Gai Town.*

Day 10 *Boat cruise on Ha Long Bay. Return to Hanoi. Dinner and overnight.*

Day 11 *Shopping and transfer to the airport.*

FV11A   HCMC/Danang/Hue/Hanoi/Ha Long Bay (11 days - 10 nights)

Price Schedule:

1 Person (A) US$1750, (B) US$1400, (C) US$1200

2 (A) US$1340, (B) US$1090, (C) US$990

3-6 (A) US$1210, (B) US$960, (C) US$860

7-10 (A) US$1160, (B) US$900, (C) US$810

11-14 (A) US$1130, (B) US$880, (C) US$780

15 and up (A) US$1080, (B) US$850, (C) US$750

Single room request (A) US$360, (B) US$220, (C) US$120

FV15A   HCMC/Mekong Delta/Dalat/ Nha Trang/Danang/Hue/Hanoi/ Ha Long Bay/Hanoi (15 days - 14 nights)

Day 1   *Arrival at TSN Airport. Transfer to hotel. Half-day city tour with stops at Independence Palace, the Historical Museum and the War Museum. Traditional Vietnamese music show. Dinner and overnight.*

Day 2   *Morning visit to the Cu Chi Tunnels. Afternoon HCMC city tour with stops at a lacquerware product center, the War Museum, Chinatown and various significant pagodas. Dinner and overnight in HCMC.*

Day 3   *Visit to the Mekong Delta. Boat cruise on the Mekong River and visits to Vinh Trang Pagoda and the Dong Tam Snake Farm. Return to HCMC. Dinner and overnight.*

Day 4   *Trip to Dalat. Hotel check-in and general city tour. Dinner and overnight.*

Day 5   *City tour and visits to Prenn Datala, Camly, Damry Waterfalls. Also Gougah, Linh Son Pagoda, Bao Dai's Palace, Minh Tam Flower Garden, Xuan Huong Lake and the Valley of Love. Dinner and overnight in Dalat.*

Day 6   *Travel to Nha Trang. Hotel check-in. Sea and sunbathing as well as visits to Husband's Rock, Tri Nguyen Aquarium, Po Nagar Cham Towers and the Marine Biological Research Institute. Dinner and overnight.*

Day 7   *Trip to Quy Nhon. Visit to Quang Trung King's House. Dinner and overnight.*

Day 8   *Trip to Danang. Dinner and overnight.*

Day 9   *Visits to the Cham Sculpture Museum, the ancient town of Hoi An, China Beach and Ngu Hanh Marble Mountain. Car trip to Hue. Hotel check-in, dinner and overnight.*

Day 10   *City tour of Hue with visits to the Hue Citadel and the mausoleums of Tu Duc, Khai Dinh and Minh Mang. Afternoon boat trip on the Huong river with a stop at Thien Mu Pagoda. Dinner and overnight in Hue.*

Day 11   *Fly to Hanoi. Transfer to hotel. Visits to West Lake and Tran Quoc Pagoda. Dinner and overnight.*

FV15A	HCMC/Mekong Delta/Dalat/ Nha Trang/Danang/Hue/Hanoi/ Ha Long Bay/Hanoi (15 days - 14 nights)

Day 12   *City tour with stops at Ho Chi Minh's Mausoleum, West Lake, 1-Pillar Pagoda, Hoan Kiem Lake, the Fine Arts Museum, Nghi Tam Flower Garden, Dong Xuan Market and the Old Town area. of Hanoi. Dinner and overnight.*

Day 13   *Trip to Ha Long Bay. Visits to Yen Lap Lake and Hon Gai Town.*

Day 14   *Boat cruise on Ha Long Bay. Return to Hanoi. Dinner and overnight.*

Day 15   *Shopping and transfer to the airport.*

Price Schedule:

1 Person	*(A) US$2370, (B) US$1880, (C) US$1600*
2	*(A) US$1800, (B) US$1440, (C) US$1290*
3-6	*(A) US$1620, (B) US$1270, (C) US$1130*
7-10	*(A) US$1560, (B) US$1210, (C) US$1070*
11-14	*(A) US$1510, (B) US$1160, (C) US$1020*
15 and up	*(A) US$1470, (B) US$1120, (C) US$980*
Single room request	*(A) US$480, (B) US$280, (C) US$160*

INDEX

Where in the World is USA TODAY?

EVERYWHERE...

In over 90 countries around the globe,
USA TODAY's International Edition
brings world travelers all the news from home,
along with special features for Americans abroad.
Look for us whenever you travel in Europe,
the Middle East, Asia and the Pacific.
Because wherever you go – there we are.

Get the latest travel & entertainment information faxed instantly to you for just $4.95*

The new Fielding's fax-on-demand service.

Now get up-to-the-minute reviews of the best dining, lodging, local attractions, or entertainment just before your next trip. Choose from 31 U.S. and international destinations and each has five different category guides.

Take the guesswork out of last-minute travel planning with reliable city guides sent to any fax machine or address you choose. Select just the information you want to be sent to your hotel, your home, your office or even your next destination.

All category guides include money-saving "best buy" recommendations, consensus star-ratings that save time, and cost comparisons for value shopping.

Fielding's Cityfax™ now combines the immediacy of daily newspaper listings and reviews with the wit and perspective of a Fielding Travel Guide in an easy-to-use, constantly updated format.

Order a minimum of two or all five category guides of the destination of your choice, 24 hours a day, seven days a week. All you need is a phone, a fax machine, and a credit card.

5 different category guides for each destination

❶ Restaurants

❷ Hotels & Resorts

❸ Local Attractions

❹ Events & Diversions

❺ Music, Dance & Theater

Choose from 31 destinations

1 Atlanta	18 New York City
2 Baltimore	19 Orlando
3 Boston	20 Philadelphia
4 Chicago	21 Phoenix
5 Dallas	22 San Diego
6 Denver	23 San Francisco
7 Detroit	24 San Jose/Oakland
8 Hawaii	25 Santa Fe
9 Houston	26 Seattle
10 Kansas City	27 St. Louis
11 Las Vegas	28 Tampa/St.Pete
12 L.A.: Downtown	29 Washington DC
13 L.A.: Orange County	
14 L.A.: The Valleys	**INTERNATIONAL**
15 L.A.: Westside	30 London
16 Miami	31 Paris
17 New Orleans	

Order each category guide faxed to you for $4.95, or order all five guides delivered by U.S. Priority Mail for just $12.9. (plus $3.50 shipping and handling), a savings of $8.30!

Fielding's Cityfax™

CALL: 800-635-9777 FROM ANYWHERE IN THE U.S.
OUTSIDE THE U.S. CALL: 852-172-75-552
HONG KONG CALLERS DIAL: 173-675-552

Order Your Fielding Travel Guides Today

BOOKS	$ EA.
Amazon	$16.95
Australia	$12.95
Bahamas	$12.95
Belgium	$16.95
Bermuda	$12.95
Borneo	$16.95
Brazil	$16.95
Britain	$16.95
Budget Europe	$16.95
Caribbean	$18.95
Europe	$16.95
Far East	$19.95
France	$16.95
Hawaii	$15.95
Holland	$15.95
Italy	$16.95
Kenya's Best Hotels, Lodges & Homestays	$16.95
London Agenda	$12.95
Los Angeles Agenda	$12.95
Malaysia and Singapore	$16.95
Mexico	$16.95
New York Agenda	$12.95
New Zealand	$12.95
Paris Agenda	$12.95
Portugal	$16.95
Scandinavia	$16.95
Seychelles	$12.95
Southeast Asia	$16.95
Spain	$16.95
The World's Great Voyages	$16.95
The World's Most Dangerous Places	$19.95
The World's Most Romantic Places	$16.95
Vacation Places Rated	$19.95
Vietnam	$16.95
Worldwide Cruises	$17.95

To order by phone call toll-free 1-800-FW-2-GUIDE
(VISA, MasterCard and American Express accepted.)

To order by mail send your check or money order,
including $2.00 per book for shipping and handling (sorry, no COD's) to:
Fielding Worldwide, Inc. 308 S. Catalina Avenue, Redondo Beach, CA 90277 U.S.A.

Get 10% off your order by saying "Fielding Discount"
or send in this page with your order

Introducing first hand, "fresh off the boat" reviews for cruise fanatics.

Order Fielding's new quarterly newsletter to get in-depth reviews and information on cruises and ship holidays. The only newsletter with candid opinions and expert ratings of: concept, ship, cruise, experience, service, cabins, food, staff, who sails, itineraries and more. Only $24 per year.

Fielding's "Cruise Insider" Newsletter is a 50-plus page quarterly publication, available at an annual subscription rate of only $24.00, limited to the first 12,000 subscribers.

Call 1-800-FW2-GUIDE to reserve your subscription today.
(VISA, MasterCard and American Express accepted.)

Favorite People, Places & Experiences

ADDRESS:	NOTES:

Name

Address

Telephone

Name

Address

Telephone

Name

Address

Telephone

Name

Address

Telephone

Name

Address

Telephone

Name

Address

Telephone

Name

Address

Telephone

Favorite People, Places & Experiences

ADDRESS:	NOTES:

Name

Address

Telephone

Name

Address

Telephone

Name

Address

Telephone

Name

Address

Telephone

Name

Address

Telephone

Name

Address

Telephone

Name

Address

Telephone

Favorite People, Places & Experiences

ADDRESS:	NOTES:

Name

Address

Telephone

Name

Address

Telephone

Name

Address

Telephone

Name

Address

Telephone

Name

Address

Telephone

Name

Address

Telephone

Name

Address

Telephone

Favorite People, Places & Experiences

ADDRESS:	NOTES:

Name

Address

Telephone

Name

Address

Telephone

Name

Address

Telephone

Name

Address

Telephone

Name

Address

Telephone

Name

Address

Telephone

Name

Address

Telephone